Africa Every Day

Ohio University Research in International Studies

This series of publications on Africa, Latin America, Southeast Asia, and Global and Comparative Studies is designed to present significant research, translation, and opinion to area specialists and to a wide community of persons interested in world affairs. The series is distributed worldwide. For more information, consult the Ohio University Press website, ohioswallow.com.

Books in the Ohio University Research in International Studies series are published by Ohio University Press in association with the Center for International Studies. The views expressed in individual volumes are those of the authors and should not be considered to represent the policies or beliefs of the Center for International Studies, Ohio University Press, or Ohio University.

Executive Editor: Gillian Berchowitz

Africa Every Day

FUN, LEISURE, AND EXPRESSIVE CULTURE ON THE CONTINENT

Edited by

Oluwakemi M. Balogun
Lisa Gilman
Melissa Graboyes
Habib Iddrisu

Ohio University Research in International Studies
Africa Series No. 94
Ohio University Press
Athens

Ohio University Press, Athens, Ohio 45701
ohioswallow.com
© 2019 by Ohio University Press

To obtain permission to quote, reprint, or otherwise reproduce or distribute
material from Ohio University Press publications, please contact our rights and
permissions department at (740) 593-1154 or (740) 593-4536 (fax).

Printed in the United States of America
The books in the Ohio University Research in International Studies Series
are printed on acid-free paper ⊗ ™

27 26 25 24 23 22 21 20 19 18 17   5 4 3 2 1

Library of Congress Cataloging-in-Publication Data

Names: Balogun, Oluwakemi M., editor. | Gilman, Lisa, 1969- editor, author.
  | Graboyes, Melissa, editor. | Iddrisu, Habib, editor.
Title: Africa every day : fun, leisure, and expressive culture on the
  continent / edited by Oluwakemi M. Balogun, Lisa Gilman, Melissa
  Graboyes, Habib Iddrisu.
Other titles: Research in international studies. Africa series ; no. 94.
Description: Athens : Ohio University Press, 2019. | Series: Ohio
  university research in international studies, Africa series ; no. 94 |
  Includes bibliographical references and index.
Identifiers: LCCN 2019028624 | ISBN 9780896803237 (hardcover) | ISBN
  9780896803244 (paperback) | ISBN 9780896805064 (pdf)
Subjects: LCSH: Leisure--Africa. | Popular culture--Africa. |
  Africa--Social life and customs--20th century. | Africa--Social life and
  customs--21st century.
Classification: LCC DT14 .A3435 2019 | DDC 960--dc23
LC record available at https://lccn.loc.gov/2019028624

Contents

Acknowledgments

In spring 2016, four University of Oregon faculty members involved in the university's vibrant African Studies Program came together to begin work on this project. Each of us comes from a different disciplinary background and conducts research in different parts of the continent. Sociologist Oluwakemi Balogun's focus is gender, nation, and beauty in Nigeria. Folklorist Lisa Gilman studies gender, performance, heritage, and politics in Malawi and more recently Zambia. Historian Melissa Graboyes examines topics related to global health, ethics, and biomedicine in East Africa. Music and dance scholar and practitioner Habib Iddrisu writes about dance and cultural change in Ghana and the global context. As scholars with a broad set of experiences, backgrounds, and professional foci, we had a few goals for this volume. First, we wanted to create a book that would be useful in the classroom for undergraduate students who have had little exposure to or direct experience with Africa. We had each felt frustrated identifying course materials that portrayed the continent in its full complexity without undue focus on oppression, corruption, poverty, or suffering. The second goal was to create a book that was lively, interesting, and accessible to students, especially at the undergraduate level. We wanted a book full of chapters that were as fun to read as the exciting topics they described. Finally, we wanted to create a scholarly work that would make a persuasive argument (understandable to college students) about why studying clothing, food, or dating could be just as significant as examining politics, the economy, or warfare.

With these goals in mind, the editors distributed the call for abstracts far and wide, intent on ultimately creating a volume with geographic, chronological, and thematic diversity. We were especially committed to including contributions by those currently living and working on the continent, and from independent and junior scholars. Though we initially intended to include only fifteen essays, we were surprised to receive ninety-five abstracts—far more than we had anticipated. We were delighted by the response and the high quality of the proposals. After much deliberation, we decided to increase the volume to twenty-nine essays while reducing the length of each chapter, agreeing that providing students with a more expansive scope would be preferable to fewer, longer pieces. The essays were selected first and foremost for their engaging topics, though we also considered geographic and temporal breadth.

In a project of this magnitude there is much labor, both explicit and hidden. All four editors participated at different stages and in different ways, and it's worth noting the many contributions made. Melissa Graboyes and Lisa Gilman served as coordinating editors of the project, originally conceiving of the volume and managing logistical requirements. This included procuring a book contract and doing major planning for a symposium associated with the project. Graboyes was responsible for coordinating the creation of all maps, managing three student research assistants, and preparing the full manuscript for its initial and final submission. Gilman was responsible for the final production stages prior to publication. All editors participated in the review of abstracts, selection of chapters to be included, multiple rounds of editing, and providing feedback to contributors.

We wish to acknowledge the many people and institutions that were involved in this book as contributors, champions, and helpers. First and foremost, we are grateful to the authors for their thoughtful and creative contributions. Thank you each for your patience in working with us through the multiple revisions, the frustratingly small word limit, and the complicated communications that sometimes resulted from so many cooks being in the proverbial editorial kitchen.

In the spirit of creating a volume that integrated multiple perspectives and was responsive to perceived gaps in African Studies, the editors invited contributors to participate in a two-day symposium held at the University of Oregon and a roundtable panel at the African Studies Association. The overall project benefited tremendously from these active and lively exchanges. The symposium was held in February 2017, with the editors and twelve authors providing feedback on early drafts while discussing emerging themes and the challenges of writing for an audience of undergraduate students. In November 2017, editors and contributors came together to dialogue during a roundtable, "Everyday Life on the African Continent: A Collaborative Book Project," at the annual African Studies Association meeting. Our process has surely taken longer and created more work, but we also think it has greatly enhanced the volume as a whole.

In addition to a lot of hard work, books also take money to produce. We would like to gratefully acknowledge the financial support provided by various units at the University of Oregon. The two-day symposium was generously supported by the African Studies Program, the Center for the Study of Women in Society, the Folklore Program, the Oregon Humanities Center, and the Office of Academic Affairs. Contributions from these units allowed the editors to offer travel bursaries for many participants flying from Africa and for junior and independent scholars. More generally, the annual Academic Support Account funds provided to faculty members for research expenses allowed us to employ a set of students and former students to help with many parts of the book. We are grateful to the Oregon Humanities Center and the University of Oregon's College of Arts and Sciences for contributing additional funds to offset production costs.

Thank you, Chris Becker for producing all the maps so professionally. We are indebted to the undergraduate students of University of Oregon's Clark Honors College who worked as research assistants with Graboyes during the many stages of this process. Clara Gorman and Rhaine Clarke were detailed, dedicated, and a joy to work with in the initial compilation of the volume. Rachel Conner was invaluable at the end stages, diligently and systematically keeping track of the many details that come with working with twenty-nine authors.

The editorial staff at Ohio University Press has worked hard to move this volume to completion. Gillian Berchowitz's enthusiasm and guidance was constant from the early stages, and we are very appreciative. We owe the excellent quality of the final product to the detail-oriented rigor of Nancy Basmajian and the numerous other members of the press's team who worked on different phases of this project. The two anonymous reviewers provided many suggestions on how to better frame the introduction and the importance of this volume as a whole. We are grateful to Laura Fair for reading and commenting on earlier versions of the introduction, which helped streamline and strengthen our thinking. In the Clark Honors College, Melissa Graboyes benefitted from the help of Laurie Notaro when working on images for the book, Daphne Gallagher when thinking through the introduction, and Shelise Zumwalt's assistance in the busy days of printing and compiling the final manuscript. Finally, each of us struggled with the balancing act of juggling teaching, research, service, and editing this volume with the demands of our families. Thanks to our children and spouses for putting up with so many demands on our time.

Introduction

Everyday Life in Africa
The Importance of Leisure and Fun

OLUWAKEMI M. BALOGUN AND MELISSA GRABOYES

In her influential 2009 TED Talk "The Danger of a Single Story," the Nigerian author Chimamanda Ngozi Adichie warns of the perils of the dominant narrative of Africa: "a place of beautiful landscapes, beautiful animals, and incomprehensible people, fighting senseless wars, dying of poverty and AIDS, unable to speak for themselves and waiting to be saved by a kind, white foreigner."[1] Famine and conflict are real and deserve sustained attention, but this narrow focus on chaos and decline pathologizes a vast and diverse continent.

The essays in this volume offer those who have little or no direct exposure to the continent numerous counternarratives to the "single story," offsetting the overemphasis on perennial crisis that saturates Western media sources, portraying daily life in Africa as nothing but hardship, violence, and despair. This volume is meant as a corrective that depicts the agency of Africans in their daily lives. To do this, it provides narratives capturing everyday life and ordinary experiences, sharing insights into the lives of individuals whose perspectives would otherwise remain hidden, emphasizing creativity, leisure, and pleasure in order to "bring a little fun" to the study of Africa.[2]

The framework of everyday life thus grounds the analytical focus of this volume. We define everyday life as the ordinary and extraordinary aspects of lived experiences and daily practices that provide valuable insight into broader social issues. By centering everyday life, these essays critically examine the multiple perspectives that enrich the complex social realities and imaginaries of life on the African continent.

Scholars have associated everyday life with the ordinary, both in terms of mundane, routine, and quotidian experiences, but also in recognition of the importance of the daily lives of ordinary people.[3] This approach brings to light perspectives that may have otherwise been ignored.[4] The topics covered in this book are broad, which we hope will capture the unevenness of daily life, full of contradictions and inconsistencies, in ways that raise real challenges for the study of the everyday but also yield innovative findings.

This collection contributes to wider Africanist scholarship, including the literature on leisure, folklore, and popular culture on the continent, and general understandings of Africa in three ways. First, building on previous scholarship, we maintain that studying everyday life has intrinsic value. This volume highlights the agency of individuals, often in relationship to cultural groupings. It also centers unconventional sources and sites outside of official records and recognizes the ambiguities and textures of social life. As renowned anthropologists Jean and John Comaroff note, "the very significance of the quotidian lies in its paradoxes."[5] This approach allows us to adjust how we understand and frame larger structural transformations, interpret cultural forms, and respond to social change. Second, studying the everyday reveals insights about many other aspects of society and culture, with topics such as clothing, music, dance, or social media use providing valuable context to questions related to politics, technology, economics, and gender relations through illuminating societal values, norms, and unstated codes.[6] As Bea Vidacs wrote in relation to studying sport, it "can throw into relief political processes on the ground and their local interpretations."[7] Finally, we argue that recognizing fun, pleasure, and creativity in everyday life does not negate the reality of hardship for many on the continent. We do not romanticize everyday life in Africa. Indeed, we spotlight that some of the social issues that cause deprivation or disorder may be productive realms for thinking about the central themes of this volume.

We recognize that our broad mandate invites accusations of exhibiting a desultory approach or even callousness about "important" issues. But the continent is vast and varied, and through case studies we seek to show the diversity of daily experiences of Africans. We caution readers not to misunderstand and believe life in Africa is ever-cheerful, and to avoid infantilizing stereotypes of Africans as naïve and carefree. Even Africans whose lives are riven with the constraints of poverty, warfare, rampant corruption, or the effects of ecological disasters may experience pleasure. Challenging circumstances create hardship; they also animate the lived experiences of people.

The Kenyan author Binyavanga Wainaina wrote in his satirical piece, "How to Write about Africa," that "taboo subjects" include "ordinary domestic scenes, love between Africans (unless a death is involved), references to African writers or intellectuals, mention of school-going children who are not suffering from yaws or Ebola fever or female genital mutilation."[8] And from this tongue-in-cheek advice we depart, assembling writings on "off-limits" topics such as courtship and new love, intellectuals and novelists in 1970s Dar es Salaam, and children playing at a park in Namibia.

Conceptual Approaches to Everyday Life

The everyday life approach has been pursued in a number of specific fields, each with its own intellectual trajectory and theoretical traditions. Within sociology, the groundwork for the approach was laid in the 1920s and 1930s but took off in the 1950s and 1960s as a critique of macro-approaches toward society that emphasized large-scale social processes and institutions. The field used everyday life as a lens to understand the relationship between self and society and peel back layers of taken-for-granted aspects of social interaction and the organization of daily life.[9] Inspired largely by symbolic interactionism, which examines how individuals construct social worlds through shared and contested meanings to understand the underlying social patterns of language, emotions, and action, this approach examines everyday behavior, beliefs, and symbols to explain social norms, change, and stability. The study of everyday life, primarily through firsthand observation, is a cornerstone of cultural anthropology, illuminating cross-cultural contexts and detailing the tacit dimensions of conflict, resistance, and social bonds.[10]

This volume builds on decades of scholarship in the broad area of social histories in Africa, where it was recognized that daily activities revealed larger social, political, and economic dynamics. The growth of social histories of Africa allowed for a focus away from macro-politics, colonization, and biographies of powerful men. These new social histories took the forms of micro-histories, biographies, and ethnographies of previously ignored populations. Books began to document the lived experiences of women, slaves, prostitutes, and sharecroppers. Works such as Marcia Wright's *Strategies of Slaves and Women*, Charles van Onselen's *The Seed Is Mine*, and John Chernoff's

Hustling Is Not Stealing provide granular details about how individuals on different parts of the continent, in varied time periods, lived their lives.[11] Though focusing on individuals, these books recognized the larger, limiting constraints that governed their subjects' lives, even as they documented the agency of a multilingual bar girl without formal education and a poor sharecropper in South Africa. These new social histories often drew extensively on oral sources, life histories, and other creative uses of sources.

Everyday life is also at the core of folklore studies, in line with Barbara Kirshenblatt-Gimblett's definition of folklore as "the aesthetics of everyday life."[12] The field's populist approach considers *all* people and *all* types of expressive practices to be equally deserving of scholarly attention. In line with folklore studies, the essays in this volume evidence that creative activities can have instrumental value, in that the pragmatic activities of everyday life, such as fishermen and car repairmen at work, can be expressive and artistic. The analysis of the interplay between the aesthetic and pragmatic across cultural forms and social groups has produced better understandings of the arts as "one of the chief media through which ideas about race, class, gender, or other dimensions of identity are inculcated, debated, and resisted."[13] Oral tradition is one of the many important genres of folklore that allows closer study of socialization, communication, and political negotiations.[14]

The scholarship on popular culture in Africa examines the production of material objects, expressive culture, performance, and arts with close attention to content, circulation, and the social context of their creation. Karin Barber (2018) traces the development of popular culture as a field of inquiry in African studies that began with ethnographic studies of the 1930s and continues with the role of media and technology in the global flows of cultural forms. Her landmark edited volume *Popular Culture in Africa* (1997) delineated the concept of popular culture as a "product of everyday life," recognizing its blurriness and its connection to identities and ideologies.[15] Popular culture emerged as a concept to capture inventive cultural forms that defied categorization into strict binaries between African heritage and European-inspired aesthetics, in addition to demarcations based on generation, class, and social setting.[16]

While the fields of African folklore and popular culture stress the cultural expression of ordinary people in the public domain, the closely related field of leisure studies has been associated with the elite and focused on consumption in private domains within the context of Africa's changing political economy.[17] Akyeampong and Ambler's introductory essay in a 2002 special issue on "Leisure in African History" made clear a few important points that this volume also engages with. First, what constitutes leisure in Africa has changed over time. Meanwhile, boundaries of race, ethnicity, gender, class, and age affect the meanings of leisure. And, as they put it, "leisure is not a fixed or natural category but a fluid phenomenon, variously understood and historically specific."[18] That special issue called for a reimagining of leisure from the perspective of those seeking pleasure, and we believe that many of the essays in this volume speak to that challenge.

Everyday life topics, even if not framed around "the everyday," represent a rich vein of scholarship. Recent books exploring subject matters such as hip-hop, car culture, and spaces like barbershops have made noteworthy contributions to analyzing everyday life in Africa.[19] Other scholars have used the everyday life approach to study institutions such as the informal economy, political culture, religion, and domestic life as well as social conditions like violence and corruption.[20] Other works bridge a focus on popular culture and leisure activities, such as Phyllis Martin's research on dance and night life in colonial Brazzaville, Jean Allman's work on fashion, Peter Alegi's writings about soccer in southern Africa, and Laura Fair's study of popular recreation in colonial Zanzibar.[21] These works and many others link subjects like clothing, music, and sport to political change and new forms of identity making, showing they are important topics in their own right.[22]

Contributor Essays

The essays in this volume overlap with one another in ways related to geography, time period, theme, and disciplinary approach. All of the authors consider aspects of daily life, like using cell phones, watching YouTube videos, shopping at malls, and working. Some chapters feature activities not all Africans can enjoy, such as joining an elite men-only tennis club, going to the movies, or attending a wrestling match. Other chapters reflect on the meaning of special occasions like fasts, feasts, weddings, and new-year celebrations. And a handful reflect on ubiquitous aspects of daily life that we rarely examine, such as cars and the camaraderie that comes from working creatively and productively with others.

Many chapters explore the ways in which African popular culture has been in dialogue with the rest of the world. They present ample evidence that forms of leisure and popular culture in Africa are best discussed in terms of indigenization, adaptation, and appropriation rather than as static binaries of European/foreign/global and African. Matthias Krings (2015) argues that rather than understanding global culture in Africa—like the remaking of Hollywood scripts in the Nigerian film industry—as mimesis or imitation, we should pay close attention to the cultural transformations occurring.[23] Many of the essays in this volume center contingency influenced by changing internal and external forces to disrupt assumptions about the fixed nature of social practices and meanings in everyday life. Essays such as Charlotte Grabli's examination of the daily use of radio in 1950s Leopoldville (present-day Kinshasa) argue that, while it was initially a tool of colonial propaganda, local radio programming adapted the technology to fit African musical tastes in ways that reconfigured public space. Jacqueline Mougoué shows how women's sporting activities such as football (soccer), the "world game," which came to Africa through colonialism, became a way for urban elites to demarcate the regional superiority of Anglophone Cameroon. Other chapters focus on how localized traditions are deeply tied to a specific place and time, such as "traditional" practices like Yoruba bridal showers in Nigeria or funeral practices in Zambia. These examples and many others throughout the volume highlight how dynamic social practices remain locally meaningful.

The essays are grouped into seven sections: Celebrations and Rites of Passage; Socializing and Friendship; Love, Sex, and Marriage; Sports and Leisure; Performance, Language, and Creativity; Technology and Media; and, Labor and Livelihoods. We encourage readers to read the book in ways that are meaningful and productive to their own objectives.

Celebrations and Rites of Passage

Rites of passage such as weddings, births, coming-of-age ceremonies, and funerals are typically set aside temporally and spatially from "everyday life" as special occasions. But they have important social functions that expand outside the set time of the event, providing opportunity for commentary about politics and community expectations surrounding gender, age, and ethnicity.[24]

Erin Nourse describes a Malagasy Islamic hair-cutting ceremony for a newborn baby, where an ethnically and religiously diverse group of family and friends gather to welcome the newest member into their community. Nourse shows how these types of rituals serve as a meeting point where participants reaffirm their social positions and navigate shared group membership. Similarly, Abiola Victoria Ayodokun and Osuolale Joseph Ayodokun analyze *ekún-ìyàwó*, a form of poetry and bridal shower celebration among some Nigerian Yoruba communities, highlighting the importance of ritual ceremonies in demarcating kinship ties. Through poetry recitations, familial blessings, and gifts, brides absorb many of the obligations that accompany their new status. Prince Lamba's chapter on "funeral swag" explores how burial rituals in Zambia have shifted from somber occasions to flamboyant affairs that highlight changing ideas about gender difference and social status. The transformations he pinpoints are due in part to the commercialization of mourning through hired caterers, professional wailers, ostentatious outfits, and lively musicians, linked to larger global trends, urbanization, and generational differences within the country.

Picking up on the theme of rituals, Hadeer Aboelnagah writes about Egyptian feasts that bring people together across religions. She remembers as a child taking delicacies enjoyed during Ramadan to her Christian neighbors, and correspondingly enjoying their offerings at Christmas. Aboelnagah describes the social importance of food in crafting joint histories, shared norms, and public displays of tolerance (as when Christians refrain from eating in public during Ramadan). Scott M. Youngstedt examines the rising popularity of New Year's Eve celebrations with heavy drinking and firecrackers in Niger. The outdoor parties present an opportunity for men and women to socialize together publicly and for citizens to feel like they are taking part in a global ritual. The rowdy behaviors function as a "ritual of rebellion" that questions the social order while still reaffirming its importance.

Socializing and Friendship

These four chapters address friendship in various contexts and forms—in exclusive clubs that emphasize wealth and masculinity, as forms of public conspicuous consumption, and between children during play. Martha Ndakalako-Bannikov recollects her own childhood in Namibia. Her essay draws on the particularities of Tank Park, where a tank rested among the jungle gyms and swing sets. The tank was "an uncommon memorial to childhood," an odd piece of material culture, the remains of a long-fought war. Without denying narratives of trauma and war that loom in Namibia's recent history, Ndakalako-Bannikov makes a persuasive case for remembering something as ordinary as children's play. Deborah Durham focuses on another communal gathering space—the malls of Botswana—where insights about fashion, consumerism, and social relationships abound. She recognizes the importance of the malls as gathering spaces for intergenerational exchanges of information, reaffirmations of kin and friendship ties, and sharing gossip. As with other chapters in this volume, Durham indicates that work and pleasure blur: people run errands and complete chores at the mall, but also experience the pleasure of seeing and being seen.

Daniel Jordan Smith and Omotoyosi Babalola further take up the connections between status and social relationships. Both authors consider friendship, class, and moral codes in male-dominated social spaces. Smith's ethnography takes us inside a tennis club in southeastern Nigeria to explain the centrality of money in the construction of masculinity. Club members spend lavishly and generously to assert their authority, generate praise from peers, and build friendships in ways that largely reproduce hierarchies of gender, age, and class. The chapter connects micro-level actions in the social club with macro-shifts in Nigeria's uneven political economy. Babalola focuses on Nigerians who enjoy going to nightclubs on weekends, a lifestyle that constitutes "turn it up" party culture. She traces the intensifying demands of urban life in megacities like Lagos that create stressful lives but also lubricate a vibrant nightlife. Male-oriented bars, dance clubs, and food joints encourage extravagant spending, drinking, and unabashed entertainment. Here as in Smith's tennis club, several-million-naira bar tabs are not just about boasting about money, but part of an assertion of affluent and influential masculinity.

Love, Sex, and Marriage

From the friendship explored in the prior section sometimes grow deeper connections of love, intimacy, and desire in the context of romantic relationships—which is the topic of the next set of chapters.[25]

Dorothy L. Hodgson's account of youth courtships and flirtations that flourish at moonlit celebrations emphasizes explorations of sexual freedom. Based on long-term ethnographic observations in Maasai communities in the Rift Valley of Tanzania, she argues that these festivities stimulate sexual play as well as young people's understanding of group membership, connection, and gender. Steven Van Wolputte pulls from extensive ethnographic fieldwork among Himba communities in Namibia to question assumptions about patriarchy in polyamorous sexual relationships through examining partners' joking, intricate kinship ties, and expressions of fulfillment. Van Wolputte argues that international discourses casting such wives as helpless victims obscures the complex power relations and mutual pleasure that undergird these partnerships. Like Hodgson, who explains how intimate gendered relationships are subject to change under larger social forces like colonialism, urbanization, state control, religious institutions, and NGOs, Van Wolputte emphasizes that shifting moral expectations have direct consequences on how sexual relationships are socially legitimized.

Lara Rosenoff Gauvin's chapter also takes up love, courtship, and marriage (*cuna*). She describes how, under the dramatically changing circumstances of postwar northern Uganda, daily life goes on in modified forms after decades of war, violence, and displacement. She focuses on challenges youth face while raised in internally displaced persons camps through the experiences of two couples and the limitations they face in courtship rituals. Conflict often draws international attention or assistance, and in this case the chapter makes clear that the concern of the international community did not match local priorities to restore community relations. In the communities where Rosenoff Gauvin was based, people described everyday encounters such as courtship and marriage as central to rebuilding in the postwar situation. As with Ndakalako-Bannikov's focus on children's play, Rosenoff Gauvin does not undermine the seriousness of war or its long-term effects; rather, she provides a nuanced picture of how daily life continues in modified ways.

Sports and Recreation

Four chapters present different ways of participating in sports and athletic pursuits on the continent. During the colonial era, leisure activities were tightly controlled, with clear examples of acceptable and unacceptable ways to spend free time—whether women should play sports, what young boys should do, what young men should not do. What was deemed acceptable was tremendously revealing of colonial priorities and expectations about age, gender, and class. Africans responded with subtle forms of resistance and obvious forms of appropriation and adaptation to heavy-handed programs. For example, soccer was introduced as an appropriate leisure activity, but Africans around the continent quickly made it their own, stretching the game to allow for female teams, elaborate aesthetics, and political commentary.[26] Across a wide time span, this section demonstrates how people construct recreational activities in ways that are socially meaningful.

Issahaku Adam and Akwasi Kumi-Kyereme draw attention to the contemporary leisure activities of people with disabilities in Ghana, who are often stigmatized and ostracized. Drawing on interviews, they describe leisure activities that might seem surprising: a young man who lost a leg who uses crutches playing soccer; a blind woman enjoying television. These examples reveal alternate ideas to the dominant narratives of what constitutes sport and leisure, who participates, and their meanings.

Expanding on the theme of rethinking normativity, Jacqueline Mougoué's and Cheikh Tidiane Lo's chapters show how varied institutional actors use sporting cultures to craft social understandings of femininity and masculinity to both buttress and destabilize assumptions. Mougoué uses archival research to describe the political history of women's participation in athletic activities in 1960s and 1970s Anglophone Cameroon. She traces how governing elites and influential journalists marshalled political leisure to represent Anglophone Cameroon as autonomous, progressive, and competitive. Conversely, Lo's work on Senegalese folk and professional wrestling analyzes the public spectacle of masculinity at these popular events. Through media analysis and first-hand accounts, he argues that men's bodily movements, technical skills, and artistic expressions present an image of masculinity centered around honor, prestige, and strength. Lo points to the many meanings of these wrestling events: a pathway for social mobility, a rite of passage into manhood, a communal gathering, and a way to create national identity. Other works have traced wrestling across the Atlantic world, yet another form of continental contact and exchange.[27]

The understandings of masculinity central to Lo's chapter also function in the boys' clubs created in post–World War II colonial Lagos that Michael Gennaro discusses. While these clubs sought to corral youth who colonial officials considered "wayward" by using sport to ease transitions into adulthood, multiple sources recount the camaraderie and friendships that the boys created and maintained there. Like other contributors to this volume, Gennaro emphasizes that Africans adapted and adopted colonial creations to fit local needs and interests.

Performance, Language, and Creativity

The next set of essays explores how people use daily forms of communication that capitalize on wordplay and performative culture as a form of social commentary and shifting communal boundaries. Alex Perullo and James Nindi explore Tanzanians' use of humor to stave off fatigue on long claustrophobic journeys on public transportation and through comedy shows. These critical conversations and performances provide biting social critique on pressing issues like crumbling infrastructure or changing urban dress codes. Lisa Gilman and Paolo Israel center performance in order to understand inventive cultural forms and historical legacies. Gilman focuses on *chilimika* dance competitions in Malawi, which offer performers opportunities to build community and engage in bottom-up forms of cultural creativity. Israel focuses on the life of Mustafa Bonde, a Mozambican masquerade master whose playful renewal of ancient traditions speaks to larger complexities of cultural change, personal struggle, and shifting social landscapes of colonialism, war, and resistance.

Mokaya Bosire's essay on Sheng, a form of slang common among youth in urban Kenya, reveals how linguistic vernacular remains at the heart of social life. Sheng shows up across Kenyan society: in mobile phone texting, social media, hip-hop, stand-up comedy, and slam poetry. By studying its structure and uses, Bosire reveals ingenious linguistic play that facilitates communication between people who speak different languages. Maya Angela Smith explores the YouTube show *Journal Rappé*, a product of the global digital age targeted at those in Senegal and the global diaspora, as a form of "edutainment" that combines Wolof and French, exposing new ways of thinking about language. Smith showcases the innovative ways that the hosts

blend rap, video, and news to convey satire, commentary, and information. For Bosire, Sheng's fast-moving expressions help illustrate re-
configurations around group identity in Kenya's ethno-linguistically
diverse urban spaces, while, for Smith, language becomes an engine to
propel political transformations for Senegalese communities. Taken
together, these contributions push us to think about linguistic artistry in the context of social change.

Technology and Media

The next four chapters document varied engagements with technology and media and show how people make these cultural products
meaningful in their local contexts. In an essay on film translation in
Tanzania, Birgit Englert and Paul Moreto explore how Tanzanians
have adapted films from the United States, India, China, and Korea
to make them relevant to their lives. A creative industry of young
men who provide translations in Swahili has garnered local fame by
adding contextual information, ignoring some lines while elaborating
other parts, and "adding a certain *vionjo* (flavor) to the film that makes
it more entertaining to the audience."

John Fenn explains that the increased availability and affordability
of cell phones in Malawi has facilitated communication and collabo-
ration between people across rural and urban settings. His chapter
documents creative ingenuity, such as entrepreneurs developing
battery-charging businesses to serve the many Malawians whose
homes do not have electricity. Charlotte Grabli's chapter explores
how the public address system, with speakers installed throughout
Kinshasa, Belgian Congo, in the 1950s to facilitate colonial control,
became a pleasurable part of daily life. This appropriation of a colonial
tool and technology to create "the musical landscape of the colonial
town" is particularly subversive.

Just as African residents in Kinshasa demanded music from around
the globe, Laura Fair shows the deeply global nature of the leisure of
many Zanzibari youth in sold-out screenings of kung fu, blaxploitation, and Indian films, and musical shows featuring R&B, funk, and
rock-n-roll in packed disco dance clubs. Some films raised questions
of justice, fairness, and equity while others provided visuals for act-
ing on true love and models of what "modern" love might look like.
Fair also draws our attention to how young couples could escape the

oversight of older generations in cinemas. All these chapters hint at Africa's history of global engagement with forms of popular culture and technology including music, film, and gadgets.

Labor and Livelihoods

Joshua Grace's chapter brings us in a slightly different direction, focusing on a creative interaction with technology (the automobile) and the Tanzanian auto garages and mechanics participating in everyday acts of repair and expertise. Grace questions and undermines narratives of technological dysfunction and brokenness, presenting Tanzania as a place of innovation by studying car garages in Dar es Salaam and the resourcefulness required to keep cars running. Through narratives of individual mechanics, he inverts the idea of dysfunction as failure, presenting it as "an opportunity to learn, to tinker, to modify and remake vehicles, to stimulate the mind, to create new designs, and to have fun."

Emily Callaci's chapter focuses on generational change, the draw of the big city, and the friendships cultivated in urban spaces. She explores the lives and friendships of the male Tanzanian authors of Swahili detective novellas written in the 1970s. Their friendships, which Callaci demonstrates are foundational to understanding their work, developed under conditions of police harassment, housing shortages, evictions, and slum demolitions. Yet the precariousness of daily life only intensified the bonds. Demonstrating the crosscutting themes prevalent in the volume, Callaci recounts how these young men made their way, generating original art while maintaining friendships.

Eric Debrah Otchere's essay examines the everyday life activities of canoe fishermen in Ghana. The chapter captures the role of singing in making their difficult work achievable. Through a call-and-response rhythm, these songs coordinate effort, invite group participation, teach life lessons, and cultivate creative spaces amid grueling work. This chapter calls attention to how music can provide space to engage with daily realities and public controversy.

In the final chapter, Bill McCoy discusses patient activities at the missionary Mbuluzi Leprosy Hospital in Swaziland in the 1950s, and particularly their growing of *dagga* (marijuana) on the hospital grounds. Selling dagga to neighboring South Africa provided some with needed funds, but represented just one of the challenges Swazi patients raised to the moral and social norms foreign missionaries advanced. The chapter is a good reminder "of just how thin the lines often are that separate leisure activity from the political and economic realm," What occurs in the everyday can be pleasure, drudgery, and legal or not.

This volume recognizes the richness of everyday life in Africa through a series of case studies that provide local context while shedding light on many broader questions of history, economics, politics, and society. However, we recognize these are only case studies and there are many important topics that these chapters did not address. These include precolonial time periods, which limits our ability to timestamp how and why leisure, popular culture, and understandings of everyday life have changed since those periods. Moreover, none of these essays directly engage with queer sexualities.[28] These essays also do not explicitly discuss how notions of beauty and fashion are locally rooted and connected to media, relationships, and labor.[29] Nonetheless, we believe we make a valuable contribution by drawing out complex analytical stories about intimate relationships, recreational activities, expressive cultures, and media and technology use. By centering these multilayered stories about everyday life, we can begin to fulfill Adichie's mandate to use many stories "to empower and to humanize."

Notes

1. Chimamanda Ngozi Adichie, "The Danger of a Single Story," video of presentation at the TEDGlobal 2009 conference, July 23, 2009, quote at 6:15, https://www.ted.com/talks/chimamanda_adichie_the_danger_of_a _single_story/transcript?language=en#t-1053011.

2. Paul Tiyambe Zeleza, "Introduction: The Creation and Consumption of Leisure: Theoretical and Methodological Considerations," in *Leisure in Urban Africa*, ed. Paul Tiyambe Zeleza and Cassandra Rachel Veney (Trenton, NJ: Africa World Press, 2003), viii.

3. Stephanie Newell and Onookome Okome, eds., *Popular Culture in Africa: The Episteme of the Everyday* (New York: Routledge, 2014); Toyin Falola and Augustine Agwuele, eds., *Africans and the Politics of Popular Culture* (Rochester, NY: University of Rochester Press, 2009); Wale Adebanwi, ed., *The Political Economy of Everyday Life in Africa: Beyond the Margins* (Suffolk, UK: James Currey, 2017).

4. Emmanuel Akyeampong and Charles Ambler, "Leisure in African History: An Introduction," in "Leisure in African History," ed. Emmanuel

Akyeampong and Charles Ambler, special issue, *International Journal of African Historical Studies* 35, no. 1 (2002): 5–6; Andreas Eckert and Adam Jones, "Introduction: Historical Writing about Everyday Life," in "Everyday Life in Colonial Africa," ed. Adam Jones, special issue, *Journal of African Cultural Studies* 15, no. 1 (June 2002): 5–16.

5. Jean Comaroff and John L. Comaroff, *Of Revelation and Revolution*, vol. 2, *The Dialectics of Modernity on a South African Frontier* (Chicago: University of Chicago Press, 1997), 30–31.

6. Philip M. Peek and Kwesi Yankah, eds., *African Folklore: An Encyclopedia* (New York: Routledge, 2004).

7. Bea Vidacs, "Through the Prism of Sports: Why Should Africanists Study Sports?," *Africa Spectrum* 41, no. 3 (2006): 337.

8. Binyavanga Wainaina, "How to Write about Africa," *Granta* 92 (Winter 2005): 91–96, published on the *Granta* website January 19, 2006, https://granta.com/how-to-write-about-africa.

9. Patricia A. Adler, Peter Adler, and Andrea Fontana, "Everyday Life Sociology," *Annual Review of Sociology* 13 (1987): 217–35; David A. Karp, William C. Yoels, Barbara H. Vann, and Michael Ian Borer, *Sociology in Everyday Life*, 4th ed. (Long Grove, IL: Waveland, 2016); Devorah Kalekin-Fishman, "Sociology of Everyday Life," *Current Sociology* 61, no. 5/6 (2013): 714–32.

10. Mwenda Ntarangwi, David Mills, and Mustafa Babiker, eds., *African Anthropologies: History, Critique, and Practice* (London: Zed Books, 2006).

11. Marcia Wright, *Strategies of Slaves and Women: Life-Stories from East/Central Africa* (Cambridge, UK: James Currey, 1993); Charles van Onselen, *The Seed Is Mine: The Life of Kas Maine, a South African Sharecropper 1894–1985* (Cambridge, UK: James Currey, 1996); John M. Chernoff, *Hustling Is Not Stealing: Stories of an African Bar Girl* (Chicago: University of Chicago Press, 2003).

12. Barbara Kirshenblatt-Gimblett, "The Future of Folklore Studies in America: The Urban Frontier," *Folklore Forum* 16, no. 2 (1983): 175–234. See also Simon J. Bronner, "Folklore Movement," in *American Folklore: An Encyclopedia*, ed. Jan Harold Brunvand (New York: Routledge, 2006)

13. Giovanna P. Del Negro and Harris Berger, "New Directions in the Study of Everyday Life: Expressive Culture and the Interpretation of Practice," in *Identity and Everyday Life: Essays in the Study of Folklore, Music, and Popular Culture*, ed. Harris M. Berger and Giovanna P. Del Negro (Middletown, CT: Wesleyan University Press, 2004), 3.

14. Kwesi Yankah, *Speaking for the Chief: Okyeame and the Politics of Akan Royal Oratory* (Bloomington: Indiana University, 1995); Isidore Okpewho, *Once Upon a Kingdom: Myth, Hegemony, and Identity* (Bloomington: Indiana University Press, 1988).

15. Karin Barber, ed., *Readings in African Popular Culture* (Bloomington: Indiana University Press, 1997).

16. Karin Barber, *A History of African Popular Culture: New Approaches to African History* (Cambridge: Cambridge University Press, 2018).

17. Zeleza and Veney, *Leisure in Urban Africa*, 105–24.

18. Akyeampong and Ambler, "Leisure in African History," 5–6.

19. Msia Kibona Clark, *Hip-Hop in Africa: Prophets of the City and Dustyfoot Philosophers* (Athens: Ohio University Press, 2018); Todd Cleveland, *Following the Ball: The Migration of African Soccer Players across the Portuguese Colonial Empire, 1949–1975* (Athens: Ohio University Press, 2017); Lindsey B. Green-Simms, *Postcolonial Automobility: Car Culture in West Africa* (Minneapolis: University of Minnesota Press, 2017); Brad Weiss, *Street Dreams and Hip Hop Barbershops: Global Fantasy in Urban Tanzania* (Bloomington: Indiana University Press, 2009).

20. Matthew Engelke, "Past Pentecostalism: Notes on Rupture, Realignment, and Everyday Life in Pentecostal and African Independent Churches," *Africa: Journal of the International African Institute* 80, no. 2 (2010): 177–99; Terence Ranger, *Dance and Society in Eastern Africa, 1890–1970: The Beni Ngoma* (Berkeley: University of California Press, 1975); Emmanueal Akyeampong, *Drink, Power, and Cultural Change: A Social History of Alcohol in Ghana, c. 1800 to Recent Times* (Portsmouth, NH: Heinemann, 1996); William J. Baker and James A. Mangan, eds., *Sport in Africa: Essays in Social History* (London: Africana, 1987).

21. Phyllis Martin, *Leisure and Society in Colonial Brazzaville* (Cambridge: Cambridge University Press, 1995); Jean Allman, ed., *Fashioning Africa: Power and the Politics of Dress* (Bloomington: Indiana University Press, 2004); Laura Fair, *Pastimes and Politics: Culture, Community, and Identity in Post-Abolition Urban Zanzibar, 1890–1945* (Athens: Ohio University Press, 2001); Peter Alegi, *Laduma! Soccer, Politics and Society in South Africa* (Pietermaritzburg: University of KwaZulu-Natal Press, 2004).

22. Laura Fair, "'It's Just No Fun Anymore': Women's Experiences of Taarab before and after the 1964 Zanzibar Revolution," in "Leisure in African History," ed. Emmanuel Akyeampong and Charles Ambler, special issue, *International Journal of African Historical Studies* 35, no. 1 (2002): 61–81; Kelly Askew, *Performing the Nation: Swahili Music and Cultural Politics in Tanzania* (Chicago: University of Chicago Press, 2002).

23. Matthias Krings, *African Appropriations: Cultural Difference, Mimesis, and Media* (Bloomington: Indiana University Press, 2015).

24. Roger D. Abrahams, "Toward an Enactment-Centered Theory of Folklore," in *Frontiers of Folklore*, ed. William R. Bascom (Boulder, CO: Westview, 1977).

25. The edited volume *Love in Africa* is a source for more in-depth readings. Jennifer Cole and Lynn M. Thomas, eds., *Love in Africa* (Chicago: University of Chicago Press, 2009).

26. Cassandra Ogunniyi, "Perceptions of the African Women's Championships: Female Footballers as Anomalies," in *Women's Sport in Africa*, ed.

Michelle Sikes and John Bale (New York: Routledge, 2016); Lisa A. Lindsay, "Trade Unions and Football Clubs: Gender and the 'Modern' Public Sphere in Colonial Southwestern Nigeria," in *Leisure in Urban Africa*, ed. Paul Tiyambe Zeleza and Cassandra Rachel Veney (Trenton, NJ: Africa World Press, 2003); Todd Cleveland, *Following the Ball*; Alegi, *Laduma!*; Peter Alegi, *African Soccerscapes: How a Continent Changed the World's Game* (Athens: Ohio University Press, 2010); Laura Fair, "Kickin' It: Leisure, Politics and Football in Colonial Zanzibar, 1900s–1950s," *Africa* 67, no. 2 (1997): 224–51; Fair, "Ngoma Reverberations: Swahili Music Culture and the Making of Football Aesthetics in Early Twentieth-Century Zanzibar," in *Football in Africa: Conflict, Conciliation and Community*, ed. Gary Armstrong and Richard Giulianotti (New York: Palgrave Macmillan, 2004).

27. T. J. Desch Obi, *Fighting for Honor: The History of African Martial Art Traditions in the Atlantic World* (Columbia: University of South Carolina Press, 2008).

28. Scholars like Ashley Currier, Marc Epprecht, Stella Nyanzi, and Zethu Matabeni demonstrate how intimate relationships, cultural representations, and political organizing that center queer peoples and perspectives provide innovative avenues that challenge normative understandings of the relationship between sex, gender, and sexuality and open new possibilities for imagining potential futures. Zethu Matabeni, *Reclaiming Afrikan: Queer Perspectives on Sexual and Gender Identities* (Athlone, South Africa: Modjaji Books, 2014); Ashley Currier, *Out in Africa: LGBT Organizing in Namibia and South Africa* (Minneapolis: University of Minnesota Press, 2012); Marc Epprecht, *Hungochani: The History of a Dissident Sexuality in Southern Africa* (Montreal: McGill–Queen's University Press, 2004).

29. Oluwakemi M. Balogun and Kimberly Kay Hoang, "Refashioning Global Bodies: Cosmopolitan Femininities in Nigerian Beauty Pageants and the Vietnamese Sex Industry," in *Global Beauty, Local Bodies*, ed. Afshan Jafar and Erynn Masi de Casanova (New York: Palgrave Macmillan, 2013).

Part 1

Celebrations and Rites of Passage

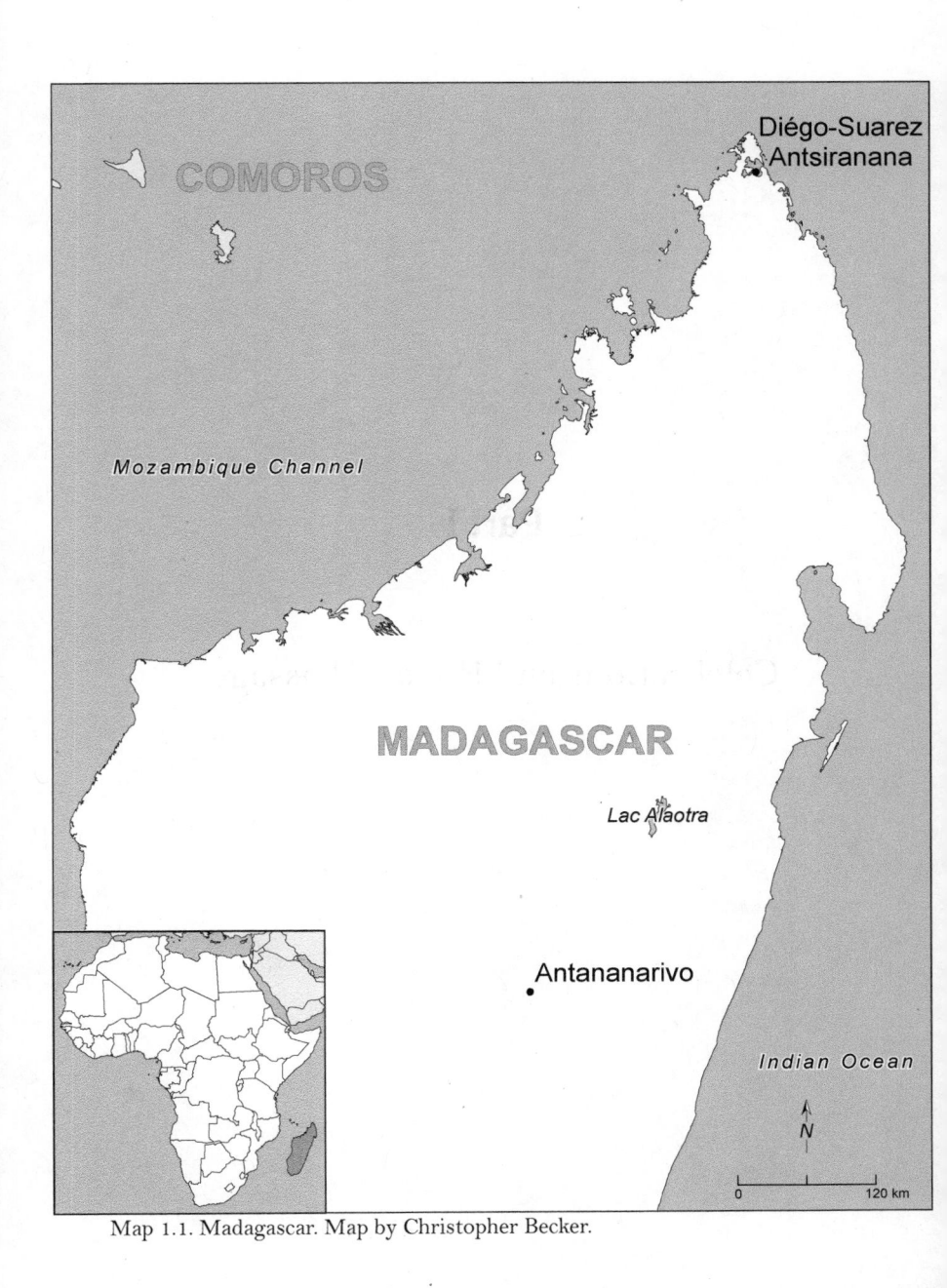

Map 1.1. Madagascar. Map by Christopher Becker.

1

Hosting a First Haircutting in Diégo Suarez, Madagascar

ERIN NOURSE

This chapter explores the social and ritual dimensions of a Malagasy baby's *aqiqah*, an Islamic welcoming ceremony. This ethnographic account of a university student's hosting of an aqiqah is based on research conducted from September 2011 to June 2012 on birth rituals and rites of initiation for the newly born in Diégo Suarez, Madagascar, where I lived with my husband, Ben. I interviewed approximately fifty informants in Malagasy and French, or a combination of the two, as Malagasy often code-switch (i.e., alternate) between the two languages. A few interviews were conducted in English. I also attended religious ceremonies and participated in typical Diégo everyday activities. All participants' names are pseudonyms.

Parents living in pluralistic urban contexts such as Diégo Suarez, a port city at the northernmost tip of Madagascar, use the birth of a child to contemplate and construct complex family histories and religious identities—their own, as well as those they wish to instill in the emerging life of the newly born. Such celebrations offer participants the space to discuss concerns regarding the appropriateness of certain religious practices, race and identity issues, and what it means to be Malagasy.

In places like Diégo, where many live far from their ancestral homelands (*tanindrazana*) and extended kin, rites for newborns are sometimes creatively invented by an increasingly diverse and aspirational generation of young people. These and other "traditional" rituals are traditional only in the broad sense of the word, in the way that most of us cast our ritual innovations as linked with the models from our past. They are informed by Malagasy family customs in addition to encounters with social difference, as Christians, Muslims, and traditionalists increasingly include one another in their religious festivities.

Traditions of Haircutting in Madagascar

Madagascar, the fourth-largest island in the world, lies in the Indian Ocean off Africa's southeast coast. It is known for its biodiversity. However, as home to peoples of African, Asian, and Arab descent, its cultural diversity is equally captivating. Travelers have long been intrigued by Malagasy practices of ancestor veneration; in particular, the burial and reburial (exhumation) customs of the Merina of the central highlands have been well documented.[1] By contrast, this essay examines beginning-of-life ritualizing activities among northern coastal groups. I highlight haircutting, in the context of a baby's aqiqah, as one of the ways Malagasy introduce the newly born to the obligations they have as descendants of ancestors—the customs (*fady*), taboos (*fomba*), and ritual practices that make them who they are today.

In Madagascar, it is common to cut or shave a young child's hair. Sometimes, haircutting is part of a ceremony or rite of passage; other times, it is simply part of an infant's conventional everyday care. While the origins are unclear, we know ritual practices in honor of birth are more than a few generations old.[2] Haircutting traditions of Madagascar's early Indonesian, East African, and Arab Muslim inhabitants likely contributed to contemporary practices. Some trim their children's hair a few days after birth as part of a traditional blessing (*joro*) or in conjunction with the Islamic practice of holding a sacrifice seven days after a birth (aqiqah); others shave babies' heads at multiple points during infancy; and some perform haircutting ceremonies once a child has cut its first teeth, at a ceremony called *mampiravaka tsaiky* (literally: to bejewel the child) where children are adorned with heirloom necklaces that link them to those—both alive and gone—who have worn the same jewels.[3]

In rituals, haircutting cleanses the child of any pollution (*maloto*) she or he might have acquired while passing through the birth canal, socializes the child, and transitions infants from something ambiguous to a fully integrated human. Haircutting cuts across religious communities and ancestral lineages, with specific prayers, food, and ritual objects shaping the child in distinct ways. Haircutting is rarely performed in isolation from other cultural and religious practices such as naming ceremonies, baptisms, sacrifices, circumcisions, and traditional ancestral blessings (joro), which also shape children's identity, but it is nevertheless an important means by which Malagasy instill what it means to be Malagasy and a member of a community.

Situating Diégo Suarez, Madagascar

Named after two Portuguese explorers said to have discovered the island in 1506, Diégo Suarez is the capital city of the northernmost province of Madagascar. A heterogeneous cosmopolitan port city, it has many lures, including a large university, teaching hospital, military base, naval shipyard, fish processing plant, and several administrative centers. Diégo has a long history of enticing people to its shores—longer than is implied by the so-called Portuguese "discovery" of Madagascar in the sixteenth century.[4]

When I returned in 2011, the third time since 2004, Diégo's streets were lined with hurricane-damaged French colonial-era buildings and shiny new tourist hotels. Pedestrians, cyclists, motorists, yellow taxis, children in school uniforms, chickens, stray dogs, and street vendors selling mangoes, pickled mango chutneys, and *sambos* and other fried treats crowded its streets. The city's inhabitants included Malagasy from all over Madagascar as well as Indo-Pakistani immigrants, Comorians, Yemini Arabs, and French expatriates.

Celebrating the Birth of Hakim

In January 2012, Ravaka and Nasreen stopped me at the University of Antsiranana's library. Nasreen wore a long blouse, skirt, and *hijab* (head scarf), and Ravaka wore a T-shirt and jeans. They shared that Nasreen's friend had given birth and would host an aqiqah, the Islamic tradition of sacrificing an animal at the occasion of a birth. "We're still looking for the goats," Nasreen explained. "If we find the goats in time, the ceremony will take place this Saturday."

At seven a.m. on Saturday, Nasreen and her neighbor, Khalisah, were preparing food for the ceremony. On the concrete porch that encircled their dormitories, they sorted rice, looking for tiny stones. As guests arrived, women congregated around the rice, children played tag in the courtyard, and men readied the space for the slaughtering of the goats. In anticipation, Nasreen's five-year-old son Aasim began to cry, which prompted Nasreen to escort all the children inside for a *dessin animé* (cartoon). Outside, in accordance with the customs of *halal,* the prescribed method of slaughter for Muslims, men prayed over the animals, laid the goats to face Mecca, and, with a quick slice of a knife across their jugular veins, spilt their blood upon the ground.

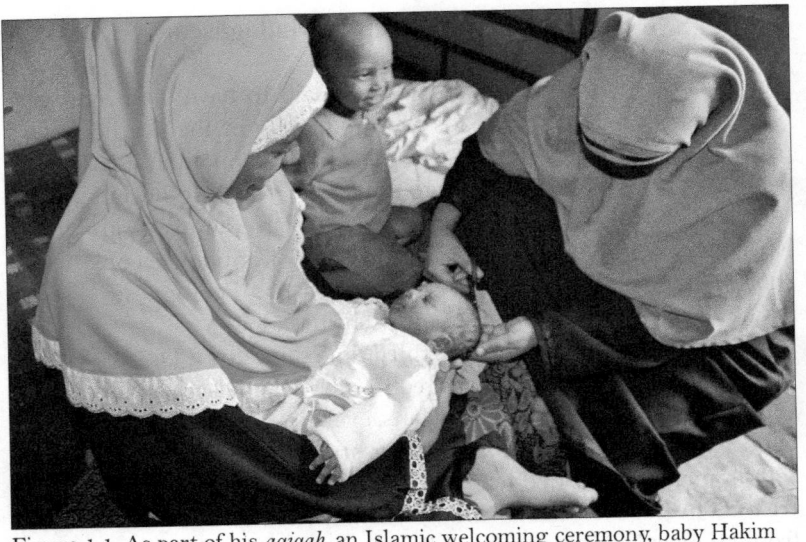

Figure 1.1. As part of his *aqiqah*, an Islamic welcoming ceremony, baby Hakim receives his first haircut. With her three-year-old daughter looking on, Nasreen, the host of the ceremony, carefully snips away Hakim's hair as he lies in his mother's lap. Source: Erin Nourse.

Aasim reemerged, deeply curious about the men's work. Across the courtyard, women prepared the feast. One scraped out the inside of a coconut and then pressed water through the shredded coconut meat. Others cut goat meat, sliced cucumbers for a salad, and peeled potatoes for the stew.

At midmorning, the newborn guest of honor, asleep and bundled in blankets, arrived in an interior room where the haircutting would take place. Rahimah held her tiny infant Hakim as Nasreen cut his hair by gracing his scalp with ordinary household scissors while he slept. Few observed this intimate procedure, save a couple of women and a handful of children. Only once did he cry, provoking his mother, who wore a long dress and hijab, to unabashedly pull her clothing aside to console him. As he suckled, Nasreen removed the remainder of the downy hair that covered his head.

Nasreen gathered the handkerchief she had used to collect the hair, shook it into a piece of white paper, rolled it up, and handed it to a man standing in the doorway. The hair would be weighed at a local *épicerie* (small grocery), and gold would be bought in proportion to its weight. They would give the gold to the poor, as a token of gratitude for the child's birth. Though the baby was unaware of the ceremony on his behalf, other children were not. They were in and out of the room, tried to touch the baby, and observed with infectious grins.

The meal was served unceremoniously. Unlike some haircutting events, no ritual speeches (joro) or requests for blessings from the ancestors were made. Instead, the gathering was casual. The sixty or so guests were relatives, friends, and schoolmates—part of the community to which baby Hakim now belonged. The attendees were diverse in age, religion, and nationality. Adult members of the Muslim community ate indoors in separate spaces according to their gender, while young children, regardless of gender, shared their own space outside.

Children changed into the gorgeously decorated religious dress, complete with hijab and hats (taqiyah). Ben, my research assistant Édith, and about a dozen of Nasreen's non-Muslim friends gathered around a table on the outdoor thatched patio. We sat in chairs and were given plates, forks, and spoons, while Muslim participants ate on the floor with their hands from communal silver platters atop traditional Malagasy eating mats (lamaka). The rice was seasoned with coconut milk and cinnamon accents and tasted of the fire on which it had been cooked, a taste distinct from that of rice cooked over gas or charcoal for more common, nonreligious occasions.

Those at our table discussed the goat meat. Some didn't typically like goat because "it smelled," but they liked how Muslims cooked it in a curry sauce with turmeric, onion, garlic, tomato sauce, and potatoes. Osman, a gregarious Muslim and an international student from the Comoros, an island country to the northwest of Madagascar, sat at the table with the non-Muslims. Telling jokes, he code-switched between Malagasy, English, French, and Comorian Swahili. Some found his use of Comorian Swahili amusing, given that the northern dialect of Malagasy has enough Swahili borrowings to make his language sound simultaneously strange and familiar.

Osman complained about burqas, loose outer garments some Muslim women wear to cover their entire bodies in public (as opposed to hijabs, which typically cover just the hair and neck), and about Malagasy perceptions of Comorians. He argued that Muslims who dress in burqas are "adding to," or perhaps altering, the traditions of the Prophet and his wives. He seemed well versed in the theological arguments against wearing burqas, but less so in the religious rationale behind some Muslims' decision to do so. He appeared embarrassed that Muslims who wear burqas in Madagascar are usually thought to be Comorian, since he viewed such garments as sinful. "Sometimes,"

Figure 1.2. Two men work together to slaughter two goats according to the customs of halal. The goats will then be cooked in a curry sauce and served over rice to attendees of the ceremony. Source: Erin Nourse.

he countered forcefully, "they are pure Malagasy." He also complained that most Malagasy think Comorians are "very black." Others concurred that they used to think this, too, but agreed that Comorians come in all shades and dress in various styles, "just like Malagasy." "Though, to win the Miss Comorian contest," Omar explained, "you have to have very black skin and you have to have curly hair. We have to stand up for ourselves," he proclaimed, designating dark skin as a source of pride.

"What about in Madagascar?" Ben inquired. The Malagasy students agreed there were no criteria for skin color for the Miss Malagasy contest. However, conversations I have overheard and my knowledge of tensions between lighter-skinned Merina, an ethnic group of mixed racial origin from the central highlands, and darker-skinned coastal groups made me wonder otherwise. While staying in Antananarivo, the capital of Madagascar in the heart of its Central Highlands region, I remember one Merina mother's concern that her children might look "black like the father," a disappointment to her, given that her family had been so careful to preserve their lighter skin. By contrast, while walking around Diégo, I recall students who boldly spoke of the beauty of blackness.

Omar's concerns about Malagasy impressions of Comorians were evidence of the tensions between Malagasy and migrants to the island, including Comorians, who make up one of the largest migrant groups in northern Madagascar. In Diégo, interaction, and even intermarriage, is common among people of diverse backgrounds. Yet, stereotypes exist about the city's Comorian and Indo-Pakistani migrant communities, and about Malagasy highlanders versus northern coastal groups. Communal gatherings provide opportunities to confront these stereotypes. Omar's assertion that burqas are worn by both Comorian and Malagasy Muslims sheds light on the complexity of religious identity in both the Comoro Islands and Madagascar. The discussion about the criteria for winning beauty contests speaks to the racial hierarchies and racial pride that exists in both countries. It is within these multifaith, multiethnic spaces that people assert and question boundaries in terms of nationality, ethnicity, and religion.

Rites of Blessing in a Pluralistic Community

This aqiqah ceremony celebrated in the courtyard adjoining two Malagasy families' homes in student housing at the University of Antsiranana served multiple purposes. First, Hakim was surely blessed. He was declared worthy of a sacrifice and feast, socialized with the blades of scissors, and fully welcomed into the life of his community. We all learn of our physical, cultural, and even spiritual environments long before we are conscious of the overt meanings attached to them. The smells of roasting meat and the feel of scissor blades provide children, even sleeping ones, with a visceral, preverbal sense of what it means to belong to a community.

Second, the ritual also made an impression on the older children present, who, in their donning of religious garb and witnessing of a child's haircutting, observed what it meant to be Muslims in Madagascar. Similarly, adults, in gathering and feasting together, created and reflected on their bondedness as members and friends of a particular religious community. On that day, being in this community meant gathering in the courtyard on a rainy day, with young and old together, Muslims and Christians alike.

Third, the ceremony was an opportunity for Nasreen to invest in her community. While her devotion to Islam has waxed and waned through the years, her faith community has become increasingly important. Raised by her grandmother after her Malagasy mother and Yemeni father separated, Nasreen describes her relationship to God as the only constant in her life. She hit a kind of rock bottom in secondary school, when, after falling in love with her then-Christian boyfriend, she was sent away to school in a nearby town in her family's effort to end the relationship. Despite a lack of familial support, the love between Nasreen and her boyfriend endured. He eventually converted to Islam and the two married, moved to Diégo, and now have four children. Far from relatives and extended kin, the Diégo ummah has become an important community in which they choose to invest their time and energies.

Lastly, the ritual provided space for conversation and social merriment that highlighted how gathering and eating together can be a sacred act. Ordinary acts of slaughtering an animal, cooking, eating, and haircutting can become sacred when they are done before witnesses and with a spirit of intentionality. When Malagasy women wake early to sort rice and prepare the coconut milk, spices, and vegetables, they help to cast the day with its proper investment of meaning. When men say prayers over a slaughtered animal, they offer something to God, that God may in turn bless the community. It is the purposefulness with which normal everyday activities are performed that make them transformative for all those involved.

Birth rituals offer communities a chance to gather together in celebration of a new child's life. They are opportunities to remember (and re-member) what it means to be part of a particular family or religious community. As part of the necessary tools of sacrifice and other rites of passage like circumcision and haircutting ceremonies, spears, knives, and scissors not only mark moments as sacred but also provide for those present a sense of the occasion's seriousness, as participants simultaneously remember the past and reenvision the future. Haircutting ceremonies are common throughout Madagascar, practiced by Muslims, Christians, and the nonaffiliated. But it is the manner in which they are performed, the specific foods that are eaten, the inherited family customs (*fombandrazana*), and the prayers uttered that enable orchestrators to shape initiates into particular kinds of people.

Guests at this ritual came from varying backgrounds but were unified as members or friends of a specific Muslim community in Diégo Suarez. It provided space for discussions about the appropriateness of certain religious acts and modes of dress within Islam; about what it means to be "purely" Malagasy or "purely" Comorian; and about ethnicity, skin color, and religious orthodoxy. Rituals such as this one are spaces where questions of one's identity are worked out, not only among the in-crowd, but also with and among those external to the religious community. In pluralistic settings, both engagement with difference and immersion in a cohesive community give us a sense of who we are. And while such conversations can and do occur anywhere, the birth of a child serves as a particularly salient moment to think about one's own religious heritage and markings.

Notes

1. For more information on the burial customs of Merina, see Maurice Bloch, "Death, Women and Power," in *Death and the Regeneration of Life*, ed. Maurice Bloch and Jonathan Parry (Cambridge: Cambridge University Press, 1982). See also David Graeber, "Dancing with Corpses Reconsidered: An Interpretation of *Famadihana* (in Arivonimamo, Madagascar)," *American Ethnologist* 22, no. 2 (May 1995): 258–78; Pier M. Larson, "Austronesian Mortuary Ritual in History: Transformations of Secondary Burial (*Famadihana*) in Highland Madagascar," *Ethnohistory* 48, no. 1/2 (Winter/Spring 2001): 123–55.

2. William Ellis, *History of Madagascar*, 2 vols. (London: Fisher, Son, 1838); Chase Salmon Osborn, *Madagascar: Land of the Man-Eating Tree* (1924; repr., Somerville, MA: Heliograph, 2012), 279.

3. For more on haircutting and other birth rituals, see Gillian Feeley-Harnik, "Childbirth and the Affiliation of Children in Northwest Madagascar," *Taloha: Revue de l'Institut de Civilisations—Musée d'Art et d'Archéologie, Antananarivo* 13 (2000):135–72; Maurice Bloch, "Zafimaniry Birth and Kinship Theory," *Social Anthropology* 1, no. 1b (February 1993): 119–32; Erin Nourse, "Turning 'Water Babies' (Zaza Rano) into 'Real Human Beings' (Vrai Humains): Rituals of Blessing for the Newly Born in Diégo Suarez, Madagascar," *Journal of Religion in Africa* 47, no. 2 (2018): 224–56.

4. For more on the history of Diégo, see Virginia Thompson and Richard Adloff, *The Malagasy Republic: Madagascar Today* (Stanford, CA: Stanford University Press, 1965), 269; Solofo Randrianja and Stephen Ellis, *Madagascar: A Short History* (Chicago: University of Chicago Press, 2009), 20; Timothy Insoll, *The Archaeology of Islam in Sub-Saharan Africa* (Cambridge: Cambridge University Press, 2003), 194.

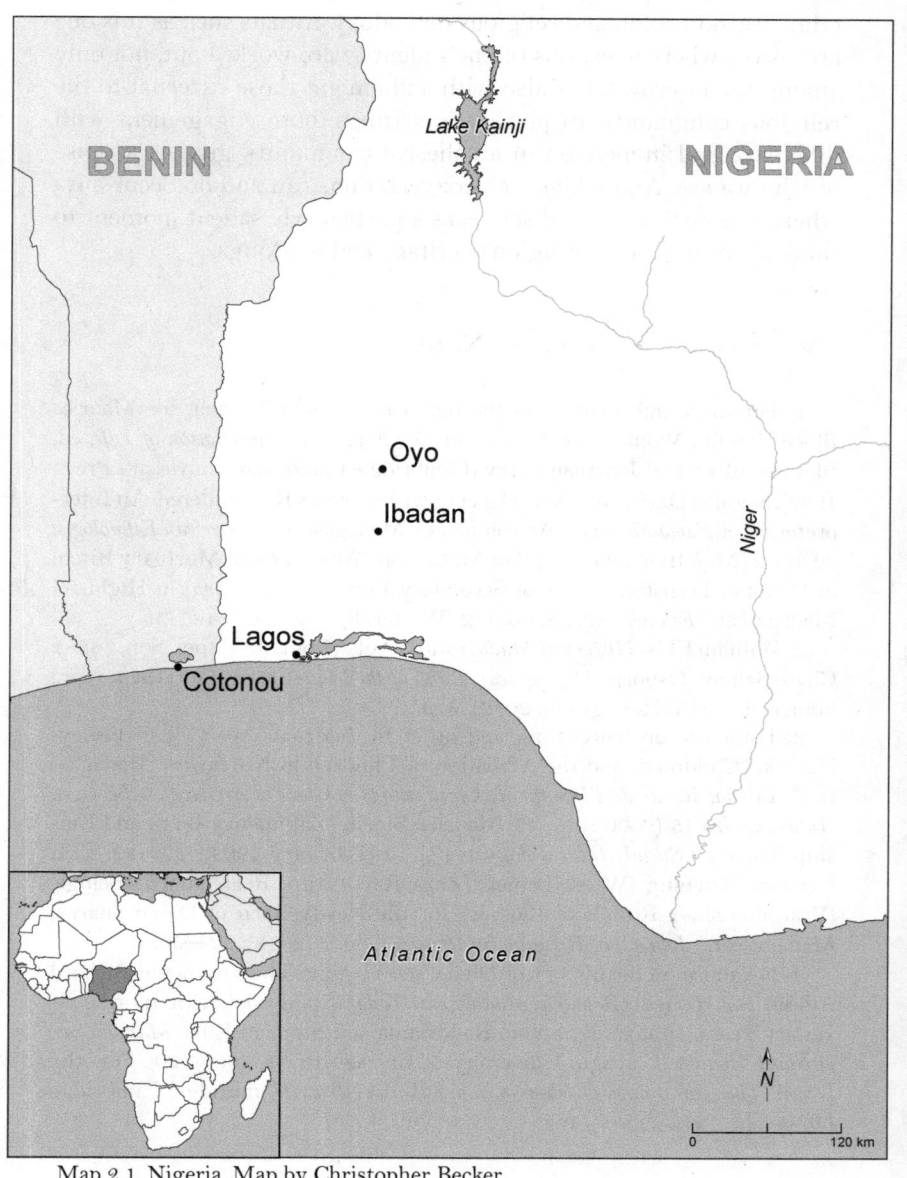

Map 2.1. Nigeria. Map by Christopher Becker.

2

Ekún-Ìyàwó

An African Bridal Shower in Yorubaland

ABIOLA VICTORIA AYODOKUN AND OSUOLALE JOSEPH AYODOKUN

Mo kuru, moyiira
Mo wa wole niwaju re iwo baba mi
Mo wa ki o wure fun mi ki nto ma lo
Ire re nire orisa o

I bow down in reverence.
Bowing before you my father, I am paying homage before I
    embark on my journey.
I am here to be blessed by you.
Your blessing is that of a god.

The Yoruba people are an ethnic group located in West Africa, of which the largest population today lives in the Republic of Nigeria. Yoruba people speak a language that consists of diverse and mutually intelligible dialects throughout the region.[1] Marriage is a culturally specific social institution and practice that cuts across ethnicity and race around the world. Like many other groups, Yoruba people place a high value on marriage. For the Yoruba, marriage involves a lot of ceremony and splendid display, lasting for days.[2] Among the Yoruba, people practice Islam, Christianity, and traditional religions. However, religious cleavages are minimized in favor of communal pan-Yoruba identity and intermarriage remains common.[3] While today Christianity and Islam hold sway in most Yoruba families, traditional wedding ceremonies continue to have social significance. "Traditional" in this sense means the cultural ways of exchanging marriage vows between the intending couple and their family. Few weddings are considered complete without a traditional ceremony, even if they now also involve a religious (Christian, Islamic) or legal ceremony.[4]

This chapter focuses on the continued role of such traditional practices by looking at *ekún-ìyàwó* (bridal lament), which is a type of bridal shower and poetic chant performed by women on their wedding day. It is a ceremonial ritual typical in some, though not all, Yoruba communities. This paper is based on direct observations and in-depth interviews conducted with ten elderly women in Ibadan and Oyo towns, in Oyo State in southwest Nigeria, between December 2014 and January 2017. These women were known for their mastery of different Yoruba singing cultures, and at one point in time they sang and trained brides on how to sing ekún-ìyàwó. We explore the performance of ekún-ìyàwó in its social context, examining how the ritual addresses the bride's shifting social relationships. More specifically, ekún-ìyàwó serves as training ground for new sets of expectations about marriage, love, and family as the new bride transitions into a different role. These relationships can sometimes extend beyond the family members physically present at the marriage ceremony to encompass other social relations, such as with the bride's ancestors. As we will see, everything about the bride on her wedding day speaks to three sets of people: herself, her family, and the groom. Therefore, understanding how a bride must behave on her wedding day tells us about the relationship between individuals and society and the performance of the social self through marriage in Yorubaland.[5]

Performing Ekún-Ìyàwó: From Rehearsing to Addressing the Family

Traditionally, when a man is ready to marry his bride, he will usually send a message to the family of the bride-to-be. He will also send gifts known as *erù-ìdána* (dowry or bride-price) to be presented to the bride's family, which must meet their specifications. Once the dowry is paid in full, the bridegroom's family then proposes that a day be set for the marriage ceremony. The interval between the proposal date and the actual date of the marriage ceremony could be a few weeks to several months; there is no fixed time span.

As soon as the date for the wedding is confirmed, the bride must begin to prepare for the marriage ceremony. One of her key tasks is to learn and perfect her knowledge and skill of singing the ekún-ìyàwó. She must also string her waist beads, called *bèbèdí*, which are associated with women's sexuality among the Yoruba. Primarily a traditional female beauty enhancer, they are worn to accentuate femininity and beauty, drawing focal attention to the hips, buttocks, and thighs, as well as their movement. For young Yoruba women, wearing beads is also a symbol of female maturity as they are worn as proof that they have begun menstruation and are ready for marriage; hence, the many gifts of beads to young brides. The preparation before, like the marriage ceremony itself, is a collective endeavor in which close and extended family members are involved. Different family members play varied roles, and the women of the bride's family are responsible for teaching the bride what to do on the marriage ceremony day. The bride-to-be works one-on-one with a teacher every evening to prepare. Family members select an expert within the family to teach the bride-to-be on the basis her singing ability and style. In Yorubaland, some women are known for their expertise in singing traditional genres of songs, such as *rárà*, a chanted song often sung at funerals and other special occasions. Mrs. Sanni, an elderly woman who participated as a singing teacher, remarked that the bride's teacher cannot be the mother of the bride; she could be a wife in the bride's family, although not necessarily junior in status to the mother of the bride. Mrs. Adijat, a woman in her early sixties who has trained many brides on how to sing ekún-ìyàwó, explained that the most important criterion is that, prior to the time of the bride's marriage ceremony, there should be some degree of cordial regard among the bride, her mother, and the teacher.

The training starts by teaching the bride how to walk on the night of her marriage ceremony. Touching any obstacles with her legs while she simply walks around or on her way to the groom's house is considered taboo. The next stage of the pre-wedding training is learning the ekún-ìyàwó, long-form poetry that brides chant to express their feelings about a transient state. The lyrics are usually words of prayer, rendered in a tone that represents the bride's own prayers and sincere plea for blessings from the people who stand in for the bride's gods. There are also some personal expressions of self-praise and beauty, concluding that it is only the groom who has the right to access the expression of her beauty within the intimacy of marriage. The fact that the bride can add lyrics that fit her situation shows the flexibility and expressive nature of ekún-ìyàwó.

> Ori mi wadoriowo
> Idi mi wa di idiileke o
> Ileke ti e ba ka ti o bape
> E wipekioko si mi labe aso
> Ohunmogbewayenbelabeaso
> Enhinenhinenhin . . .

My head commands a huge wealth
My waist becomes adorned with beads
The beads you count but found incomplete
Ask my husband to check under my cloth
My purpose my pride is hidden beneath my cloth
Enhinehinehin . . .

Ekún-ìyàwó is a complex genre employing stylistic devices such as anadiplosis (repetition of the last word of a preceding clause), anaphora (repetition of a word at the beginning of successive clauses), and epiphora (repetition of a word at the end of successive clauses).[6] It is usually learned line by line so that the bride will not make mistakes or forget the lyrics. The bride is expected to learn the lyrics at her leisure. The teacher will then call her into her own room for rehearsals, which will last several weeks before her wedding night.

Once the bride has learned the ekún-ìyàwó, she is ready for her wedding day. On the morning of her wedding day, the bride will be showered with gifts. As family members and friends of the family arrive in the house or compound, their first point of call is the bride's room. She is usually in her room with her friends and some female members of her family. The teacher takes charge by helping the bride get dressed during various wardrobe changes throughout the day. The guests will place a gift in her hands, usually clothes and other wearable items such as earrings or beads. It is expected of the visiting family members to give a gift, but the type and value of the gift is determined by the giver.

The family of the bride is expected to feed all the guests on the wedding day, so the day is known for much joyful cooking and drinking. There is a lot of excitement and singing from the morning onwards by the agemates of the bride, with drummers accompanying the singing. As the evening gets near, one of the women in the family will come to the big room or the section of the family compound where the elders of the family are seated. These elders will include the parents of the bride and the grandparents of the bride if they are still alive. In addition, there are other family members from both sides of the bride's family. The teacher also acts as the facilitator of the singing session. After ensuring that everyone is seated, she announces to the gathering that the bride is about to be brought out for her performance of ekún-ìyàwó and that everyone should get ready to play their role.

Everyone to whom the bride will sing will prepare a gift, and this time it is usually a monetary gift. The actual amount of money is not what matters; the key point is that the individual gives the bride money after she sings. However, before giving cash to the bride, the first cultural gift is to shower prayers on her, with a specific focus on certain aspects of her marital and economic life—such as enjoying her husband's house, prayers that she will bear children who will grow up to be a blessing to her, that her children will be successful and renowned in her husband's family, and that she, too, will succeed in all her endeavors. Every person for whom the bride sings is free to pray for the bride, focusing on any aspect of her life. The subsequent cash gifts belong to the bride, and this is thus the second time the guests and her parents will be showering her with gifts.

The singing is done solely by the bride; it is forbidden for anyone to join her. The bride is expected to sing with a veil over her face, a sign that she is prepared for her groom. The first person she will sing for is her father, to be followed by her mother. Kneeling down before him, the bride begins with a traditional invocation of each of her parents' symbolic position as god.

> Mo kuru, moyiira
> Mo wawoleniwaju re iwo baba/yeye mi
> Mo waki o wure fun mi kinto ma lo
> Ire re nire orisa o
>
> I bow down in reverence.
> Bowing before you my father, I am paying homage
>   before I embark on my journey.
> I am here to be blessed by you.
> Your blessing is that of a god.

This song is considered to be auspicious because it is an accepted tradition that a child pays homage to her parents as a mark of respect before embarking on major events in life. The invocation to the ancestors through the biological parents of the bride is done intermittently while singing the song. Lines of the lyrics are often drawn out with the sound of sobbing. The ambience and the lyrics, together with the usual emotions that prevail on such occasions, usually cause the bride to weep, sometimes joined by her mother and other female members of the family. The bride who does not weep while singing the ekún-ìyàwó is usually considered to be a very brash daughter who lacks emotion. For any bride, this is an undesirable characterization on such a day, so every bride is encouraged by her tutor to weep while singing.

The bride may kneel down and sing her ekún-ìyàwó for at least twenty people, and sometimes more for those brides with larger families. Whenever the bride sings kneeling down in front of any family member, paternal or maternal, that individual she is kneeling before is seen as occupying the position of a god, and thus has the capacity to invoke eternal blessings on the bride. The bride, therefore, receives a spiritual shower of blessings through her ancestors, whom everyone that she sings for represents. This act of showering the bride with prayers focuses on her life as a married woman, wishing her a peaceful childbearing experience and praying that her children will be prosperous in life so that in her old age she will be cared for by them. Since family members present the bride with both monetary and other, spiritual gifts, this ceremony is also a bridal shower. The requests for prayer and parental blessings through song is a dimension that makes the Yoruba bridal lamentation unique. Ekún-ìyàwó is sung to plead for blessings for the bride from her ancestors, as represented by the people for whom she knelt down to sing.

Cultural Context and Social Change

Ekún-ìyàwó is a cultural practice that is full of excitement and expression in Yoruba society. It brings to the fore the core tradition of communality in the fact that every member of the bride's family, paternal and maternal, is committed to support both the bride and her parents, as enacted through the performance. It also showcases the response of the family members, in which these relationships are made concrete for all onlookers to appreciate. It is a time to show support to the bride and her family. The liminal position of the bride allows her to bind her family members together at her moment of transition into married status. The family members the bride sings for contribute materially and spiritually to the well-being of the bride and her family as a result of her singing.

Ekún-ìyàwó is closely linked to other aspects of Yoruba culture. First, it brings to the fore the fashion-consciousness of the Yoruba people, as the bride will be seen dressed in various outfits throughout the day. The family members also appear in their best dress. Second, the ekún-ìyàwó heightens the shared conviviality of the day. The bride's friends usually take the lead in singing throughout the day and as they escort the bride to her husband's house. It is only when the bride is ready to sing her ekún-ìyàwó that silence is observed, as that moment is considered sacred. The shared conviviality of the day thus again highlights the threads of sociality that link the bride, her family, and the rest of her guests.

However, Western influence is having what we consider to be a negative effect on this very important tradition. Principally, individualism is now gaining ground among Yoruba families, and some families are now wary of each other in ways that they were not previously, often due to religious differences. For instance, some people consider collecting gifts and kneeling down before someone whose faith is different from that of the bride or her parents undesirable. Another factor is that many young women, especially in the cities, do not have enough deep knowledge of the Yoruba language to perform ekún-ìyàwó or lack family members with enough familiarity to teach it. Therefore, today ekún-ìyàwó continues to be performed only at weddings in very rural societies of Yorubaland. In the cities, the brides are usually excused from singing ekún-ìyàwó. Nonetheless, even in the city, the other aspects of the bride's symbolic transition remain intact, such as the covering of the bride's face with a veil, the practice of parents and family members praying for the bride in the open, and the family members' material and spiritual contributions, suggesting that the moment of marriage continues to bear its significance as a moment of change even among urbanized Yoruba.

Ekún-ìyàwó is a complex, entertaining, and emotional art that illuminates the communal nature of Yoruba traditional weddings and highlights the role of the verbal arts in recognizing and sustaining relationships between individuals and other members of their society, including the ancestors. Anyone who watches a performance of ekún-ìyàwó will be left with no doubt that, like any good performance art, it has the capacity to hold our attention and leave its traces on us long after its final words have been sung.

Notes

1. William Bascom, *The Yoruba of Southwestern Nigeria* (Prospect Heights, IL: Waveland, 1984).

2. Nathaniel Akinremi Fadipe, *The Sociology of the Yoruba* (Ibadan, Nigeria: University of Ibadan Press, 1970).

3. Insa Nolte, Olukoya Ogen, and Rebecca Jones, eds., *Beyond Religious Tolerance: Muslim, Christian and Traditionalist Encounters in an African Town* (Woodbridge, UK: James Currey, 2017).

4. J. S. Eades, *The Yoruba Today* (Cambridge: Cambridge University Press, 1980).

5. Kwame Gyekye, *African Cultural Values: An Introduction* (Philadelphia: Sankofa, 1996).

6. Olalere Waheed Raji and Rasaq Atanda Ajadi, "A Stylistic Analysis of Ekun Iyawo," *Research on Humanities and Social Sciences* 3, no. 9 (2013): 143–48.

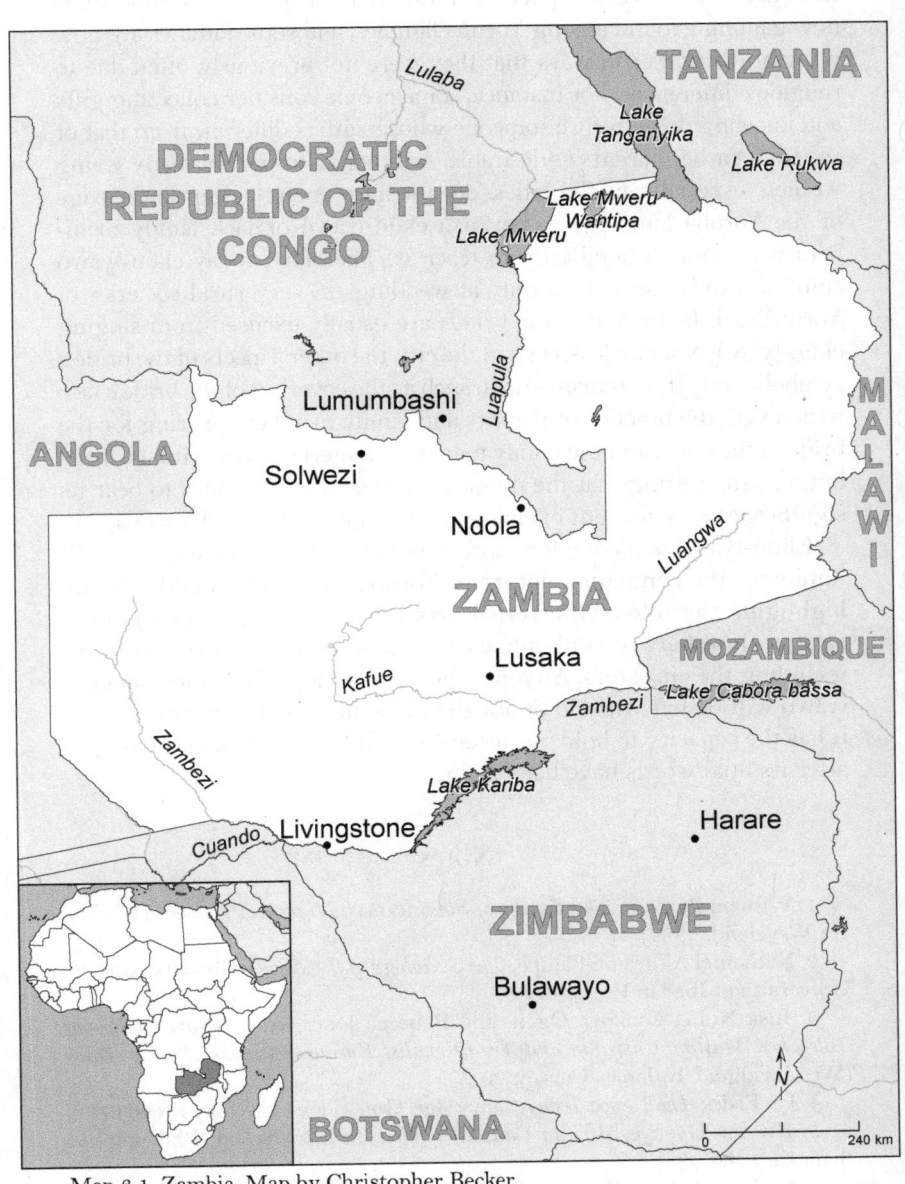

Map 3.1. Zambia. Map by Christopher Becker.

3

Funeral Swag

A Celebration of Death in Urban Zambia

PRINCE F. M. LAMBA

Across African cultures, dead ancestors are treated with fear and veneration, with funeral rituals serving as a way of demonstrating respect. Traditional and modern aspects of mourning have now been fused, incorporating luck, ancestor worship, and urban life. Likewise, death in Zambia has been associated with somberness and observed under strict adherence to cultural norms. Traditionally, funeral gatherings are major community events in Zambia to which one does not require an invitation to attend. However, the organization of funerals has over time evolved tremendously, especially in urban areas. New practices have been incorporated and changed the general outlook and character of present-day funerals from entirely solemn occasions to flamboyant affairs with delicious foods, expensive drinks, and a deep sense of fashion and socializing. This essay discusses an emerging cultural context that offers new perceptions of death and funerals in the country. It describes a trend, commonly referred to as "funeral swag," that creates opportunities for the expression of high-end lifestyles on the occasion of death. Funeral swag represents a slew of nontraditional behaviors during funerals. However, traditionalists believe these new practices bring misfortune to the living and the dead and are in direct violation of centuries-old rules that encourage silence and solemnness, and shun socializing.[1]

Zambia is a large, landlocked, southern African country spanning the plateau of south-central Africa. It is 290,586 square miles (752,614 square km) in area, which makes it slightly larger than Texas. On October 24, 1964, Zambia became independent of the United Kingdom and established Lusaka as its capital city, located in the south-central

region. Zambia as a country can be divided into two major demographic regions, based on levels of development: urban and rural.
Lusaka and other cities found in the most industrialized and developed areas, stretching from Livingstone in the south to Solwezi in
the northwest, commonly known as the "line of rail" (following the
country's main railroad route), are the core economic hubs and constitute the urban region. The rest of the country is largely rural. Still,
Zambia is one of the most urbanized countries in sub-Saharan Africa
and, as a result of the urban influx, diverse ethno-linguistic groups interact regularly. Many contemporary Zambian households, especially
those in cities, are exposed to the media, technology, and influences
of Western urbanized cultures, from internet cafes to hip-hop music.[2]
However, the majority of the country's poor population still live in the
rural areas.

Historically, funerals in Zambia are big occasions both in villages
and cities. Death, however, assumes a different character in these two
contexts, primarily because of the differences in the level of adherence to cultural practices and the socioeconomic status of residents.
Traditionally, women and men separate; the men stay outside and the
women remain in the house of the deceased.[3] During the mourning
period, grief is shown through wailing, singing, and dancing and becomes an emotional affair. In rural areas, the whole village walks to
the burial place to pay their last respects after long speeches about
the departed and expressions of gratitude for donations and support have been delivered. After burial, the mourners return to the
funeral house, where homemade meals are served together with locally brewed traditional beverages, both alcoholic and nonalcoholic.
Tradition and cultural norms take precedence and "dos and don'ts"
are strictly adhered to according to local practices regarding death
and funerals.

In urban contexts, the character of funerals changes: features of
funeral swag are introduced and become evident. The phenomenon
is mainly practiced in Lusaka and other major towns found along the
line of rail and occasionally in the regional capital cities. Funeral swag
has steadily established itself as a sociocultural activity in urban areas,
especially among youth, members of the educated middle class, and
wealthy populations. These privileged groups adopt new ways of life
that value change, and which they perceive to be classy and symbols
of high social status.

Funeral Rites and Funeral Swag

According to tradition, when a death occurs all possible means of communication are used to spread the sad news.[4] Soon after, friends and relatives from across the country converge on the funeral house. The grief-stricken friends and relatives mourn and sob together. Some may even roll on the ground with grief. Women remain inside the house while men mourn from outside, regardless of the weather conditions. Women dress modestly, wearing old, simple dresses with *chitenje* (dyed fabric) wrapped around them and tennis shoes or *pata-pata* (flip-flops). Their hair may be uncombed and they are expected to wear headscarves, without much makeup on. Men are expected to wear casual or old clothes, too, with worn-out shoes or sandals. Wearing black is optional. Music, food, and beverages form a significant part of funeral events. Conventionally, depending on the bereaved family's religious orientation, religious music or traditional dirges are sung. The food and beverages are home-cooked meals, locally prepared within the premises of the funeral house either by female church members, neighborhood friends, or ordinary sympathizers. These meals, drawing from wide-ranging menus, are cooked in large pots on big bonfires and braziers based on traditional recipes.

These above-mentioned funeral rites stand in contrast with funeral swag, which refers to an emerging sociocultural practice that presents extraordinary opportunities for personal amusement and creative expression during traditionally somber moments on the occasion of death. It is a local adaptation of the "after-tears parties" practiced in South African urban townships, born out of interactions between people from the two countries and their proximity to each other.[5] While the South African parties are held after the burial of a deceased person, Zambian funeral swag is a cumulative process practiced throughout the entire mourning period, before and after burial. Funeral swag has become an integral feature at most urban funerals, with some connecting them to increasing westernization in the country.

Facets of funeral swag include trendy fashion, music, food and beverages, socializing and networking, as well as other customs and manners usually considered untraditional and culturally unacceptable at funerals. In contrast to the plain outfits expected at traditional funeral rites, funeral swag promotes wearing fashionable outfits. For example, funeral swag dress codes include bereaved family and close relatives wearing uniform designer attire. It is not uncommon today for women to wear trousers, put on heavy makeup, and generally exhibit their acumen in fashion, a trend that would have been considered taboo in the past. Dressing for funerals has increased creativity and created income-generating opportunities for fashion designers. There are no longer clothing restrictions for men and women; the emphasis is on looking sophisticated.

There are also conspicuous changes taking place with regard to music and food served at funerals. Upon returning from the cemetery, mourners are welcomed by a smorgasbord of delicious foods and beverages, sometimes prepared by professional caterers. In the case of music, lively recorded genres are played instead of solemn music to soothe and entertain people as they enjoy their meals. Playing popular religious and secular music creates a party-like environment, resulting in sporadic dance performances, especially by youths and members of the tribal cousinship (ethnic group).[6]

In the meantime, people take time to socialize: old friends and relatives catch up, relationships are renewed, and new acquaintances are made. The extent of socializing at funerals is slowly developing

Figure 3.1. Mourners dressed in uniform funeral attire showcasing the fashion element of the swag. Source: Prince Lamba.

Figure 3.2. Male mourners gather around a casket in swag style: classy dress code, "staged" mannerisms, and printed T-shirts. Source: Prince Lamba.

funeral gatherings into ordinary rendezvous for merrymaking. To some extent, funerals are refashioned into everyday events for social networking, especially among the youth. For instance, for young people, leaving a funeral house to go out for a drink or some form of a "good time" is now a common practice in urban areas. When darkness falls, they hang around in intimate couples and sometimes spend romantic moments in nearby cars. Many serious intimate relationships begin with socializing at funerals. On the other hand, long-lasting business relationships among elders have also been achieved through networking at funerals. All in all, this extent of mingling and personal indulgence during funerals nowadays includes practices that many consider a violation of cultural etiquette with regard to funerals.

New Creativity

It is said that the only thing that is constant in life is change, a process that is common in all aspects of human life, including funerals. Change in life may take place in a gradual way through a process of continuity or as complete, radical transformation. Funerals in urban Zambia have in this regard been going through a gradual process of continuity and change through which some aspects are discarded and new ones are introduced. Since culture embodies human behaviors and beliefs that are susceptible to change and surely do change over a period of time, it is evident that culture is dynamic.

It is no longer an issue of holding on and preserving a cultural practice but a question of how long this can be effectively sustained, especially in a cosmopolitan society that is rapidly responding to modern global trends. The transformation of urban funerals in Zambia has given rise to a new social context in which participants are increasingly finding personal amusement. The occasion of a funeral is also an opportunity that promotes creativity among diverse players. Arguably, a funeral scene in the city today represents a sense of high life and has become a hive of activities that involve style, creativity, and attention to detail in the event's organization. Behaviors and practices which were once intolerable, such as elegant dressing, multiple-course nontraditional meals, free gender mixing (sometimes leading to romance and dating), high levels of alcohol consumption, and lively music are now common features at most urban funerals of the educated middle and upper classes.

Elderly citizens and traditionalists find it hard to comprehend the new phenomenon, with many saying the tradition of holding a dignified funeral for their loved ones has been lost. Brian Meleka, 72, from Lusaka, said that when he was growing up, funerals carried with them respect, humility, and honor. Another female senior citizen, Lupasha Kasapo, 68, also of Lusaka, adds that "No elderly person approves of what is done in this day and age during funerals, but there is very little we can do, as we are often disregarded and called backward."

On the other hand, Zambian youth and the allegedly enlightened segment of society have various reasons for embracing the funeral swag phenomenon, highlighting some intergenerational conflict. They argue that funeral swag is a celebration and remembrance of the life of a deceased loved one. "No one goes to a celebration dressed in ragged clothes and looking downcast," explains thirty-year-old Daniel Mubanga. Grace Mumba, a teenager, also adds, "In dressing smartly, eating good food and socializing at funerals, we express the fraternal and happy relationships we had with the person that had died." Professor Sichalwe Kasanda from the University of Lusaka further elaborates that "it is believed that when one dies, he/she remains within the premises of the funeral house. For this reason, the surviving relatives and friends gather together and make huge bonfires to wade off the spirits of the dead, as they are believed to be lingering around. In all this, the African spirit of Ubuntu promotes dining together, regardless of whether the event is painful or celebratory."[7] Kasanda's comments can be seen as an indirect confirmation of funerals being a form of celebration—though quite a unique celebration, one may say. These cultural understandings and blended foreign practices have resulted in funeral swag.

Moreover, funerals of celebrities have become heightened occasions for swag. The inclusion of performing artists in the funeral program is now common and referred to as the "artistic send-off," which normally takes place at a convenient venue capable of accommodating a variety of artistic performances in remembrance of a departed celebrity. In Lusaka, the artistic send-offs usually take place at the city's only public theater hall, the Lusaka Play House, or right at the cemetery. In either case, the stage is set and necessary equipment and props are put in place as several artists take turns performing. Unlike other types of funerals, funerals of celebrities take funeral swag to the maximum level in every aspect: the music is lively and deafening, mourners dress to impress, mixed gender interactions become freer, public consumption of alcohol and food increases, people's conduct becomes extreme and inclined to foreign behaviors.

Creativity is an important ingredient in funeral swag, which generates and sustains business. Fashion designers use their talent and imagination to design appropriate outfits for their clients; caterers diligently apply their cooking skills to prepare delicious meals and drinks; undertakers come up with innovative services; sociable mourners employ tactful networking skills to achieve maximum mutual benefits with fellow mourners; professional mourners (who are trained and hired to wail and weep) use creative tactics to attract attention and win approval—the list is endless. In all instances, the level of ingenuity is amazingly orchestrated not only to please the concerned but also to motivate other people to practice funeral swag.

As change is inevitable, it is equally important that the process of change is managed in order to prevent undesirable social outcomes. However, the challenge here lies in who has the right to determine what is desirable and undesirable, especially in this era of globalization, fast-paced high-tech systems of communication, and media platforms. All of these elements have the potential to influence human behavior as well as change people's cultural practices. Similarly, the aspirations of local social classes for upper-class lifestyles have equally fostered the practice of new cultural trends such as funeral swag. This is true of the Zambian situation, where elite classes and celebrities desire extraordinary lifestyles that they believe embody modernity.

Undoubtedly, urban funerals today have created a new sociocultural context for people to express themselves through funeral swag. Despite facing some opposition from the elderly and traditionalists, the funeral swag phenomenon has come to stay. It is a new culture in which participants find relevance through one's death. With funeral swag, they mourn the dead, they celebrate the life of the dead, they show companionship and sympathy, they rededicate relationships, and at times find love. Marissa Abruzzini, writing about the after-tears parties of South Africa, sums it up: "Everyone grieves differently, even in cultures with strict funeral rites. What is a case of disrespect to an older person can be a young person's vital coping mechanism after losing someone they love. As this new tradition continues, we'll likely see it evolve even further and outgrow some of its more disrespectful components."[8]

In conclusion, funeral swag is a new sociocultural phenomenon that showcases changing ways of life that are steadily eliminating myths and beliefs about death and funerals in Zambia. It is a neotraditional practice that defies stereotypes and offers new perspectives and knowledge about a socially and culturally developing and changing Zambian community.

Notes

1. See Marissa Abruzzini, "The Evolution of After-Tears Parties in South Africa," blog post, SevenPonds.com, January 5, 2017, http://blog.sevenponds .com/cultural-perspectives/the-evolution-of-after-tears-parties-in-south-africa.

2. Scott D. Taylor, *Culture and Customs of Zambia* (Westport, CT: Greenwood, 2006).

3. John Katebe, "A Guide to Conducting a Zambian Funeral," Kwite Online, November 4, 2011, http://kitweonline.com/kitweonline/discover-kitwe /culture/a-guide-to-conducting-a-zambian-funeral.html.

4. John Chowa, personal communication, February 19, 2017.

5. T. H. S. Setsiba, "Mourning Rituals and Practices in Contemporary South African Townships: A Phenomenological Study," PhD diss., University of Zululand, 2012.

6. Jackson Kalumba, personal communication, February 7, 2017.

7. Sichalwe Kasanda, personal communication, February 7, 2017.

8. Abruzzini, "The Evolution of After-Tears Parties in South Africa."

Map 4.1. Egypt. Map by Christopher Becker.

4

Beyond Religion

Food, Decoration, and Songs of Egyptian Feasts

HADEER ABOELNAGAH

Egypt is one of the most populated countries in Africa and one of its most diverse cultural centers. More than ninety-four million people, Muslims and Christians alike, call it home, though about 90 percent of its population is Muslim. Egypt's ancient and complex history earned its designation as "the cradle of civilization," and among Arabs and Egyptians its known as *um al-donia*, or "mother of the world." Geographically, Egypt spans the northeastern corner of Africa and, in the Sinai Peninsula, the western edge of Asia. This location allowed it to become the meeting point of many cultures, prompting the cross-fertilization of languages and religions that shapes daily life. With a diverse heritage stretching back several millennia, the uniqueness of contemporary Egyptian culture is largely due to the fact that it mirrors myriad Pharaonic, Coptic, and Islamic roots.

Despite their religious significance, the occasions detailed in this chapter, namely Ramadan, Eid al-Fitr, Christmas, Palm Sunday, and Sham al-Naseem, represent celebrations that tie Egyptian people together across religious differences. Some of these feasts are also celebrated in other areas of Africa. Yet, in Egypt, they have a special flavor that reflects its rich cultural background. Variations may occur between rural and urban areas and from one generation to another. However, the basic practices remain unchangeable, as they form the heart and soul of the country. As a native of Egypt, I invite you to explore some of the country's popular feast dishes, decorations, and songs. *Belhana wel shifa* (bon appétit).

Ramadan

It is the first day of Ramadan (the Muslim holy month of fasting) and the whole family is here. It is almost sunset, time to set the table and prepare for *iftar*, the special meal for breaking the fast. It will be the first thing eaten since dawn. Long hours have been spent reading the Quran, praying extensively, and preparing delicacies especially for this month. The streets are almost empty except for speeding cars and some pedestrians racing to arrive at their destination before the *athan*, or the call to prayers, which officially ends the day of fasting.

Allahu akbar, Allahu akbar	الله أكبر الله أكبر
God is greatest, God is greatest	

These words are part of the traditional call to prayers. During Ramadan, the call for *maghrib* or sunset prayer officially ends the day of fasting. The highly anticipated loud boom of the iftar cannon also marks the end of the day and the beginning of long festive nights. The iftar cannon dates back to the tenth century and, though it is not a religious custom, it became a Ramadan tradition to hear the cannon or its recording on the radio twice a day—the first to announce the start of fasting and the second at sunset to announce the end of it.[1] The sounds of Quran recitations, heard on the radio and from mosques, fill the air with the spiritual atmosphere of the holy month.

"Ramadan Gana" (Ramadan is here) is the most popular Ramadan song in Egypt and serves as an announcement of Ramadan's beginning. Although maybe not as popular among younger generations today, the song is still frequently heard from televisions and radios everywhere, throughout the thirty days of fasting.

Ramadan has come	رمضان جانا
We are happy to see it again	وفرحنا به
After its absence	بعد غيابه
It has been a long time	وبقاله زمان
Sing with us for the whole month	غنوا معانا شهر بطوله
Sing and say: welcome Ramadan	غنوا وقولوا أهلاً رمضان
Ramadan is here: welcome Ramadan[2]	أهلا رمضان رمضان جانا

The month of fasting begins—like all lunar months in the Islamic calendar—with the sighting of the new moon, which is marked with a special event. Afterward, fasting is officially announced. However, for many Egyptians just hearing this song on the radio is enough to know that Ramadan has begun.

Dates, water, and cold drinks like *qamar el din* (made by soaking dried apricot paste in sugary water) are served as satiating treats that break the daylong fast. Other examples of favorite Ramadan beverages include *tamr Hindi* (a delicious chilled drink made by boiling tamarind seeds and adding other ingredients) and another made from the hibiscus flower. These drinks are welcome on the table after a long day of not eating or drinking anything.

Ramadan is also a time for charity and other giving. Iftar tents and partitions are erected in almost every neighborhood to host the needy, travelers, and those who are spending the month away from their families. The colorful tents are made of colorful *khamiya* fabric, which is traditionally red with yellow, green, and blue geometrical shapes, inspired by Islamic art, that have become iconic symbols of the holy month. The traditional khyamiya fabric is a uniquely Egyptian design which used to be handcrafted by folk artists. Contemporary adaptations of the original designs are now used as Ramadan decoration in homes, commonly on cushions and table linen,

Figure 4.1. Ramadan decorations. Source: Mawadah Nofal.

and for women's dresses, skirts, and handbags. The word *khyamiya* is a derivative of the Arabic word *khyma*, which means tent, referring to the setting for many Ramadan gatherings over the centuries and even today. It is also the name of a village that specializes in making this special fabric.

The dishes served in the iftar tents are usually simple ones like *feta*, meat, vegetables, and sometimes dessert. Feta is made from dried bread soaked in lamb or beef broth and topped with white rice, seasoned with a garlic and vinegar sauce. It is a dish typically served at the two major Islamic feasts, Eid al-Fitr (the small feast after Ramadan) and Eid al-Adha (the big feast of *hajj*—pilgrimage to Mecca). Eid al-Adha means "festival of sacrifice," referencing the slaughter of sheep during the time period. Feta is also served during Christmas and at other large gatherings where people eat together.

The dishes served in private family gatherings are slightly different. Stuffed vegetables and more sophisticated recipes are considered the prize after each day of fasting. Desserts are the most popular, as they compensate bodies with sugar after the long hours of fasting. *Kenafa* is the queen of all desserts: it is a fine delicacy made from thin layers of dough, traditionally filled with mixed nuts or crème, soaked in syrup, and garnished with nut sprinkles. *Qataeif,* a type of pancake also filled with nuts, then fried and soaked in heavy

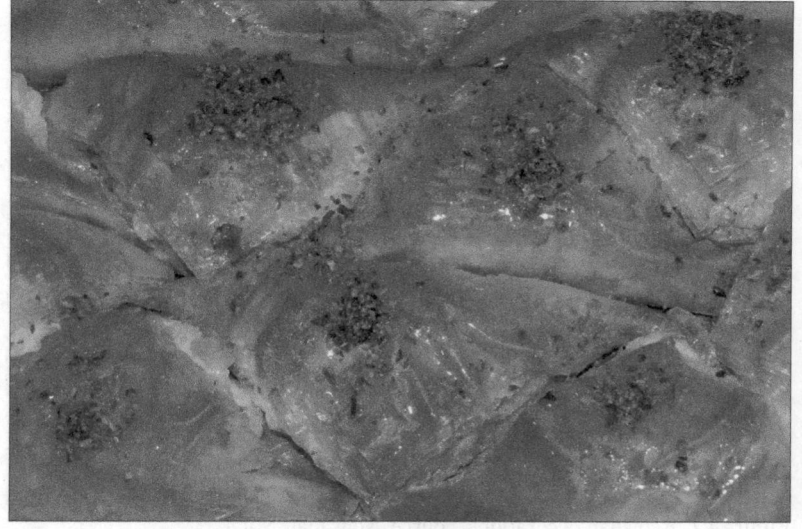

Figure 4.2. Homemade baklava. Source: Mawadah Nofal.

Figure 4.3. Ramadan lanterns. Source: Rima Rahwanji.

syrup, is another common Ramadan dessert. Baklava and *khoshaf,* the latter made of dried mixed fruits soaked in sugary water and chilled, are other special Ramadan desserts. In the last few years, innovative alterations have been made to these desserts. For example, newer kenafa-inspired recipes use mango, berries, or other fruits instead of the typical nuts-and-raisin filling. When served with ice cream, whipped cream, or chocolate toppings, kenafa is even more appetizing.

The lantern or *fanous* is a symbol of Ramadan, providing a festive feel. Historically, it was used for lighting, since people usually stay up late during Ramadan and wake to eat *sohour* (a pre-dawn meal) when it is still very dark. Now it is mainly used for decoration. It is an important gift for children to celebrate the month, and it is also used as an incentive to encourage fasting. Today's fanous use batteries and can play traditional music, looking much different from older glass, candle-lit lanterns.

In Egyptian society, strong ties are frequently maintained across social differences. This is best shown through the mutual respect Muslims and Christians show toward others' religious rituals. For example, in many parts of Egypt, especially in rural communities, Christians refrain from eating in public during the month of fasting.[3] Sharing food is another example of social contact: homemade

Ramadan dishes like kenafa and qataeif are sent as gifts by Muslims to Christian neighbors, who return the gesture during Christian feasts. This custom of exchanging food may not be as widely practiced now, but it has contributed to Egypt's solidarity throughout its long history. As the only daughter in my family, one of my happiest childhood memories is of lovingly taking a dessert dish to our Christian neighbors.

Ramadan is more than a month of fasting. In Egypt as in many Muslim countries, it is a time for compassion, charity, family gatherings, and generosity. The twenty-nine or thirty days of fasting—depending on the lunar calendar—end with a big celebration known as Eid al-Fitr (festival of breaking the fast). Chants from all the *masjid*s (mosques) start right after the dawn prayer.

Allahu akbar, Allahu akbar	الله أكبر الله أكبر
Laa ilaha iila Allah	لا إله إلا الله
Allahu akbar wa lillahi al-hamd	الله أكبر ولله الحمد

God is greatest, God is greatest
There is no God but God
God is greatest and all praises are due to Him

Everywhere in Egypt, like in any Muslim country, these chants are repeated again and again, filling the air with blessings and happiness. A full month of fasting has been completed and the celebration begins. Dates and coffee or tea are a quick breakfast to declare the completion of the fasting ritual. Then, people usually attend Eid prayers in mosques or more often in public parks and open areas. Prayer areas are usually decorated with balloons or handmade colored-paper decorations. Large numbers of men, women, and children arrive in their new clothes. Buying an Eid outfit and wearing it for the first time on Eid morning remains a dear childhood recollection. On the way back from the prayer, firecrackers are heard everywhere, and street vendors sell small toys and colorful balloons to the crowds.

After the early morning prayer, a heavy breakfast spread, which includes cookies called *kahk*, awaits families when they return home or gather in the "big house," the grandparents' home. Home-baked kahk, often in decorative dishes covered with a nice napkin, are sent to neighbors. In particular, such gifts are given to Christians or to

Muslim families who didn't bake at home due to extenuating circumstances like a family death. As young children, we got to make our own kahk to give to cousins and friends. The dishes that held the gifts of kahk are frequently returned during Christian feasts, if the kahk were given to Christians, or simply given back filled with nuts and dates—but they are never to be returned empty.

Christmas

Though the majority of Egyptians are Muslims, Christianity is freely practiced. Christians and Muslims alike are especially proud of the fact that the holy Christian family (Mary, Joseph, and Jesus) were sheltered in Egypt.[*] Christmas is mainly celebrated by Christians, but lately it has become a more inclusive feast. Though similar to Western traditions in terms of food, decorations, and gatherings, in Egypt it has its own unique flair, especially in the streets of big cities like Cairo and Alexandria. Street vendors sell Ottoman red hats (*tarboush*) along with colorful, locally made "Egyptianized" Christmas decorations similar to those made during Ramadan. Every year, creative plastic trinkets and colorful paper crafts are displayed and sold at traffic stops. The traditional feta dish fills the tables of Christmas gatherings along with roasted turkey or lamb. Most Egyptian Christians are Coptic (Eastern Orthodox), so January 7 is observed as a national holiday, since Coptic Christians celebrate Christmas on this day. The night before, bells ring from ornately decorated churches. The smell of *bokhour*, or aromatic woodchips, wafts from churches and homes of Christians along with scents of butter and vanilla from kahk sweets, the exact type made by Muslims during their feasts. In some years, Christmas and one of the two *birams* (Muslim feasts) coincidently occur at the same time, since Muslim feasts follow the lunar calendar, which shifts from year to year in relation to the Gregorian calendar. These times when the whole country is gathered in one big feast are extraordinary.

Palm Sunday

Palm Sunday (Al'ahad as-Sa'af, or as-Za'af) is generally a more Egyptian-feeling celebration than Christmas because it's a more important holiday for Egypt's Coptic Christians. During the fifty-five days of Lent, no meat is consumed. Egyptian Muslims respect this period of fasting, with many restaurants preparing alternative recipes that do not include any animal products. In addition, friends and neighbors include vegetarian dishes if Christians are invited to their gatherings. Palm Sunday is the last Sunday before Easter, which marks the end of Lent.

Lent fasting was memorable to us as young Muslim children, since we got the most delicious homemade *koshari* and *besara* from our Christian neighbors. Koshari is a delicious vegetarian dish of rice and black lentils topped with fried onions and garlic sauce. Besara is another particularly aromatic Egyptian vegetarian dish made from mashed boiled beans with coriander, garlic, herbs, and fried-onion garnish. As the family's official dish carrier, I used to smell and taste them before anyone else, which was a satisfactory reward for transporting the dishes.

Al'ahad as-Sa'af is not just a Christian feast, it officially announces the beginning of spring. The streets near churches are decorated with palm leaves. This feast is a beautiful carnival, as flowers and small bamboo and palm-leaf crafts are sold in the streets. It is also the season for silkworms and chicks, which are decorated and sold in front of schools. Though perhaps less common now, it has been a habit of Egyptians to buy these small animals and palm leaves as gifts for children, friends, and neighbors. Growing up, it took me some time to realize that Palm Sunday is a Christian feast, as I enjoyed the little handmade palm-leaf craft pieces. I still enjoy hanging them on apartment doors as decorations. During this celebration, fireworks are heard everywhere. The week before Easter is known as "patience week," since it marks the end of Lent fasting. On Easter Sunday, early morning prayers announce the long weekend's two-fold celebration, when Egyptians celebrate two occasions—Easter Sunday, which is a Coptic feast, and on the following day the originally Pharaonic Sham al-Naseem.

Sham al-Naseem

Sham al-Naseem, or "sniffing the breeze" in Arabic, is a popular sunrise-to-sunset folk carnival that Egyptians have celebrated since the time of the pharaohs. It announces the beginning of spring, and it usually occurs the Monday after Coptic Easter Sunday. In ancient Egyptian Pharaonic culture, the celebration symbolized the revival or return of life through the coming of spring. Preparation for this annual outing comes a few days before the event. It begins with growing different seed samples at home, which is considered an act that will bring blessings and prosperity to the household. The carnival is best seen on the Nile River banks, from Aswan in the far south to the northern city of Ras El-Bar (the tip of the land), where the river pours into the Mediterranean. Families and friends gather in huge numbers to celebrate the feast of the spring the same way their ancestors hailed life.[5]

The Nile has always been the heart and soul of the country, and this feast in particular derives its meaning from the life that the river brings to the land and its people. Many of those partying in the parks and cruising the Nile may pay little attention to the symbolic references of the food they have brought in heavy baskets and stuffed bags. Dried and salted mullet fish known as *feseikh* was invented by ancient Egyptians in order to preserve the fish, since it is regarded as a gift of the blessed river. Green onions, lettuce, and *malana* (young, green chickpeas) are used in a side salad served to lessen the heavily salted taste of the fish and to praise the freshness of the spring. Though feseikh remains popular, some Egyptians prefer the taste of smoked fish to feseikh's salty flavor. Homemade spicy chickpeas and homegrown fenugreek seeds are also traditional snacks of this feast that are still popular today.

Egg coloring is a favorite activity for young children, typically done in the early morning before going out, or sometimes on the night before to save time. Traditionally, organic colors made from beets and hibiscus petals were used to color the eggs with reddish or purple colors, along with parsley for green and onion peels for yellow. All coloring substances were gathered from the local environment to show respect for nature and the continuation of the life cycle. Conversely, children nowadays find food colors, crayons, or stickers more attractive and colorful than traditional eco-colors.

Besides these long-lasting traditions that most Egyptians have practiced for years, regardless of their awareness of their historic implications, some more recent customs have become equally popular. For example, "El Donia Rabee" (It is springtime) has been a cheerful national song for nearly half a century, whose lyrics are memorized by most Egyptians. It was written in Egyptian vernacular by an adored

Egyptian folk poet, the late Salah Chahin, for energetic crowds to join in, in welcoming the breeze and the jovial atmosphere.

It is spring time	الدنيا ربيع
And the weather is pleasant	والجو بديع
Cancel all serious talks	قفلي على كل المواضيع
Cancel . . . Cancel . . . Cancel	قفل . . . . . قفل . . . قفل
Don't tell me about this	لا تقلي كاني
Don't tell me about that	ولا ماني
What is the need to do this or that?	كاني ماني أيه؟
Now it is spring time	ده الدنيا ربيع
The dried leaves have become fresh and green	لشجر الناشف بقى ورور
The birds are becoming active and playful	والطير بقى لعبي ومتهور
When are we going to have fun?	واحنا حنفرفش إمتى أمال
If not now? In September?![6]	دلوقتى ولا في سبتمبر

Throughout the country, in crowded parks, on the edge of the Suez Canal, in the Sinai Peninsula, or at north coast resorts, the atmosphere remains festive. Egyptians regard this day as a national occasion they can't miss.

Feasts in Egypt have their own flavor, with rich cuisine that is shared by Egyptians from diverse backgrounds. Though most of its feasts have religious origins, their folk roots are apparent. Beyond religious differences, food sharing or, as I like to call it, "traveling dishes," is one of the social habits that have kept these feasts lively for centuries and maintained the social fabric of the country. Egyptian feasts reflect the long history and cultural richness of people who enjoy laughing, singing, and relishing the taste of special dishes they've assembled for each occasion.

Notes

1. Ahmad Bahgat, *Ramadan Diary*, trans. Nermeen Hassan (Cairo: General Egyptian Book Organization, 1988), 47–48; F. Morsi, *Ramadan Encyclopedia* (Cairo: General Egyptian Book Organization, 2013), 129–30, my translation.

2. Morsi, *Ramadan Encyclopedia*, 131–36, 227, my translation.

3. Bahgat, *Ramadan Diary*, 59.

4. Joann Fletcher, "Pharaonic Egypt," in Matthew D. Firestone, Michael Benanav, Thomas Hall, and Anthony Sattin, *Egypt*, 10th ed. (Franklin, TN: Lonely Planet, 2010), 134.

5. Firestone et al., *Egypt*, 158.

6. My translation from Arabic. Salah Chahin, *Azjal Sihafiyah* (Cairo: Al-Ahram Center for Translation and Publishing, 2007), 94.

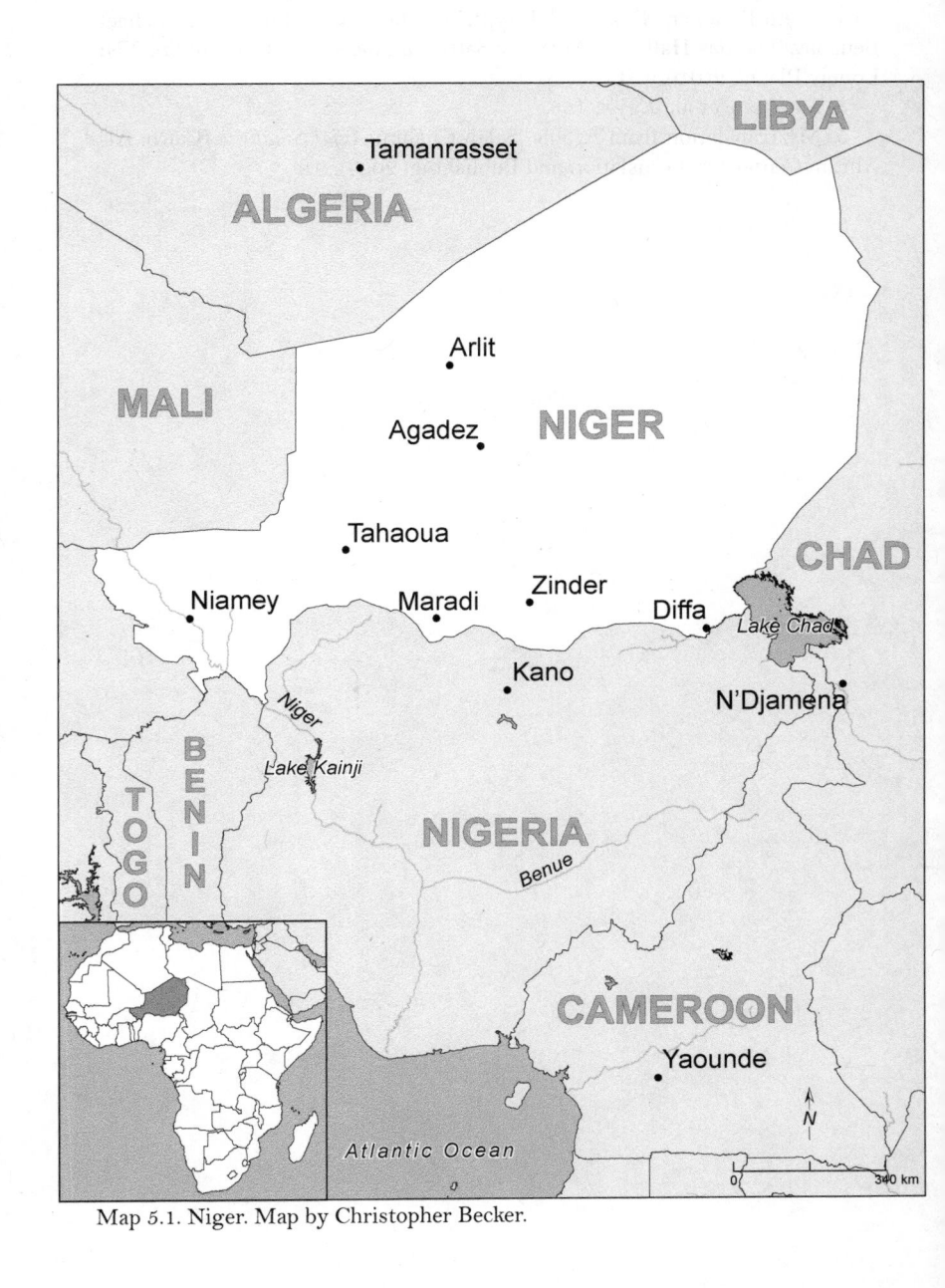

Map 5.1. Niger. Map by Christopher Becker.

5

New Year's Eve in Niamey, Niger

SCOTT M. YOUNGSTEDT

Abderrahmane Sissako's film *La vie sur terre* eloquently depicts the last day of the twentieth century in Sokolo, Mali, highlighting how the village is simultaneously isolated from and connected to globalization and modernity.[1] Sissako presents a place mired in poverty, separated by a vast technological divide, where people who get around on foot, bicycles, and donkey carts live "life on earth." The people of Sokolo, nevertheless, are connected to the world at large through the appropriation of global popular culture, the letters and remittances from the global Malian diaspora, and ubiquitous radios that are often tuned to Radio France Internationale (RFI), which is extremely popular in all of the former colonies of France in West Africa. While the people of Sokolo strive for global inclusion in many ways, they have no interest in New Year's Eve. RFI's upbeat reports of global universalism at the dawn of the new millennium are unconvincing to them.

Until 2005, most residents of Niamey, Niger, similarly regarded New Year's Eve—of the Gregorian calendar—as merely an ordinary day, even though New Year's Day has been a national holiday since the French colonial era. Then, everything dramatically changed in December 2005. That year, and ever since, New Year's Eve has been marked with exuberant celebration in Niamey. This chapter describes the various ways that New Year's Eve is observed in this Sahelian capital and offers explanations for their emergence over the past thirteen years. It draws from anthropological research, including sixty structured interviews, dozens of informal conversations, and participant observation—in house parties, bar hopping, and musical performances—during New Year's Eve festivities in Niamey in 1991, 2003, 2005, 2007, 2008, 2009, 2012, 2013, and 2016. Most interviews and conversations were conducted in Hausa, a major ethnolinguistic group in West Africa; a minority were completed in French.

Situating Niamey, Niger

Niger (population eighteen million) is a stunning place marked by sharing, faith, conversation, laughter, patience, family, friendship, dignity, knowledge, community, and hope—even though it consistently rates as the world's least developed country. Located in West Africa, Niger is one of the hottest and driest countries in the world. Until 1900, Niamey consisted of a collection of fishing villages on the banks of the Niger River. The French reached Niger by the late nineteenth century and established full control by 1922 when Niger became a French colony. France chose Niamey as the capital of Niger in 1926 primarily due to the reliable water supply of the Niger River. Today, Niamey is a sprawling city with nearly two million residents. Niger gained its independence in 1960, but has maintained close ties with France, and retains French as the national language.

Islam arrived peacefully in what is today Niger in the eleventh century via North African traders and preachers. As in much of West Africa, the urban aristocracy and select city dwellers first embraced Islam. It was not until the nineteenth and twentieth centuries that Islam made great gains in Niger, spreading to most urban residents and advancing significantly in rural areas. Today, 98 percent of Nigeriens are Muslims, and many participate in Sufi brotherhoods. In the past twenty-five years, a growing number of anti-Sufi, conservative, reformist Islamist sects promoted by Saudi Arabian and Nigerian movements have gained significant prominence in the Nigerien religious landscape. About 1.5 percent of the population practices Christianity. Almost all Christians in Niger reside in cities, primarily Niamey and Maradi.

Letting Loose on New Year's Eve

Since 2005, residents of Niamey begin visibly and audibly preparing for New Year's Eve by mid-December. City streets as well as shops and restaurants are decorated with festive strings of multicolored, flashing lights and tinsel. Shop windows and billboards sponsored by local and transnational companies display colorful images with "Happy New Year" wishes. Every night for at least two weeks, boys set off firecrackers from about 9:00 p.m. until past midnight—the only time of year when firecrackers are heard in any substantial numbers.

People then celebrate New Year's Eve in various ways. City streets are clogged with honking traffic and milling crowds of people until sunrise. Youth are particularly loud, tossing firecrackers all night. Their male *fada* (neighborhood associations) rent sound systems for staging hip-hop dance parties on the streets, many of which last all night. They invite young women to join them, presenting a rare opportunity for public gender mixing.

Niameyans of all ages and ethnic groups visit family and friends. Some stay only briefly for greetings and gift exchanges. Cloth fabric, jewelry, and cell phones are the most common presents. Others, particularly the wealthy, middle-aged, and elderly, host extravagant house parties. These typically last for several hours and feature watching talent shows and comedies on television, snacks such as peanuts and crackers, juice and soda, recorded or DJ-provided music, and conversation. Shortly before midnight, elaborate dinners are served. These feature delicacies typically reserved only for special occasions such as Muslim holidays, baby-naming ceremonies, and weddings, including roasted lamb stuffed with couscous and large, whole fried Nile perch—the prestige fish of the Niger River. Participants take a brief pause from their meals at midnight to shake hands and offer their best wishes for a prosperous and healthy new year to all who are present.

New Year's Eve is by far the busiest night of the year for drinking and live musical performances, including hip-hop, Nigerien "desert blues," reggae, jazz, and Niamey beats. Men and women, youth and elderly, rich and poor, drink, dance, and laugh the night away, filling all of Niamey's nightclubs, casinos, and normally placid neighborhood bars. The wealthy pay 100,000 Francs Communauté Financière d'Afrique (FCFA), equivalent to $200, or more per couple to gather in posh restaurants, hotels, and private clubs—a conspicuous display of consumption where the per capita daily income is about 500 FCFA ($1). The poor and middle class assemble in small smoky bars to drink bottles of Bière Niger or Flag for 500 FCFA each. Many residents save money for weeks to drink several bottles of beer on New Year's Eve. Circles of middle-aged women consume beer as quickly as servers can deliver it. Old men stumble from one bar to the next. Most of these revelers drink and dance only one night a year: New Year's Eve. Some

Figure 5.1. Bombino and his band warming up in a makeshift performance space created exclusively for New Year's Eve. Source: Scott M. Youngstedt.

energetic Niameyans enjoy these activities by lighting firecrackers with friends in the early evening, continue on to visit house parties, and end the night in bars. Niameyans spend a lot of money on New Year's Eve, providing a significant economic boost for taxi drivers, gas stations, cloth merchants, butchers, bars, and restaurants. Niamey returns to normal by the end of New Year's Day.

Explaining the New Popularity of New Year's Eve

This radically new form of flamboyant celebration defies simple explanations. Niameyans do not seem to understand it. When questioned about it, they typically offer only vague, brief explanations, such as "It is fun," "The people like to imitate the rest of the world," and "Why not?" However, Youssoufou, a key participant in my research for twenty-seven years, offered a more comprehensive interpretation.

> The 31 December celebration came with colonization. It fell short a long time ago because the population associated it with Christian manifestations. But little by little, after many Nigeriens travelled all over the world, they came back with

Figure 5.2. Bombino and his band performing on New Year's Eve in Niamey. Source and copyright: Eric J. Schmidt.

Figure 5.3. Jesters getting people in a celebratory mood on New Year's Eve in Niamey. Source: Scott M. Youngstedt.

more knowledge about the celebration and realized that it
is not religious. The population accepts that it's just to welcome the New Year. And since we have TV, we can see what
is happening anywhere in the world. This event occurs once
a year, and people celebrate it with exaggeration. We break
the rules (loud music, bars, etc.) and no one complains. During the year, it's the only noisy evening. The year is ending,
and the population is so glad to welcome the New Year with
many wishes to relatives, friends, neighbors, etc.

Youssoufou's comments are representative of the views of many Niameyans. The French initiated the celebration of New Year's Eve in
Niamey during colonialism, and a tiny minority of Niameyans joined
them. However, many Niameyans thought of the holiday as part of
Christmas and rejected it for this and other reasons.

It is important to note that although a broad cross-section of the
urban population celebrates New Year's Eve in one way or another,
roughly as many Niameyans—particularly conservative imams (Muslim scholar-leaders), their congregations, and the elderly—object to
it. Many regard it as a Christian holiday and are appalled by what
they perceive as morally repugnant, flagrant debauchery—particularly the consumption of alcoholic beverages, public gender mixing,
and loud noise throughout the night. Two factors explain why some
think of New Year's Eve as a Christian celebration. First, it occurs
just one week after Christmas Eve, which is also stereotyped in Niger
as featuring alcohol. Many Niameyans think that New Year's Eve
celebrates "the birth of the Prophet Jesus." Second, even though it is
rarely referred to as such in Niamey, by coincidence December 31 is
also the day of the Feast of Saint Sylvester I, a fourth-century pope
of the Catholic Church. This holiday is observed in France and many
other European countries. Some imams repeatedly emphasize these
points, especially the former. For example, Elhadji Aboubacar, in a
radio address, explained, "A good Muslim does not let his family
celebrate New Year's Eve because it is a Christian holiday and we
have our own holidays to thank Allah for all that he gives us. December 31 is a night for youth to get together to get drunk, and to engage
in debauchery, and hence it is a night that is forbidden to Muslims."

I offer four mutually inclusive explanations for the emergence in
2005 of New Year's Eve as an important holiday in Niamey. First, the
initial raucous celebration of December 31, 2005, followed Niamey's

successful hosting of the fifth Francophonie Sports and Arts Festival of December 7–17, 2005, which brought athletes and artists from France, Haiti, Senegal, Tunisia, Vietnam, and forty-five other member countries of the Organisation Internationale de la Francophonie to Niamey. In addition to enjoying the competitions, many Niameyans surged into the streets and bars to listen or dance to live music throughout the festival. The celebratory mood in Niamey persisted through New Year's Eve. In punctuating their Francophonie experience through observing New Year's Eve in a boisterous style, Niameyans "chose" one last way to feel included in a global community. This Francophonie afterglow assessment accounts in large part for the observance of New Year's Eve in 2005, but does not explain why celebrations of New Year's Eve have continued since.

Second, New Year's Eve celebrations in Niamey function as a "ritual of rebellion."[2] Max Gluckman identifies religious and royal ceremonies in southeastern Africa that allow believers and subjects to briefly and symbolically express their displeasure with authority. He explains that these ritualistic protests, in complex ways, renew the unity and authority of religions and monarchies. Gluckman argues that rituals of rebellion are possible when the social order is sufficiently sure of itself to allow its opposite to be temporarily indulged. They are "steam valves" that ultimately preserve or even strengthen the existing social order. As Youssoufou put it, "we break the rules (loud music, bars, etc.) and no one complains."

As in all rebellions, loyalists who defend the status quo are pitted against rebels who challenge it. Indeed, Niameyans articulate polar opposite views about New Year's Eve. The loyalists, in this case the "proper Muslims," oppose the celebration of this holiday because they associate it with Christianity, alcohol, gender mixing, and loud noise—the key points of contention, as highlighted earlier. Others think that even quiet house parties without alcohol among families represent a betrayal of Islam. Many interviewees voiced their strong opposition to New Year's Eve. For example, Mohammadou, a twenty-five-year-old man, declared, "Above all it is a menace for Muslim people because it is a hallucination of the youth." Aichatou, a twenty-eight-year-old woman, stated, "Participants enjoy non-Muslim holidays that include debauchery; this is forbidden in Muslim holidays." Nigerien anthropologist Cheiffou Idrissa explained, "It provides an opportunity for youth to get drunk, to fight in the bistros, and drive drunk, causing accidents and fatalities. However, it seems that the horrible consequences for the revelers makes many of them think twice and only do this once a year." In sum, many Niameyans who do not participate in boisterous public celebrations regard those who do as rebels without a good cause.

For the rebels, this celebration of New Year's Eve involves "symbolic inversion" that leads participants to experience "collective joy."[3] They engage in joyful ritualistic rebellion against global economic inequality and against Nigerien Islam, particularly its emphasis on gender segregation and the prohibition of alcohol consumption. Particular actors express their discontent through these specific perspectives in ways that appear to be reckless, joyous abandon. For example, youth cry out for recognition and in protest of their marginalization through the explosive noise of their firecrackers and rap music and their mixed-gender dance parties on the street. According to a young man of the Zarma ethnic group, "New Year's Eve is important because it permits certain Nigeriens to distract themselves, and to make new relationships with the opposite sex." Making noise with strangers leads to a special type of collective joy. Women challenge patriarchal Nigerien Islam by asserting, for one night, the right to assemble in public to drink beer like men. A middle-aged woman from the Hausa ethnic group expressed to me, while out drinking with her group of female friends, "I am a good Muslim and Allah will forgive me tomorrow for what I did tonight. It may take a little longer for my husband to forgive me."

Youth, women, and men engage in *pleurer-rire* at house parties, on the streets, and in bars and restaurants. Mariama, a thirty-six-year-old Tuareg woman, believes that New Year's Eve offers "a special moment of unwinding or releasing of tension, and opportunity to receive big gifts." *Pleurer-rire* is a peculiar term that functions as a double entendre. When translated as "the laughing cry," it refers to humor that is good enough to make one laugh hard enough to cry. When translated as "the crying laugh," it refers to situations that are bad enough to warrant crying but are countered with laughter. The latter is akin to the sentiment expressed in the most popular Hausa proverb used in Niamey: "Zaman duniya sai hank'uri" (only with patience can one make it in the world). Through one night of release, Niameyans find it more bearable to return to their daily lives of economic insecurity on the periphery of the global economy. According to Yacouba, an unemployed father of six children, "New Year's Eve marks the joy of the end of the year, and a new life that begins and promises to be better."

Third, residents of Niamey feel they are consuming and making local a ritual that has global cachet. The newness of the celebration is also an important part of its appeal. The statement, "The people like to imitate the rest of the world," cited earlier, tells part of the story. The celebration of New Year's Eve in Niamey involves a symbolic assertion of global inclusion through mimesis. Marking the day in ways that are perceived to be just like how other people around the world who have access to economic modernity do, some Niameyans claim membership in the modern global community. "They think celebrating New Year's Eve proves that they are modern," according to Mamane, a twenty-eight-year-old. Having a time when they are really celebrating with many people across the globe including relatives in Paris, Dakar, and New York is appealing and is only possible with a solar calendar. Niger's uniqueness is also integrated into the celebration. Niameyans have made the holiday local by emphasizing the same sorts of activities found in their Muslim holidays and rites of passage—greetings and conversation, gift giving, and feasting.

Fourth, although New Year's Eve celebrations are essentially new, they circle back to an older Nigerien value: the value of public, loud, communal fun. For many Nigeriens, fun used to involve activities such as farm work parties in which men hoed while women clapped and sang to urge them on, followed by drinking millet beer. Weddings typically featured music and dance. The rise of conservative Islam over the past twenty-five years—what Abdoulaye Sounaye calls the "re-Islamization" of Niger—has suppressed these types of fun.[4] For example, men and women are increasingly segregated, millet beer is very hard to find now, and most wedding ceremonies no longer include music. To celebrate New Year's Eve in a public, loud, gender-integrated way is to reclaim an important value that has been driven underground.

Heretofore having largely ignored the holiday, Niameyans have celebrated New Year's Eve with enthusiasm for over a decade now. Niameyans have creatively adapted a global celebration in their own ways. They draw from global, local, new, and old resources to address their concerns and grievances and to express their joy and desire for inclusion in the wider world. For some Niameyans, the observance of New Year's Eve serves as a ritual of rebellion and form of symbolic inversion involving resistance to abject poverty and certain conservative interpretations of Islam. They find collective joy in rebellion,

whether their resistance is deliberate or not. For many other Niameyans, New Year's Eve is simply about coming together in playful
solidarity to have fun.

Notes

1. Abderrahmane Sissako, dir., *La vie sur terre*, VHS (San Francisco: California Newsreel, 1998).

2. Max Gluckman, *Order and Rebellion in Tribal Africa* (London: Cohen
and West, 1963).

3. Edith Turner, *Communitas: The Anthropology of Collective Joy* (New York:
Palgrave Macmillan, 2012).

4. Abdoulaye Sounaye, *Islam et modernité: Contribution à l'analyse de la ré-
islamisation au Niger* (Paris: Harmattan, 2016).

Part 2

Socializing and Friendship

Map 6.1. Namibia. Map by Christopher Becker.

6

Tank Park's Children

Recreational Activities of Namibian Children
in Oranjemund during the 1980s

MARTHA NDAKALAKO-BANNIKOV

Tucked at the bottom tip of Namibia's west coast is a secluded town, Oranjemund, and at its eastern edge is Tank Park. Large and lined with tall, branchy evergreens, carpeted by soft perennial grass, and generously furnished with playground equipment, it was the perfect place for children to exhaust their energies. While jungle gyms and swing sets are common in play areas, ancient Sherman war tanks make for an unusual sight in such a space. However, such a tank—stationed in the park's southeast corner and painted a bright, child-enticing blue and red—was the defining feature of this park and its main attraction for many years. Children came from all over Oranjemund to play in the popular Tank Park. In their reminiscing many years later, this playground serves as a nostalgic and necessary byway on their journey back to childhood days of fun.

In the hopes of capturing some of the delight that memories of the park evoke, I utilize a folkloric approach to provide an insider perspective on Oranjemund childhood. This essay makes use of written correspondence with four of the town's now-adult children, along with my own recollections. It also includes posts from Oranjemund Online, a web-based forum for the Oranjemund community around the world, and excerpts from the *Oranjemund Newsletter.* Focusing on experiences that occurred between 1980 and 1990, I explore the various diversions Oranjemund children engaged in, particularly at Tank Park.

Historical Context

Namibia is a coastal country, previously named South West Africa. The country was colonized twice, first by Germany in 1896 and then by South Africa in 1921, after the League of Nations granted South Africa administrative authority of Namibia.[1] Thereafter, South Africa, Namibia's neighbor to the south, began plans to incorporate Namibia—defining the country as another of its states and implementing apartheid rule.[2] Namibians declared war with South Africa, and on August 26, 1966, the first battle of the Namibian War (1966–89) was fought, finally leading to the country's independence on March 21, 1990.[3] Due to Oranjemund's secluded location and status as a closed town at that time (public access is limited without a valid permit), much of the turmoil that occurred in the rest of the country as a result of the war did not directly impact its residents.

Oranjemund is a small town located on the southwest tip of the Namibian coast, only twelve kilometers from where the Orange River flows into the Atlantic Ocean: hence its name, which means "Orange Mouth" in German. The town was formally established in 1936 and owes its existence to the discovery of diamonds in the area in 1928, when Consolidated Diamond Mines (CDM), an affiliate of the De Beers Group of Companies, began mining there.[4] Oranjemund began as a collection of single-room shacks built to house the miners who came from various parts of Namibia, South Africa, and Europe to work at the mine, and eventually expanded to include housing and facilities for their families.

As with most settlements, Oranjemund is governed hierarchically, but, because it was a company-owned town, the discrepancies in social standing, while existing, were more diffused. For example, at the time, all the children attended the same top-tier, company-sponsored private school. During the last few, particularly violent years of the Namibian War, Oranjemund was an attractive location for many Owambo, Herero, Nama, and other indigenous Namibian workers to raise their families. This was also the case for the Scottish, Welsh, English, German, and other non-indigenous workers who came to Oranjemund, because it was with families in mind that the town developed, providing houses with large yards and playgrounds interspersed throughout the town where children could play close to their homes. Tank Park was a favorite.

Figure 6.1. The author and her sister, Rebekka, on a recent visit to Oranjemund. Source: Martha Ndakalako-Bannikov.

Tank Park: Childhood Recollections

One might think that during the final decade of Namibia's war for independence, the tank's conspicuous presence in the park would have been a constant reminder of the country's embattled state, but this was not the case. Naftal Negongo has resided in Oranjemund since 1979 and writes wistfully of the park, "The exercise of recollecting my childhood memories of the Tank Park can't be done without an innocent chuckle and the shedding of a nostalgic tear."[5] Similar sentiments are evident in forum member Ebben's recollections on Oranjemund Online.

> We lived opposite the tank park . . . and a whole [lot] of shenanigans went down in that park. That is where Billy Linekar used to blow impressive smoke rings. . . . I almost died coughing when I tried imitating him. Fights, broken arms—from falling of [*sic*] swings, clandestine meetings in the tank on how to take over the world by our gang "the Pink Ladies"—read "Grease 2"!!!! It was also my refuge when I knew my Mom was going to whip my hide for doing something wrong—which was daily! . . . It was . . . beautiful in the mornings covered in a blanket of mist . . . gemsboks

grazing—I preferred to think of them as unicorns. . . . Also tried to convince my twin sister in that park that we were adopted. She didn't buy it.[6]

Penehafo Ndakalako also thought fondly of the park. Having lived in Oranjemund from 1981 to 2010, she happily remembers playing in the park "all day, until just before the sunset." While she admittedly did not enjoy playing in the tank—"I probably climbed into the tank one time, [but] it was dark, cramped and it reeked of urine"—she nevertheless refers to it as "a treasure."[7] Thus, rather than a reminder of war, for Tank Park's now-adult children the tank serves as an uncommon memorial to childhood.

The many afternoons I spent playing in Tank Park with my best friend, Zara, comprise my fondest childhood memories. I lived in Oranjemund from 1979 to 1997, across the street from Tank Park, and Zara frequently came to my house pushing a doll-sized stroller, which sometimes held a doll whose looks matched her blonde hair and blue eyes. Usually, however, the stroller held her cat—docile and dressed in a baby-doll dress and bonnet. We then crossed the street into the park—Zara pushing her pram and I mine, complete with an uninteresting baby doll. On these days we picnicked, Zara rocking

Figure 6.2. The tank at Tank Park, Oranjemund, 2015. Source: Martha Ndakalako-Bannikov.

her dressed-up feline pet and I my inanimate doll, wishing it was a cat. When we did not have our "babies" with us, our games were more challenging.

Tank Park was surrounded by tall eucalyptus trees and other ever-greens whose branches intermingled high above the ground, and it was a thrilling game among Tank Park's children to climb a tree at one point and attempt to traverse the park's boundary by passing from tree to tree where the branches met. Tips circulated as to the best trees to start at and the firmest branches to use as crossings, but no one completed the rectangle (although many boasted they had). Zara and I spent many afternoons high in those branches navigating precarious crossings. When we discovered particularly sturdy branches and shady alcoves, we played there for a while. On these occasions we picnicked in our "tree-homes," packing sandwiches and fruit into backpacks to haul up into the branches, where we whiled away the hours while other children played other games in the park beneath us.

The park had all manner of playground equipment and, naturally, children made use of these, redefining the apparatuses' prescribed uses to intensify their play. Penehafo Ndakalako recounts these games, one being "Blind man's bluff, on the witches' hat. As long as I wasn't 'It.'"[8] A witch's hat functions like a merry-go-round but is taller and conical in shape—like a witch's hat. Blind man's bluff is a game typi-cally played in an open area, and so playing it on the witch's hat was far more precarious. The base—the hat's "rim"—was a wooden seat-ing platform a few inches off the ground. As the hat spun, it shifted from side to side, depending on the weight of the people it carried. Ndakalako explained that, to play blind man's bluff on this device, "you'd stand on the planks, where you're supposed to sit, holding onto the bars and move away from 'it' either clockwise or anti-clockwise, while 'it' tried to catch you by doing the same, but with closed eyes."[9] The last person captured would be "it" for the next game.

While this game challenged the vestibular system, Ndakalako men-tioned another game that allowed those who dared to participate to experience the impossible act of flying—if only for a moment: "I . . . loved the roundabout, but I was always too scared to play that game where you'd hang on with your hands only and somebody would push it round and round, [and] when it got to a high speed you'd let go and go flying."[10] The highlights of this game were the exhilarating seconds spent soaring through the air—before hitting the ground in a tumble of arms and legs.

I remember a similar fanciful game involving the swings. The older children frequently told the younger ones that one day, to get to Heaven, we would need to leap onto the clouds, and the best way to practice this was to jump off the swings—in mid-swing, and the higher, the better. So, we swung as high as we could and at the highest point in the swing's forward arch we launched our bodies into the air and landed tumultuously on the grass. This "practice" required courage, but Ndakalako recounts a far more daring game on the swings: "there was that game where someone would get on the swing and somebody else would push them, until the person on the swing made a 360-degree turn. The other kids would stand there shouting, 'COMPLETELY, COMPLETELY!!' I never tried that though."[11] While these games were admittedly rough-and-tumble, incurring more than a few injuries, including broken arms from falling off swings, not all the activities were so challenging.

The park's ample space also allowed for diverting fun that did not involve any playground equipment. Negongo tells of a day when he and

A group of young boys went about looking for a . . . spot to build ourselves a hangout den. We found a perfect spot amongst the trees where a small thicket had grown. . . . After great exertion and over a period that seemed to stretch over an entire afternoon, there was a large rectangular hole. . . . [We] placed a large wooden board over the mouth of it and then placed some soil on top, to . . . hide it from passersby. A side shaft was then dug and presto, we had an access tunnel to our den. We soon realized that it was very dark inside, so we ran to a friend's house and returned with a candle and a match box in hand. We had great fun therein but it didn't last very long, as we hadn't considered that the park's irrigation system would wet the surrounding soil and compromise the structure's integrity.[12]

Alicia van Rooyen remembers a less labor-intensive but nevertheless "awesome childhood memory": "My favorite memory of the tank park is play with my cousins. . . . Our game was to jump over the 'clouds' if this makes any sense. The clouds would make shadows on the grass and we would see over how many we could jump. Today, to most this would sound silly, but for a six-year-old . . . this was the best game ever. When our legs couldn't jump anymore we would just lay there and find shapes in the clouds."[13]

These diverse and imaginative games demonstrate some of the collective play undertaken at Tank Park. This communal recreation mirrored the town's sense of community, which was bolstered by its parent company, CDM.

Oranjemund: Recreational Activities within the Community

Oranjemund's remote location and small population meant that the residents of the town became close, and CDM did much to encourage this. The company extravagantly sponsored many town events, and, as such, class differences were not immediately apparent, especially for children. Angie Ndinelago Nampala, who lived in Oranjemund from 1981 to 2003, discusses one such event: "the Children's Christmas Party . . . took place every December, a couple of weeks before Christmas. Our parents would choose and register what they wanted us to receive as Christmas gifts. . . . In fact each child got whatever they [*sic*] parents wanted. . . . The company paid for it all." She adds, "In 1983, I got a bicycle. That I appreciated wholeheartedly but did not use it, at all, as I could not ride a bicycle then. My siblings enjoyed it for many, many, many years."[14]

As Christmas is a summer occasion in the southern hemisphere, the "Children's Christmas Party," or "Christmas Tree" was held in the fashion of a town fair with Ferris wheel rides and bumper cars, adults costumed as cartoon characters, iced lollipops, and, the most anticipated, Father Christmas himself. An article in the *Oranjemund Newsletter* describes 1987's event in the following manner: "A rather green-looking Father Xmas disembarked from the helicopter wobbling around in search of his land legs, obviously wishing that his reindeer had been more serviceable! Together with his entourage of Maya the Bee, Donald Duck, the Pink Panther and Bugs Bunny, they attempted to spread goodwill amongst the youngsters. But the only act of goodwill the kids were truly interested in was Father Christmas's official opening of the gift stalls. There was no doubt though that the fireworks display was the 'highlight' at this year's function."[15]

"Christmas Tree" was a much-anticipated summer event during those years, but the more frequent summer weekends spent by the water are, for me, fonder recollections. Saturdays fishing for catfish at the Orange River were a favorite pastime of mine (as well as for Nda-kalako, who writes, "remember how the barbel catfish would still be alive when we got home?"), along with Sunday afternoon barbecues at the beach.[16] These frequently involved multiple families, and while our parents prepared the food, we children played.

The Atlantic's icy Benguela Current traversing the southwest African waters meant that, often, instead of running to play in the breaking waves, children waited until the last second before racing away from them. Once out of energy, a group of us would lie down in a circle in the damp sand an arm's length from each other and, with one hand, dig vertically into the ground a little way and then horizontally until our hands met in the middle. The peculiar sensation of our wet fingers touching underground as we lay with an arm buried to our shoulder, trying to guess whose fingers we were touching, delighted us.

The Value of Multiple Narratives

The above recollections draw from a period of ten years in Namibian history, years from which one could recount many other narratives with different emphases. The popular narratives concerning Namibia—and Africa in general—are often distressing, stories that rightly demand attention and action. And yet, with the prevalence of such narratives it becomes easy to assume that difficulty is all that defines the lives of the people encapsulated. Namibian novelist Neshani Andreas expresses the writer's difficulty of balancing the demand for narratives of trauma against her own narrative preference and experiences: "Writers were expected to write about great events, to glorify the past and the present, to glorify people. . . . My struggle was different. . . . I was not involved in high-profile political activities. I had to write about other things: travelling in overcrowded minibuses, selling and buying at markets, about sickness, witchcraft and church, about ordinary things."[17]

With the dominance of single-perspectival narratives of "catastrophe," it is easy to forget that the experiences of any life vary. Steven Feierman elaborates this point concerning historical narratives, pointing out that to understand a people's narratives or histories is to excavate the "palimpsest of social forms" in which they are enmeshed.[18] Lived lives, in other words, are never as unassuming as they first appear, and during the Namibian War, Namibians continued nevertheless, navigating the necessities, discomforts, and pleasures of everyday life. The narratives told above about Tank Park may seem trivial—child's play—but they significantly define the identities of the individuals to whom they belong. Perhaps these reminiscences of Oranjemund's now-adult children about happy, bygone days, intrinsically bonded to an old red-and-blue army tank resting in their playground, are a testament to human dignity, to the aptitude of people—even in difficulty—to find pleasure and some peace.

Notes

1. Marion Wallace, *A History of Namibia: From the Beginning to 1990* (Oxford: Oxford: University Press, 2013), 131.

2. Wallace, 205, 218.

3. Wallace, 268, 273.

4. Martin Boer and Robin Sherbourne, *Getting the Most Out of Our Diamonds: Namibia, De Beers, and the Arrival of Lev Leviev,* Institute for Public Policy Research Briefing Paper 20 (Windhoek, Namibia: IPPR, 2003), 2–3.

5. Naftal Negongo, "Re: Tank Park Document," personal communication, December 7, 2016.

6. Ebben, comment on "The Tank Park," Oranjemund Online, July 17, 2007, www.oranjemundonline.com/Forum/index.php?topic=25.0.

7. Penehafo Ndakalako, "Tank Park Questions," personal communication, December 13, 2016.

8. Ndakalako, "Tank Park Questions"

9. Ndakalako, personal communication, December 14, 2016.

10. Ndakalako, December 14, 2016. A roundabout is a merry-go-round.

11. Ndakalako, December 14, 2016.

12. Negongo, "Re: Tank Park Document."

13. Alicia van Rooyen, personal communication, November 24, 2016.

14. Angie Ndinelago Nampala, "Re: Tank Park Questions," personal communication, December 3, 2016.

15. "Children's Xmas Tree," *Oranjemund Newsletter,* December 4, 1987, 4.

16. Ndakalako, "Tank Park Questions."

17. Neshani Andreas, "Neshani Andreas: A Passion for Writing," interview by Erika von Wietersheim, originally published October 2004 in *Insight Namibia* (Windhoek), The Free Library, December 1, 2004, https://www.thefreelibrary.com/Neshani+Andreas:+a+passion+for+writing-a0131994511.

18. Steven Feierman, "Africa in History: The End of Universal Narratives," in *After Colonialism: Imperial Histories and Postcolonial Displacements,* ed. Gyan Prakash (Princeton, NJ: Princeton University Press, 1995), 53.

Map 7.1. Botswana. Map by Christopher Becker.

7

"Have You Been to All the Malls?"

The New Mall Scene in Botswana

DEBORAH DURHAM

"You Must Go to Them All"

Late in 2014, I was driving two university students back to their houses in Gaborone, Botswana's capital city, after seeing the latest *Hunger Games* film. We inched along in traffic on the busy A-1 roadway, passing industrial workshops and houses near the city's core. Here and there were small older shopping venues, two stories, typically organized in an L shape around a parking area. The main road would lead us to the cavernous indoor mall named after its anchor store, Game, before stretching into the countryside, where cattle, donkeys, and goats wandered out of the dusty, acacia-thick bush in front of speeding cars. Far behind us was the new Airport Junction Mall, with elegant restaurants, shoe, clothing, music, computer, and home goods stores, and its two supermarkets, termed "hyper-markets." Malls were typically anchored by chain grocery stores, often two, which ensured constant traffic.

From the backseat of the car where the girls sat, a voice asked, "Have you been to all the malls yet?" Laughing, I commented that the shops were all the same. "But you must go to them all," they both said earnestly.

Botswana's Malls: Past and Present

All those malls to go to! By 2017, more malls, some larger than before, had opened in Gaborone. It seemed that all the larger villages had a mall. Much had changed since my last stay in 2000, when the first of the "new" shopping malls in Gaborone had just opened. I had done anthropological research in Botswana throughout the 1990s in Mahalapye, a large urban village a couple hours' drive from Gaborone. Many residents engaged in agriculture in plots outside the village and at cattle posts (communal land) further out. Few subsisted entirely on agriculture, relying in part on income from jobs or remittances from kin working elsewhere. Roads were sandy, pitted, winding ways between irregularly shaped compounds of mudbrick rondavels (dwellings) and small cement-block houses. A central area had government offices, a hospital, banks, and a variety of shops, including furniture stores and large wholesalers whose goods made their way into little "general dealers" throughout the village. Many of the older shops sat surrounding a large open, dusty area where buses pulled off the main road. This area was sometimes called "the station," but more often "the mall." Botswana did not have the thriving street markets common in West Africa, but a few people set up small shelters from which they sold cooked food and snacks to travelers. However, most preferred the fried chicken from a takeaway eatery down the road. People sometimes said they were going to the mall and sometimes said they were going "to town" (*ko mollong* or *ko toropong* in Setswana, the Tswana language).

Figure 7.1. Main mall in Gaborone, Botswana. Source: Deborah Durham.

Figure 7.2. Main mall in Gaborone, Botswana. Source: Deborah Durham.

When I returned to Botswana in 2014 and again in 2017, I stayed in the capital city with its growing array of shopping malls. In the early 1990s, the main mall in Gaborone was a long, open walkway at the center of the city. It stretched from the parliamentary and ministry buildings at one end to the city council buildings at the other, lined with foreign embassies, shops, and one of the city's two premier hotels. A couple of blocks away, an open parking area surrounded by small shops with a few eateries and tailoring enterprises was called "the African Mall." By the 2000s, the mall that lay at the center of the city—still there—was not one of the malls that the university students thought I should visit. This downtown mall was now primarily a transit point for pedestrians; embassies had moved and premier hotels were elsewhere. The students strongly warned me against buying food in its "dirty" grocery stores. Vendors set up tables, selling used clothing, dried beans and vegetables, and CDs of gospel, rap, and American country music. One woman called it, in English, a "flea market."

The malls that the students thought I should visit surrounded the city: they were their own spaces, distinct from the city itself. In some ways, my return in 2014 was a double move: from an urban village to the capital city, and from the 1990s to the 2010s. By 2014, even Mahalapye had an elegant new shopping mall, just to the north of town—too far, really, to walk to—and next to a gleaming luxury hotel that hosted government conferences. It served as a venue for elite weddings, removed from the dusty compounds and crowds of hungry fellow-villagers.[1]

In the 1990s urban village, people went down to the mall to pick up needed things at the shops and do errands at a government office. You could buy limited things at little "general dealers," later called "tuck shops," scattered throughout the village. These were one-room affairs selling nonperishable necessities—soap, toilet paper, candles, tea, sugar, a few sweets, and matches for wood fires and paraffin lamps. No one went to this mall without an errand to bring them there, except, perhaps, schoolchildren loitering and mixing on their way home from school. From where I lived, it was a moderate walk, perhaps half an hour; for others, the mall might be closer or considerably farther. One hoped for a ride from one of the few cars and pickup trucks ("bakkies") in the village, but no taxi or other transport was available. Most people thoroughly enjoyed being seen in a car, even a knocked-up old model, if they could wangle a ride. People, women especially, usually bathed and dressed in better clothes to go to the mall, frequently stopping as they got closer to wipe the accumulating dust off their shoes. Anthropologist Wim van Binsbergen has explained that such preparations ritually protect oneself in the foreign (European) urban space. Elsewhere, I have argued that bathing and dressing well are connected with ideas of active citizenship in the liberal democracy.[2] The more mature people were, the slower they walked down to the mall, displaying their dignity. Because of the time involved, people often sent children to the mall instead to pick up a bit of meat for mid-day supper or paraffin for lamps. Children were told to jump to it—to run—to their errands.

Going to the bus-station mall was fun, even if you only went to stand in long lines to pay the water bill for the compound standpipe or to buy a new coal-heated iron for your aging clothes. High school students wandered around in clusters that formed and reformed, talking and laughing, with boys holding each other's hands and girls pretending to disdain boys' attention. Older women enjoyed going into clothing stores and looking through the limited selection of clothes, rarely buying but often making demands of the shop assistants. The assistants themselves responded slowly to demands, sometimes with a surly demeanor. It was a contest of status in which the customers tried to order the assistants around, as if they were children or household subordinates, and the assistants resisted. The shop assistants, often in uniforms, were among the few people with regular jobs in the urban village. If you knew the assistant already, the exchange morphed into teasing and ended in laughter. At the mall you ran into other people you knew, both from your own ward and from one of the sixteen others scattered across the sprawling village. Seeing others, seeing who they were with or what they were doing, talking with them about visitors and relatives, who was going where, who was visiting here, the illnesses of acquaintances, and the conditions at cattle posts or agricultural fields sustained a sense of shared social connection.

Fifteen years later in Gaborone, you didn't need an errand to take you to a mall. Some people might walk if it wasn't too far, but more often they made their way in minivan buses, shared taxis that waited to be filled at designated spots, or the private cars that increasingly clog roadways. People of almost all ages, though few elderly, came to the shopping malls. Of course, some were there to shop for the old staples of mealie-meal, cooking oil, tea, milk, or sugar. Today's essentials might also include purchases of fresh grapes, jars of hot atchar, and disposable babies' diapers. Some bought packets of prepared foods at the grocery stores—chicken and samp (similar to hominy), or beef stew and rice, in clamshell packaging, with a mayonnaise-rich salad on the side. Some were looking for special-occasion clothing for themselves or to be given to a relative, for a vase or wine glasses or another decorative item to gift for a party or wedding. Many were just checking out the fashions, whether at a shop with well-known Western fashion lines (Ralph Lauren, Izod) or one with cheap, affordable tops. Both types of stores always seemed full of younger people holding up shirts as salespeople—now quite helpful—hovered around. At Game City (a large store similar to Target), I listened to two women in their thirties discuss in English the relative quality and desirability of kitchen appliances in the long row of toasters, microwaves, stand mixers, blenders, and the like. Their crisp and clear English switched to Setswana as they moved along and began to gossip about people they knew. Though it was a hot November day south of the equator, the front of the store had rows of artificial Christmas trees, ornaments, and suggested gift items. Secondary school students—very few in school uniform—played pinball or wandered in groups, laughing and watching each other surreptitiously. At another shopping complex, River Walk Mall, some looked at the posters outside the movie theater or headed inside. Young couples and families ate fast-food ribs or

Figure 7.3. New shopping mall in Botswana. Source: Deborah Durham.

slices of pizza. More established people sat at Mugg & Bean, a coffee shop/restaurant with outdoor seating, or went to the casual dining chain Nando's (though both stretched their wallets). At night, some of the larger malls filled with diners seeking drinks at happy hour and finer fare late into the night, eating Mexican, Latin American, Lebanese, Irish pub-style, and Thai cuisines.

Shopping and Showing Off

Going to the mall (bus station) in Mahalapye in the 1990s and going to the malls (big shopping and dining centers) in Gaborone in 2014 had much in common. Women still paid close attention to their clothing, knowing they would be evaluated for the neatness of their outfits. Going to the mall often combined work—the need to stock the house with necessities, buy a gift, or at least pick up some little thing—with pleasure. Some of that pleasure came from looking at things for sale, much came from being in the crowds of people, seeing and being seen. And then there was the opportunity—usually seized—to pick up something delicious to eat, even if, in the 1990s, it was a small bag of chutney-flavored crisps, and in the 2010s pizza, ribs, or an ice cream cone.

But so much had changed. It is fun to assess the styles of clothing in stores, but now these styles point to a global fashion world and not the limited regional styles available in 1990. People now like to be seen with their purchases: a prospective entrepreneur looking for a business opportunity told me that my suggestion of home-delivered groceries would never be popular in Botswana. People, she said, wanted others to see them with full shopping carts leaving the grocery stores for the parking lots. In the nineties, in the village, one's purchases were often a loaf of bread, cabbage and soup cubes to flavor it, or a small packet of meat. People seeing these modest purchases would jokingly demand that the purchaser share the small packet of meat, or expect a mealtime visit.[3] Now, people at malls were buying mock-leather skirts, decorative pillows, coffee makers, wine glasses, and all sorts of goods—and the people buying were from a range of ages. In the 1990s, in the urban village, one rarely saw an older teen purchasing anything more than candy or food for the family meal that day. Most children and teens in Mahalapye wore older, hand-me-down clothing and had one good outfit for special events. People's clothes were judged most often on their cleanliness, neatness, and the way they were worn. Now, in urban Gaborone's malls and in Mahalapye, young people were at shops buying fashionably ripped jeans, T-shirts with an array of ersatz Disney or University of Boston motifs, Nike and Soviet sneakers, and whimsical baby clothes. People only bought household goods out of real need in the 1990s—even enameled tin bowls and mugs, cast-iron pots to sit over a fire, basins for laundry and baths, and blankets for sleeping and wearing were often borrowed from a neighbor and only occasionally purchased. Yet more rarely, an item of furniture, a wardrobe, bed, or velvet-upholstered sitting-room suite was bought by layaway or on monthly installments—and people loved to gossip when payments were missed and furniture items disappeared from someone's house. Money went to consumables: the water bill, paraffin, batteries, food. Now, malls offered opportunities to browse and purchase an amazing array of goods, from knickknacks to computers and flat-screen televisions.

The Stress and Pleasure of Middle-Income Status

What had changed? Of course, the change for me involves moving from an urban village to the capital city, but there are new malls in Mahalapye, too. One obvious place to look for the sudden growth of malls is money. At independence in 1966, Botswana was one of the poorest countries in the world, with very low levels of education and most income sent back by labor migrants in South Africa. By 2014, the World Bank rated Botswana an upper-middle-income country, with GDP per capita at over $7,000 and a purchasing power parity (a number for comparing income across countries) of over $15,000 per year. That income is highly skewed (the Gini coefficient, which measures income inequality on a scale of 0 for complete equality to 100 for complete inequality, was 61 in 2014), and many people earned less than $100 per month, if they earned anything at all. However, these formal measures do not include the substantial redistribution of income and resources, typically to extended family members and lovers, that circulate in the informal economy. Economic growth has been accompanied by considerable property speculation in the 2010s. The mushroom growth of new malls reflects, too, attempts to develop local properties, with developers reaping considerable profits, chain stores doing fairly well with their deep reserves of stock, and smaller local businesses opening and then quickly closing in a saturated mall market.

There is so much more to buy these days. In the 1980s and '90s, most goods came from or through South Africa, whose apartheid regime was under economic sanctions by most of the world. In the 1990s, Chinese immigrants had just begun to appear, selling watches or plastic household goods on the streets, accompanying Chinese investment and infrastructure improvement projects. Today, the global commodities that flow into post-apartheid South Africa also flow into Botswana, and cheaply manufactured goods from China stock shelves. Clothing, in particular, has gotten very inexpensive and is available in a wide array of styles. Additionally, the increasing availability of electricity in homes, both in town and in many villages, spurs desire for coffee makers, televisions, or at least electric irons.

Along with this influx of goods from around the world, and an increasing means to access them, there is growing exposure to global media. In the 1990s, the few people who had televisions could watch American soap operas like *The Bold and the Beautiful*, American comedies like *The Cosby Show*, and ads for dish soaps and other goods on South African stations that depicted African families in distinctly middle-class, well-stocked households. By the 2010s, cellphones and social media, along with proliferating televisions with hundreds of satellite channels, transmitted images of a world awash in consumer-driven leisure, cooking, and home improvement.

Forms of leisure persist, and new ones have arisen—where there once were choir practices and fund-raising concerts in candle-lit rooms in the village, choirs now practice to produce CDs for sale. Well-advertised concerts in large venues now include local and regional pop stars. Soccer clubs in dusty fields have been joined by exercise studios, and young people flock to Tlokweng, a village in the middle of the continent, for its annual "beach party." But fun is also found in a more everyday venue, the shopping mall. In the mall, even those who scrape by on salaries of $100 a month, like the shop girls themselves, surround themselves with the illusion of consumer plenty, and perhaps sometimes manage to buy themselves a cheap Chinese T-shirt for $3 or a piece of pizza. People of all income levels go into debt for all those household goods, or for the cars to get them to the malls, with consequences ranging from losing the goods, to retiring to the cheaper village home, to despairing and committing suicide.[4] But if the fun of the malls is in their excess—the numbers of people flocking to them, the ability to display a full shopping cart (at least, after payday at the end of the month), or the impressive array of consumer goods assembled there in shop after shop, on shelves and shelves of microwaves, on racks and tables of clothing—then of course one should go to *all* the malls, as the girls in my backseat told me.

Notes

1. On new wedding practices in Botswana, see Rijk van Dijk, "The Social Cocktail: Weddings and the Innovative Mixing of Competences in Botswana," in *Transforming Innovations in Africa: Explorative Studies on Appropriation in African Societies*, ed. Jan-Bart Gewald, André Leliveld, and Iva Peša (Leiden: Brill, 2012); and Jacqueline Solway, "'Slow Marriage,' 'Fast *Bogadi*': Change and Continuity in Marriage in Botswana," *Anthropology Southern Africa* 40, no. 1 (2017): 309–22.

2. Wim van Binsbergen, "Making Sense of Urban Space in Francistown, Botswana," in *Urban Symbolism*, ed. Peter J. M. Nas (Leiden: Brill, 1993); Deborah Durham, "Did You Bathe This Morning? Baths and Morality in Botswana," in *Dirt, Undress, and Difference: Critical Perspectives on the Body's Surface*, ed. Adeline Masquelier (Bloomington: Indiana University Press, 2005).

3. I have written about how these demands for things—"give me that bread!"—were important ways of distinguishing relationships of independent equality or unequal dependence. See Deborah Durham, "Soliciting Gifts and Negotiating Agency: The Spirit of Asking in Botswana," *Journal of the Royal Anthropological Institute*, n.s., 1, no. 1 (March 1995): 111–28.

4. On debt and suicide in Botswana, see Julie Livingston, "Suicide, Risk, and Investment in the Heart of the African Miracle," *Cultural Anthropology* 24, no. 4 (November 2009): 652–80. For a full study of debt in South Africa, see Deborah James, *Money from Nothing: Indebtedness and Aspiration in South Africa* (Stanford, CA: Stanford University Press, 2014).

Map 8.1. Nigeria. Map by Christopher Becker.

8

Sociality, Money, and the Making of Masculine Privilege in Nigerian Sports Clubs

DANIEL JORDAN SMITH

In contemporary Nigeria, the relatively gender-segregated character of social life means that men's relationships with each other dominate their daily lives. Further, male peer groups constitute a central arena for the performance of both social class and masculinity. Competent manhood is increasingly tied to having money and spending it in ways that are conspicuous (and even ostentatious) and yet at the same time generous. For elite men in urban settings, sports clubs are attractive arenas in which to build politically and economically valuable social networks, display wealth, demonstrate masculinity, and consolidate their class position. While at some level many of the men who join and regularly participate in club activities recognize these benefits, in everyday discourse they mostly emphasize just having fun.

Drawing on decades-long experience with men's tennis clubs in southeastern Nigeria, in this chapter I explore the importance of leisure, pleasure, and male camaraderie in the making of masculine privilege. A curious mix of formality and informality characterizes men's behavior in the clubs, practices that simultaneously subvert and reinforce hierarchies of age, wealth, and power that exist outside these venues. The character of everything from evening drinking sessions to attending the funeral of a fellow club member's parent is at once highly ritualized and yet also frequently spontaneous and profoundly intimate. For these elite men, male-only social spaces offer opportunities to escape and debate perceived challenges to their manhood, while at the same time they affirm their social position through the pleasurable celebration of their successes as men.

Masculinity and Money at a Nigerian Tennis Club

Owerri is a small city of about half a million people in Imo State, in the heart of the Igbo-speaking region of Nigeria. Igbos are one of Nigeria's three largest ethnic groups, numbering close to thirty million people. I have lived and worked there periodically since 1989, often conducting research as a cultural anthropologist. While I joined a club there to play tennis, it eventually became a source of rich ethnographic data about a range of interesting topics, including politics, inequality, and gender. Located on the outskirts of town, Owerri Sports Club is a particularly masculine space. Most often there are few women—and frequently no women—present.

During one of my visits to the club, JMJ arrived in his new Mercedes Benz for an evening tennis game. When the men sitting in chairs arranged by the side of the court saw him enter, they chanted in unison, "JMJ, 2.6 Billion!" In fact, "2.6 Billion" was JMJ's nickname at the club, a kind of late-twentieth-century version of praise names that have long been a part of masculine culture in southeastern Nigeria.[1] Traditionally in Igbo society, men's praise names referenced attributes like skill in warfare or wrestling, excellence in farming, or some honorific associated with a man's character, such as wisdom or oratory prowess.[2] JMJ's praise name referred to the fact that he had a lot of money. No one knew exactly how much, but 2.6 billion was an imagined number of naira (the Nigerian currency) so large that even a very rich man would be flattered by it. JMJ's fellow club members did not, however, lavish him with so much attention simply because he had a lot of money. The praise name signaled that he was also generous in spending it.

JMJ showed off his brand-new Wilson Hammer racket, then the latest model that no other club member had yet acquired. After playing a brief game of doubles, he joined the assembly of men gathered for a long evening of beer, food, and boisterous conversation that always began in earnest just after the sun set and the tennis ended. The club's president formally initiated the evening's proceedings, banging a large gavel that looked like it belonged in a courtroom. Once the president called the club to order, everyone was expected to join the group and participate, at least until enough alcohol pulled things again toward more informal interaction later in the evening.

Figure 8.1. Men socializing at a tennis club in Nigeria. Source: Daniel Jordan Smith.

Once the group came to order, the president addressed the men: "My trustee, my patrons, my vice president, my general secretary, my financial secretary, my sports secretary, the captain of tennis, my champion, all other celebrities, ladies and gentlemen." The president had looked around the assembled group to see who was present so as not to forget to acknowledge each club officeholder in attendance. The club had at least two dozen formal offices or recognized positions, and each time someone addressed the club as a group it was expected that he mention each official by his title. Further, it was important to recite them in their order of prestige. Because the president was speaking, he did not mention himself, but normally the order would be the president, the trustee(s), the patron(s), the vice president, past presidents, and so on down the hierarchy, every address concluding with "all other celebrities, ladies and gentlemen." The fact that every man there could be a celebrity (or at least that every man might think of himself as such) is a feature not only of the club's culture, but also of masculine social life in southeastern Nigeria more generally. Igboland is, after all, the place about which the anthropologist Richard Henderson titled his 1972 ethnography

The King in Every Man, signaling this common male expectation that every man is entitled to respect.[3]

Of course, the fact that they had the financial wherewithal to join a club, play tennis, and spend several evenings out drinking beer with their mates meant that these particular men constituted part of the town's elite. But, in reality, the men at the club varied considerably in their wealth and status, even if none was poor. Still, they often liked to point out that they were equals once inside the club premises. There was indeed some truth in this. Men of a wide range of ages and differing political and economic clout interacted with an equality that wouldn't be possible outside the club. Further, when at the club, all the men generally deferred to club officeholders, even if those relations reversed hierarchies of age, wealth, and power that prevailed outside the club. Yet, in other ways, the club not only reproduced wider social disparities, it also accentuated them. Men at Owerri Sports Club were intensely attuned to status and to the recognition that comes with it. In many respects, this magnified quite common patterns in southeastern Nigeria, particularly regarding the importance of money as a marker of men's social position. Nigerian society is marked by significant social and economic inequality. Although joining a tennis club is only possible for men who are relatively elite, most people in contemporary Nigeria aspire to a middle-class lifestyle. Proving masculinity is increasingly linked to demonstrating one has the money to be in the middle class.

After the opening formalities, the president reminded the men that the following weekend they were expected to attend the burial ceremony of the late mother of one of the club's members. Everyone was tasked with paying a burial levy that would become the club's collective contribution to the event. He then explained that he was opening the floor for members to make additional contributions to the funeral.

Several members addressed their mates. Each speaker went through the entire list of assembled club officers and celebrities before offering a contribution over and above the set burial levy. They offered their contributions in cash or as a number of crates of beer. Everyone knew the exact price of a crate of each of the several types of beer that were available at the club. The announced contributions were followed by a collective "Ohhwaayyy!" The shout suggested mock surprise at the size and generosity of the gifts and conveyed genuine appreciation.

To encourage more donations, the president called for clapping in unison to thank the donors—six claps for smaller amounts, twelve claps for larger amounts. He instructed the club's social secretary to lead these collective claps, which in club parlance were known as six-gun and twelve-gun salutes.

Later, after a period of quiet conversation, JMJ stood up and asked the president for the floor. As he stood, his rotund belly protruded between his tennis shirt and shorts. Before formally addressing the club, JMJ raised his hand and shouted "Ahhheee, club!," in response to which the assembled men chanted in unison, "Club!" As is common in southeastern Nigeria, the men sometimes spoke in Igbo, sometimes in English, and often in a mix of the two. JMJ shouted again and the group responded. Then he shouted, "Ahhheee, tennis!," and the men responded, "Tennis!" The "ahhheee" salutation was a dramatic mode of address. It simply meant "greetings" or "attention," but it created the expectation that the speaker had something bold or important to say. The men expected a flamboyant performance from JMJ. He began, "My president, my trustee, my patrons, my general secretary." By this hour of the evening, even these Igbo men, who had a seemingly insatiable appetite for formal recognition, expected that conventional forms of address be cut short. JMJ obliged and followed "my general secretary" with "all protocols observed." At the beginning of the evening's festivities this would have been perceived as too curt. But later on, after several rounds of drinks, when every "celebrity" had been recognized numerous times, the men seemed to welcome the respite from the formal protocol. So, when JMJ uttered "all protocols observed," the men let out a collective "uhhhweee," signaling that they eagerly anticipated whatever he had to offer.

JMJ did not disappoint. He announced that he would contribute ten crates of beer and a goat to the upcoming burial ceremony. Other men had contributed between one and four crates of beer. JMJ's donation generated whoops and shouts of "2.6 Billion!" JMJ then added that all the evening's fine gestures needed to be properly "washed down." With that, he ordered three crates of beer and a plate of pepper soup for everyone. At this the men whooped again. The president called the group to order again and instructed the social secretary to lead the men in a "twenty-one-gun salute," this number of claps being reserved only for the largest and most remarkable donations. By the end of the synchronized clapping, several men had lost the beat, but so much beer had flowed and was still yet to come that no one objected and the president did not impose any fines.

When the crates of beer JMJ pledged were brought out for consumption, the president called on a new applicant to the club to distribute them. This man, in his mid-thirties, had the unenviable task of making sure the beer was distributed in order of social status. The distribution of beer (or anything shared among men) mimicked the traditional distribution of kola nuts made famous in the Igbo author Chinua Achebe's novels.[4] I had been asked to do this when I first applied to join the club, and the men took great delight in both my successes and my mistakes. The same was true for this new Nigerian comrade, though the expectations that he get it right were higher than in my case. At the club, the beer had to be distributed in the same order as the formal greetings: to the president, the trustee, the patrons, and so on. Learning the hierarchy of club offices was relatively easy, but beer had to be distributed to everyone, not just club officers. Once one had served the club officials, the order of distribution then reverted to social status overall. In other words, one needed to know each man's perceived ranking in society.

Monetary wealth played an ever-larger role in shaping these male-peer-group social rankings, but its prominence also produced conflict and discontent. Being able to "perform" monetarily is one of the paramount ambitions of Nigerian men, and certainly, having lots of money and using it in socially appropriate ways are the surest means to secure the admiration of other men. But as in other domains of men's lives, in male peer groups the rise of money as the most important marker of manhood comes with much ambivalence and breeds discontent. The ambivalence and discontent reflect uneasiness about rising levels of inequality. Although most men aspire to a middle-class lifestyle and the comforts and recognition that come with money, they also lament the greed, the disparities, and the emphasis on individualism that accompany these changes. Even as JMJ was showered with praise for his generosity, in his absence I sometimes heard his peers criticize his ostentation or speak derisively about the political corruption that enabled his great wealth. Publicly, having lots of money appeared to bring rich men nothing but admiration; behind their backs it generated much criticism.

Money, Intimacy, and Men's Relationships with Each Other

Many aspects of how men demonstrate friendship or allegiance with each other happen in very public ways. In trying to show support to a fellow club member, spending money to demonstrate one's affection and loyalty is a key means for enacting sociality and expressing solidarity. Men's public displays of monetary backing for their peers are not only highly visible; they are also heavily scrutinized. A man's economic and political status is shaped by how much money he has, but his moral status depends, in part, on whether the amount he spends is seen as stingy or generous relative to his "size." In other words, while money translates into power, virtue is determined by perceptions of generosity and sincerity.

But not all of the dynamics of money and intimacy in men's relationships with each other unfolded in such public ways. Indeed, one of the markers of deep friendship and intimacy between individual men manifested itself in the willingness to trust another to know about one's financial difficulties and seek help. In my many friendships at clubs in Nigeria, I learned about men's financial vulnerabilities and the often-quiet help they sought from each other. For example, one of the better tennis players at Umuahia Sports Club (another club I joined in the town of Umuahia in Abia State, where I also did anthropological research) was a man named Kelechi. On his modest teacher's salary, the expenses of club membership were onerous even in the best of times. To make matters worse, at various periods during both military and civilian regimes, the Abia State government would fail to pay salaries for long stretches of time. During one span of several months without pay, Kelechi's father became seriously sick and was hospitalized for several weeks. These financial shocks left Kelechi in dire straits. He eventually approached Ezeife, one of his best friends in the club, for a loan. Ezeife, in turn, approached me and a couple of other club members to contribute enough cash to see Kelechi through until the government paid salaries.

During this period, many club members knew of Kelechi's situation. While people asked about his father and club members lamented and made jokes about the government's failure to pay salaries, no one ever sympathized publicly about Kelechi's financial situation, much less mentioned the fact of our loan. To do so would have been seen as unnecessarily exposing our friend's vulnerability. Until salaries were paid and Kelechi was able to right his financial situation, many people bought him beers, the president ordered the club's financial secretary to overlook his lapsed monthly dues, and no one expected him to open a can of new tennis balls. But it was taboo to openly discuss his predicament in front of him. As ostentatious as these men could be about showing off or celebrating someone's money if he had plenty, for a friend they could be equally protective when he did not.

Of course, the willingness to loan Kelechi money and treat his situation discreetly was something Kelechi had earned in his relationships with his friends and fellow club members. Such help and discretion could not be taken for granted. I observed other instances in which financial debts accrued in ostensibly private arrangements exploded into public disputes. When a man failed to repay a debt in the amount of time that his creditor expected, sometimes that creditor would make the dispute known to others, looking for mediation and pressure to pay the debt. But it was rare to air such conflicts at the club, because to do so was seen as shameful for both parties. When it happened a handful of times over the years, all the men lamented that money had spoiled a friendship and introduced conflict into club comradery.

In Nigeria, particularly in the southeast, the performance of masculinity is judged heavily by how men spend their money. Nigerian men's desire for money is not only, or even mainly, about individual greed. Instead, it is deeply tied to sociality and to the yearning for and rewards of social recognition. In Nigeria's gender-segregated social world, male peer groups are major arenas in which men spend their time and their money to seek social recognition and rewards. Despite its dark side, spending money animates and lubricates many important social networks to which men belong. The sense of belonging— so palpable in the tennis clubs—often triumphs over the discontent that the struggle for money can bring.

Notes

1. Afam Ebeogu, "Onomastics and the Igbo Tradition of Politics," *African Languages and Cultures* 6, no. 2 (1993): 133–46; Obododimma Oha, "Praise Names and Power De/constructions in Contemporary Igbo Chiefship," *Culture, Language and Representation* 7 (2009): 101–16.

2. Chinwe M. A. Nwoye, "Igbo Cultural and Religious Worldview: An Insider's Perspective," *International Journal of Sociology and Anthropology* 3, no. 9 (September 2011): 304–17.

3. Richard N. Henderson, *The King in Every Man: Evolutionary Trends in Onitsha Ibo Society and Culture* (New Haven, CT: Yale University Press, 1972).

4. Victor C. Uchendu, "'Kola Hospitality' and Igbo Lineage Structure," *Man* 64 (March/April 1964): 47–50.

Map 9.1. Nigeria. Map by Christopher Becker.

9

"Let's Turn It Up"

Effervescent Night Life in Nigeria

OMOTOYOSI BABALOLA

To "turn it up" colloquially means having a good time, alluding to the impulse to blast music at maximum volume. This phrase is widely used with reference to the lively weekend nightlife in Nigeria's urban centers. Nigeria is an ethnically and religiously heterogeneous nation with diverse cultural practices, yet this party lifestyle cuts across age, gender, religion, and class, though largely dominated by upwardly mobile men who are moving into higher socioeconomic positions.[1] The "turn it up" spirit integrates a variety of foods, fashions, places, and people that locate many Nigerians in a survive-or-surrender mentality. To many urban Nigerians, this lifestyle is a way to release accumulated stress, calm personal pressures, and get refreshed for the upcoming week. The frequency of this practice is dependent on a number of factors, such as financial capabilities, religious affiliation, and place of residence.

Living in Nigeria can be tough, especially with major economic challenges such as the frequent backlog of unpaid salaries. Problems such as bad roads, erratic or no electric power supply, intense traffic jams, and internet network issues can be overwhelming, hence the need to turn it up as a form of escape. Many Nigerians, especially those in Lagos—one of the fastest-growing cities in the world, Africa's most populous city, and Nigeria's economic center—are pleasure seekers who love to hang out with friends to have fun. In this essay I draw from interviews and participant observation of people and places in Nigeria to highlight this tension between precariousness and pleasure to show how nightlife persists as a strategy to seek distraction and relief from the social realities of urban Nigeria.

Nightlife Party Culture: Gender, Class, and Urban Leisure

The "turn it up" lifestyle is a lively, predominantly male-driven culture within clubs, comedy shows, and sports venues, centered mostly in Lagos. Nigeria is a patriarchal society where women and girls are still largely discriminated against. A plethora of sociocultural factors have contributed to and maintained existing social inequalities that constrain the activities of women.[2] Though women socialize and seek entertainment in other ways, there are unwritten rules that prohibit them from partaking freely in the activities described in this essay. Women are expected to use the weekend for house chores, styling their hair, cooking special meals, helping the children with homework, and other so-called "women's duties."[3] Therefore, salons, religious centers, marketplaces, and malls are likely places to find women socializing. Those who go against this norm by frequenting bars and nightclubs are considered by many to be immoral. As a result, most women who want to be perceived as responsible stay away from these activities altogether. However, there are women who are actively involved in nightlife. An acceptable way for a woman to be seen in clubs and bars is if she is accompanied by a man. Some young women go to clubs and bars occasionally to celebrate a major achievement or to mark a public holiday. Moreover, there are "bar girls" employed to serve and wait on customers. Nevertheless, the low proportion of women to men as customers in these places makes urban nightlife a predominantly male-dominated activity.

In contemporary urban Nigeria, with the growing prevalence of demanding nine-to-five white-collar jobs, nightlife and weekend party culture serves as a means of escaping social drudgery. For example, Daramola Olukayode, an architect, opined, "'Turn it up' culture is the sole reason why some Nigerians have not committed suicide." Similarly, Philip, a civil servant, shares a common sentiment, viewing nightlife as a personal necessity.

> [At night] is the only time I have on my own to relax and catch fun after a hectic day. As a civil servant, I work in Ikeja [one of the busiest areas in Lagos], I wake up 5:30 a.m. everyday [*sic*] to go to work and come back around 8:30 p.m. Some times, I come back around 9:00 p.m. depending on the level of the traffic and this happens from Monday to Friday. On Saturday, I use that for my laundry work.

So you find out that the only time I have to relax and enjoy myself with my friends is at night. I do not go out everyday [*sic*]. It is only on weekends especially, Saturdays and Sundays. As a bachelor, I have less to think about when I hang out.[4]

For some Nigerians, no matter how insolvent they are, they find the money to "turn it up." It is so important, especially to men, that Goke Ajayi, an accountant, explained, "If I owe N5000 [naira], and all I make in a day is the same N5000, I will plead with my creditor to wait and I will use the money for *faaji* [enjoyment and relaxation]. Anything can wait [but] not my turn it up money." Additionally, people use "turn it up" time to network by expanding existing circles of influence. For example, they might land a contract over a bottle of beer and *asun* (spicy goat-meat barbecue).

Much of "turn it up" culture flourishes in Lagos, a megacity with an estimated population of twenty-one million.[5] The city of Lagos has two main geographical divisions, the Mainland (e.g., Yaba, Surulere, and Agege) and the Island (e.g., Lekki, Victoria Island, and Marina), which are connected by the Third Mainland Bridge. Class stratification falls along this geographical divide: the Island is home to the very rich while the Mainland is populated largely by middle and lower economic classes. Most people living in the city of Lagos work on the Island among high-end neighborhoods located in and around the creeks of Lagos Lagoon. This area is home to leading, well-paying corporate establishments where many Lagosians aspire to work. A majority of employees who work on the Island cannot afford to live there because of exorbitant housing rates. Thus, they rent more affordable dwellings on the Mainland, the landlocked area of Lagos. To get to work on time, most employees must leave home by 5:00 a.m. to maneuver the Third Mainland Bridge's congested roadways. Commutes can take as long as three to six hours depending on traffic flow. As a result, many men in the corporate world do not wait until weekends to have fun. Weekday evenings, with the exception of Mondays, which many Nigerians revere as the start of the workweek, are spent at nearby bars, clubs, and relaxation centers to wait out rush-hour traffic before driving home. Starting Tuesday evenings, these hotspots start to fill up as people begin to loosen up. On Thursday evenings, when workloads start to ease up, clubs, lounges, and sports bars experience a large surge of customers. Many in particular look forward to Friday as a time for climactic and epic fun, referring to the day as TGIF (Thank

God It's Friday). Aside from the aforementioned conventional "turn it up" peak times and places, entertainment entrepreneurs—those who make money through recreational activities—strategically organize events around public holidays and weekends to promote relaxation, partying, and overall having a good time.

Clubs, Bars, and Lounges

Nigerian cities, like those in other cosmopolitan places, are replete with clubs, lounges, and bars, each of which attracts its own type of clientele. Because of its extreme metropolitanism, Lagos has more sophisticated bars and clubs compared to many other cities in the country. They include venues like Ntyce, Club 57, Escape Nightlife, and Caliente.[6] In the morning and early afternoon hours, the staff busily prepares by cleaning, stocking up, and cooking. Most clubs open in the evening around 4:00 p.m, with a major uptick in business around midnight.

Allen Avenue is one of the busiest neighborhoods in Lagos and is known for its lively nightlife. It is also a commercial hub of Lagos's Mainland where major companies and landmarks like the prominent Alade Market are located. On this booming street, expensive cars are parked alongside bustling pedestrians. Inside a typical club, DJs blast loud musical compilations all night with bright colors lighting the venue, which attracts young and upwardly mobile patrons. Customers vocalize their enjoyment by singing along at the top of their lungs, holding bottles of alcoholic beverages in their hands. Sometimes, especially on Thursday and Friday nights, popular artists and entertainers perform shows, with guests making special requests. A major component of Nigerian clubs is the VIP section, which is exclusively reserved for the rich and famous, who enjoy privacy, comfortable seating, and premium drinks.

As in other parts of the world, drinking alcoholic beverages is a big part of nightlife in Nigeria. There are a number of drink options and the menu choices are largely influenced by financial status and individual preferences. Both alcohol and herbal mixtures are popular and seen as not only intoxicating and therapeutic drinks, but also aphrodisiacs. People order herbal alcohol drinks like Alomo Bitters, Baby Oku, and Orijin, which they mix with more costly beverages. The herbal concoctions have a high percentage of alcohol, sometimes 40 percent and upwards. Those with more discretionary funds imbibe

Moët champagne, Grey Goose, Belvedere, or Cîroc vodka, or other imported beverages. On weeknights, many restrict their consumption so as not to get drunk and be hungover for work the next day. But on weekends, some men let their guard down and drink excessively.

Some Nigerian men engage in extreme "turn it up" practices. In one viral example, a group spent a whopping ten million naira (about $60,000 at the time) during a single night at Escape Nightlife. For comparison, the lowest-paid civil servant on level 01 is paid N226,800 per annum; thus, it would take them the equivalent of over forty-four years of work just to pay the Escape bar tab.

For those without as much disposable income, fun is still possible, though it is quite different from that of people with more money. They "turn it up" by visiting roadside bars, pepper soup joints, and *suya* spots (suya is a tasty meat kebab prepared with peppery spices) as opposed to high-end bars, clubs, and lounges. With N2,000 (about five dollars), an individual can engage in forms of amusement in more affordable spaces. An example of a very popular suya spot is University of Suya (not an actual university), located on Allen Avenue and in Ikeja and Yaba, Lagos, a place with an assortment of suya made with chicken, gizzards, beef, intestines, or pork. No matter your financial status, there is a place to "turn it up" in Nigeria.

Figure 9.1. A man sells *suya* in the Asokoro section of Abuja, Nigeria. Suya is thinly sliced strips of meat cooked over an open fire, often on a wooden skewer. Source: Mark Fischer, creative commons. https://www.flickr.com/photos/fischerfotos/18361384221/in/photolist-Cccs5H-tYwTQ2-DZ4SH6.

Comedy Shows

In addition to the club scene described above, comedy shows featuring popular and up-and-coming standup comedians are also common destinations for Friday and other evenings. On average, tickets sell for N5,000 (about $15) for regular admission and N10,000 (about $30) and upwards for VIP tickets. In Lagos, a six-person table can cost up to three million naira (about $10,000). All tables are usually sold out before the night of the event. In slower-paced parts of the country, similar tables are usually much cheaper and can be as low as N100,000 (about $300). Some of the headline comedy shows include AY Live, Funny Bone Untamed, Basket Mouth Uncensored, and Crack Ya Ribs. Comedians make jokes ranging from hot-button political issues to everyday humorous topics. Any way one looks at it, an entertainment show in Nigeria is always a win-win for customers, performers, and entrepreneurs alike.

Sport Bars and Viewing Centers

Other places for fun in Nigeria are venues to watch televised sports, especially ones that feature soccer games. Viewing centers are typically affordable to the general populace. They are medium-sized halls constructed with wooden planks and benches for viewers to sit on. Those who patronize them are predominantly men between the ages of eighteen and forty. These places are usually very crowded, boisterous, and entertainment-filled. Tickets can be as low as N80 (twenty-five US cents, an amount affordable to almost everyone) for Premier League matches, roughly N100 for international Champions League matches, and about N150 (about 50 cents) for three matches. These halls usually accommodate about fifty to one hundred spectators who watch sports events on large television sets that are connected to the cable network. Outside the hall is a board with details about the matches throughout the course of the week. In contrast to viewing centers, sports bars are fancier, with modern facilities geared toward economic elites. Star soccer matches draw customers, so clubs make provisions for built-in sports bars to attract rich clientele who are ready to splurge.

One might find a few women patronizing viewing centers or sports bars, perhaps one woman for every fifteen men. But, in general, women who enjoy soccer tend to watch sports at home. Soccer is a very male-dominated sport in Nigeria, and many Nigerian men support major European football clubs like Chelsea, Barcelona, Manchester United, Arsenal, Real Madrid, Manchester City, and Liverpool. Local football teams also have large followings and die-hard supporters. Some of the popular local clubs in Lagos include the Apapa Golden Stars, Bridge Football Club, and Ikorodu United. Most young adults who patronize these viewing centers have access to cable networks in the comfort of their homes, but, as Yemi Daramola explained in an interview,

> It is more fun to watch it here in public, with friends. We start by arguing and analyzing the strength and weaknesses of our favorite players like Zlatan Ibrahimovic, Eden Hazard, Neymar Dasilva-Santos, Lionel Messi, or Christiano Ronaldo. We can also roar when our club scores a goal. We can throw jeers at the supporters of the losing team. We argue about the match on our way back home. We analyze our favorite players before the match begins. After a star match, we are left with mixed emotions in the viewing centers. The fans of the winning team sing all sorts of abusive and celebration songs at the fans of the losing team. For instance, we sing songs like:
>
> > Winner oh oh oh winner!
> > Winner oh oh oh winner!
> > Chelsea you don win oh winner!
> > Patapata you go win forever winner!
> > Loser oh oh oh loser!
> > Loser oh oh oh loser!
> > Arsenal [or the losing club] you don lose oh loser!
> > Patapata you go lose forever loser!
>
> The losing team sure pays us back in the same coin when the table flips. It is just a pleasant experience for us and it really calms us down.

Men enjoy watching these matches in public spaces with friends, whether at a viewing center or sports bar, leading to an increase in clubs, bars, and pepper soup and asun (spicy goat meat) joints that incorporate viewing soccer free of charge into their spaces to lure fans. The walls are often adorned with pictures of popular clubs and players. Some customers play snooker (billiards) as a side attraction at these venues. Viewers often order bottles of beer and cigarettes, especially when their club is winning the game. Weekday matches are shown at night so that men can go to sports bars and viewing centers on their way home from work.

Against the backdrop of long-standing social culture in Nigeria, "turn it up" activities flourish. There is a common assumption that weekends, starting from Friday, must exude merriment. Many men and some women use the weekend to consume foods and alcohol of choice and to hang out with their friends after a long week of hard work, activities which are differentially shaped by gender, class, and location. This prevalent trend features maximum levels of fun in different forms and places. In spite of the nation's myriad challenges, these forms of leisure have not been compromised. This chapter ruptures a commonly held misconception that Nigerian social life remains overshadowed by poverty, corruption, and other societal problems. As much as these factors are undeniably present in the country, Nigerians also enjoy themselves, as is evident from "turn it up" party lifestyles. Regardless of people's social class, income or level of exposure, there is a place for them to "turn it up" and feel a sense of belonging. This effervescent nightlife has become an integral part of urban Nigerian weekend culture that has been and continues to be embraced by its people, against the backdrop of shifting social realities in the country.

Notes

1. Mark O. C. Anikpo and Josiah D. Atemie, eds., *Introduction to Nigerian Socio-cultural Heritage* (Port Harcourt, Nigeria: Osia International, 1999), 1–2.

2. Godiya Allanana Makama, "Patriarchy and Gender Equality in Nigeria: The Way Forward," *European Scientific Journal* 9, no. 17 (June 2013): 116; Morolake Omonubi-McDonnell, *Gender Inequality in Nigeria* (Lagos: Spectrum, 2003).

3. I. E. Nwosu, "Gender Role Perceptions and the Changing Roles of Women in Nigeria," *International Journal of Agriculture and Rural Development* 15, no. 3 (2012): 1240–46.

4. Anozie Egole, "Clubbing, Night Life, Only Way to Ease Stress—Lagosians," *Vanguard* (Lagos), August 4, 2012, https://www.vanguardngr.com /2012/08/clubbing-night-life-only-way-to-ease-stress-lagosians.

5. See www.lagosstate.gov.ng for more information about Lagos State.

6. "Unveiling the 6 Hottest Clubs in Lagos," *Encomium*, April 19, 2015, http://encomium.ng/unveiling-the-6-hottest-clubs-in-lagos.

Part 3

Love, Sex, and Marriage

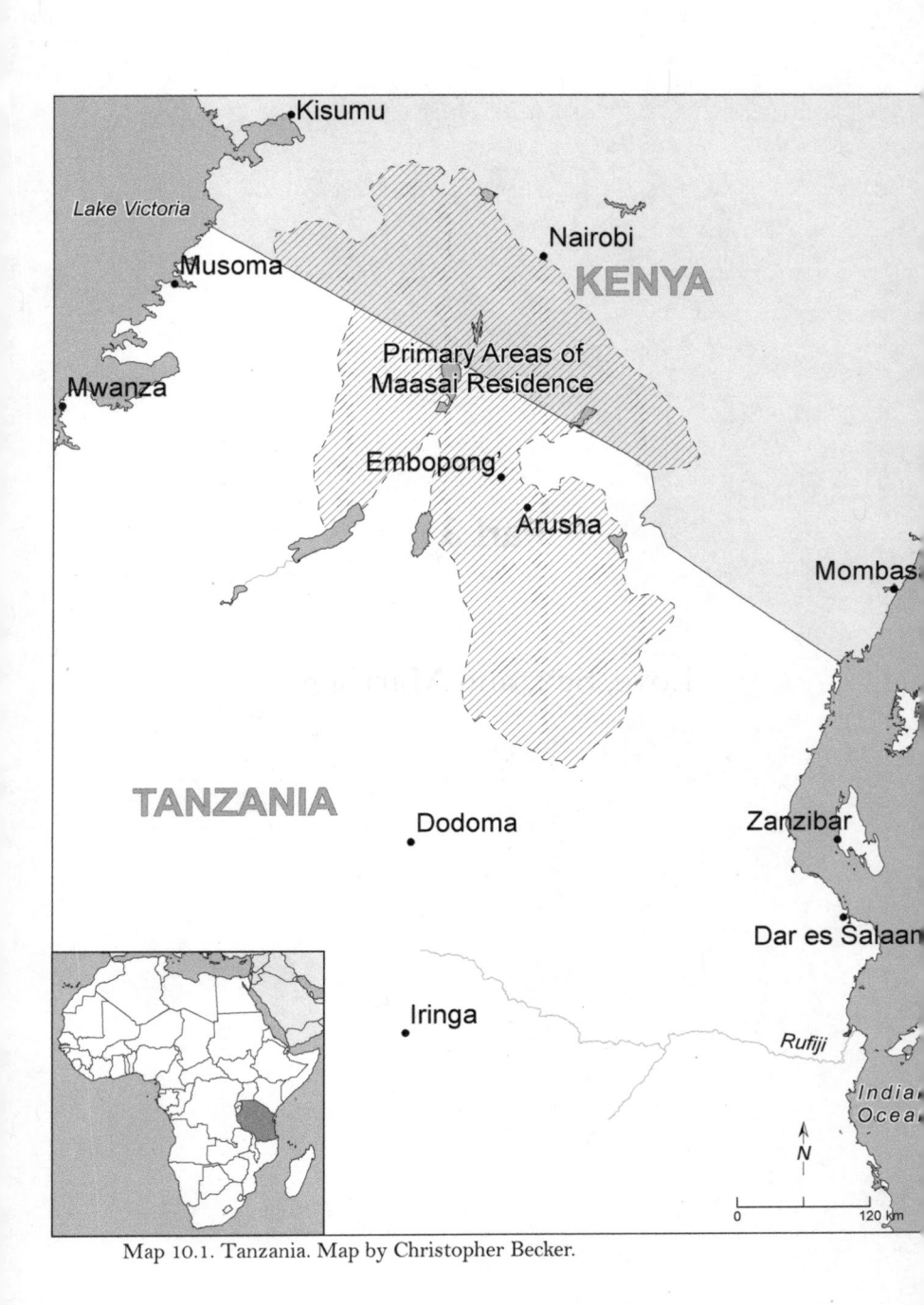

Map 10.1. Tanzania. Map by Christopher Becker.

10

Young Love

Dancing by the Light of the Moon in Tanzania

DOROTHY L. HODGSON

Embopong' is a Maasai community in the remote, dry Rift Valley of Tanzania. By day, life can be hard: long treks for water and wood, scavenging for bitter weeds, milking goats, escaping the relentless dust and heat in the cool of mud-walled homes. But in the past, during nights with a full moon, the dreary drudgery of everyday survival was forgotten as young men (*ilmurran*) and girls (*ntoyie*) danced all night together to the joy and encouragement of their elders. Ilmurran chanted in low, guttural rhythms, pierced by shrieks as they competed with one another to jump as high as possible. Ntoyie, dressed by their mothers in their finest beads and clothes, shimmied their wide beaded collars up and down as they praised these young men in song: "He who killed the lion! He who stole my heart! He, the most brave and fierce!"

Being Maasai

I first witnessed one of these moonlight celebrations in 1992, during my two years of dissertation field research with three communities of people who self-identify as "Maasai" in northern Tanzania. Maasai was a term that emerged in the mid-1800s to describe people who spoke the Maa language and relied primarily on herding animals (cattle, sheep, goats, and donkeys) for their livelihoods. I had already spent over three years working in community development throughout Maasai areas in northern Tanzania, but rarely spent the night in people's homesteads. I was therefore unaware of their sometimes lively nightlife—at least when the moon was full. As an anthropologist studying gender and social change, however, I usually slept in people's homes or in my small blue tent pitched next to my host's home, inside the safety of the high thorn fences that ringed the homestead's cluster of six to ten round homes and a central livestock corral.

Of the three communities I worked in, Embopong' was by far the most desolate. Set on the dry side of Monduli Mountain, the scattered homesteads received little rain throughout the year. The one permanent water trough was usually broken, so women often walked miles to collect precious water for their households, carrying it back in large plastic containers on their heads and strapped to their donkeys. Farming was impossible, although every year some intrepid souls tried, only to watch their corn and beans wither in the fields. Even raising cattle, the prized livestock that anchored Maasai livelihoods and sense of collective being, was too difficult for most, as it required long treks for water, grass, and salt. As such, households kept most of their cattle with kin or "stock friends" in other communities. They relied instead on sheep and goats, browsers that could subsist on the scant vegetation of scraggly cactuses, thorn trees, and tough grasses that dotted the landscape.

To help feed their households, able-bodied (and sometimes not-so-able-bodied) women would walk miles up the mountain to farm small plots they had received from extended kin (often in exchange for herding the kin's browsers with their own), or even further down the other side to the weekly market in Monduli, the nearest town, to try to sell the wild weeds and greens they had laboriously gathered. Young men pursued money in many ways: buying and selling livestock, walking or biking to Monduli to purchase small goods (such as matches, flour, sugar, or dried beans) to bring back and sell at higher prices, or seeking work as guards in distant cities or as guides and trekkers for the large big-game hunting firms that hosted wealthy European and American clients. Older, married men visited one another or far-flung age-mates (men who were initiated together) and clansmen (men of the same clan) to share news (about the weather, politics, family events), resolve disputes, and reinforce social networks. The very elderly, men and women, stayed home, caring for small children in their parents' absence. Older girls supervised their younger siblings and assisted their mothers with cooking and cleaning. Older boys herded the livestock, scrambling over the dirt paths with their sticks and dogs to manage the often-unruly animals (while sheep and goats may be domesticated, they are not very obedient).

Like Maasai living elsewhere in northern Tanzania and southern Kenya, families in Embopong' had endured decades of neglect and sometimes active dispossession and discrimination by first the German and British colonizers and, later, after Tanzania gained independence in 1961, the elite, educated Africans who took power. Key moments included their forced removal by British colonial administrators from their most fertile lands and permanent water supplies into the Masai Reserve in the early 1900s in order to contain and control them (and open up their former lands to more "productive" peoples like British settlers and African farmers); a disastrous attempt by the British to grow wheat on the fragile rangelands near Embopong' to supply African troops during the Second World War that produced permanent dust bowls instead of food; repeated campaigns by first the British and later African politicians to force Maasai to abandon their clothing, hairstyles, and jewelry so as to at least look "modern"; and occasional development projects by the state or, later, non-governmental organizations (NGOs) that focused more on the quality of livestock than the welfare of people. As a result of these and other policies and practices, Maasai lost control of and access to huge areas of their former land (much of it to national parks and game reserves for wild animals); suffered stark inequities in the provision of quality healthcare, education and other social services by the government; and felt deeply disrespected by other Tanzanians, especially elites.[1]

Celebrations and Courtships through Dance and Song

Despite these sometimes daunting challenges to their lives and livelihoods, everyday life was still filled with small pleasures and joys: mothers and fathers cuddling small children, shared laughter at the silly antics of toddlers, whispered gossip about possible love affairs, visits from friends and family. Families and neighbors came together for larger celebrations as well, such as male and female initiation ceremonies and weddings, especially during the rainy season with its relative plenty of milk, meat, and water.[2] Guests enjoyed roasted meat, sour milk, milk tea, home-brewed honey beer or alcohol, and other fare.

At a female initiation ceremony that I was invited to in Embopong', the men and women clustered together by gender inside and outside the homestead, sitting or standing in small groups. In the late afternoon, after the ceremony was completed and food had been served, about thirty girls (ntoyie) and twenty young men (ilmurran) started dancing together in the central corral. The girls were dressed in their finest clothes, with layers of multicolored beaded ornaments draped on their heads and necks, wire coiled on their arms and feet, and delighted smiles on their faces. Feet on the ground, they swayed their bodies and necks back and forth, chanting soaring songs of praise for the exploits, bravery, and beauty of the ilmurran. The older girls, in their teens, stood proudly and boldly at the front of the semicircle, while younger girls, some clearly dancing for the first time, hid shyly behind their older sisters. At first, the ilmurran stood in small, chatty groups, chuckling together as they watched the girls and listened to their songs. They, too, were dressed in their finery: clean red cloths cinched by belts at the waist, ornate braided hairstyles, beaded ornaments on their wrists and ankles. And soon they joined in. Clutching long, thin, polished sticks against their sides, they faced the girls in a semicircle and began chanting in low murmurs and grunts. Each took a turn, often two at a time, moving to the center of the circle to jump straight up, as high as possible, to the encouraging shrieks of their friends. As the dancing and singing continued, older married women sometimes joined on the sidelines, swaying and dancing in an embodied memory of their youth. I even spied some elder men at the edge of the corral mimicking the ilmurran, recalling their own days of youthful energy and glory. Eventually, the dancing and singing subsided, and the older girls and young men wandered off to the

edges of the homestead to pursue their flirting and courting away from the watchful gaze of their elders.

By dark, ilmurran and their girlfriends would snuggle together inside houses built solely for ilmurran (who were not supposed to sleep in their mother's or any woman's home during this period, until they became junior elders and could marry). Until Christianity began to influence Maasai ideas of "morality," ilmurran and ntoyie were encouraged—indeed, expected—to engage in sensuous touching and

Figure 10.1. Two festively dressed *intoyie* (girls) posing with their *ilmurran* (young men) friends in Embopong', 1992. Source: Dorothy Hodgson.

sexual play, to develop their erotic techniques and to pleasure one another. The one practice that was forbidden was penile intercourse, for fear of making an uninitiated and unmarried girl pregnant. But, like young people elsewhere, they adapted themselves: a young man would often rub his penis between a girl's upper thighs until he ejaculated. Although I was never able to record the songs of the ilmurran and ntoyie at these large ceremonies, I understood most of the verses. Ntoyie would praise certain groups of ilmurran and even individuals by name, complimenting them on their bravery, handsomeness, and feats in cattle raids and battles. But they would also criticize and condemn other men for being weak and fearful. Ilmurran, in turn, would sing their own praises, boasting about the cattle they had stolen, distant travels, and the beauty of their favorite animals. Naomi Kipuri, a Maasai anthropologist, recorded and translated several Maasai songs from her homestead. One song, by a girl named Saetuan, praised her group of ilmurran and rebuked the ilmurran from another clan, the Nkidong'i—and their girlfriends—for being cowards.

Irrepeta e Saetuan

Nkuapi naamanya ilitiyan lang'
Ino nkena mincho kilang'

Oyiayio hoo laleyio ehoyiaayio
(Chorus, repeated after every verse)

Emanya ole kipuri owuasa
Le ng'oto Nakae Ilmotioo

Nemanya ilmeori eiriamari
Lololkatira Embirika

Nelo amanya enkerai oolmurran
Le ng'oto kitai oltepesi

Nemanya ole Esho lolgisoi
Le ng'oto Ntitai eneika

Nelo amanya ologeli osur atua
Enting'ida naishuyie Nkunyinyi

Amen isiankikin tena kop
Neisulaki inoonkidong'i

Sasin ilmurran lirorierie
Neima nkiri enkuretisho

Era kulo tualan okuni
Linkodo nkg'i nikiya

Kinkonyaitie oltuala oikodo nkumok
Lole Sampurri loolpapit

Kiwaita temanyata ole Ping'ua
Isototo nkayiok erashe

Kiwaita ole Rakua lolgisoi
Oishuyie Naingolingola

Enchira naanetu nkidong'i
Ole Ping'ua lempere olkiteng'

Praise song of Saetuan

Count the locations where our bamboos[3] live
And miss not any

The proud Ole Kipuri of Nakae's mother
Lives at Ilmotioo

The identical twins of Ole Olkatira
Live by the waterhole

The warrior's son of Kitai's mother
Lives at Oltepesi

Ole Esho of the ring of Ntitai's mother
Lives at the high ground

The thicket of *ologeli*
Holds the proud one of Nkunyinyi

I despise the young women of this country
Especially those of the Nkidong'i [a clan]

The warriors with whom you talk are thin
And their flesh is drenched with cowardice

Three bells have you decorated[4]
But we have taken them

We have repatriated the highly decorated bell
of Ole Sampurri with long hair

At the *manyatta* [homestead] we have taken Ole Ping'ua
While you the diviner boys are gathered[5]

We have taken Ole Rakua with the ring
The one who lives by fighting

You the Nkidong'i may cry bitterly
For Ole Ping'ua with the spear that is worth an ox[6]

As Saetuan's song suggests, young men and girls bonded together in rival groups. While they might pair off for an evening, they did not form long-term couples. Instead, each girl had several boyfriends, named according to whether they were her most or least favorite. Conversely, young men courted multiple girls, as well as seeking secret affairs with married women (a story for another time).

By March 1992, after almost six months back in Tanzania, I had witnessed several of these large, public, daytime ceremonies. Often there would be some lingering activity in the evening, such as drunk elder men regaling each other with stories and young wives cleaning up from the event or chasing down small children for bedtime. But, with darkness, the homesteads quickly quieted down, as they did on more routine evenings. Women and children stayed in their houses as the women cooked and served the evening meal, prepared children for bed, and soon dampened the hearth fire and crawled into their own beds to sleep. Ilmurran often wandered about, moving between homesteads to ensure everyone's safety, quietly visit their girlfriends, or congregate together under the thorn trees to chat, eat, and sleep. I would usually sit with my host (every married woman has her own house) and her family through dinner, then retire to her guest bed or my tent as the fire dimmed.

But one evening, as I prepared myself to sleep in my tent after dinner, a group of six ntoyie and four ilmurran started gathering outside in a nearby clearing between two houses. Although not in their finest ceremonial clothes, both the girls and young men were dressed up with beads and clean cloths. I could see everything clearly because the night sky was brilliantly lit by the full moon. As I walked over to join a group of married women who were watching, the girls began singing together in their high-pitched voices, facing the young men, who sat together on the ground. Soon the young men started humming in their rhythmic, low-pitched register. The mood was playful and joyous, as the girls and men sang together, grinning, laughing, and flirting. After about fifteen minutes, four other ilmurran walked over, greeted the seated ilmurran, and teased the ntoyie (to their shrill delight). Shortly, all the ilmurran stood up, faced the ntoyie, and continued singing. The men began dancing, taking turns jumping in the center, walking towards the ntoyie, then back to their space. At times, adult women like my friends Ndari and Katimwa (both mothers of girls in the group) joined in the singing, even dancing on occasion. The dancing went on and on for what seemed like hours as I watched, mesmerized by the moonlit music and movement. At times the pace of the singing and dancing was fast, at other times it slowed down. Finally, exhausted, I wished everyone a good night. After crawling into my tent and changing, I settled into my sleeping bag. The ilmurran and ntoyie soon quit dancing and singing and seated themselves on a skin mat near my tent. Eventually, I fell asleep to the sound of their laughter and raucous joking, which I assume continued into the early morning.

Continuity and Change

Over the years, I witnessed similar moonlight festivities in Embopong' and elsewhere, but none of these events had the same magic as that first night. By sharing this story of everyday joy, I hope to unsettle claims that conflate material poverty with lack of pleasure, to evoke the exuberance of the moment, and to provide a glimpse into the everyday social and sexual lives of young men and women at a certain historical moment. Of course, gender relations, like other dimensions of life, are dynamic and change over time, as they did both before and after that moonlit evening in March 1992.[7] Since that time, I have witnessed both dramatic and gradual changes in the lives of and relationships between ntoyie and ilmurran. As more and more girls now join their brothers in primary school and, increasingly, secondary school, few have the time for or interest in such pastimes. Indeed, as more Maasai have become Christians, their moral codes have transformed, so that now the sexual freedoms and pleasurable pursuits of girls and boys are increasingly condemned as "sinful" rather than celebrated and, in the case of female initiation, even criminalized as illegal.[8] For some religious denominations, especially Pentecostalism, even the clothing and beaded jewelry that were proudly worn by young people in Embopong' and elsewhere is forbidden.[9] Land grabs and other forms of political disenfranchisement, economic dispossession, and social inequality have accelerated, forcing more Maasai men and women to abandon pastoralism and diversify their livelihoods by seeking work as traders, workers, miners, and tourist attractions.[10] Life has therefore become more challenging in remote communities like Embopong'. But young men and women still find ways to flirt, court, love, couple, and, occasionally, dance, even if these practices have taken on new meanings and forms.[11] Now their dancing may take place to the sounds of Bongo Flava (Tanzanian hip-hop) under the light of solar-powered lamps, as, dressed in blue jeans, T-shirts and tight crop tops, they shimmy and sing with each other.

I have not slept in a homestead for some time. But I still hope that a few young people still feel the seductive pull of the full moon when it brightens their homesteads, tempting them to gather together outside one more time to dance and sing.

Notes

1. The history of these policies and practices and their consequences for Maasai communities are described in my books, particularly Dorothy L. Hodgson, *Once Intrepid Warriors: Gender, Ethnicity, and the Cultural Politics of Maasai Development* (Bloomington: Indiana University Press, 2001); and Hodgson, *Being Maasai, Becoming Indigenous: Postcolonial Politics in a Neoliberal World* (Bloomington: Indiana University Press, 2011).

2. For detailed description and analysis of the meaning and gender dynamics of initiation, weddings, and other rituals, see Dorothy L. Hodgson, *The Church of Women: Gendered Encounters between Maasai and Missionaries* (Bloomington: Indiana University Press, 2005).

3. "Bamboos" refers to the tall, thin ilmurran.

4. Ilmurran often wear bells around their ankles when they are dancing.

5. All diviners come from the Nkidong'i clan. See Hodgson, *The Church of Women.*

6. The song is reprinted from Naomi Kipury, *Oral Literature of the Maasai* (Nairobi: Heinemann Educational Books, 1983), 218–20.

7. See, for example, the cases described in Dorothy L. Hodgson and Sheryl A. McCurdy, eds., *"Wicked" Women and the Reconfiguration of Gender in Africa* (Portsmouth, NH: Heinemann, 2001).

8. Dorothy L. Hodgson, *Gender, Justice and the Problem of Culture: From Customary Law to Human Rights in Tanzania* (Bloomington: Indiana University Press, 2017).

9. Hodgson, *The Church of Women.*

10. Hodgson, *Being Maasai*; Hodgson, *Gender, Justice.*

11. See, for example, Jennifer Cole and Lynn M. Thomas, eds., *Love in Africa* (Chicago: University of Chicago Press, 2009); Sylvia Tamale, ed., *African Sexualities: A Reader* (Nairobi: Pambazuka, 2011).

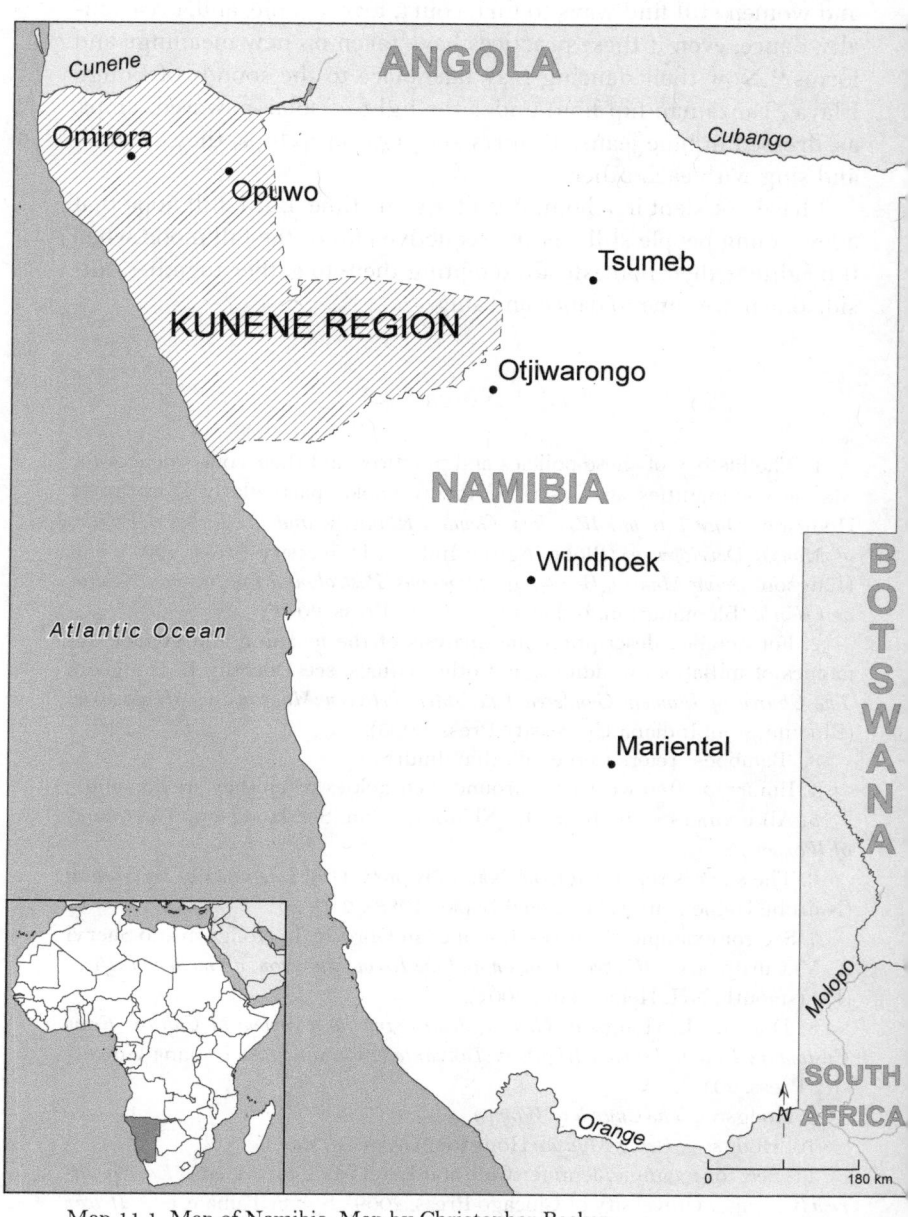

Map 11.1. Map of Namibia. Map by Christopher Becker.

11

Love, Play, and Sex

Polyamory and the Hidden Pleasures of
Everyday Life in Kaoko, Northwest Namibia

STEVEN VAN WOLPUTTE

Kazandu and I were sitting in Arsenal Bar (again), enjoying our beer and chatting away. Two women joined us. Both were sipping from the large bottle of Tafel Lager they just bought. The oldest one, I guess in her early twenties and obviously pregnant, came to stand closer to Kazandu. While sipping their beers, the two of them were laughing and joking. Then I saw Kazandu's hand sliding up her skirt. While they continued their conversation, he started to massage her pubis. Then the two women walked away. "What was that about, *erumbi* (senior brother)?" "*Omuranwe wandje* (my cousin)," he replied. These two words sufficed as an explanation.[1]

The day after, I met with Katjambia Tjambiru, daughter of the legendary leader Vetamuna Tjambiru of Etanga. Over the years—the material presented here is based on anthropological fieldwork from 1995 until the present—our paths had crossed several times, but now she had invited me to discuss something important.[2] A few articles had appeared the year before in the *Namibian*, the leading national newspaper, that discussed the practice of "wife-swapping" or "wife-sharing," quite common in this part of the world.[3] This practice, locally known as *okuyepisa*, is usually depicted as a husband being required by the rules of hospitality to "offer" his wife to his friends and visitors. Similar accounts circulate regularly on social media, eliciting emotional and predictable comments.

The Inhabitants of the "Last Wilderness"

Katjambia and I met in the garden of her political party's headquarters in Opuwo, the capital of the Kunene Region, Namibia.[4] Namibia is a country in southern Africa that with its 318,772 square miles is almost twice the size of California, yet home to only 2.4 million inhabitants. Sometimes referred to as "Africa's last colony," Namibia celebrated its independence on March 21, 1990, after a protracted freedom struggle against the South African apartheid regime. One of the battlegrounds was here, in the country's northwestern corner, often referred to as Kaoko.

After independence, Opuwo grew from an administrative outpost and military camp into a bustling melting pot of various groups, each with its history and background. Among them are the Himba, most of whom inhabit the arid mountain savannah outside town and whose economy and social and political life predominantly revolve around livestock. Since 1990, Namibia has become a popular tourist destination, with Kaoko and especially Himba women in their leather attire as one of its exotic attractions. Tour operators represent Kaoko as a remnant of a so-called "traditional Africa." This idea, shared with most development workers, government officials, and church leaders, portrays Himba society as naturally conservative and governed by harmful cultural practices such as the "sharing" or "inheriting" of women, considered particularly disadvantageous to women and girls.[5]

It was precisely this that Katjambia wanted to discuss. Sitting in the shade of an acacia tree, we exchanged greetings and soon found ourselves debating Himba gender roles in the face of modernization and development. Toward the end of our conversation, she urged me to help her tell "the other story," that practices such as "wife-sharing" (or, rather, both women and men having sexual partners outside marriage, with the implicit consent of the spouse) are not *necessarily* bad and that, and here I borrow the words of Everjoice Win, not every woman in Kaoko is "poor, powerless and invariably pregnant, burdened with lots of children, or carrying one load or another on her back or her head."[6]

Sex and Marriage Require Joking . . .

Himba women and men sharply distinguish between parallel cousins (the children of the father's brother and of the mother's sister) and cross-cousins (the children of the father's sister and of the mother's brother). The former are referred to as brothers and sisters, and fall under the incest taboo. The latter are considered to be *ovaramwe* (cousins), the preferred partners in sexual relations and in marriage. Also, they are under the mutual obligation to joke, which can take the form of explicit language and behavior, sexual teasing, flirting, touching, playful bantering, or, as in the opening diary fragment, behavior that otherwise would be considered (very) inappropriate. Cross-cousin joking relationships are closely intertwined with marriage and sexual relationships: they involve the same partners.

Besides this cross-cousin joking, intimate relationships are also embedded in what people refer to as "the work of matriclans" (*ongura yomaanda* or *okukurasana*), By birth, everyone belongs to both a patriclan (*oruzo*) and a matriclan (*eanda*).[7] Members of each matriclan are in a joking relationship with members of at least one other matriclan. Matriclan joking may take the form of ritual insulting contests or, more commonly, derogatory comments about one's family background, for instance during important ceremonies, such as a funeral or marriage. A third joking relationship exists between members of the same age group, especially for men. This usually involves practical jokes and pranks among age group members and their spouses.

These three forms of joking ideally converge in marriage and sexual relationships. For instance, the marriage partner that families seek out for their daughter or son ideally belongs to her or his joking matriclan. Also, women and men prefer their sexual and marriage partner to be one of their cross-cousins, while women partake in the joking between the members of their husband's age-group. Both marriage and sex thus involve a multilevel joking relationship, with failure "to play" (*okunyaanda*) being considered as sufficient reason for divorce (*omahanikiro*). The latter is fairly common and not looked down upon: it is easier to divorce your husband than to abandon your lover, one woman explained.

. . . But Marriage Does Not Require Sex

For my female interlocutors, however, marriage is not all *that* important. For bachelors it signifies an important stage of their lifecycle: their marriage makes them an adult and grants them the right to start a homestead. However, women's marriage status is hardly significant (it is, for instance, nowhere expressed in jewelry or attire). Rather, what matters is the transition from girl to childless young woman, to mother-of-one, to adult woman, a status visualized in the belts and jewelry they wear.

Vignette: The "Hidden" Love Belt

Women in traditional attire wear several belts indicating their status as a mother, from girl (*omukazona*) to childless young woman (*omusuko, evare*), to mother-of-one (*omberipa*), to adult (*omukazendu*). Underneath their clothing, however, they also wear a "hidden" metal-bead loin belt (*etanda*), which one participant referred to as the "love belt." She wears it when travelling and at night, when receiving her boyfriend, but not when she is with her husband. People explain that it functions to "give better grip" and because of the association of metal beads with ancestors and fire, to protect the woman's womb and promote pregnancy (*okuyakanisa*, "to light a fire").

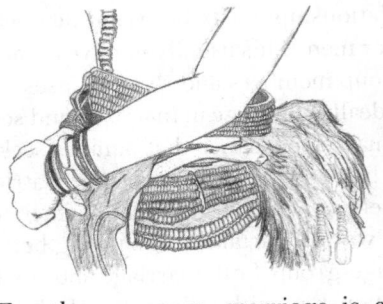

Figure 11.1. Women wear the "love belt" (*etanda*, or, more archaically, *etuku*, from the root *tuka*, "to churn") underneath their clothing. It is made from metal beads held together by rope and leather bands. Drawing by Steven Van Wolputte.

For these women, marriage is an exchange or union between families that has little to do with exclusive rights or even sex between individuals. This is especially true for first, often arranged marriages that women commonly dismiss as *otjisanekero* (make-believe) or *oviporoporo* (fake). Usually, such unions are considered to be consummated after a brief ceremony during which the bride and groom literally "eat meat" together (*okurya [onyama] motjoto*): they share a piece of mutton in a ceremonial shelter erected for the occasion, after which the bride returns to her father's homestead.

Most marriages are not prearranged but generally referred to as *okuwaka* (stealing [a bride]). Unlike what the idiom suggests, this expression refers to a couple deciding to elope together, with or without their families' permission.

Figure 11.2. The party of the groom tries to "steal" the bride, while she is being "defended" by her sisters. This results in a ritual but playful fight accompanied by throwing stones and insults. Drawing by Steven Van Wolputte.

Sitting by the fire, Muingona obviously savored the memory as she recounted how Mutjinde one day came to steal her from her then husband, Veripi T. He had been her long-time lover and teenage crush, and she cherished the idea of him giving up his entire herd just to be with her. (Field notes, Omirora, November 12, 1995)

Polyamory: To Make Someone Hide

Women and men, however, also engage in extramarital relationships. These relationships are seen as vital to the health and well-being of the individual, family, and society. They are more than just flings (though these occasionally happen). Instead, they consist of long-lasting, durable bonds based on affinity, attraction, and intimacy. They are firmly grounded in kinship, embedded in gift exchange (between partners and families), and subjected to ancestral interdictions (a pregnant woman, for instance, is supposed to abstain from sex except with her husband; he is supposed to sleep only with her).

As noted above, extramarital relationships are called okuyepisa, "to make someone hide or dodge," often wrongly translated as "wife-sharing" or "wife-swapping." A more accurate translation is polyamorous relationships.[8] These relationships constitute an institution, as does marriage. However, as the example of the "love belt" suggests, among Himba they are supposed to stay submerged and implicit.

> Yesterday evening, finally, and to our relief, our evening company stood up and left. Only Vezemburuka remained seated. To our surprise he pulled out his neckrest and blanket, and installed himself under a tree. "Why?" I asked, "your homestead is just nearby." "Yes, but I arrived after dusk, and maybe my wife is receiving someone," he explained, implying that he

did not want to surprise his wife with her lover. (Field notes, Omirora, March 9, 1996)

These relationships rarely surface in public discourse. They constitute a public secret, as spouses usually know of their partner's relationships. More so, they are being negotiated between spouses: a husband may, for instance, object to a particular relationship. Women also choose their lovers, and may, as in the example below, oppose their husband's choice. At the same time, ideally at least, these relationships remain shrouded in joking and playfulness.

> Joroka laughed. "You know what Katira did? After they got married last week, Mezeri [her husband] asked her to go and arrange him a night with Uaripi, that popular girl, which she promised. But then she went straight to this other girl, Njandee—you know her, she is not that popular—and told her that Mezeri fancied her and would visit her that night. Njandee agreed. And then Katira went back home and told Mezeri what she had done. And he went like, "No, not that one!" (Field notes, Omirora, April 26, 1996)

Polyamory, Freedom, and Pleasure

Below the surface of overt discourse is another, less visible, but equally tangible or sensuous reality that is implied, joked about, suggested, but hardly ever made explicit. Much of this reality gets lost in translation. *Okuriwa* (also *okupingena*), for instance, is often translated as "wife-inheritance." In anthropological jargon it is known as levirate, and refers to when a widow marries her deceased husband's brother. Rather than as a harmful practice, it should be understood as a way of securing a widow's livelihood. During a short ceremony, she is offered different chops of meat that each represent a person. She then chooses who she wants to go and live with. In a similar vein, "stealing" a wife refers not to kidnapping, but to a ritualized playful fight (including mutual insults and stone-throwing) between the party of the groom trying to "steal" the bride and her relatives trying to "prevent" this from happening.

Unsurprisingly, Himba women do not recognize themselves in the portrait of passive, subjugated victims painted by developmentalist discourse.[9] During our conversation, Katjambia emphasized that, even if women share the same husband, "it is not the man [husband] who makes the lady happy. It is the boyfriend.''[10] For Katjambia and many other women and men in Kaoko, active engagement in polyamorous sexual relationships contributes to people's beauty and moral standing (both connoted in the word *nawa*) and to their position as a full, competent members of society. It creates lasting bonds, prevents *eruru* (envy), and makes someone's blood "work" (*ombindu mai ungura*), meaning that engaging in multiple sexual relationships makes someone more attractive and desirable. It is an almost moral responsibility, as women recommend looking for a "good bull" (*ondwezu ombwa*; here, lover) to have strong, healthy, and happy children who make the house (*ondjuwo*, the female space, but also womb, matriclan, or ancestress) thrive. In this context, polyamory is a source of personhood, of fullness, maturity, and woman- or manhood.[11]

This idea of multiple sexual relationships as a precondition to maturity and personhood, or the mere thought of a polyamorous sexual regime, is at odds with a moralizing discourse on (especially female) sexuality and with ideal/typical family relationships as envisioned by the Namibian government (which promotes the nuclear family as the foundation for a future industrial society), the churches (which promote monogamy and condemn extra- or premarital sex), or NGOs (which perceive polyamory as detrimental to people's health and/or women's emancipation).[12] Especially in town, the postindependence elites and aspiring middle classes have embraced romantic love, companionate partnership, and monogamy—also celebrated in television serials and cosmopolitan popular culture—as models of intimacy and identification.[13]

This, however, is not the case everywhere, and certainly not in the rural areas. Many of my female interlocutors felt that converting (*okutanaura*) or leaving tradition (*okupita kombazu*; also *okuhita moveta*, to enter the law) would mean forsaking their sexual liberty and freedom in return for a vague promise of redemption. They cited the example of pastors picking a husband from among their followers, or the double morality when it comes to male versus female "adultery." They did not use these terms, but in general they claimed that turning away from their "harmful" tradition and committing themselves to one man (*okuhakasana pomurumend' umwe*) would mean to subject themselves to a patriarchal and moralizing discourse on marriage, sexuality, and womanhood that would leave little place for pleasure, joking, or love.

Himba polyamorous relationships are part of a sexual regime that is often misunderstood by agents of development committed to the ideal of monogamy and companionate, romantic love. Most of these contemporary discourses continue to focus on sexuality in the function of reproduction, marriage, or disease and fail to acknowledge the importance of fun, pleasure, and intimacy. A similar absence characterizes popular representations of Africa in general and of the Himba in particular: pictures of parents cuddling a child or of a couple in love are hard to find, and not because men or women do not cuddle children or don't fall in love. Polygamy or polyamory do not exclude friendship, companionship, love, or intimacy. Or pleasure.

This chapter has emphasized female agency and freedom. Nevertheless, gender equality in Kaoko is still a distant goal. Girls, for instance, have less access to formal education, despite the relative egalitarianism of Himba social relations and despite, at the national level, one of the world's most equitable set of laws. What Katjambia warns us is that "woman" is not a single, universal category, and that "mistaking category for person" or an essentializing and universalist discourse on emancipation is at risk of weaving its own "epistemology of ignorance."[14] This failure to understand women in traditional dress and shining with red ochre as anything other than "married off, "given" in marriage, "shared," or "inherited" pushes women's voices further to the background and is in danger of reproducing the gender inequalities it tries to combat. It is, in other words, important to listen to how women themselves think and feel about the practices that involve them, before univocally dismissing these practices as harmful.

Acknowledgments

The research for this chapter was made possible by a grant from the Research Foundation Flanders (FWO–RFF) on The Politics of Love: Urban Development, Intimacy and the Future in the Northern Kunene Region, Namibia (no. 150911N).

Notes

1. Diary fragment, Opuwo, November 4, 2014.
2. I spent a first fieldwork period (1995–98) mostly in the villages and cattle posts of Omirora, a rural region in western Kaoko. I have continued my research via regular visits to the region. Over the years, my focus has shifted to Opuwo, the regional capital.

3. Tjikunda Kulunga, "Chief Encourages Sharing of Wives with Friends," *Namibian*, October 18, 2013, http://www.namibian.com.na/index.php?id =115402&page=archive-read; "Traditional Women Confess to Oppressing Men," *Namibian*, October 25, 2013, http://www.namibian.com.na/index .php?id=115747&page=archive-read.

4. Namibia knows twelve officially recognized languages, not counting the many dialects. Otjihimba is a local vernacular of the larger Otjiherero language group. It also means "Himba tradition" or "the Himba way."

5. Chia Longman and Tamsin Bradley, eds., *Interrogating Harmful Cultural Practices: Gender, Culture and Coercion* (Burlington, VT: Ashgate, 2015).

6. Everjoice J. Win, "Not Very Poor, Powerless or Pregnant: The African Woman Forgotten by Development," in *Feminisms in Development: Contradictions, Contestations and Challenges*, ed. Andrea Cornwall, Elizabeth Harrison, and Ann Whitehead (London: Zed Books, 2007): 79.

7. A clan is a descent group that traces descent to a common ancestor. Patriclan membership is transmitted through the father; matriclan membership through the mother.

8. Sheff defines polyamory as "a form of relationship in which people openly court multiple romantic, sexual, and/or affective partners. With an emphasis on long-term, emotionally intimate relationships, practitioners see polyamory as different from swinging—and from adultery. . . . Both men and women have access to multiple partners in polyamorous relationships, distinguishing them from polygynous ones in which only men are allowed multiple (female) partners." Elisabeth Sheff, "Polyamorous Families, Same-Sex Marriage, and the Slippery Slope," *Journal of Contemporary Ethnography* 40, no. 5 (2011): 488.

9. Katjambia's story is a case in point. In 2008, she took the Ministry of Local and Regional Government to court over its refusal to recognize her claim to the stool of her father and instead appoint her—male—competitor.

10. Katjambia Tjambiru, recorded interview, November 5, 2014, Opuwo.

11. In Himba society, there are no illegitimate children. Husbands (should) recognize all children born in their household, regardless of who the genitor is. If the mother is not married, her father takes this role.

12. James Ferguson, *Expectations of Modernity: Myths and Meanings of Urban Life on the Zambian Copperbelt* (Berkeley: University of California Press, 1999).

13. Rachel Spronk, *Ambiguous Pleasures: Sexuality and Middle-Class Self-Perceptions in Nairobi* (New York: Berghahn Books, 2012).

14. "Mistaking category for person": Marshall Sahlins, "What Kinship Is (Part One)," *Journal of the Royal Anthropological Institute* 17, no. 1 (March 2011): 13. "Epistemology of ignorance": Vivian M. May, *Pursuing Intersectionality, Unsettling Dominant Imaginaries* (New York: Routledge, 2015), 190.

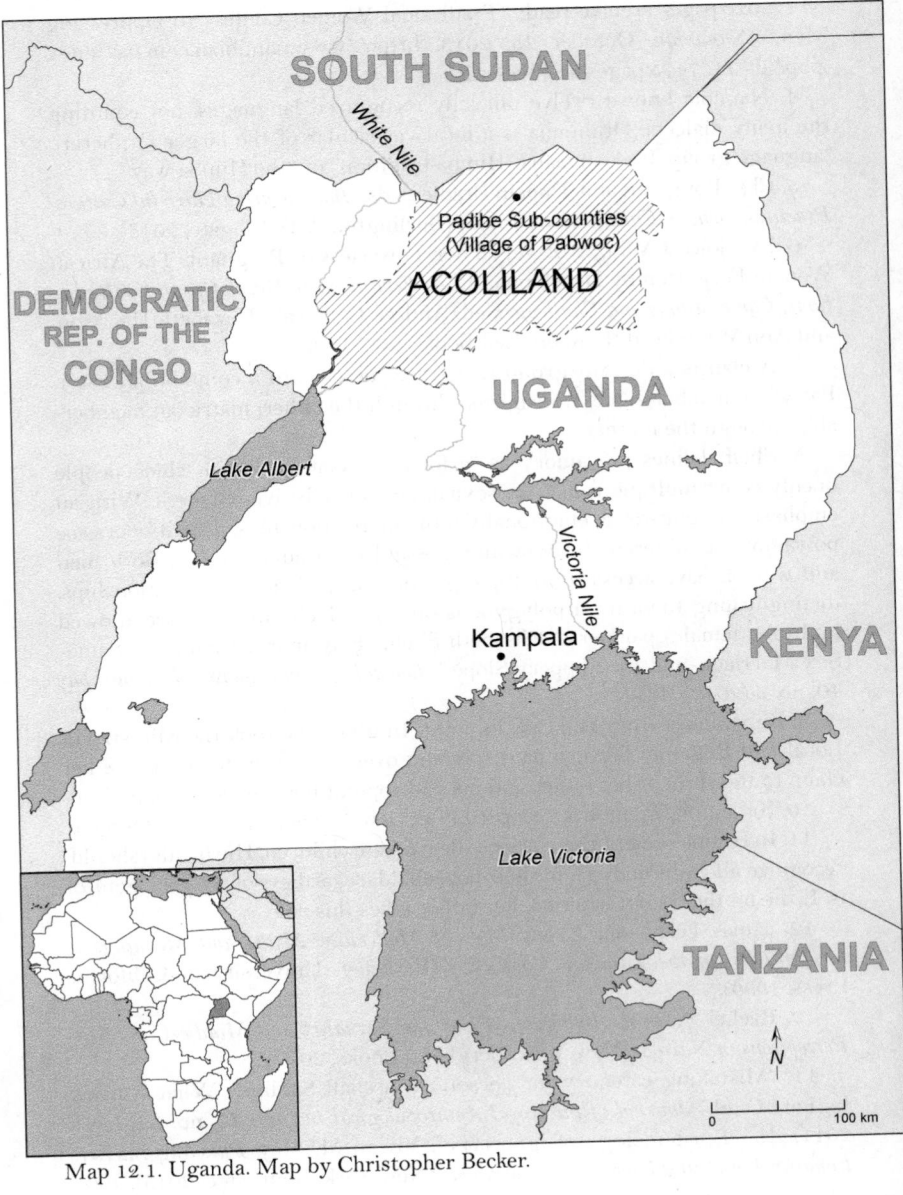

Map 12.1. Uganda. Map by Christopher Becker.

12

Love in and after War

Courtship (Cuna) in Rural Acoliland, Northern Uganda

LARA ROSENOFF GAUVIN

Sixty-five-year-old female: War made us go to the camp, and culture eroded there. Courtship, and other things . . . nowadays, girls get pregnant so fast! But before, imagine, boys were supposed to go to the girl's parents' house and remove their shoes in front!

Twenty-three-year-old male: But that is a good thing, before it was very hard to get a woman, we had to wait until we were almost thirty, but now, even us very young, we all have women from the camp!

It was 2012 when I first encountered people's extreme interest in *cuna* processes (love, courtship, marriage) in postwar and postdisplacement rural Acoliland, Northern Uganda.[1] The above exchange was part of a heated debate that I attended while I was living in my host family's homestead in the village of Pabwoc. At the time, I was conducting research on how rural communities were "moving on" after the two decades of war between the Lord's Resistance Army (LRA) and the Ugandan government (1986–2006). As an anthropologist, I was interested in the everyday activities and practices in which people engaged as they rebuilt their lives, livelihoods, and communities after the extensive violence and displacements that they had experienced. In my everyday interactions with my host community, in the village survey I conducted, and in my engagement with a youth group's programming, cuna was repeatedly discussed and debated as a key practice that had been deeply affected by the years of war and displacement.

My stay in 2012 was part of my cumulative time of eighteen months over eight visits to Northern Uganda since I first visited during the war in 2004. My research grew out of the relationships and experiences I had had with various people who self-identify as Acoli while visiting Padibe Internally Displaced Persons' (IDP) camp between 2006 and 2008. The Acoli are a group of people who speak Acoli Luo—a language I eventually learned—and who predominantly live in Northern Uganda and South Sudan.

This fieldwork took place about three years after the rural population in Acoliland finally left the squalid IDP camps to which they had been forced during the war. In contrast to international concerns about formal justice after periods of war and violence, high levels of angst regarding intergenerational relationships and *tekwaro* (indigenous knowledge) monopolized local popular discourse about the effects of the war in the postconflict period.[2] The circumstances of displacement had overturned the intergenerational social structure of the Acoli, and many elders, parents, and counselors alike complained that the war destroyed tekwaro.[3] Although the Acoli word *tekwaro* is generally translated as "culture," the word itself has a large semantic range (like "culture") that includes history and tradition. I use Gloria Emeagwali's definition of tekwaro as indigenous knowledge, "the cumulative body of strategies, practices, techniques, tools, intellectual resources, explanations, beliefs, and values accumulated over time in a particular locality."[4]

Thinking alongside the postconflict angst over tekwaro and people's pervasive interest in the war's effects on cuna, this chapter explores how, even in the midst and wake of the horrifying conditions of wartime violence and forced displacement, it is important to acknowledge the importance of the everyday to people's lives. Cuna continues to be a fundamental practice for the building and rebuilding of relationships and community. This chapter explores how youth engage in cuna practices in the contemporary postdisplacement and postconflict everyday, and the ways that cuna works to provoke intergenerational participation with tekwaro. This participation is always important, yet its recognition is particularly crucial to conversations about how groups of people work to remake social relationships and rebuild lives and communities in the aftermath of forced intracommunity war.

Justice and Everyday Social Repair

The LRA-government war is rooted in events that occurred in 1986 when President Museveni and his National Resistance Army (NRA)

seized power after a five-year guerilla war. Some defeated Acoli soldiers from the previous government's military took to the bush to
form various rebel groups, and eventually reorganized as the LRA
under the leadership of Joseph Kony in 1990. With a lack of popular support, the LRA abducted tens of thousands of their own Acoli
children and forced them into their ranks. As the war progressed,
Museveni's NRA also conscripted other Acoli youth into the military,
further contributing to what Opiya Oloya calls unprecedented "Acoli-
on-Acoli violence."[5] At the same time, the government displaced 90
percent of the population from their lands into squalid IDP camps
where deplorable conditions caused over a thousand excess deaths
per week.[6]

As many Acoli have pointed out when expressing their worry over
a "destroyed" Acoli culture, living through two decades of forced
intracommunity war where civilians were "squeezed from both sides"
deeply affected people's will and ability to engage with tekwaro.
First, survivors recount that their forced dependency on international non-governmental organizations for access to food for survival
exposed them to many "sensitization" programs that ideologically
challenged the authority of Acoli indigenous knowledge (tekwaro),
and along with it, indigenous governance and law. The infiltration of
born-again churches into the IDP camps was also mentioned, as they
further challenged tekwaro as "backward" and "satanic." Second, the
overcrowded conditions within the IDP camps made parental control
difficult. On their ancestral lands, comings and goings were highly
visible, and indigenous governance and law functioned to regulate a
more public and observable everyday life. Third, 90 percent of rural
Acoli survive from subsistence agriculture, and their wealth is found
in livestock. During the war years, either the LRA or the military
raided or sanctioned raids of all livestock in rural areas. The resulting destitution furthered people's disengagement from many tekwaro
practices, like cuna, for example, that demand material exchanges to
cement newly formed social relations. Amidst this generalized angst
over tekwaro, youth, adults, and elders repeatedly lament that the
ideological and spatial dimensions of IDP camp life, in addition to
the prevalent violence, had completely disorganizing effects on vital
courtship and marriage practices that both highly impact and rely
upon indigenous governance and law.

Centering intergenerational relations and indigenous knowledge
to questions of how war-affected people can move on with their lives

diverges from much policy and practice that remains framed from a Western legal understanding, particularly the field of "transitional justice."[7] Recent scholarship, however, has questioned transitional justice assumptions that mostly manifest in the forms of trials and truth commissions. It questions whose versions or "fictions" of justice ultimately lead to the rebuilding of community and social relationships.[8] Researchers call instead for attention to localized, contextualized practices that survivors *actually* engage in during the *everyday* to rebuild their lives and relationships.[9]

Thinking alongside the Acoli community's angst regarding cuna, tekwaro, and intergenerational relationships during the war years, I learned that multigenerational engagement in cuna—widespread and everyday practices concerned with love, courtship, and marriage—in contemporary rural Acoliland serves as a significant site for the everyday, difficult, and ongoing work of social repairing after two decades of forced intracommunity conflict.

Cuna—Courtship, Love, and Marriage

Augustine and Fiona are from the rural Padibe sub-counties. Augustine is my host family's eldest son and my longstanding research assistant. I was living in the same homestead as Augustine and his extended family in 2012 when his and Fiona's cuna activities began. While neither had been abducted by the LRA, they and their families were displaced from their homes, and, like all families in Northern Uganda, both have close relatives who were abducted and killed during the war.

Shortly after the war, Augustine and Fiona established that they were interested in one another. Augustine began the cuna process by checking with his uncles to make sure that he was not related to Fiona in any way. Restrictions on whom one can marry (incest taboos) are far-reaching in the Padibe sub-counties. Whole villages and groups of villages (clans, subclans, lineages) are deemed ineligible for marriage through one's father's, mother's, or grandmother's lines. In fact, Pabwoc elders said that it should ideally be checked back seven generations, but that today four or five generations are generally accepted.

Having no genealogical relations, Augustine and Fiona were able to proceed. The first time that Augustine brought Fiona to his family's homestead, she was brought to my hut under the guise of being my "guest." Fiona, usually exuding a quiet confidence, had looked very nervous when I saw her earlier that week. I had asked if she was excited, and she replied, "I just want to be able to do everything right when I come to Pabwoc!" Soon after I ushered Fiona in and gave her a place to sit, there was a knock on my door. It was Augustine's two aunts and his father's brother's wife. They exclaimed, "apwoyo kelo welo" (thank you for bringing a visitor). All the women in the homestead, except for Augustine's mother, joined us for lunch, which they had meticulously prepared. The women followed aspects of te-kwaro. For example, Fiona did not eat meat on that visit, nor was she supposed to eat with Augustine's mother for the first few visits. After Aunt Santina discreetly tucked a crumpled shilling note under the lip of Fiona's bowl, she finally began to eat. Small amounts of money were given to Fiona by the women throughout the different visits to symbolize advancement to the next "level" of familial relations. The change in relationship was also symbolized through the gradual shar-ing of different kinds of food; she eventually shared all foods with Augustine's mother in a future visit.

I was also present when Fiona came to stay in the village for a week, a few months after that first visit. She was much less nervous, and there was no ruse this time—she was no longer pretending to be my guest. Augustine had also, in the meanwhile, visited Fiona's mother with a friend. As per cuna regulations—which he asked his uncles about—he removed his shoes in front of the home and crawled in on his hands and knees. Augustine's family also had had time to fully check up on Fiona's background and had approved the union. That night, Augus-tine's father welcomed Fiona. Ceremoniously, everyone present added words of welcome and wisdom. Fiona stayed with Augustine in his hut this time and cooked in the main kitchen hut with Augustine's sisters. She was also permitted by the women to eat meat.

The prospective partners had obtained the consent of both their close and extended kin, yet formal negotiations for bridewealth had not yet begun. Bridewealth is the term for the "gifts" (including money, animals, and other items) given to the bride's family by the groom's family. The bride's family names an amount, taking into ac-count the bride's socioeconomic status. The initial demand begins a process of lengthy negotiations between the two families before they finally agree the night before the official Acoli wedding.

On that second appearance in Pabwoc, Fiona had planned to visit her family for a few days before returning to her schoolteaching job in another district, but unexpectedly stayed in the village with us for a few extra days. Nobody thought much about it until Augustine and I returned to the homestead one evening and his brother handed him a letter from Fiona's family. They accused him of eloping with Fiona and demanded money. Augustine exclaimed that he had tried to do everything right, to follow cuna with respect. Clearly embarrassed and frustrated, he didn't know what to do. His mother heard him talking loudly and came out of the kitchen hut to ask what was going on. When he told her, she laughed loudly. She explained that he should fully involve his father and uncles from now on, and that it was just part of the whole bargaining and negotiating process of cuna.

I have followed how these negotiations have continued to play out. For example, five years later, Augustine has still not fully paid the bridewealth. This is normal, as the average bridewealth typically represents a very large sum of money. After Fiona and Augustine had daughters in 2013 and 2016, Fiona's family began demanding *luk*, extra funds to "legitimate" children born before the full bridewealth payment. The massive and ongoing financial debt between the groom's family and the bride's ideally assures continued negotiation, involvement, and thus active and ongoing social relations between the two extended families.

A second, very different example is that of Beatrice and Kilama, a younger couple who met in Padibe IDP camp just as people began

Figure 12.1. A scene from day two of an Acoli wedding celebration—the cake cutting. Padibe West sub-county, Northern Uganda, 2012. Source: Lara Rosenoff Gauvin.

planning to leave in 2007. Like almost one-quarter of youth in Acoliland, Beatrice and Kilama were abducted by the LRA for a period of
time.[10] In 2007, back in Padibe IDP camp, Beatrice became pregnant
with Kilama's child, but he was in prison nearby. Beatrice's brothers (her parents are deceased) had begun building huts back on their
ancestral land. They planned to leave the IDP camp and return home
later that year. Beatrice was waiting for Kilama in the IDP camp, hoping to move with him back to his land.[11] When I asked her if she
was sure that she should wait for him, suggesting that maybe she
should go with her brothers instead, Beatrice answered firmly, "but
he is my husband. He is a good man, and I believe that he is innocent.
We will live together as a family." I was worried about her, partially
because she was young and pregnant, but also because I had learned
that her situation—and that of her unborn child—were uncertain in
terms of where they "belonged," due to their lack of participation in
cuna and their resulting unsanctioned union. In Acoliland, I was told,
land claims are most straightforwardly granted through the husband
or father's clan; they are largely patrilineal. Without participating in
aspects of the cuna process, Beatrice and her child's social and material standing were precarious. Strictly speaking, this was the case due

Figure 12.2. Kilama Amos,
Aceng Beatrice, and Kisumu
Vita. Kilama and Beatrice met
while they were displaced by
the war between the Lord's
Resistance Army and the
Ugandan Government. Vita
was born in Padibe Internally
Displaced Persons camp in
2008. They are pictured here
after they returned to Lotibol
village, Padibe East sub-
county, Northern Uganda, in
2012. Source: Lara Rosenoff
Gauvin.

to a *lack* of involvement of the couple's extended families in negotiating monetary exchanges necessary to legitimate the couple (e.g.,
bridewealth [*lim akumu*] and luk). I learned that part of the extreme
interest in lapsed cuna processes during the war was because their
lapse had completely disorganized many women and children's rights
to access and claim land.[12]

Kilama was released six months later and built a hut for his new
family on his ancestral land. I visited and had a chance to meet him and
their new baby. He told me that he loved Beatrice. He thought she was
the nicest and most hardworking woman around, not like many Acoli
girls who were spoiled by camp life. His gaze followed her around
their hut on the outskirts of what had been the camp. He watched her
admiringly as she cooked dinner and fed their infant. Beatrice's brothers began demanding luk soon after. They now have four children.
As Kilama slowly pays Beatrice's extended family, Beatrice and their
children are becoming officially legitimized and incorporated into his
clan. This happens practically through an exchange of funds, but *socially* because her husband has enlisted adults and elders from his extended kin to negotiate with Beatrice's extended kin. Like Augustine
and Fiona's case, the involvement of both young people's kin in these
negotiations constitutes a public contract, involving witnesses and
initiating a range of social relationships that will ideally assure the
children's, and the couple's, continued legitimacy and rights within
their clans and villages.

Through the cuna process, both Augustine and Fiona, and Beatrice
and Kilama, engage with adults and elders, build intergenerational
relationships, and acquire indigenous knowledge. Tracing their extended genealogies to check that they are sufficiently unrelated and
learning specifics of the cuna practices works to catalyze these relationships that also legitimize young people's status as adult members
of their communities.

Cuna and Everyday Social Repairing

In Acoli Luo, there is no indigenous word for "justice." When speaking
of the rectification of wrongs after crime, for example, the term *roco wat*
(restoring relations) is used. As the two cases illustrate, cuna serves as
an everyday, particularly widespread process for roco wat by creating
intergenerational social relations through youth's engagement with

tekwaro. After two decades of forced intracommunity violence and a decade of displacement that struck at the very heart of Acoli sociality, this kind of participation and negotiation is an important site of everyday social repair and reconciliation, or roco wat.

It is important to consider that processes like cuna—which engage people in tekwaro—are not simply "traditional" practices that act as static reproductions of social power and authority. Understanding cuna practices as everyday sites of interaction, encounter, and negotiation is a useful way to think through how cuna engages multiple generations in tekwaro and, therefore, what cuna does as a dynamic, multifaceted process in these contexts.[13]

It is also useful to remember that cuna practices are based on the same framework of engagement with tekwaro and Acoli law ways that have historically served as sites for the creation of personhood, for the negotiation of gendered and generational social relations and authority, and for adult initiation in indigenous governance organizations (clans, as an example) and communities. Attending here to contemporary cuna processes shows that important social-repair practices are based on everyday interactions that depend on multigenerational participation in and negotiation of tekwaro. Highlighting community capacity and knowledge, the frameworks that engage people in tekwaro—in this case, cuna—should be recognized as important practices of everyday social repair, reconciliation, and a localized form of transitional justice in these postconflict and post-displacement settings.

Notes

1. I use the Luo spelling "Acoliland" and "Acoli" rather than the Anglicized "Acholi" throughout this work following Acoli poet and scholar Okot p'Bitek.

2. Lara Rosenoff Gauvin, "In and Out of Culture: Okot p'Bitek's Work and Social Repair in Post-conflict Acoliland," *Oral Tradition* 28, no. 1 (March 2013): 35–53.

3. Kristin E. Cheney, *Pillars of the Nation: Child Citizens and Ugandan National Development* (Chicago: University of Chicago Press, 2007).

4. Gloria Emeagwali, "Intersections between Africa's Indigenous Knowledge Systems and History," in *African Indigenous Knowledge and the Disciplines: Anti-colonial Educational Perspectives for Transformative Change* (Rotterdam: Sense Publishers, 2014).

5. Opiyo Oloya, *Child to Soldier: Stories from Joseph Kony's Lord's Resistance Army* (Toronto: University of Toronto Press, 2013).

6. Ugandan Ministry of Health, *Health and Mortality Survey among Internally Displaced Persons in Gulu, Kitgum and Pader Districts in Northern Uganda* (Kampala: Ministry of Health, 2005).

7. Alexander Laban Hinton, "Introduction: Toward an Anthropology of Transitional Justice," in *Transitional Justice: Global Mechanisms and Local Realities after Genocide and Mass Violence*, ed. Alexander Laban Hinton (New Brunswick, NJ: Rutgers University Press, 2010).

8. Kamari Maxine Clarke, *Fictions of Justice: The International Criminal Court and the Challenge of Legal Pluralism in Sub-Saharan Africa* (Cambridge: Cambridge University Press, 2009).

9. Rosalind Shaw, "Displacing Violence: Making Pentecostal Memory in Postwar Sierra Leone," *Cultural Anthropology* 22, no. 1 (February 2007): 66–93; Pilar Riaño-Alcalá and Erin Baines, "Editorial Note," in "Transitional Justice and the Everyday," ed. Pilar Riaño-Alcalá and Erin Baines, special issue, *International Journal of Transitional Justice* 6, no. 3 (November 2012): 385–93.

10. See Jeannie Annan, Christopher Blattman, Khristopher Carlson, and Dyan Mazurana, *The State of Female Youth in Northern Uganda: Findings from the Survey of War-Affected Youth (SWAY)* (Boston: Feinstein International Center, 2008).

11. People who self-identify as Acoli and live in rural areas are, for the most part, patrilocal. Meaning, a wife moves to her husband's family's land to live.

12. As a result, many clans and villages now have a higher percentage of daughters and daughters' children residing in them.

13. As Rice emphasizes in her work on abduction marriage in South Africa, these practices serve as a primary site of negotiation about gender, rights, and generational authority. Kate Rice, "Ukuthwala in Rural South Africa: Abduction Marriage as a Site of Negotiation about Gender, Rights and Generational Authority among the Xhosa," *Journal of Southern African Studies* 40, no. 2 (2014): 381–99.

Part 4

Sports and Leisure

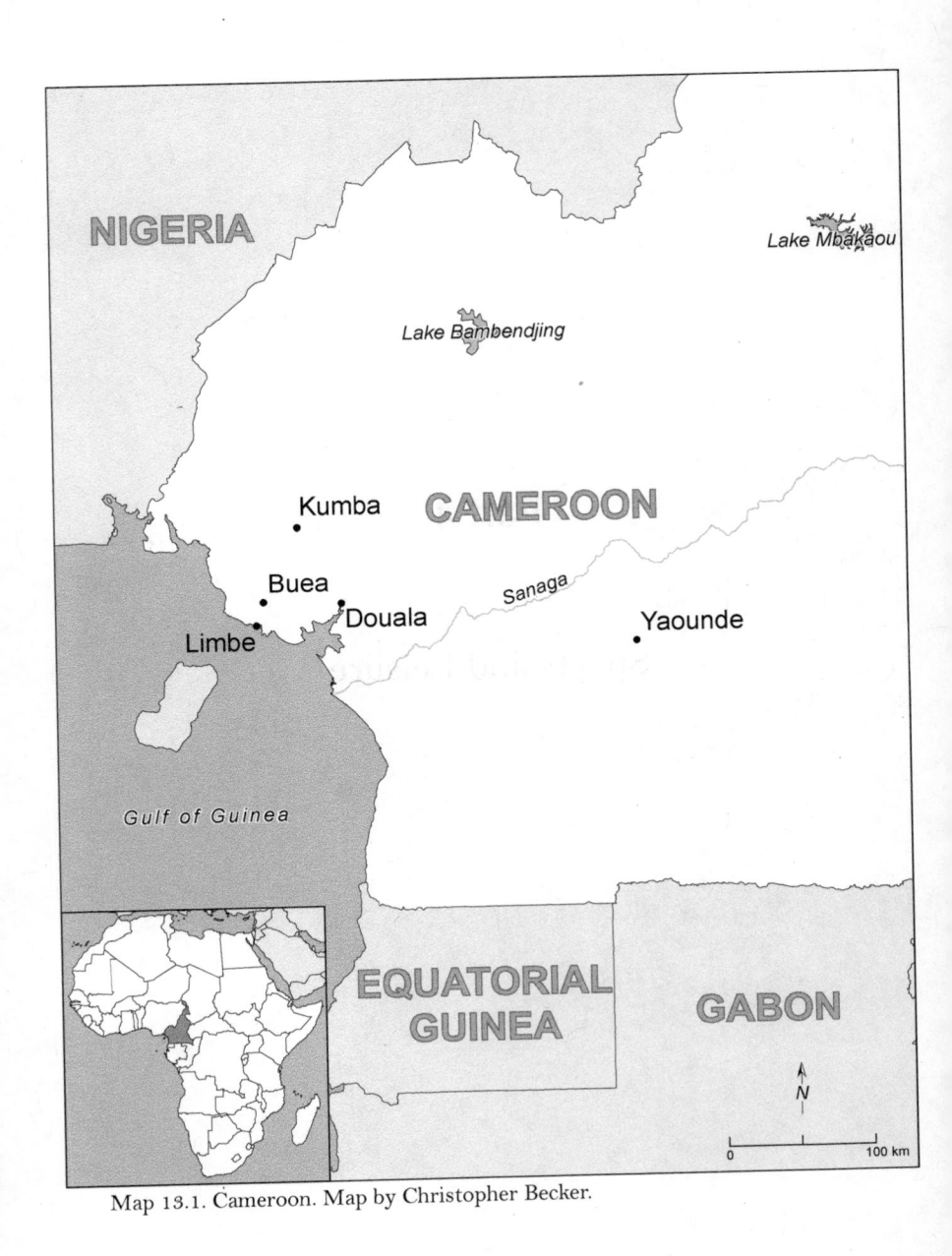

Map 13.1. Cameroon. Map by Christopher Becker.

13

"Where Are All the Women Who Used to Be Good Athletes in Their School Days?"

Sports, Gender, and Leisure in English-Speaking Cameroon, 1960s–1970s

JACQUELINE-BETHEL TCHOUTA MOUGOUÉ

At five o'clock in the morning in Buea, the capital of the Anglophone Southwest Region of Cameroon, a family friend and I headed to an exercise class in the Molyko Omnisport Stadium. On the way, she remarked, "I'm determined to cut down," meaning lose weight, recalling that adult women had avoided exercise when she was growing up in the 1970s. Although some Cameroonian subcultures still consider a robust body size evidence of good health and prosperity, being overweight increasingly stigmatizes women. Women in Cameroon are increasingly appreciating the physical and mental health benefits of exercise regimens and organized sports. On arrival, despite the early hour, we saw that exercise groups and all-male soccer teams had crowded the stadium. The women, many of them wearing colorful African-print head wraps, dominated the exercise groups.

Positioned in West-Central Africa, Cameroon neighbors Nigeria, Chad, and the Central African Republic and encompasses a minority of English-speaking towns, reflecting British administrative legacies in a predominantly French-speaking country. My research in Buea indicates that neither disinterest in fitness nor discouragement of women's athleticism drove the dominant anti-exercise culture of the 1970s. Women's participation in *formally* organized sports teams, such as soccer, was not widely accepted in the 1970s and is still not. However, unlike in the early postindependence period, *informal* exercise regimes have become more acceptable, and health campaigns addressing obesity have promoted acceptance of informal exercise, such as aerobics, for Cameroonian women. My 2011–12 research in Buea demonstrated that, then as now, economic stratification, geographic positioning, and shifting gender-norm expectations contributed to Anglophone Cameroonians expressing conflicting ideas about formally organized sports and informal exercise regimens for women.

This chapter draws from political and social history. It uses English-language archival records in Cameroon, such as official government documents and newspapers, to analyze ideas about gender, sports, and leisure in urban Anglophone Cameroon. It examines how, in the 1960s and 1970s, Anglophone Cameroonian women created, contested, and occupied their leisure time in the early period of independence. This discussion reaffirmed and challenged gender norms, social positioning, and citizenship. Sports and leisure were spaces of negotiation where formally educated urban elites transformed politics, culture, and society. While older women today contend that the culture discouraged women from exercising in the 1970s, primary sources suggest that many individuals in urban regions strived to normalize formal and informal women's sports for nationalist, social, and cultural purposes. I contend that formally educated female elites asserted that participation in sports and exercise made Anglophone female citizens happy by socially emancipating them. Through this politicized leisure, which included participation in organized sports, women represented Anglophone regions of Cameroon as a socially progressive nation compared to others around the world. Readers who wrote to newspapers responded with conflicting opinions, suggesting that women's participation in organized sports teams both fractured and advanced ideal gender norms. Examining women's participation in organized and informal sports allows us to think more complexly about gender ambivalence and its connection to crafting new African national identities in the early postindependence era.

Urban elites sought to regulate varied forms of women's leisure and expressivity as part of their efforts to communicate the emergence of Anglophone Cameroon as an autonomous nation-state. Britain and France had divided modern-day Cameroon between 1922 and 1961. In 1961, British-ruled areas became part of the Federal Republic of Cameroon, which consisted of two sociopolitically autonomous states—the West Cameroon State (Anglophone, comprising the current Southwest and Northwest Regions of Cameroon) and the East Cameroon State (Francophone). The political dominance of Francophone Cameroon contributed to growing perceptions amongst the Anglophone urban elite that the Francophone state threatened their shared traditions and political and cultural identity based on British administrative legacies. Anglophone Cameroonian political elites—politicians, government workers, and the wives of politicians—strived to delay their incorporation into the Francophone regime by emphasizing differences, real and manufactured, between the previously British- and French-administered regions. Anglophone political elites saw organized sports as one way to preserve their Anglophone identity and autonomy as a nation-state. In 1968, for example, one sports writer for the *Cameroon Telegraph* attributed his countrymen's proficiency at soccer to their British heritage: "Any football scholar understands the difference between football being played in former French [c]olonies and that played in former British territories. . . . British football is hard and swift, while the French play is cool and slow."[1]

The period under consideration brought expanded formal education and job opportunities for women, changes individuals applauded as social progress, but which also occasioned anxiety over the loss of African cultural values.[2] The notion that women played a key role in communicating the sociopolitical advancement of English-speaking regions of Cameroon led many individuals to encourage women to participate in organized sports like men.

Gender, Time, and Leisure in Urban Anglophone Cameroon

Research on changing notions of leisure in Africa demonstrates that European rule and the existence of Christian missions influenced the order of time and space in urban Africa, particularly among the educated elite. Colonial powers, through the introduction of sports, hoped to exert "social control" and redefine Africans' perception of leisure, which they believed was unorganized. Colonial officials and Christian missionaries considered organized sports an important dimension of colonial hegemony, feeling that the rules would teach Africans obedience, bravery, and perseverance. However, colonial governments seemed more interested in developing organized sports for male members of African society, such as soccer and rugby. Conversely, women focused on "[g]oing on errands or joining friends for strolls" or "found dance at church services and participation in church activities" to be acceptable leisure activities.[3]

During British rule in Cameroon, Christian missionary groups played a significant role in establishing women's approach to leisure by imparting European gender norms in which "good" women

Figure 13.1. Female students play netball at the Teachers Training College in Kumba, an English-speaking city in the southwestern region of Cameroon, 1953. Source: The National Archives of the UK (TNA).

focused on domestic activities, endeavoring to "create 'good' Christian wives and mothers." Women's associations also demarcated elite women's suitable domestic activities, contributing to definitions of ideal femininity. For example, the Women's Corona Society organized children's parties, needlework competitions, and various educational presentations on embroidering, baking, and flower arranging in Buea and Limbe in the late 1950s.[4]

Although schools introduced girls to sports programs by the early twentieth century, women had fewer opportunities after graduation. They were hampered by a "lack of financial resources, sponsorship, and training amenities that affected all Africans," in addition to stereotypes and gender segregation in organized sports.[5] Urban women's daily activities, which contrasted with those of their rural counterparts, were confining, and they "had to be much more careful about transgressing the boundaries of respectability than rural dwellers." Regularly visiting "beer halls and other public drinking venues, for instance, often marked younger women as loose or available."[6] Various national initiatives in 1960s and 1970s Anglophone Cameroon sought to change that perception by providing opportunities for women to participate in athletics and by asserting that women's athletic activities were respectable and denoted the social progression of Anglophone Cameroon.

Sports, Progressiveness, and Citizenship

Anglophone Cameroonian elites sought to demonstrate that they were as socially advanced as their European and African counterparts. Women's participation in sports and competitions indicated "good" citizenship and the social progressivism of the nation. Thus, women were obliged to participate in organized sports to support the Anglophone nationalist campaign. Both the West Cameroon government and its hegemonic Francophone successor developed government initiatives to improve women's sports culture. They succeeded: in 1960, 1,000 girls were members of the Athletic Federation (boys, 5,335); in 1975, girls totaled 4,000 (boys, 10,000). There were 105 women's basketball and handball teams in 1960 and 900 in 1975.[7]

Government texts encouraged women's participation in sports, asserting that, through purposeful leisure, women's athletic activities highlighted the social progress of the nation. The Women's Cameroon National Union, the women's wing of the country's national political party, released a short booklet, *Faces of the Cameroonian Woman*, in 1975. It exemplified the government's emphasis on emotional expressivity in promoting leisure activities. Asking "how many fights were fought and how much prejudice had to be overcome before public opinion admitted that a woman could take part in sports contests[?]," it connected sports to temporary liberation from the kitchen, as a way to achieve "health and physical, as well as mental balance" and "a sane and healthy body," which it termed "a major trump in a world where they [women] have to fight every day in order to conquer their place as full-fledged citizens." Women were to fulfill domestic obligations as well as nationalist endeavors that sought to emphasize progress-driven unity in the country. Further, the booklet avowed that Cameroonian women's "physical fitness was equal and sometimes even superior to that of her sisters in other countries," concluding that "[j]ust as high school and university education, participation in sports has helped with the Cameroonian girl's emancipation."[8] The booklet implied that women were responsible for emancipating themselves and for combatting societal stereotypes. Thus, political ideologies about leisure stipulated that "free" time was not just for women to pursue their own individual interests; it was also time in which women should "work" and "fight" to develop the nation-state.

The Cameroonian state connected women's participation in sports to emancipation, but it also limited the extent of that liberation. *Faces of the Cameroonian Woman* cautioned that the reader must "remain African and retain her own true nature which is the fruit of her ancestral and traditional heritage."[9] While political elites sought to stress women's participation in sports as a sign of social progress, they also held women responsible for upholding imagined ideas about an African "authenticity"—a "real" African cultural heritage independent of European ideals. Yet, simultaneously, they sought to indigenize, or Africanize, some of these new cultural expressions, such as women's participation in organized sports, to align them with broader nationalist rhetoric. Thus, the state endeavored to limit the boundaries of women's emancipation even as it endorsed their liberation through sports participation.

Sports and Normative Gender Ideals

Newspaper records suggest urbanite elites similarly supported sports—even while recognizing limitations in their encouragement—in support of the progress of the nation. Female journalists argued that Cameroonian women's participation in sports was an antecedent to their being as progressive as their European and African counterparts. Journalist Clara Manga's 1963 column in the *Cameroon Champion* was typical: "The average Cameroon woman, as soon as she gets married and has one child[,] feels too old and big to take part in any form of sports." Thus, while women might subscribe to ideal gender norms and engage in domestic activities through marriage and motherhood, they nevertheless failed to embrace acceptable contemporary cultural expressions that would signal the progress of Anglophone Cameroonian societies and support nationalist endeavors.

Manga noted that "wives and mothers [took] part in sports" in European nations and other African nations, such as Ghana and Nigeria. She advanced sports participation as an ideal feminine activity and chided her readers for lagging behind, comparing the plight of Cameroonian womenfolk with *other* African females who she deemed to be more socially progressive and cosmopolitan. While scholars underline how educated African elites in the postcolonial period have compared themselves to Westerners, they pay less attention to how Africans have favorably or unfavorably compared themselves with people from other African countries. Manga's comparison of her compatriots' sports participation with those of Ghanaians and Nigerians suggests how postcolonial African women have measured themselves against both continental and international gender norms to shape standpoints on women's athletic activities and use of leisure time. Manga also asserted that Cameroon needed "a real well-organised Women's Athletic Association" to encourage the same level of sports participation as their African counterparts, and less "class distinction amongst women."[10] She proposed that sports might break down class boundaries and foster camaraderie among women. But Manga's lamentations also illustrate that socioeconomic position informed just *who* engaged in leisure activities. Her 1963 observations and the 1975 government text, *Faces of the Cameroonian Woman,* demonstrate that, while women's participation in sports reflected larger ideas about the progressiveness of Cameroon, it also identified the *type* of woman suitable for conveying such messages. Formally educated women more easily accessed sports than did women of lower economic status; the latter lacked financial resources and faced time constraints.

In a 1962 article in the *Cameroon Champion,* an unknown journalist similarly criticized women's indifference toward sports. She (assuming the writer was a woman) reflected on her "last tour in the East Cameroon," in which she had seen "that girls can run faster than boys." The columnist lamented the "draw back spirit in women" in West Cameroon as indicative of a "great weakness in the women['s] field of sports" and exposed these female counterparts as noncompetitive with "their sisters in the East."[11] Like Manga, the journalist described women who forewent sports as lazy, thus emphasizing that indolent use of leisure reflected a larger failure to fight for West Cameroon's emancipation and social progress.

Others described women's sports as challenging normative gender ideals. In October 1964, Sarrah Agbor, a light-middleweight boxer, knocked out her male opponent, H. Nitty, in two rounds in front of a thousand-strong audience in Limbe. The *Cameroon Times* printed a review of the match: "Both boxers started very fast, but Nitty rained heavier punches. . . . Sarrah dashed out of her red corner like a wounded lioness. Spectators leapt to their feet as Sarrah cornered Nitty and rained blows in preparation for the kill. Nitty escaped to the centre of the ring for a breather, but the Amazon was on him like lightning. The end came fast. . . . Nitty's legs became rubber and wobbled. He crashed on the canvas, dazed." Following the match, Agbor, allegedly "still looking fresh," told a reporter, "what a man can do, a woman can [do]."[12] She dared any woman "who thinks she can contest my right as a boxer" to a boxing match with her. Agbor's declarations—or threats—implied that she derived pleasure in challenging the supposed biological differences between men and women. Her statements highlight how some women found pride in their athleticism when participating in sports. Such women's experiences provide a lens for understanding how they sometimes found it pleasurable to challenge dominant gender codes of behavior for women.

Clara Manga criticized men who objected to women's sports and blamed a "rude and unkind" public for opposing their involvement, rather than women's laziness, as others had. Manga lamented the lack of a female referee in a netball match and urged women to "rise to the call and come forward to improve women's sports in an Independent Cameroon."[13] The *Cameroon Times* ran a letter from a reader from Limbe who, while agreeing women should referee netball matches, ultimately argued that "women cannot officiate without the help of men for they cannot take a firm decision when officiating in any sports competition." The author pointed to women's previous officiating of netball matches, which, in the author's opinion, went poorly.[14] The letter implied that women referees in the 1960s, like those of their contemporary global counterparts, face sexism because of their leadership positions in a patriarchal sports world. Thus, female referees may be "seen as deviant in these male-defined roles."[15] Clearly, as women crossed—or challenged—cultural barriers to their participation in athletics, the role of gender and authority in sports informed perspectives about leisure, femininity, and citizenship duties in Anglophone Cameroon.

In the 1960s and 1970s, formally educated urban Anglophone Cameroonians endeavored to regulate forms of leisure and expressivity by women to show that Cameroon was a socially progressive nation. Consequently, a relationship began between state policy and women's involvement and how they might take pleasure in a leisure activity that brought individual autonomy and communicated the national and global sociopolitical advancement of Cameroon. Discussions of women's involvement in sports evidenced a societal ambivalence about changing gender norms for women. While political elites sought to regulate and monitor formally educated women's leisure activities so that they adhered to recognizably indigenous cultural forms, some women, like Sarrah Agbor, reveled in their physical prowess and used sports to break the boundaries. Today, in Cameroon, women's participation in exercise and organized sports teams continues to signal the social advancement of the nation. When Cameroon's national women's soccer team, the Indomitable Lionesses, qualified for the 2014 Women's World Cup, their coach explained to a BBC reporter its impact on women's social emancipation: "We have more girls playing soccer, we are better organized—with this qualification, many things will change."[16] Indeed, when the Indomitable Lionesses were runners-up at the 2016 Africa Women Cup of Nations, one Cameroonian fan asserted that "Women's football is popular in Cameroon. We all know the team and we know what they do," thus demonstrating how women's use of leisure time continues to be a primary site for the public (de)construction and performance of gender, and nationalism, in Cameroon.[17]

Notes

1. "The Pinching Spot in Our National Team," *Cameroon Telegraph*, December 20, 1968, 5.

2. Jacqueline-Bethel Tchouta Mougoué, "Intellectual Housewives, Journalism, and Anglophone Nationalism in Cameroon, 1961–1972," *Journal of West African History* 3, no. 2 (Fall 2017): 74.

3. Emmanuel Akyeampong and Charles Ambler, "Leisure in African History: An Introduction," in "Leisure in African History," ed. Emmanuel Akyeampong and Charles Ambler, special issue, *International Journal of African Historical Studies* 35, no. 1 (2002): 9, 10, 11; Phyllis M. Martin, *Leisure and Society in Colonial Brazzaville* (Cambridge: Cambridge University Press, 1995), 3.

4. Melinda Adams, "Colonial Policies and Women's Participation in Public Life: The Case of British Southern Cameroons," *African Studies Quarterly* 8, no. 3 (Spring 2006): 1, 5, 12, https://sites.clas.ufl.edu/africa-asq/files/Adams-Vol8Issue3.pdf.

5. Kathleen Sheldon, *African Women: Early History to the 21st Century* (Bloomington: Indiana University Press, 2017), 242.

6. Akyeampong and Ambler, "Leisure in African History," 10.

7. Women's Cameroon National Union, *Faces of the Cameroonian Woman* (Yaoundé, Cameroon: Ateliers Graphiques du Cameroun, 1975), 109.

8. Women's Cameroon National Union, 109.

9. Women's Cameroon National Union, 89.

10. Clara Manga, "Women and Sports," *Cameroon Champion*, May 29, 1962, 3.

11. "Women Too in the World of Sports," *Cameroon Champion*, June 12, 1962.

12. "Boxing Sensation: Woman Licks Male Opponent," *Cameroon Times*, October 6, 1964, 1.

13. Manga, "Women and Sports," 3.

14. "Women Are Incapable Referees," letter to the editor, *Cameroon Times*, July 15, 1967, 2.

15. Kamiel Reid and Christine Dallaire, "'Because There Are So Few of Us': The Marginalization of Female Soccer Referees in Ontario, Canada," *Women in Sport and Physical Activity Journal* 27 (2019): 13.

16. "Nigeria Reclaim African Women's Title," BBC Sport, October 25, 2014, https://www.bbc.com/sport/football/29739296.

17. "Africa Women Cup of Nations Kicks Off in Cameroon," *Guardian*, November 20, 2016, https://www.theguardian.com/world/2016/nov/20/africa-women-cup-of-nations-cameroon-opening-ceremony-football.

14

"We Are Building the New Nigeria"

Lagos, Boys' Clubs, and Leisure, 1945–60

MICHAEL GENNARO

In post–World War II Nigeria, the British colonial government appointed Africa's first social welfare officer, Donald Faulkner, to study the rise in crimes committed by boys and young men in large cities like Lagos. After months of research and interviews, Faulkner believed that the increase in juvenile delinquency and the rise of "wayward youth" could be traced to the breakdown of "traditional" family homes and institutions as found in villages, leading young boys and men to engage in unrestrained and thus dangerous leisure practices.[1] Faulkner's response to this colonial crisis was to create Boys' Clubs, multisport facilities equipped for table tennis, football, cricket, boxing, and others, since he believed sports—particularly boxing—taught discipline, confidence, courage, and "character."[2] Although Faulkner established the Boys' Clubs, he made sure that the young men who joined and the Nigerian communities at large were responsible for their upkeep and maintenance, soliciting financial support and patronage from elite Nigerians. These facilities were meeting spaces for young men to gather and discuss politics, the city, sports, and women. Furthermore, these clubs were safe and structured places for young boys to have fun in a dynamic and changing urban environment.

This chapter examines the history of the Boys' Club Movement in post–World War II Nigeria, focusing on the case study of Lagos, where the first Boys' Clubs were created. While recognizing the British origins of the club and the function the colonial government hoped the clubs would serve, namely, creating proper gentlemen and curbing juvenile delinquency, I will also explore the importance of the space itself as a site for leisure, camaraderie, and fun for Nigerian boys from all social classes. When we think of colonialism, we tend not to

Map 14.1. Nigeria. Map by Christopher Becker.

think of things like leisure pursuits or having fun; however, along-side developing nationalism, resistance to oppression, and the unfair practices of colonial rule, Africans in the colonies did have fun and leisure time and fought to protect and shape the spaces in which these activities occurred.[3] Their participation in various sports were some of the most treasured memories of the Nigerians I have interviewed, where they learned to be "men" and where they could gain the skills to navigate the new colonial urban city and its contours.

Boys' Clubs: A Post–World War II Phenomenon

After World War II, the British made a concerted effort to shape Nigerian social and private lives in response to alarming trends in the rapidly growing urban centers.[4] Between 1931 and 1950, Lagos grew in population from 126,000 to 230,000, and a significant part of this large-scale migration was young men and boys under twenty.[5] The ending of war brought with it new urban problems. Since Lagos was the economic, social, and political epicenter of the colony, it attracted many people who were in search of jobs and opportunities.[6] The postwar period also saw a rise in unemployment, and with it a rise in (both actual and perceived) crime. In the public imagination, it was the youths who were the main culprits of the criminal activities and it was they who needed "reforming."[7] As children needed to be protected from bad influences, lest they grow up to become criminals, the colonial government and Nigerian elites saw the need to raise children "properly" as a crusade of the postwar period. With this in mind, the colonial government hired Faulkner to investigate the rising trend in crime and juvenile delinquency and to come up with a solution. The Boys' Club Movement, as it came to be known, grew beyond the contours of juvenile delinquency and reforming wayward youths. The movement swept most of Lagos's youths and young men into its fold, inculcating a generation of Nigerians within the cult of sportsmanship.

The Threat of Juvenile Delinquency

As the editor of the *Nigerian Daily Times* (*NDT*) lamented in 1947, Nigerian youths were too often wandering the streets without any leisure activities or clubs to "fill [their] vacant times." Male youths were seen as a danger to society because they ran the risk of becoming juvenile delinquents.[8] Nigerian Patrick Graham, appointed the social welfare officer and Faulkner's second-in-command, told the new Boys' Club patrons and officials that "the causes of juvenile delinquency were lack of filial respect for parents, dull homes and ignorance of parents."[9] Colonial officials placed the blame on "faulty home discipline, while others have found difficulty in adjusting themselves to urban conditions."[10] By late 1947, colonial officials perceived youths to be passing their time in "improper leisure" pastimes, leading them into juvenile delinquency.[11]

The Creation of the Boys' Club Movement

The presence of so many young men and the concurrent increase in crime in Lagos prompted the colonial government to study the problem of wayward youths and later to hire Faulkner. This selection had an incredible impact, as Faulkner was an avid sportsman who believed Boys' Clubs would prevent wayward youths from becoming delinquents because the sports offered at the clubs would craft character, "pluck," and gentlemanliness by filling the idleness of urban life.[12] As the *NDT* reported in 1948, these spaces were "designed to afford youths recreational and cultural amenities, and a congenial atmosphere in which they can spend their evenings far away from the maddening crowd."[13] By doing so, youths had a venue that not only provided "games to check idleness and juvenile delinquency," but also taught them useful skills and traits, like teamwork, courage, and "the spirit of tolerant and common citizenship."[14] Graham told members of the press in 1951 that the central aim of the Boys' Club Movement was to train youths to become "useful citizens of tomorrow."[15] This strategy went hand in hand with crafting proper gentlemen, or, as the *Nigerian Daily Service* called it, "the character of the coming generation."[16] Faulkner decided that one way to turn wayward boys into proper gentlemen and useful citizens was by placing the running of the clubs on the boys themselves, thus giving them a measure of control over their leisure space. The boys annually voted for the president, vice president, and secretary positions of the club, in the hopes that they would learn responsibility, respect, and democratic functions—traits that Faulkner deemed necessary for adulthood and citizenry. By 1951, there were over forty such clubs with a membership of over five thousand boys in Lagos alone, and they expanded throughout the colony to almost every city and town by the end of the decade.[17]

The Boys' Clubs were open to all boys up to age twenty-one, neighborhood-based, and open during the daytime (since many boys did not attend school) and into the evening. As long as the boy paid his fees—most cost 1–10p a month, when the average monthly salary was £5, or 1,200p—he had full access to the club and its facilities. According to my interviews, while the clubs offered classes and taught technical skills to the youths, the most popular reason so many joined was access to sporting facilities, coaching, and competitions.[18] Although the clubs were intended to reform delinquents, they attracted Nigerians from all social classes, from former juvenile delinquents to schoolboys from elite schools. By 1949, the Boys' Clubs were making a name for themselves in crafting useful citizens. Those living in the various neighborhoods of Lagos saw a noticeable difference in the boys and in the level of crimes committed, as well as the new attitudes of many youths. "Old Tony," a Nigerian writer for the *Nigerian Daily Times* wrote in 1949, "This movement gives hope, great hopes for the future of our boys especially as some parents and public-spirited leaders are giving their support and encouragement." For Old Tony and others, the rising tide of the juvenile delinquency "menace" was finally showing signs of turning. Old Tony hoped that the Boys' Clubs would "thrive and forge ahead and spread not only all over the township [Lagos], but here and there throughout the country."[19] Sports were seen as necessary to craft proper men and citizens, a major reason why Nigerian elders supported the Boys' Club movement. For example, residents of Apapa, a suburb of Lagos, showed their support when the community donated seventeen pounds (British currency) for a new clubhouse and sporting equipment in 1949.[20] Old Tony recognized the value of this contribution: "it is comforting to know that the foundation is already laid: Football, Table Tennis, and Boxing are in progress in many of the clubs."[21] The success of the early clubs at curbing juvenile delinquency prompted local elites from surrounding areas in Lagos to want clubs in their areas. But make no mistake, it was more than simply the troubled boys, the colonial government, or local elites that drove the success of the clubs.

While the colonial government patted itself on the back for the good work that the clubs performed, one very important reason for the rapid spread of the clubs was that the boys recognized the clubs as places for them, where they could learn useful skills and have fun. Many learned or improved their reading and writing skills, participated in debates, and listened to lectures about topics like good citizenship, the usefulness of sports, and proper courting. An article in the *Daily Service* in 1949 detailed the experiences of Babatunde Shoretire, a member of the Yaba Boys' Club. Shoretire described the club as a meeting place for boys of all ethnicities, a place to make friends, and where one learned humility through sport and athletics: "although I have not had the fame, that publicity, that esteem which go to sportsmen, I have come to know how to hit and be hit, how 20 contest for a prize but only one of them wins," he explained. These sporting experiences, he noted, taught him valuable lessons that went far beyond the sports field into his life in the community. Sports to a Boys' Club member "meant sweet fellowship, [and] the building of a healthy mind in a healthy body." Shoretire described his "greatest gain" as his learning the need for selfless service. Young Nigerians, he said, should learn to do things not for money or personal gain, but for "their own sakes" to craft "desirable citizenship" within them. He summed up, "From my Club, I have gained humility, I have gained something of the spirit of sportsmanship, I have developed a sense of responsibility. . . . I have made many dear friends. These are the qualities desired of a good citizen and which are not easy to develop at school."[22]

Shoretire was not alone, as thousands of young boys and men developed similar skills through their involvement in Boys' Clubs in Lagos and the rest of Nigeria in the 1940s and 1950s. Examples like Shoretire's confirmed what colonial officials believed and hoped about the clubs, but also illustrate how Nigerians used and shaped the leisure spaces provided by the Boy's Clubs.

Boys' Clubs and Masculinity

For young boys and men, being noticed by the opposite sex was important. Part of the appeal of sports, and thus Boys Clubs, was that it was a way to be noticed by girls and women. In an interview with Olu Moses in 2013, he pointed out that boxing made "girls attracted to you." For Moses, boxing at the Yaba Boys' Club gave him the local fame he craved. Almost seventy years later, he still relished the memory of the cheering crowds, especially the women. He went on to say that women loved men of good character who were also sportsmen, highlighting what many young men at the time were either told or believed: that in order to attract a desirable mate, one must be a good sportsman. Furthermore, boys and young men could use the sports arena to showcase their strength and manliness in a city where traditional rites of passage were fading in the rapidly growing modern urban culture.[23] Ideals like strength, courage, discipline, and leadership merged with physical attributes like muscle tone and athletic build to change ideal forms of masculinity into what I have called "muscular citizenship."[24] Being good at sports, having muscles, and winning athletic competitions became modes toward a new form of urban masculinity after World War II.[25] For many, the only places outside of schools that afforded the space, equipment, and competition necessary to attain these desired traits were Boys' Clubs. Looking back on their experiences, many former Boys' Club members explained to me that it was at the Boys' Clubs that they learned what it meant to be a man—both physically and socially. Thus, Boys' Clubs were not only a space to showcase manliness through sporting prowess, but also a place to fashion and act out masculinity in the presence of women.

As the 1950s progressed, the Boys' Club Movement started by Faulkner expanded beyond Lagos and spread throughout the colony. However, this was not simply a European "civilizing" success. While the colonial government praised itself for the Boys' Clubs' contribution to reforming juvenile delinquents and wayward youths, the fact remained that the Boys' Club Movement was comprised of boys from all levels of society, as well as Nigerians from all walks of life. For the boys who frequented these clubs, they were a place for camaraderie and fun, for sporting competition, and, looking back nostalgically, a place shaped by and for them. The colonial government missed what made these clubs truly remarkable: they were places that boys could go and have fun, play sports, socialize, and become men.

Notes

1. Donald Faulkner, *Social Welfare and Juvenile Delinquency in Lagos, Nigeria* (London: Howard League for Penal Reform, 1952). See also Simon

Heap, "'Their Days Are Spent in Gambling and Loafing, Pimping for Prostitutes, and Picking Pockets': Male Juvenile Delinquents on Lagos Island, 1920s–1960s," *Journal of Family History* 35, no. 1 (2010): 48–70; and Laurent Fourchard, "Lagos and the Invention of Juvenile Delinquency in Nigeria, 1920–60," *Journal of African History* 47, no. 1 (2006): 115–37.

2. For a full discussion of the significance of boxing in Nigerian society, see Michael Gennaro, "Nigeria in the Ring: Boxing, Masculinity, and Empire in Nigeria, 1930–1957" (PhD diss., University of Florida, 2016). For the importance of sport in the British mindset in building men of "character" for service in Africa, see J. A. Mangan, "The Education of an Elite Imperial Administration: The Sudan Political Service and the British and the British Public School System," *International Journal of African Historical Studies* 15, no. 4 (1982): 671–99.

3. For discussion of the importance of leisure to African studies, see Emmanuel Akyeampong and Charles Ambler, "Leisure in African History: An Introduction," in "Leisure in African History," ed. Emmanuel Akyeampong and Charles Ambler, special issue, *International Journal of African Historical Studies* 35, no. 1 (2002): 1–16.

4. Frederick Cooper, "Industrial Man Goes to Africa," in *Men and Masculinities in Modern Africa*, ed. Lisa A. Lindsay and Stephan F. Miescher (Portsmouth, NH: Heinemann, 2003).

5. Akin L. Mabogunje, *Urbanization in Nigeria* (London: University of London Press, 1969), 257.

6. Although employment was most likely the largest factor in the rise in population, Lagos was also the primary locale for demobilized soldiers from World War II, many of whom decided to stay in Lagos rather than go to their home villages and towns. See Mabogunje, *Urbanization in Nigeria*.

7. See Fourchard, "Lagos and the Invention of Juvenile Delinquency in Nigeria." For a more Africa-wide study, see Richard Waller, "Rebellious Youth in Colonial Africa," *Journal of African History* 47, no. 1 (2006): 77–92.

8. "From the Editor's Mail Bag: Recreational Facilities for the Nigerian Youth," *Nigerian Daily Times*, April 29, 1947 (hereafter cited as *NDT*).

9. "Boys Club Formed at Apapa," *NDT*, May 24, 1949.

10. Mensah Boboe, "The Work of the Probation Officer," *Nigerian Daily Service*, November 8, 1949 (hereafter cited as *DS*).

11. Fat. A. Durosinmi-Etti, "Juvenile Delinquency and Boys Club," *NDT*, August 26, 1947.

12. See Gennaro, "Nigeria in the Ring," 61–65; and "Helping Young Lagos," *West Africa*, December 22, 1951, 1181.

13. "Training Club Leaders," *NDT*, June 12, 1948.

14. E. Ade. Odedina, "Welfare Work in Enugu," *NDT*, January 22, 1951. See also Gennaro, "Nigeria in the Ring."

15. "Sportsmen on Improvement of Boys' Clubs," *DS*, January 16, 1951.

16. "Our Boys Clubs," *DS*, October 8, 1949.

17. "Activities of Boys' Club in Colony Area," *NDT*, April 6, 1950.

18. Each club had local athletes, both professional and amateur, who would coach and teach skills for free to the boys. In the case of boxing, ping-pong, and football, local stars spent many evenings teaching the boys lessons through free workshops. These were often advertised in the newspapers well in advance.

19. Old Tony [pseud.], "Our Youths' Welfare," *NDT*, January 4, 1949. At the time, there were clubs located at Kakawa (later Onikan), Bar Beach, Primrose, Ebute Metta, Yaba, Mushin, Isolo, Oshodi, Agege, Imidu, Isheri, Ikorodu, Ajegunle, Araromi, Marine Beach, Apapa, and Ijora.

20. Old Tony [pseud.], "Our Youths' Welfare." In 1949 currency, £22 would be equivalent to approximately £500 in 2005.

21. "Boys Club Formed at Apapa."

22. Babatunde Shoretire, "What I Gain from My Club," *DS*, October 8, 1949.

23. For a more detailed look at Nigerian masculinity throughout the colonial era, see Carolyn Brown, "Race and the Construction of Working-Class Masculinity in the Nigerian Coal Industry: The Initial Phase, 1914–1930," *International Labor and Working-Class History*, no. 69 (Spring 2006): 35–56; and Lisa A. Lindsay, "'No Need . . . to Think of Home'? Masculinity and Domestic Life on the Nigerian Railway, c. 1940–61," *Journal of African History* 39, no. 3 (1998): 439–66.

24. See Gennaro, "Nigeria in the Ring." The post–World War II era saw an increased awareness of, and anxiety over, creating good citizens of Nigerian youth. The ethos of sport and being a good sportsman became entwined with physical and sporting prowess. Being a good citizen could thus be taught to Nigerian youth through the various values that sport inculcated in its participants.

25. As Lindsay notes, the years after World War II saw an increase in emphasis on displays of manhood and masculinity in the public sphere, and sport was one important space where such displays took place. See Lisa A. Lindsay, "Trade Unions and Football Clubs: Gender and the 'Modern' Public Sphere in Colonial Southwestern Nigeria," in *Leisure in Urban Africa*, ed. Paul Tiyambe Zeleza and Cassandra Rachel Veney (Trenton, NJ: Africa World Press, 2003).

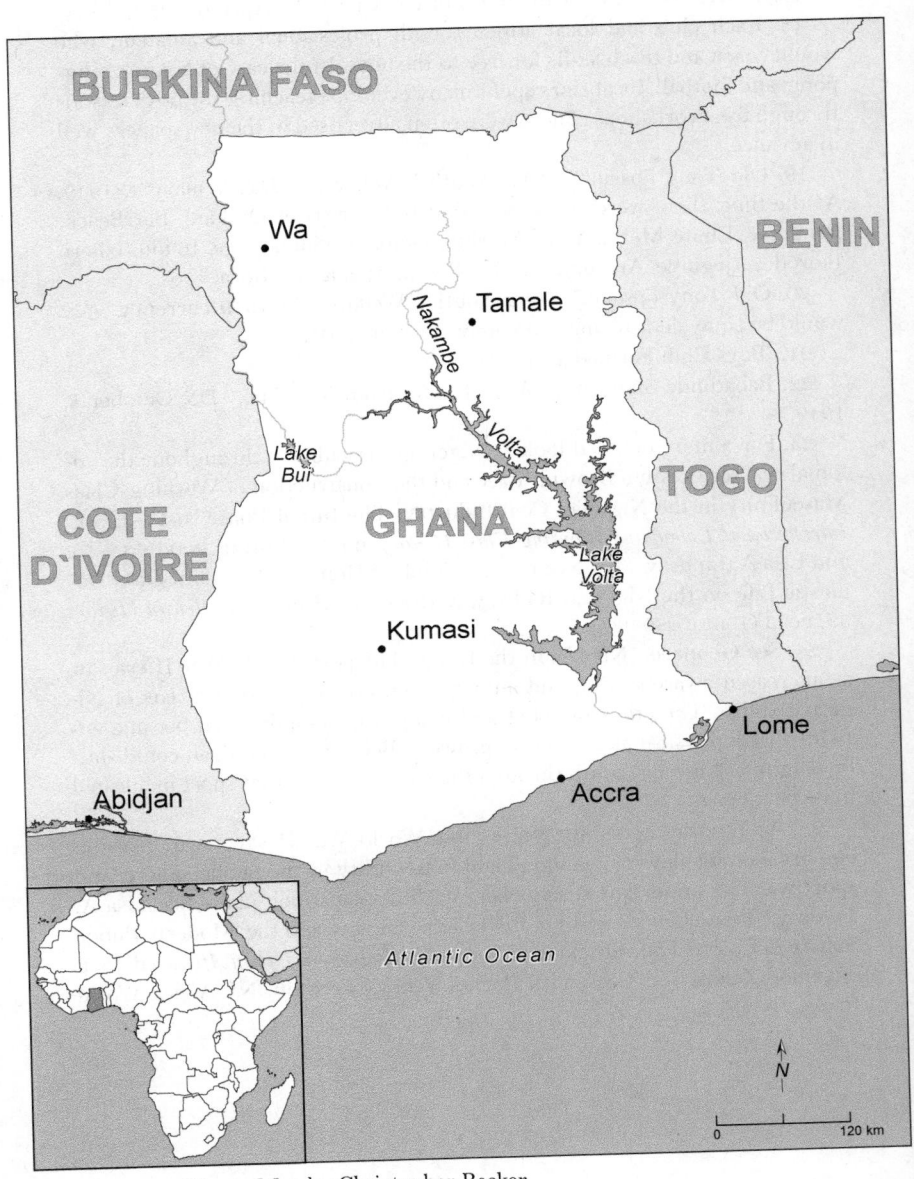

Map 15.1. Ghana. Map by Christopher Becker.

15

Leisure, Resistance, and Identity Formation among People with Disabilities in Ghana

ISSAHAKU ADAM AND AKWASI KUMI-KYEREME

Leisure provides a conducive opportunity for people to freely express themselves and influence their identities.[1] Identity is described as socially distinctive characteristics that an individual (or group of people) view as representing them.[2] Identity development involves the dual process of individuation and social relatedness. Individuation relates to the need to separate oneself from others through a process of personal identity development with a sense of agency and autonomy. Social relatedness pertains to the need for group identification by developing relationships with others and viewing oneself as being a member of a particular social group. Leisure as a sociocultural space for identity formation has rarely been discussed in relation to people with disabilities (PWDs), particularly in Africa. PWDs are expected to conform to their socially constructed identities, which often project them as second-class citizens. However, PWDs are capable of using their leisure to resist such identification. Resistance in this case typically involves people going against the socially established forms of leisure that are expected of marginalized groups of people.

Through leisure activities, PWDs can overcome certain structural and interpersonal constraints, including political, social, cultural, economic, and perceptual ones. Leisure activities afford participants greater freedom and allow for self-expression, which makes leisure an ideal avenue to counter dominant sociocultural stereotypes.[3] Nonetheless, resistance in leisure does not change the general societal power relations or identities of the subjects in question. Rather, it creates opportunities for infusing new identities and enhancing one's self-image.[4] This chapter draws on the disciplines of leisure studies, psychology, and sociology to discuss how PWDs use their leisure to resist socially constructed stereotypes in Ghana. As nondisabled people who have cared for relatives with physical impairments, the authors know that leisure provides an avenue for enhancing the well-being of PWDs.

Overview of Relevant Context

Despite being an aspect of social diversity, disability is often cast by society as something inherently negative. Globally, PWDs are often excluded and marginalized and, in some locations, even have to fight for their lives.[5] PWDs often face numerous stereotypes and discriminations in all spheres of life, including access to education, health care, and job opportunities.[6] Therefore, PWDs constitute one of the poorest segments of the world population and often live on the fringes of extreme poverty and powerlessness. The marginalization and exclusion of PWDs exists across both developed and developing countries, though with some nuances in specific contexts.

In Ghana, disability is mostly defined based on moral undertones. One perspective projects the individual with impairment as a social deviant.[7] Disability is conceived by many to be a manifestation of a punishment from a deity for sins committed by the individual with the impairment or by a relative. Another moral conception of disability portrays it as an aberration in nature's creation. Under this conception, it is believed that the path to salvation lies in being sympathetic to PWDs by being charitable to them. Whereas many followers of Christianity and Islam hold this latter view, followers of traditional African religions (characterized by worshipping spirits and lesser deities) often hold the former view.[8] To eliminate these negative stereotypes and foster the inclusion of PWDs, the Persons with Disability Law (Act 715) was enacted in 2006. Among other things, the law proclaims the rights of PWDs to education, employment, health care, and social life, including leisure.

Leisure has sociocultural connotations in Ghana. Traditional Ghanaian meanings of leisure portray it as a luxury. Leisure is regarded as something for the rich and elite who have both the time and means to exercise it. Also, being in possession of free time without having anything obligatory to do is regarded by many as a sign of laziness.[9] For this reason, Ghanaians largely engage in home-based leisure activities to escape being tagged as lazy. Meanwhile, Western education and globalization are gradually causing changes in the traditional conception of leisure, especially among the affluent and educated in major cities, who are beginning to develop routine and formal leisure lifestyles. However, most PWDs find themselves at the fringes of such transformation because they are often considered to be second-class citizens.

Description of Method and Findings

The findings presented in this chapter are based on data obtained in Ghana as part of a doctoral thesis in 2015. The thesis focused on the leisure experiences of people with visual and physical impairments in the Kumasi metropolis. Visual and physical impairments are the two leading categories of disability in Ghana and the Kumasi metropolis, hence the decision to focus on them.[10] The study employed mixed methods entailing the use of questionnaires and focus-group discussions. The findings presented here are based on the qualitative (focus-group discussion) dimension of the study. The discussions were conducted in the local language of Asante Twi. Contrary to mainstream Ghanaian expectations, PWDs engaged in structured leisure and used their leisure activities to challenge the negative sociocultural stereotypes on disability.

Engagement in "Nondisabled-Friendly" Activities

Some of the PWDs in our project engaged in activities that are conventionally thought to be outside their capabilities. Specifically, people with visual impairment watched television while those with physical impairment played soccer. While watching television is undertaken for the purpose of entertainment, enjoying television indirectly helped to challenge the stereotypes about people with visual impairment. In watching television, the people with visual impairment shared that they relied on their sense of hearing rather than sight. Enjoying television resulted in different kinds of experiences. First, based on the different levels of visual impairment, the respondents had varied experiences with television. People with partial visual impairment had better connection with television programs than those with complete visual impairment. Second, the type of television program was limited to dialogue-based programs. Respondents explained that they could better enjoy programs that were in dialogue formats than those that were programed in non-dialogue formats. In this regard, the respondents enjoyed news items as well as discussions on television and local dramas. Lastly, the people with visual impairment watched television together with their friends or relatives, who served as co-participants. A thirty-six-year-old woman and mother of two who was born with sight limitation in both eyes remarked:

> Watching television is an activity we enjoy. However, through watching television, we are able to influence the perceptions of our nondisabled relatives and friends that we can undertake some activities that they enjoy. Naturally, nondisabled people tend to underrate our abilities and mostly have the perception that we are incapable of doing certain things because of our disability. However, we have different experiences with watching television. Those who are partially sighted have better viewing experience than those who have fully lost their sight. But generally, we tend to enjoy television programs that are in dialogue forms like news items, discussion programs, and our local dramas.

The people with physical impairment reported playing soccer with their nondisabled peers. Though soccer is conventionally associated with nondisabled people, this expectation did not restrict some of the people from engaging in it, especially the males. However, playing soccer was mostly undertaken with friends and relatives and limited to the school and home environments. In both cases, the act starts with nondisabled friends or relatives who share an interest in soccer. These friends or relatives serve as the bridge through which they can break stereotypes about their disability. In the school environment, some teachers help to convince nondisabled students about the need to allow people with physical impairment to play soccer with them.

Further, participants in our study indicated that they had to adjust their abilities and skills to fit with those of their nondisabled counterparts. In specific terms, they explained that they had to get crutches that are lighter and can help them run faster to be able to compete with their nondisabled peers. Those without crutches used sticks to support the part of the leg that was either amputated or deformed. Ultimately, playing soccer was limited to those with impairment in one leg, one arm, or both arms. It was the view of the respondents that their participation in soccer positively enhanced the perceptions of nondisabled soccer players about PWDs. In some instances, nondisabled soccer players preferred to have some of the people with physical impairments as their teammates rather than other nondisabled soccer players.

The ability of some people with physical impairment to play soccer with nondisabled people not only allows them to fulfill their leisure desires, but also resists stereotypes about disability and abilities and thereby enhances the PWD's identity. A twenty-year-old man who lost the use of his left leg in a car accident at age fourteen and uses crutches and has passion for playing soccer revealed:

> We enjoy playing soccer at school and home. Because we have to play with nondisabled people, we initially encounter challenges since they doubt our abilities to play soccer. At school, some teachers and close friends help to convince nondisabled soccer players to allow us to play. At home, our nondisabled friends help to convince other players to give us the chance to play with them. As you know, this is limited to males and also those who have deformity in one leg, one arm, or both arms. For those whose impairments are more severe than this, like wheelchair users, they are not allowed to play. Even those who are allowed to play, they have to learn how to run faster to adjust to the speed of other players by using lighter crutches or sticks. But the good thing is that the negative perceptions about us change and some of them prefer to have us as teammates.

Formation of Leisure Clubs

Another strategy relates to the formation of disability-based leisure clubs. The local or popular jargon used to refer to these leisure clubs is "fun club." The leisure clubs provide the opportunity for PWDs to come together and undertake common activities such as chatting, sharing ideas and information, and playing board games such as Ludo and draughts (checkers). The goal of the leisure club is to provide its members avenues to interact and build their confidence in order to enhance their dealings with nondisabled members of society. Based on the knowledge gained from the leisure clubs, they are able to take charge of certain activities in their communities and thus help transform the attitudes of some nondisabled people. The leisure clubs are initiated and managed by the PWDs. Some leisure clubs have become synonymous with the disabled community and are associated in the Kumasi metropolis with positive identities regarding disability. A twenty-six-year-old man who lost his sight in both eyes when he was twenty-three years old and enjoys hanging around with friends and relatives shared:

> One of the things we've been able to do through leisure is to form fun clubs. These fun clubs do not only provide us with the opportunity to regularly engage in leisure but it also gives us the chance to demonstrate to nondisabled people that we're equally as capable as they are. This is because through the fun clubs we're able to organize different kinds of leisure activities and therefore show that we're not second-class citizens. The fun clubs have had positive effect as most nondisabled people now respect us for that. Also, it makes possible for all of us to engage in leisure despite the social challenges that we face.

Disabled/Nondisabled Leisure Alliance

Resistance in leisure entails the desire and ability to confront one's leisure constraints in order to overcome the societally projected image of the individual. In so doing, the individual with impairment must be willing and able to go against the socially approved leisure that he or she is expected to embrace. In this regard, the PWDs engage the assistance of some nondisabled members of society, specifically, their friends and relatives. The aim of such relationships is not to get co-participants, but rather to help them develop the relevant skills and acquire the needed resources to overcome the limitations on their ability to freely engage in leisure.

Social support as a process of interaction in relationships has the potential to improve coping, esteem, belonging, and competence through actual or perceived exchanges of physical or psychosocial

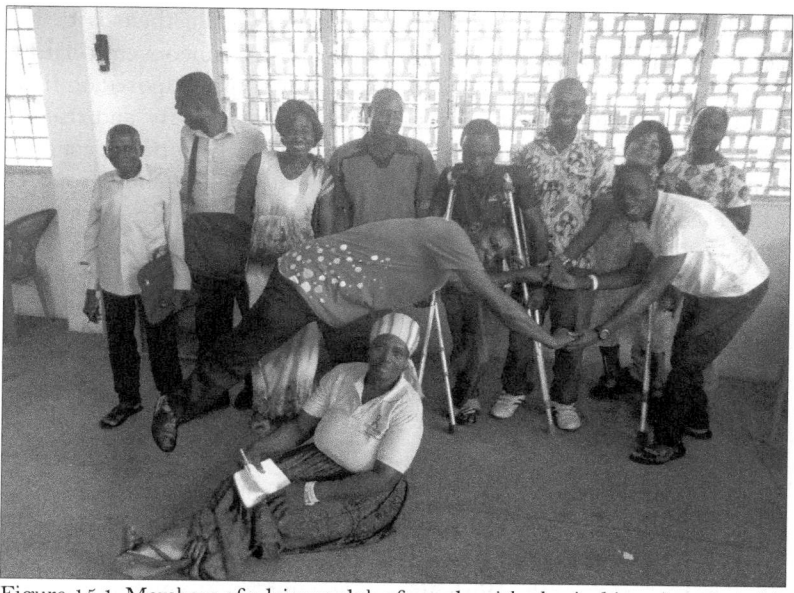

Figure 15.1. Members of a leisure club of people with physical impairment (with one of the authors standing third from the right). Source: Issahaku Adam.

Figure 15.2. Members of a leisure club of people with visual impairment (with one of the authors standing far right behind the two females). Source: Issahaku Adam.

resources.[11] These alliances are intended to provide them with the needed social support to be able to engage in those unconventional activities and thereby resist the traditional stereotypes imposed on their identities. In the context of leisure, nondisabled family and friends provide varied forms of social support to PWDs. Eventually, such alliances help equip the PWDs with the needed skills and resources to overcome the stereotypes. Meanwhile, the ability to form such alliances depends on the formal education and socioeconomic backgrounds of one's family and friends. The study suggests that people from educated families or who had educated friends found it easier to form such alliances. Similarly, those from wealthy families found it easier due to the social prestige of their families. A twenty-five-year-old man who was born with deformities in both legs and uses a wheelchair observed:

> By forming relationships with nondisabled friends and family members we're able to overcome some leisure constraints and engage in leisure activities that are originally out of our reach. Without overcoming such constraints, it is difficult to engage in such activities due to societal perceptions, meanwhile we have the abilities to engage in them. Even though we try hard to adopt this approach, it is usually easy for those whose family members/friends are educated or from rich families. For those with well-educated family/friends, it is easy because such people are mostly receptive to us [PWDs]. In the same way, those of us from rich families are naturally respected in society and so find it easy to make friends who will be willing to help us. Either way, the relationships we form help us overcome the social constraints and engage in activities that help us to gain the trust and respect of nondisabled people.

Discussion and Conclusion

The insights provided in this study bring to the fore an aspect of the changing social dynamics of PWDs' leisure spaces in Ghana. Examples of how PWDs participate in leisure and use it to challenge negative sociocultural stereotypes have not been highlighted previously in the literature. Leisure plays an important role in the lives of

PWDs by helping them to relax and have fun and serves as a context within which they are able to resist negative stereotypes.

The findings reported in this chapter highlight that leisure can be used as a tool to foster cohesion between PWDs and the larger society and eventually enhance the identities of PWDs. The relative freedom of leisure allows for self-expression and hence personal and communal identity formation. However, the ability to use leisure to influence one's identity, particularly among PWDs, requires the use of their power of agency to refuse to be what society expects them to be. By refusing, PWDs often need to collaborate with nondisabled people to aid them in freely expressing themselves in their leisure environments. While leisure spaces need to be accessible to PWDs to encourage participation, this should not lead to the segregation of leisure spaces between PWDs and nondisabled people. The focus should be on developing common leisure spaces that meet the needs of all manner of persons, including PWDs. Encouraging PWDs and nondisabled people to share common leisure spaces will aid the two groups to know themselves and enhance their identities.

The interactions that occur between PWDs and nondisabled people are an integral aspect of the ability of PWDs to individually and collectively resist stereotypes on disability. The discussions with the respondents further suggest that, contrary to popular notions regarding PWDs, they are able to exercise their power of agency. The marginalization and exclusion experienced by PWDs in Ghana has not prevented them from pursuing leisure in a positive and enjoyable manner. PWDs take initiative to construct their leisure and also use their leisure as a tool to resist stereotypes. In the restricted social environments of PWDs, they persevere and construct positive leisure spaces that they enjoy in their everyday lives.

In conclusion, leisure serves as a sociocultural space for positive identity formation among marginalized people such as PWDs. Leisure provides an avenue for self-expression and thus helps to align and define one's identity in a way one likes. However, to achieve this, one should be able to resist negative perceptions about one's identity, as this chapter has demonstrated. In this regard, the PWDs used their leisure time to break stereotypes by engaging in activities that are conventionally out of their reach. Thus, every human has the power of agency. When given the opportunity, it can be exercised, and, through that, every human can prove his/her potential. The PWDs in this study were therefore able to navigate their highly restricted environments in constructing positive leisure experiences that also enhanced their identities. The marginalization and exclusion experienced by PWDs in Ghana has not prevented them from pursuing leisure in a positive and enjoyable manner. Nevertheless, there is the need to create inclusive environments that cater to the needs of both PWDs and nondisabled people in order to foster alliances that help PWDs to exercise their power of agency.

Notes

1. Susan M. Shaw, Douglas A. Kleiber, and Linda L. Caldwell, "Leisure and Identity Formation in Male and Female Adolescents: A Preliminary Examination," *Journal of Leisure Research* 27, no. 3 (1995): 245–63.

2. Naomi Ellemers, Russell Spears, and Bertjan Doosje, "Self and Social Identity," *Annual Review of Psychology* 53, no. 1 (2002): 161–86.

3. Robert A. Stebbins, "Choice and Experiential Definitions of Leisure," *Leisure Sciences* 27, no. 4 (2005): 349–52.

4. Glenda Madeleine Jessup, Anita C. Bundy, and Elaine Cornell, "To Be or to Refuse to Be? Exploring the Concept of Leisure as Resistance for Young People Who Are Visually Impaired," *Leisure Studies* 32, no. 2 (2013): 191–205.

5. Simon Darcy, "Inherent Complexity: Disability, Accessible Tourism and Accommodation Information Preferences," *Tourism Management* 31, no. 6 (December 2010): 816–26.

6. World Health Organization, *World Report on Disability* (Geneva: World Health Organization, 2011).

7. Issahaku Adam, "Leisure Aspirations of People with Visual Impairment in the Kumasi Metropolis, Ghana," *Annals of Leisure Research* 21, no. 3 (2018): 347–63.

8. Joseph S. Agbenyega, "The Power of Labelling Discourse in the Construction of Disability in Ghana," paper presented at the Australian Association for Research in Education Conference, Newcastle, New South Wales, Australia, 2003.

9. Aaron Kofi Badu Yankholmes and Shanshan Lin, "Leisure and Education in Ghana: An Exploratory Study of University Students' Leisure Lifestyles," *World Leisure Journal* 54, no. 1 (March 2012): 58–68.

10. Ghana Statistical Service, *2010 Population and Housing Census Report: Disability in Ghana* (Accra: Ghana Statistical Service, 2014).

11. Bert N. Uchino, "Social Support and Health: A Review of Physiological Processes Potentially Underlying Links to Disease Outcomes," *Journal of Behavioral Medicine* 29, no. 4 (August 2006): 377–87.

16

Bits and Beats from Senegalese Wrestling

CHEIKH TIDIANE LO

Wrestling, practiced in rural and urban areas, is one of the most com-
pelling sports events in contemporary Senegal. It is very mediatized
and draws larger crowds every weekend than any other sport. In this
chapter, I will examine how wrestling represents a source of leisure
that is locally meaningful in Senegalese urban culture, and how the
porous lines between folk wrestling and professional wrestling in-
tersect, especially in the capital city of Dakar. This work draws from
my personal participation in wrestling ceremonies and in specialized
social media outlets. From an insider perspective also informed by
folklore studies, I emphasize the artistic expressions of wrestling as
a public spectacle, including its gender dimension. I argue that wrestling reinforces gender lines through the celebration of the male body
and masculinity. However, women singers also play a critical role in
the performance of wrestling songs, a characteristic of both what I
call "folk" and professional wrestling.

Contextual Element

Located on the west coast of Africa, Senegal gained its independence
from France on April 4, 1960, ending a three-hundred-year colonial
era. Wolof, the main language of communication and medium for
wrestling commentary, is Senegal's lingua franca, the language commonly spoken between people from different linguistic communities.
Over 90 percent of the population is Sufi Muslim, and 5 percent is
Christian. A commonality bonding these different religious communities is indigenous belief in the supernatural, an important component in wrestling culture.

Map 16.1. Senegal. Map by Christopher Becker.

In the Wolof language, two terms have emerged to refer to the forms of a wrestling festival. The first is *mbappat*, derived from the Wolof *bapp* (to fall back) and denoting the traditional wrestling festival, what I call "folk wrestling," which usually happens in the rural zones or urban neighborhoods. This wrestling festival, which originally marked the harvest festivities, has been brought to the cities through rural migration. The second is *laamb-j*, a Wolof term meaning to touch or feel with your hands that in this context represents the professionalized form of wrestling. Laamb-j is characterized by the introduction of money, which replaces other means of value important to mbappat that are associated with honorific gains. Wrestlers are called *lutteur* in French. A male-oriented sport, wrestling has become a popular event that involves all social strata, particularly the youth who constitute most local fans. To understand the centrality of wrestling in Senegalese popular culture, it is important to briefly examine the technical, ritualistic, and artistic dimension of wrestling in the urban culture of Dakar.

Technique, Ritual, and Art

The techniques of wrestling combat can be sorted into three major types. The first is called "simple wrestling" or *bëree simple*. In this type, each contestant has a grip on his opponent's waist before the match begins, and wrestlers are not allowed to use boxing punches. The aim is to bring one's adversary to the ground, making him fall on his back, front, or side. The second one, called *laamb ji* or *bëree dóor* (wrestling with punch), is like the first, except that when the match starts, the wrestlers are not gripping one another. When the umpire or referee signals the beginning, each tries to trick his opponent to throw him to the ground. In the last type called *tuur*, which is more complicated, contestants throw punches to neutralize their adversaries. The introduction of punching is said to be a Western influence from English boxing. It was first integrated into the discipline with the transformation of wrestling into a lucrative public spectacle.

A Senegalese wrestling match is a highly codified martial art involving very refined and sophisticated technical and tactical prowess. Wrestlers rigorously train their bodies to get fit and be mentally and psychologically prepared in training camps called *écuries* or *écoles de lutte* in French. The wrestler's community, composed of family, friends, neighbors, and fans, shores up its contestant to uphold its image and honor. A wrestler solicits his community's support and visits local shrines and religious guides to increase his chances of victory.

The wrestling battle is as much mystical and cultural as physical. It is along these lines that Eric S. Ross writes, "Libations are made. A multitude of specially confected talismans and charms of various kinds," such as *gris-gris* (talisman) and other types of leather amulets, "are then attached to the body."[1] Ross explains that these rituals continue throughout the event. Such bodily apparel serves aesthetic and sacramental or protective purposes. The close links between wrestling and indigenous belief systems render this sport unique to Senegal and account partly for its importance to national identity.

Wrestling as a Folk Game

I use the term "folk wrestling" to indicate the traditional and original form of wrestling mainly organized in rural or nonprofessional settings, locally called mbappat. Folk wrestling matches are customarily held right after the harvest time. They are entertainment festivals reserved for young boys. The events usually occur at night or in late afternoons, in either intra- or inter-village tournaments.

I remember when, from fifteen to nineteen years old in the 1990s, I would accompany my elder brothers to the nightly open-air mbappat in the province of Saalum, a zone encompassing the current central and western regions of Kaolack and Kaffrine. Barely lit by light bulbs under the glaring moon of the harvest season, the ring was surrounded by a thick crowd of young men and a few women. The electric atmosphere of frenzy and the dust that filled the air due to the vigorous wrestlers' feet pounding the ground to the rhythms of drums marked the wrestling arena. Small groups of dancers and the drum band were the only people allowed inside the ring before the beginning of the contests. Friends and companions would escort the wrestlers, bedecked with gris-gris, brandishing burning wood torches, and holding talismans and bottles of blessed waters prepared by the mystical marabouts. Such nightly events left indelible imprints on my childhood memories.

These wrestling festivals were bound in time and space and were marked by well-established phases. The preliminary stages were devoted to the arrival of wrestlers with their supporters. Then they proceeded to the ritual sacrifice, the dance, and the praise songs. After that, wrestlers were pitted against each other. The youngest wrestlers competed first, then the medium-weight contestants, and finally the heavyweight champions.[2]

The rewards to winners were typically not monetary, but consisted of material prizes, such as a bull, bags of rice, or other valuable items. Gradually, such prizes have been replaced by money. Folk wrestling in Senegal is still interwoven with belief systems and has played a crucial role in consolidating gender roles and the social structure, as well as in initiating young boys into values of masculinity, courage, and solidarity.[3]

Wrestling in Dakar

Laamb-j, the form of wrestling events popular in contemporary Dakar, is more professionalized and is mostly sponsored by big companies or the government. This type of professional wrestling is a lucrative event, with prizes ranging from $100 to $200,000 per match. The ceremony generally starts around four in the afternoon and ends around seven or eight in the evening.

Lightweight categories wrestle first, then the medium-weight wrestlers, then heavyweights, ending with the biggest contest, called the *grand combat*. Television stations make agreements with match promoters for exclusive coverage rights and announce the event from pre-match to post-match time, when the partner station generally interviews the champion at the end of the fight. Events are transmitted live to the viewing public. In addition to the use of punches, which differentiates pro wrestling from folk wrestling, professional wrestling follows stricter regulations.

The professionalization of the sport came into effect with the creation of the National Committee for the Management of Wrestling in 1994.[4] Before this, wrestling events used to occur at street intersections. Due to its popularity, professional wrestling began to be hosted in district soccer stadiums. Although folk wrestling is still organized in local districts, professional wrestling has become the number-one sport in most urban centers, especially the city of Dakar. In view of wrestling's critical role in youth leisure, with the help of the Chinese, the government has initiated a construction project for a National Wrestling Arena of 20,000 seats in Dakar, anticipated to host wrestling in early 2019.

Today, out of thousands of unknown or emerging wrestlers, there is a restricted circle of less than fifty famous wrestlers, comprising medium- and heavyweight athletes, who vie for the title of king of the arenas (in French, *roi des arènes*). Every year the king of the arenas is challenged, and, if defeated, the winner replaces him. There are about a dozen super- star wrestlers who are potential kings of the arenas at any given time. Other wrestlers work hard to be admitted into this privileged superstar realm, where they benefit from popular adulation and are solicited by companies for advertisements and by local and international media for coverage and to be the subject of documentaries. CNN's reporting on Modou Lo, a famous superstar wrestler, is a case in point.[5]

In Dakar, wrestling has become a huge business, closely intertwined with urban showbiz. Wrestling champions work with musicians, poli- ticians, and media celebrities to widen their networks and increase their influence. In return, the musicians and politicians use wrestlers' images and popularity to attract the masses. A parallel phenomenon that occurred with the rise of urban wrestling culture is the prolif- eration of traditional magicians, foreseers, and talisman specialists. These people profit from the wrestlers' belief in mystical powers as supernatural forces that can aid them in achieving success. Wrestling also constitutes a great economic niche for *griots* (the French name for the *géwel*, a caste group that is customarily in charge of communica- tion and oral histories in Wolof society), in addition to drummers, singers, and other performers. The entertainment component has an important role in attracting spectators and media attention.

Wrestling Fan Culture

The rise of fandom is a significant phenomenon in urban wrestling culture in Dakar. Wrestlers' market value is measured based on the number of fan clubs that support them, among other criteria such as their personal trajectory and dancing skills. Wrestlers' fans have created youth clubs and associations across Dakar's suburbs and nearby towns. Big meals are prepared on the wrestling day at the various adversaries' houses for fans who mobilize to accompany their champion to the stadium. Energetic fandom has emerged as wrestling ceremonies have developed into media spectacles in Dakar. This rise of fan clubs is particularly distinctive, as it evokes the adaptability of the game to the new urban environment.

Figure 16.1. This wrestling match pitted Mame Balla versus Pape Mor Lo in June 2013. In this image, each wrestler is thinking about the strategy to defeat his opponent, with a stadium crowded with fans and tourists taking pictures. Source: Pierre-Yves Beaudouin / Wikimedia Commons / CC BY-SA 3.0 Creative Commons. https://commons.wikimedia.org/wiki/File:Lutte_s%C3%A9n%C3%A9galaise_Bercy_2013_-_Mame_Balla-Pape_Mor_L%C3%B4_-_15.jpg

Professional wrestling in Dakar, although it is more mediatized and involves bigger amounts of money, does not eliminate folk wrestling in certain areas of the city. Innovations often occur in those urban folk wrestling contests, because they help young lutteurs to climb up to the higher sphere of pro wrestling. Those who excel in folk wrestling tend to benefit from an easy entry into professional wrestling, because they have built up the popularity to earn the trust of potential promoters. The rituals typical of folk wrestling are also permitted in professional wrestling, which keeps Senegalese wrestling distinct from wrestling elsewhere.

Wrestling and Oral Poetry

In Senegal, traditional wrestlers, beyond being athletes, are often praised for their artistic talents as dancers and poets. A few of them compose their own verbal pedigrees and praise poetry.[6] As Patricia Tang writes, "wrestlers have always been accompanied by their own special *bàkk*s." (Bàkks are rhythms and mottos that are like a "war cry" that marks the identity of a wrestling family or community.) "For example, Mbaye Gueye and Mustapha Gueye have their own *bàkk* called *Ndia ja jinne*. The *bàkk* represents the saying: '*Jinne xam seen kër, te xamuloo këram, nja ja jinee*,' which means, 'The spirits know where you live, but you don't know where they live.'"[7] In the following Wolof song, a wrestler brags about his supremacy.

> Géwelay tëgg
> Mbër mooy daan
> Boroom doolee ma tax di bakku
> Keppu ku mu mena doon
> Woolu na sama doolee
> May na ma fu ne ndam
> Te loolu mooy li am solo

> The griot bangs the drum
> But it is the wrestler who wins
> I take pride in front of the strongest
> Whoever it might be,
> I trust my power
> It gives me victory everywhere
> And that is what counts

In Senegal, historical information has long been recorded in oratory rather than in writing. In the absence of written records, poetry often documents the life histories of wrestlers' careers. Poems also evoke wrestlers' genealogies, kinships, and regional or ethnic backgrounds. Poetry plays a significant role in the psychological confrontations between wrestlers. For example, in the following praise song, originally in Wolof, a wrestler compares himself to a python, the reason why other wrestlers fear him.

> Cebbi dana màtt
> Moo tax gaa ñi
> Di ko yër di daw
> Cebbi dana màtt

> The python bites
> That is the reason why people
> Do not dare to come near it
> The python bites

In addition to being poets, some wrestlers mobilize women praise singers who know their history and traditions, as well as drummers who can play *tuu*s (rhythms) and bàkks (the wrestler's motto or war cry) that are associated with their idiosyncratic artistic taste and that speak to their personal and group identity. During wrestling matches, the praise singers exhort wrestlers on to victory through songs that emphasize their noble genealogy, or through comparison with well-known historical heroes.

These women singers come generally from the géwel caste already mentioned, a particular Wolof artistic subgroup in charge of traditional communication and music. Some of them are talented at composing wrestling songs that they practice during mbappat. Today, many of them have integrated this tradition into the professional wrestling world, where they benefit from the social esteem of the wrestling community. Arrangements are usually made for them to use microphones for their performances during the matches. Khar Mbay Madiaga and Mayé Ndep Ngom are currently among the most famous singers featured at wrestling ceremonies. The songs are repetitive and short, with invariable refrains and less frequent verses of variable length that are flexible enough to accommodate new information, depending on the occasion. A common song sung in Wolof by Khar Madiaga is

> Bayyileen seen yaaba ji te laale
> Yaaba du baaxu góor
> Laale mooy baaxu góor
> Ne bu doon laambi jigeen sax jeex na
> Aaye! Laamb bu ca góor nekkul
> Jigeen a koy moome

> Leave your pawing and attack one another.
> Fighting is a man's tradition.
> If it were women's wrestling,
> The wrestling match would have been over by now.
> If men run away from wrestling,
> Women will take it over.

Such verses are repeated by the singer and her chorus, with new elements introduced by the main singer. The song is intended to galvanize wrestlers into action, letting them know that not even women are as sluggish and fearful as they are being. Slow drumming patterns often accompany the songs.

Wrestling has become a mega-genre in which choreography and poetry are staged to accompany the actual sporting event. Music stars occasionally are invited to perform for audiences during the preliminary activities of big wrestling events. The entertainment dimension of wrestling could be the driving force of wrestling in Senegal. Many people I talked to or who were interviewed during local media reports express that they enjoy wrestling mostly for its artistic offerings.

Wrestling's popularity in Senegal makes it big business. As noted above, for the sport's superstars the rewards can be huge, with top earnings of up to two hundred thousand dollars per contest.[8] More than three thousand wrestlers, scattered across one hundred training centers, are said to possess licenses. Seeking to escape unemployment, most of the young wrestlers hope to reach success through this sport. Although only a small number of young wrestlers succeed in making a living with wrestling, the sport offers an alternative path to social mobility to youth who have lost faith in education and the challenges of finding employment. Superstar wrestlers at the time of this writing (2017) train in Europe and the United States, drive luxurious cars, and build villas, creating rays of hope for millions of young people who regard them as idols. Wrestling's growing popularity is also implicated in politics: some politicians are known to secretly or publicly sponsor wrestlers, hoping to earn their fans' electoral allegiance. Although its future is unpredictable, wrestling will undoubtedly continue to shape Senegalese urban, popular, and sporting cultures for years to come because of its rootedness in the collective imaginaries and its entertaining quality.

Today, more than in the past, wrestling provides intense moments of joy and suspense to millions of fans and lovers of wrestling inside and outside Senegal. Confronted with the ups and downs of life, the masses periodically find solace in watching and commenting on wrestling contests, relishing challenges between adversaries, victories, and cultural displays throughout the wrestling season. Senegalese wrestling is an example of a professional sport that is closely tied with local traditional cultures, yet it continues to adapt to changes in the contemporary world. Wrestling is a sphere in which masculinity is celebrated, but where women continue to play an important role as artists and guardians of oral histories.

Notes

1. Eric S. Ross, *Culture and Customs of Senegal* (Westport, CT: Greenwood, 2008), 113.

2. John Blacking, "Games and Sport in Pre-colonial African Societies," in *Sport in Africa: Essays in Social History*, ed. William J. Baker and James A. Mangan (London: Africana, 1987).

3. Buchi Emecheta, *The Wrestling Match* (Oxford: Oxford University Press, 1980); T. J. Desch Obi, *Fighting for Honor: The History of African Martial Art Traditions in the Atlantic World* (Columbia: University of South Carolina Press, 2008).

4. Ousseynou Faye, "Sport, argent et politique: La lutte libre à Dakar (1800–2000)," in *Le Sénégal contemporain*, ed. Momar-Coumba Diop (Paris: Karthala, 2002), 328.

5. See "Senegalese Wrestling: Grappling in the Land of Giants," CNN, December 22, 2016, http://edition.cnn.com/2016/12/22/sport/senegal-wrestling/index.html.

6. Momar Cissé, *Parole chantée et communication sociale chez les Wolof du Sénégal* (Paris: Harmattan, 2009), 139–44.

7. Patricia Tang, *Masters of the Sabar: Wolof Griot Percussionists of Senegal* (Philadelphia: Temple University Press, 2007), 146; italics in original.

8. Nicholas Loomis, "Pro Wrestling, Senegal Style," *New York Times*, May 24, 2012, http://www.nytimes.com/2012/05/25/sports/money-and-mysticism-mix-on-fight-nights-in-senegal.html.

Part 5

Performance, Language, and Creativity

Map 17.1. Kenya. Map by Christopher Becker.

17

Sheng

Expressivity, Creativity, and Rebellion in Nairobi

MOKAYA BOSIRE

Nairobi, the commercial and political capital city of Kenya, is an expansive and bustling city of about five million people. It is a place where old and new, national and international trends in fashion, food, and popular culture collide, change, and are shaped by the dynamism of a contemporary metropolis. Kenya's internet speeds are among the top five in Africa and Nairobi's tech valley, known as I-Hub, produces cutting-edge applications, including the world's first mobile money-transfer platform, M-Pesa.

From its founding in 1899 as a railway stop along the Mombasa-Uganda Railway, Nairobi has steadily grown in economic and political importance, attracting people from different parts of Kenya in a sustained rural-urban migration. These peoples come with distinct languages, customs, and traditions so that, together with a growing expatriate community, the city has become a melting pot of cultures. During the colonial period (1895–1963), the British imposed English as the official language of Kenya, although Swahili—which was more commonly and widely known in East Africa at the time—was used unofficially. Upon political independence from the British in 1963, Kenya continued to use English as the official language but adopted Swahili as the national language (i.e., the language of national identity). Since 2010, Swahili is a co-official language alongside English.

While English and Swahili are the co-official languages, there are forty-plus additional languages spoken in different parts of the country.[1] In Nairobi and other urban areas, sustained contact between these different linguistic groups and use of English and Swahili alongside these native languages has led to multiple negotiations of linguistic identity in the urban space. The result has been the normalization of multilingualism in urban areas, the emergence and use of language-contact varieties like code-switching and code-mixing (whereby different languages are mixed in the same word or utterance), and, especially in Nairobi, the rise of a distinct urban vernacular known as Sheng.

This essay briefly explores the use of Sheng as a voice for Kenyan urban youth by highlighting popular youth culture, as manifested in *genge* (Kenyan hip-hop) and poetry. I approach this topic from a linguistic perspective. Linguists study words and sounds of a language (what sounds are in a language and what sound combinations are allowed in a word by the language); sentences (to determine the grammatical structure); variations within a language (accents and dialects); changes in the use of a language (older versus newer forms, slang, jargon, formal versus colloquial uses); and attitudes that speakers have toward a variety of a language (accent and dialect) or one language versus another in multilingual cases. In a multilingual society like Kenya, it is intriguing to investigate the emergence, use, and staying power of Sheng in the crowded linguistic scene that is Nairobi. Data for this discussion is drawn from my ongoing research on Sheng and from web sources online.

Sheng: Evolution of an Urban Vernacular

Since many people are multilingual in Swahili, English, and at least one other Kenyan language, the question becomes: how has Sheng grown amid these different ways of speaking and why does it hold great appeal for youth in urban areas? Nairobi, the home of Sheng, is the capital and biggest city in Kenya. Established in the late 1800s during the Kenya-Uganda Railway construction, it has grown from a small rail stop into a cosmopolitan city with an estimated five million people at the start of 2017. As it grew in the years before independence in the 1960s, Nairobi attracted Kenyans seeking opportunities for work and school, many of whom did not speak Swahili or English very well. Most of these immigrants into the city were forced to live together in inner-city areas (native quarters), and, since many came from diverse ethnic communities and spoke different languages, language contact happened. That led to experimentation with code-switching and code-mixing. Children growing up subsequently made this a stable way of speaking, giving rise to a mixed code much like Pidgin in Nigeria, Spanglish (mixture of English and Spanish) in the

United States, or Camfranglais (a mixture of Cameroon French and English) in Cameroon. This code became known as Sheng in the 1980s and has become the de facto urban vernacular for Nairobi youth. Structurally, Sheng resembles Swahili, since it uses Swahili's morpho-syntax (word and sentence structure), but its vocabulary is drawn from English, Swahili, Kenyan native languages, and others. For many, Sheng is the slang version of Swahili. Below, examples 1 and 2 show the same sentence written in Sheng and Swahili, with differences italicized. The sentence structures are the same but the words used are different, and there are some morphological processes at play that do not happen in Swahili.

> 1) Sheng: Ma*pinchi* watam*sanya* viz*ii*.
> 2) Swahili: Ma*jambazi* watamw*ibia* vi*baya*.
> English: The thieves will rob him/her badly (of everything).

Sentence 1 and sentence 2 differ only in the choice of words used to express "thieves," "rob," and "badly" (*pinchi* versus *jambazi*; *sanya* versus *iba*; *zii* versus *baya*). Because of this closeness in structure between Sheng and Swahili, many have concluded that Sheng is a Swahili slang or some form of Swahili-English code-switching. These claims are, however, not supported by a thorough analysis and there are strong arguments to show that Sheng continues to be a separate code from Swahili.[2] Aurélia Ferrari states that Sheng has first-language (i.e., L1) speakers—making it an autonomous language by linguistic standards, irrespective of its hybrid nature or closeness to Swahili. This is the language that has captured the imagination and become the preference of young people in Nairobi for expressing themselves.[3]

It may be that the appeal of Sheng for many lies not only in that it is different from the established languages in the country (English, Swahili, and other native languages) but also in its lexical flexibility—its ability to manipulate meanings of existing words and to adopt words freely from other languages, making it respond to new concepts in ways other languages in the repertoire do not. This is Sheng's slangy expressivity: since most Sheng speakers can speak and understand Swahili and English, they appreciate the way words taken from those languages are then tweaked in Sheng, their meanings extended, narrowed, stretched, or completely flipped around in ways that argots and slangs deliberately manipulate and distort word-forms and meanings.

In sentence 1 above, the word *pinchi* (thief) is appropriated from English "pinch" (but the meaning is changed from the act of stealing to the one doing it), while *sanya* (steal) is coined. Other words that colorfully describe everyday life in the inner city abound. An example is *mabeast* (literally, "beasts") to describe the notorious cops—with the implied connotation of how fractious and brutal the relationship between poor urban youth and the police is. Prostitutes are termed *chips funga*, from Swahili "take-away fries," and a job is a *haso*, from English "hustle." Even ordinary names of places may undergo "Shengization"—a process of making a commonly used word sound different and acceptable to Sheng speakers. Consequently, names of neighborhoods in Nairobi like Buruburu, Makongeni, Kangemi, Eastleigh, Kibera, and downtown are *Buruu, Okongoo, Ungem, Isich, Kibich,* and *Tao,* respectively.

Whether at the bus parks waiting to board one of the notorious *matatu* (transit buses) or in the popular cafes and in hangouts and other joints frequented by the young, Sheng is the language in which you hear most young people communicate. With the explosion of cellphone use in the country, the internet has become readily available, and, with that availability, there is a huge presence of young people (and therefore Sheng) online in social media. It has also found its way into the print media, with a dedicated information website at www. sheng.co.ke, and FM radio (Ghetto FM).[4]

Nowhere is the use of Sheng more powerfully apparent as in the genres that young people care for: music, social media, slam poetry, stand-up comedy, film, and expressive media in general. In the age of self-expression and identity projection, young people strive to define themselves to each other and to the world through social media. Many among the youthful avant-garde of Nairobi feel that they belong to a new, post-tribal ethnicity and are interested in things that are quintessentially youthful, unique, chic, and contemporary. In the following section, we examine how this mixed code is used in the genres of local hip-hop, genge, poetry, and spoken word to enhance and give voice to youth identity, interests, and expression in Nairobi.

Genge Music as Voice of the Youth

Music is a potent avenue for youth expression, entertainment and activism. Hip-hop started becoming popular in Kenya in the 1990s but exploded toward the end of the decade and early 2000s. Hip-hop as a foreign (American) appropriation in the form of rap music was readily adapted to local conditions and tweaked to local settings in terms of themes and the use of Sheng as its local language. As Evan Mwangi states, global music (in this case, hip-hop) inevitably gets adapted to local conditions because music is a "site upon which the local, the national, and the global contest and negotiate" to "create a transnational and regional agenda that goes beyond individual nation-states."[5] Rap music's implied militancy found a ready audience in Nairobi's inner cities, where Sheng is not only considered transgressive but activist in standing up to the oppressive status quo. The urban poor are marginalized in many ways, including in language, since the government of Kenya does not recognize Sheng as an official language. One of the most popular genge rappers is Jua Cali (Paul Nunda), and in the song "Kuna Sheng" he sings praises to Sheng and its uniting force across these neighborhoods.

> . . . kuna Sheng ya Calif, Lakini si wote tuneelewana
> Kuna Sheng ya Buru, lakini si wote tunelewana
> Kuna Sheng ya Dandora, lakini si wote tuneelewana

> . . . there are varieties of Sheng in California, but we understand each other
> there are varieties of Sheng in Buruburu, but we understand each other
> there are varieties of Sheng in Dandora, but we understand each other

The term *genge* is used to describe a variety of hip-hop music in Nairobi connoting "gang," usually an unruly mob or group of gangsters. Genge lyrics mirror the militancy of so-called "gangsta rap," the West Coast United States version of rap music of the late 1990s that featured artists like Tupac Shakur, Ice Cube, Dr. Dre, and Snoop Dog. Gangsta rap is graphic and frequently includes violent tales of real life in the inner city. In "Ngeli ya Genge," Jua Cali describes the inner city and its life of crime, jail, violence, drugs and sex.

> Kuiba nayo siku hizi ni balaa,
> Utaagizwa kima na advising
> Pika live tunamanga,

Sukuma, chumvi na ka uganga
Chuma ngumi na teke kadhaa
Boxer vumbi na makamba
Toka nyuki asali na changa'a
Twende kwa kina Farida

Even stealing these days is a hazard
Puts your soul on the line and more trouble
Cook, live, we shall eat
Cabbage, salt, and ugali
Metal bars, fists, and kicks
Boxer, dust, and ropes
Getting out it's *nyuki, asali,* and *changa'a*
Let's go to Farida's[6]

Jua Cali raps about the casual lifestyle of stealing, ending up in jail (metal bars, handcuffs), getting out of jail to a life of cheap alcohol (nyuki, asali, and changa'a are locally available alcoholic drinks), and ending up with the call-girls ("kina Farida" refers to "the likes of Farida," in context). This theme of the hardship and lack of chances in the city that drive young people to crime and other nefarious activists underlies much of genge music. This is also the life that drives young people to protest. No longer content with that status quo, genge lyrics are militant, calling for political as well as economic change. Nonini (Hubert Mbuku Nakitare), another genge musician, says in a track called "Kataa Hio" (meaning "don't take that") that he's done with accepting the status quo.

Majamaa mtaani walimvotia
Walimake sure ameingia kwa hiyo kiti
saa ona vile hata ametupiga miti
barabara mitaani ni hizo hazipitiki
Wee kabila gani?
Kataa hiyo

Folks voted him in the hood
Made sure he got the seat
Now he just hangs out drugging
While the roads are impassable
[Being asked things like] "What tribe are you?"
Don't take that[7]

Figure 17.1. Jua Cali, the popular Kenyan musician. Source: crapudo, Creative Commons. https://en.wikipedia.org/wiki/Jua_Cali#/media/File:Juacali_2.jpg

In these lyrics, Nonini is saying enough with corrupt politicians, inept service, and petty tribalism. Urban youth resent being asked about their tribal identity—it is considered a question reeking of tribal identity politics. One of the most salient forces of Sheng is its post-tribal identity, which dovetails into an imagining of Nairobi and other towns in Kenya, and Africa in general, as places with an urban, cosmopolitan, globalized culture.

These narratives about life in the city for young people—the majority of whom are poor (the youth unemployment rate is about 17 percent) and struggling to make a living in a corrupt system stacked against them, finds voice in other genres. Nairobi's poets are increasingly and forcefully speaking to these and other concerns.

Nairobi Poetry

East Africa has a long tradition of poetry, with some of the oldest manuscripts in Swahili being either religious writings or poems. In Nairobi, poetry has taken on a new vigor and the city is awash with poetry events featuring rising poets of all styles, content, and persuasion. Some of the famous poets in Nairobi include Ngwatilo Mawiyoo, Wamathai, Sitawa Wafula, Njeri Wangari, and Wanjohi wa Makokha. According to Anne Moraa, the exponential growth of poetry and spoken word may be due to "the sheer diversity of our styles," in which traditional poetry styles fuse with hip-hop and American slam poetry influences, and innovations of beatboxing and freestyling are used to enhance "texture."[8] Slam poetry is particularly popular and there are yearly competitions held in Nairobi.

The use of Sheng in poetry makes this art accessible and pleasurable to the youth of Nairobi, many of whom identify with all things Sheng. But, significantly, it is the voice that affords young people a chance to express their views on issues dear to them: daily struggles of living (*haso*), drugs (*mamiti, matembe*), love, revolt against the status quo, and more. In the poem "Kura Yako, Sauti Yako," poet Kennet B (Odongo Kennedy Leakey), accompanied by guitarist Hakim, encourages youth to have their voices heard through the ballot.

> Amkeni, amkeni
> Kura yako, sauti yako
> wino kidoleni mwako
> ndio mabadiliko
> ya maisha yako
>
> Arise, arise
> Your vote, your voice
> The ink on your thumb
> Is the change
> In your life[9]

Another budding poet and hip-hop singer, stage name Virusi Mbaya (Peter Waweru), is famous for speaking about corrupt politicians, handouts, and lack of investment in the young. In the poem "Usinigei Doo," Virusi Mbaya lambasts corrupt politicians who, once elected, forget the electorate, buy loyalty with cheap handouts, and are busy enriching themselves with corrupt deals, poaching, and other nefarious activities while the youth suffer.

> Kuna wazee wengine wamenibore
> Hawa wasee wamekuwa maroba tangu wabuy range
> Kabla sijawachagua walitupromise change
> Saa tumewachagua wamechange hiyo promise
> Mr Politician usinigei doo,
> Nigei job niwe natafutafuta hiyo doo
> Juu ukinigei doo
> Ile siku utaenda ni usoo

> Some old men disgust me
> These guys have become robbers since the Range Rover
> Before I voted for them they promised change
> After election they have changed that promise
> Mr. Politician I don't need money handouts
> I need a job so I can make that money
> Because if I take your handout
> I will have nothing when you leave

About rampant corruption, the poet continues to lament a lack of justice, saying that the prisons and jails are full of innocent people, jailed because they had no bigger bribes to give and were therefore quickly dispatched to prison.

> Hakuwa na doo, hakuwa anatakiwa
> So jaji na prosecutor wote walihongwa
> Wakajazajaza mafile halafu nyundo zikagongwa[10]

> Without money, he wasn't any use
> So the judge and the prosecutor were bribed
> They quickly signed the papers and the gavel sounded

But life is not all gloom and doom. The city is also a place of bright lights, modernity, and love. The young poets of Nairobi talk about their exploits, joys, and heartaches, and through poems (or dramatized poems) the youth express their feelings, hopes, and desires. In "Special Dedication to Ladies," budding poet Brigeddia Poet (Francis Odhiambo Onono) celebrates his (presumed) girlfriend as the only "element" he has discovered that reacts with his heart to make a unique solution:

> Nimegusa element kadhaa kama
> Sodium, lithium, magnesium, aluminum
> Na hizo pium pium zingine
> Lakini mrembo wewe ni mdelicate
> Wewe ndio unaeza react na heart yangu
> Juu wewe ndio solute, mimi ni solvent
> Sisi ndio solution
>
> I have touched other elements
> Sodium, lithium, magnesium, aluminum
> And other like elements
> But pretty one, you are so lovely
> You are the only one who can react with my heart
> Because you are the solute to my solvent
> Together we make the solution[11]

As urban youth struggle to make ends meet in a unique urban reality of a city that fuses the traditional and the modern, the Kenyan and the global, they are forced to forge, define, and express an identity that spans historical (postcolonial, postindependence), cultural, political, and socioeconomic realities. Underlying that identity is language. In Sheng, the youth have found a voice that is neither tribalized nor colonial, but a hybrid of the languages and global influences that impact a cosmopolitan city like Nairobi. The explosion of Sheng in genge music, poetry, social media, and other genres is the arrival and triumph of urban youth on the national stage. It is the youth of Nairobi finding their voice in a world where they had been voiceless and unheard.

Notes

1. Gary F. Simons and Charles D. Fennig, eds., *Ethnologue: Languages of the World*, 20th ed. (Dallas, TX: SIL International, 2017).
2. Mokaya Bosire, "What Makes a Sheng Word Unique? Lexical Manipulation in Mixed Languages," in *Selected Proceedings of the 39th Annual*

Conference on African Linguistics: Linguistic Research and Languages in Africa, ed. Akinloyè Ojó and Lioba J. Moshi (Somerville, MA: Cascadilla Proceedings Project, 2006); Philip W. Rudd, "Sheng: The Mixed Language of Nairobi" (PhD diss., Ball State University, 2008).

3. Aurélia Ferrari, *Emergence d'une langue urbaine: Le sheng de Nairobi* (Louvain: Peeters, 2012).

4. Sheng Nation, http://www.sheng.co.ke/kamusi; Ghetto FM, https://www.ghettoradio.co.ke, and available via http://www.liveonlineradio.net/kenya/ghetto-radio.htm.

5. Evan Mwangi, "Masculinity and Nationalism in East African Hip-Hop Music," *Tydskrif vir letterkunde* 41, no. 2 (2004): 5, quoted in Chris Wasike, "Jua Cali, Genge Rap Music and the Anxieties of Living in the Glocalized City of Nairobi," *Muziki* 8, no. 1 (July 2011): 19.

6. Jua Cali [Paul Julius Nunda], "Jua Cali—Ngeli ya Genge," YouTube, November 13, 2011, posted by "GengeNairobi," video, 4:14, https://youtu.be/U2lseD8eLME.

7. Nonini [Hubert Mbuku Nakitare], "Nonini—Kataa Hio (Official Video)," YouTube, November 18, 2009, posted by "Nonini MgengeTrue," video, 4:03, https://youtu.be/-8GxtU1Rsjg.

8. Anne Moraa, "Spoken Word in Kenya: A Hunger for the Word," The Spoken Word Project—Stories Traveling through Africa, accessed October 10, 2017, http://www.goethe.de/ins/za/prj/spw/plc/nai/enindex.htm.

9. KTN News Kenya, "Life and Style: Spoken Art with Kenneth [*sic*] B and Kuni Mbichi," YouTube, January 24, 2017, video, 28:20, https://youtu.be/z9OU2CC--qw.

10. KTN News Kenya, "KTN Life and Style: Artistic Tuesday, Spoken Art—Virusi Mbaya 06/12/2016," YouTube, December 8, 2016, video, 28:38, https://www.youtube.com/watch?v=VAsibu_VkbM.

11. Churchill Show (NTV Kenya), "Brigeddia Poet—Special Dedication to Ladies (Spoken Word)," YouTube, April 24, 2015, video, 4:09, https://youtu.be/d0tcaG8V2J4.

Map 18.1. Senegal. Map by Christopher Becker.

18

The *Journal Rappé*

"Edutaining" the Youth through Senegalese Hip-Hop

MAYA ANGELA SMITH

In April of 2013, Senegalese hip-hop artists Xuman and Keyti debuted the *Journal Rappé* (*JR*) on YouTube and the Senegalese television station 2S TV. Rapping the news in both French and Wolof, they created a platform for Senegalese youth to discuss current events. In four seasons, their YouTube channel gained a hundred thousand subscribers and twenty-five million views, reflecting the success that the *JR* has had not just in Senegal but also in the Senegalese diaspora, francophone Africa, and the larger francophone world.

Realizing that most young people are not reading or watching the news but are listening to rap, Xuman and Keyti created the show as a form of "edutainment"—a balance between education and entertainment. The *JR* represents a critical space to continue a hip-hop legacy of civic engagement, using humor to offer different perspectives on how to address issues such as political corruption, poverty, and unemployment. Drawing on the fields of sociolinguistics and Africa diaspora studies to analyze their bilingual news program, this chapter explores how Xuman and Keyti utilize music to relay important information to a traditionally underserved market, the significance of multilingualism in conveying their message, and their interest in challenging the dominant narrative of Africa as synonymous with misery.

Senegal, a country of fourteen million people, has a complex linguistic profile. Because Senegal was the former center of France's West African colonies, French remains the official language, even though only about 10 percent of the population speaks it fluently and another 21 percent possess some French-language ability. More than 80 percent of the country speaks Wolof, the main national language

Figure 18.1. Senegalese hip-hop artists Xuman and Keyti of the *Journal Rappé.*
Source: Nazir Ciss.

and lingua franca (the language that people who speak different native languages use to communicate with the broader public). In addition to Wolof, there are around twenty-five other recognized national languages, including Pulaar and Sereer, whose speakers comprise about 24 percent and 15 percent of the population, respectively. Most of the population is multilingual, with the ability to speak Wolof, another national language, and perhaps French.[1] However, while most Senegalese have a robust linguistic repertoire, many do not have access to information that concerns their daily lives. The majority of news programs on state-run television are only in French, and almost all print media is in French. Furthermore, a large portion of the population is not literate. Forty-two percent of the population over age fifteen is unable to read or write, with women being particularly affected: 53 percent of women are not literate, compared to 30 percent of men.[2]

Although literacy rates are low, Senegal has made impressive gains with regard to the dissemination of information in the digital age. In the early 2000s, only forty thousand people had internet access. Sixteen years later, seven million people, more than half the country's population, have access—slightly higher than the world average.[3] More impressively, nearly everyone has a mobile phone with internet capability.[4] Seeing people in Senegal and the world using social media to create their own stories and tell their own points of view, Xuman and Keyti decided to tap into an emerging field of citizen-journalism by bringing together their love of hip-hop, education, and artistic activism. As Xuman put it, "Everyone can be a journalist or a reporter because of smart phones. We said we're going to do something. We're going to rap the news and give our own point of view on what's going on around us. . . . Instead of waiting for the revolution, we are going to be the revolution."[5] With their platform, they educate their viewers on matters that hit close to home through discourse that is readily accessible, revolutionizing the ways in which the news is disseminated as well as the relationship that everyday people have with their surrounding social environment. Because the *JR* airs on Senegalese television channel 2S TV every Friday, thirty minutes before they upload the episode online, a wide range of people—old and young, rural and urban, across class lines and the technology spectrum—can access their message both within Senegal and across the diaspora. By using online and offline platforms, they are democratizing the news both with regard to who has access to their show and the type of content and analysis they offer.

The show's opening is always the same: a black background with the bold, white, uppercase typeface of "Natty Dread Edutainment" dead center. Xuman explained that the name pays homage to both Bob Marley, who brought global recognition to the Rastafari term Natty Dread, and to legendary rapper KRS-One, whose album *Edutainment* emphasized the link between education and entertainment. The simultaneous nod to Jamaican reggae and American hip-hop highlights the importance of the black diaspora and situates the *JR* in a long tradition of socially conscious music. A percussive intro accompanies the predominantly black screen before morphing into the *JR*'s signature musical motif. High-quality graphics disrupt the blackness, as a red-and-white globe with the show's logo spins on its axis.

In the first episode of season three, Xuman enters the scene in a metallic royal-blue suit, crisp, collared, periwinkle shirt, and complementary tie.[6] He begins the newscast as he always does, with a long, drawn-out "Bonjour," before looking over at his co-host Keyti and rapping his usual opening line in French: "Bienvenue, installez-vous, on a des nouvelles pour vous…" ("Welcome, settle in, we have some news for you…"). Keyti, dressed in a navy-blue suit, white shirt, and red tie, welcomes the audience with a similar refrain, but in Wolof. Then, in French, Xuman launches into a scathing indictment of

European nations' disinterest in rescuing undocumented migrants who cross the Mediterranean Sea and often tragically drown. The migration pathways forged from a colonial past continue to inflict grave consequences on Africans in the postcolonial present. He calls attention to the victims as an image of tarp-covered corpses appears behind him. The image then switches to an aerial photograph of an overcrowded boat as he laments that the Mediterranean has become the tomb of their dreams ("le tombeau de leurs rêves"). He reminds the viewer that this is a global problem that will wind up drowning us all. Then Keyti cuts in, rapping in Wolof from a different perspective. He points out that African leaders also must step up and do something to stop emigration through political and educational means. The lack of opportunities at home forces people to risk their lives abroad. The same background images of corpses and overstuffed boats from Xuman's commentary reappear before transforming into the portraits of several African leaders to whom Keyti refers. The newscast then moves on to other topics concerning politics and education.

Each weekly, approximately seven-minute episode follows a similar format in which Xuman and Keyti offer bilingual and often differing commentary on local and global current events. For instance, in episode 24 of the first season they go from decrying the water shortages that often plague Dakar to comically lampooning people's obsession with reality television.[7] They cover wide-ranging issues with remarkable flow, and they do so with a slightly raw, detached sense of humor that manages to make the stories that they are telling—and the messages they are getting across—palatable in a way that other news sources might not be able to do.

Both Keyti and Xuman stress that they are doing more than simply reporting the news. They offer their unique opinions, rooted in social justice, because they want their audiences to see a problem from many different angles. For this reason, they also invite various guests on the show to rap their opinions on myriad subjects. In episode 9 of season one, they ask several hip-hop artists to express their view of Barack Obama's 2013 visit to Senegal and what it means to the United States, Africa, and the world.[8] Meanwhile, in season two, rapper Sister LB discusses the dangers of skin-lightening creams and how Westernized standards of beauty affect everyday women in Senegal.[9] With each episode, the *JR* deftly navigates between the wide-angle lens of macro-politics (state institutions, international-level policies, and political structures) and the granular details of micro-politics

(small-scale social interventions at the local level), making links between everyday life, civic communities, and politics.

The *JR* also conveys concrete ways that everyday people can get
involved in their communities, such as drawing attention to the sociopolitical movement Y'en a Marre ("Fed Up"), comprised of musicians
and journalists. In one episode, Keyti excerpts a music video explaining Y'en a Marre's "Dox ak sa Gox" (Walk with Community) initiative, which is a platform for participatory governance where youth
monitor how their elected officials govern.[10] In the footage, several
people wearing T-shirts with "Dox ak sa Gox" in giant letters march
through the streets of Dakar as rapper Fou Malade warns elected
officials that the people will hold them accountable. This marching
mirrors activists' on-the-ground activity, going door to door to talk
with people about the issues plaguing their communities. Indeed, the
work that various hip-hop artists do to promote civic engagement
has influenced elections (e.g., former Senegalese president Abdoulaye
Wade's failed reelection attempt in 2012). For Keyti and Xuman,
the more informed the population is, the easier it is to demand basic
rights. They highlight how music is a perfect medium for relaying information, how language use affects the reception of information, and
how their primary interest lies in showing a different side of Africa
than the image that is often exported to the rest of the world.

Natural wordsmiths, both Xuman and Keyti enjoy playing with
language. They seem particularly fond of portmanteaus, combining
words to make new ones. In addition to their focus on edutainment,
they emphasize that they are not journalists but artists and refer to
themselves as "journartists." Keyti intimated his understanding of an
artist's role when he mused, "The way the *JR* is structured—we're
in the visual era. Showing things can make us gain time. Doing it
in an artistic way can make it easier for people to understand." For
him, art is political. It serves its viewers by helping them make sense
of the world. Xuman corroborated this perspective: "Artists must be
someone who brings controversy, and from this controversy people
can have a clearer view."

Xuman and Keyti contend that the way they use hip-hop is just
a natural progression in Senegalese cultural production. Xuman explained, "We have Senghor, writers of Senegalese culture. We say we
have a role to play in this culture. And our role is to write songs
about our environment. . . . The best legacy we have is the *Journal
Rappé*." In evoking the name of Léopold Sédar Senghor, a famous

writer and the first president of Senegal, they carve out their niche in this cultural fabric. For both of them, this drive stems not only from a long line of thinkers, writers, and artists in Senegal but also from a socially engaged hip-hop foundation. Adamant about foregrounding the hip-hop origins of their initiative, they reflect on the evolution of Senegalese hip-hop from the 1980s obsession with bravado and showcasing material wealth to the contemporary prioritization of a socially conscious message.

Xuman explained how his fans demanded he produce more substantive music: "Man, we're jobless. We have societal problems. . . . As long as you have the mic, as long as you can speak for us, you have to speak something relevant. You cannot keep speaking only about yourselves." Public accountability thus forced Senegalese hip-hop artists to slowly become more political, more interested in educating the people. Keyti noted, "at the end of the day what is important to us is to build a new type of citizenship, but we can't have a new type of Senegalese if that new type of Senegalese is not well-informed." The new type of Senegalese ("Nouveau Type de Sénégalais," or NTS) refers to people who are socially engaged citizens who take responsibility for creating social change, political action, and personal accountability.[11] For Xuman and Keyti, rapping the news allows the average citizen, especially young citizens, to stake a claim in civic engagement.

While Xuman and Keyti play with genre in providing the news through rap, they also call into question the role of language in the dissemination of information. The sole use of French by news outlets severely hinders non-French speakers' quest for knowledge. Keyti conceptualized the service they provide as a duty: "We take the responsibility to make the news accessible, to give the news in Wolof, in other local languages if possible." Furthermore, he signaled the complex relationship many Senegalese have to language. "Language is something really important for a community 'cause it defines you. We've forgotten our language, or they made us forget about our language, so we got to restore that pride of using your own language and being proud of using your own language."[12] By employing French and Wolof equally, the *JR* makes a concerted effort to elevate Wolof while also acknowledging the historical legacy of French, the language of the colonizer, in Senegalese identity formation.

In explaining the French colonial strategy of demeaning local languages, Keyti remarked, "I think language is really the soul, the base of any culture. You lose a language, you lose a culture. . . . So, by stripping the essence of our languages, [the French] made us feel helpless. They made us feel nonexistent. And we tend to reproduce certain things even when we are conscious of certain things. My first linguistic revolution was with rappers." Keyti realized that the freedom and creativity inherent in hip-hop was a way of reclaiming power and culture. "The only thing that I'm really, really, really proud of, is people asking me how come you are able to say these things in Wolof? You know, it takes creativity. It takes research. You just have to go back, ask people. How can I translate this idea? . . . It is important." Rapping the news in Wolof, therefore, not only conveys content, it also dispels the myth perpetuated since French colonialism that Wolof, or any African language, is insufficient in intellectual conversations.

At the same time, using French in the newscast acknowledges the *JR*'s international reach and its position as part of a Global Africa. Keyti spoke of their audiences in nearby countries such as the Ivory Coast or Mauritania, as well as in distant countries, such as the United States, where members of the francophone African diaspora reside. Meanwhile, Xuman discussed how he is mindful of his French usage by explaining how, in the French-language newscast, he often limits the inclusion of Wolof vocabulary and tries to avoid Wolof-influenced grammatical constructions because he knows that many of their viewers are not from Senegal. "I'm trying to use really classic French. If I am using too many Wolof words in my French, depending on the subject, the message could not be understood by the people outside of Senegal." Similarly, in the Wolof-language newscast, when Keyti focuses on a topic that is of interest to a younger audience, he is more likely to include Wolof slang words. However, he tries to strike a balance so that the message is still intelligible to older audiences and to Wolof speakers from other countries.[13] In other words, both Keyti and Xuman keep the audience in mind when using Wolof and French, respectively.

Whether they are figuring out how to translate concepts in a language that their audiences can understand or trying to talk about somber issues in a way that instructs as well as entertains, Xuman and Keyti's mantra is creativity. As Keyti put it, "we can come up with creative solutions because we are creative people at the end of the day." For Xuman, this means combatting a problematic and one-dimensional image of Africa. "Most of the people—they think that Africa is misery. . . . This is ignorance, but wisdom is a weapon."[14] If they are going to facilitate the creation of a new type of Senegalese and a new Senegal, they must challenge not only how the world sees them but also how they see themselves.

Keyti and Xuman thus see their programing as combatting the fear that an onslaught of negative information often creates. Keyti offered the following perspective: "We would rather take care of [problems] while we're still able to smile rather than be angry while trying to find a solution, because most of the time the solution is not a good one when we just do it out of fear." Importantly, the positivity that the *JR* harnesses in the face of so many societal and global problems does not suggest that people should ignore these problems or be blindly optimistic. However, this viewpoint calls for a reimagining of strategy, where humor and knowledge pave the way for creative solutions.

This chapter demonstrated how hip-hop in general and the *JR* in particular champion innovative methods of knowledge production made possible by new technologies, which in turn grant the audience access to information they might not otherwise have and give voice to a sector of the population that often feels disenfranchised. It spoke to the essence of this edited volume by highlighting the creativity that Xuman and Keyti employ in addressing societal issues that afflict not just Senegal or Africa but also the world at large. The chapter also evaluated some of the successes that this type of work has had in instigating social change (e.g., getting people to vote, demanding accountability from politicians). Furthermore, it showed how the *JR* provides viewers with a nuanced depiction of Senegalese life that allows global audiences to reflect on the similarities and differences between their own experiences and those of Senegalese youth.

Notes

1. For more information about the linguistic situation in Senegal, see Mamadou Cissé, "Langues, état, et société au Sénégal," *SudLangues: Revue électronique internationale de sciences du langage*, no. 5 (December 2005): 99–133; and Barbara Trudell, "Practice in Search of a Paradigm: Language Rights, Linguistic Citizenship and Minority Language Communities in Senegal," *Current Issues in Language Planning* 9, no. 4 (November 2008): 395–412.

2. Central Intelligence Agency, "Senegal," *The World Factbook*, accessed February 16, 2017, https://www.cia.gov/library/publications/the-world -factbook/geos/sg.html.

3. Senegal has 50.7 percent internet penetration, compared to the world average of 50.1 percent. Internet World Stats, "Internet Users in Africa: June 2016," accessed February 16, 2017, http://www.internetworldstats.com /stats1.htm.

4. Senegal had 14.7 million mobile lines by March 2015. Information about Senegal's digital access can be found at "Senegal Mobile Subscribers Reach 14.7 Million at end-March," *Telecompaper*, last modified July 6, 2015, https://www.telecompaper.com/news/senegal-mobile-subscribers-reach -147-million-at-end-march—1091056.

5. All quotes are from my interview with Xuman and Keyti in October 2015, unless otherwise stated.

6. "Journal Rappé [S03] EP 01 avec Xuman et Keyti," YouTube, May 8, 2015, posted by "JT Rappé," video, 7:32, May 8, 2015, https://www.youtube .com/watch?v=lgUQ_xBs0nQ.

7. "Journal Rappé [S01] EP 24 avec Xuman et Keyti," YouTube, October 4, 2013, posted by "JT Rappé," video, 5:36, https://www.youtube.com /watch?v=KqfND-ynq2o.

8. "Journal Rappé [S01] EP 9 avec Xuman et Keyti," YouTube, June 21, 2013, posted by "JT Rappé," video, 5:27, https://www.youtube.com /watch?v=yHevxCIF4d4.

9. "Best of Journal Rappé 2 (Invités) avec Xuman et Keyti," YouTube, October 25, 2013, posted by "JT Rappé," video, 7:39, https://www.youtube .com/watch?v=MiGgqskvFlc.

10. "JTR Medley (English Subtitled)," YouTube, May 22, 2015, posted by "JT Rappé," video, 10:01, https://www.youtube.com/watch?v=2kfiq8mpn14.

11. For more information about the concept of NTS, see Sarah Nelson, "The New Type of Senegalese under Construction: Fadel Barro and Aliou Sané on *Yenamarrisme* after Wade," *African Studies Quarterly: The Online Journal of African Studies* 14, no. 3 (March 2014): 13–32, https://asq.africa.ufl .edu/files/Volume-14-Issue-3-Nelson.pdf.

12. Jake Warga, "Rapping the News in West Africa," NPR, *All Things Considered*, January 15, 2015, audio podcast, 3:30, accessed February 16, 2017, http:// www.npr.org/2015/01/15/377527029/rapping-the-news-in-west-africa.

13. Wolof is also spoken in neighboring Mauritania and the Gambia as well as in places that have experienced migration from these Wolof-speaking regions.

14. Warga, "Rapping the News in West Africa."

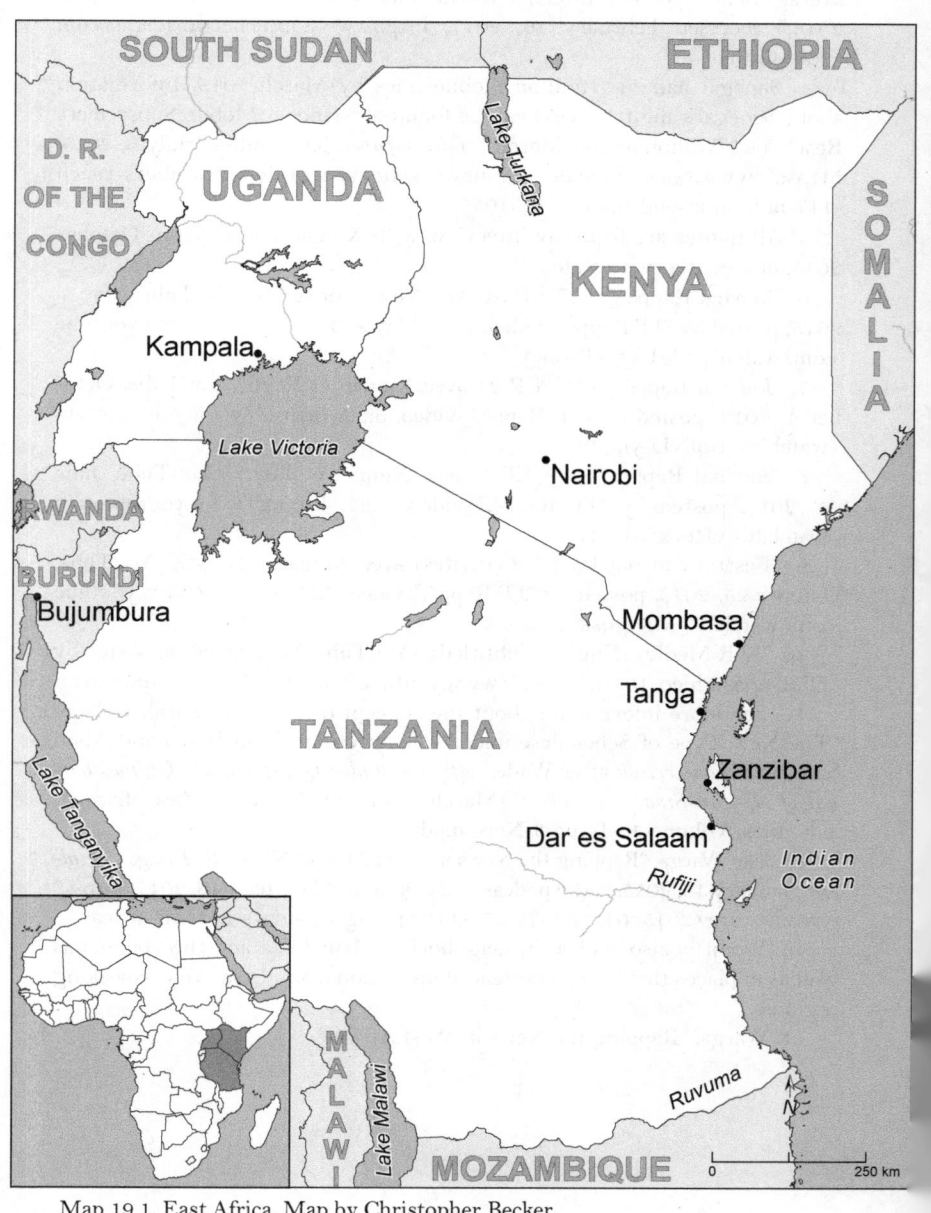

Map 19.1. East Africa. Map by Christopher Becker.

19

Teeth Appear Themselves
Laughter and Humor in East Africa

ALEX PERULLO AND JAMES NINDI

In many parts of East Africa, people travel between towns and within cities in minivans or trucks converted into public buses. The drivers and conductors pack the buses with people, and when seats remain unoccupied, the driver waits until he has enough customers to fill all seats. Filling the bus entails stuffing the vehicle with enough paying customers that passengers become envious of those walking outside, even in the heat of the day. In this claustrophobic environment, people tend to talk to each other, share stories, and commiserate. It is as if the bus becomes a temporary micro-community of shared experience. To get through this journey, where people pay to be packed into a vehicle with one another and, often, to sit in traffic, they try to enjoy their time together rather than lament their predicament.

Both authors ride these buses frequently. Once you get over the lack of airflow, let alone air conditioning, you realize that there is something magical about *some* of these journeys. Conversations emerge about social norms and politics, recent environmental issues, or a bit of news read in the local paper. While subdued conversation takes place on many of these rides, often a bus ride is so full of banter you would think you were at a family gathering. Our collaborative fieldwork shows how these rides are microcosms for many aspects of East African life. Passengers tell long stories, pulling you into the trials of their lives or into narratives about someone they know. It is customary for storytellers on these rides to raise their voices so that all can hear the story being told. And many rides entail laughter, a few of them turning into long, memorable stretches of gut-wrenching amusement, despite the lack of personal space.

On one such ride in Dar es Salaam—a coastal Tanzanian city of about four and half million people—Perullo sat in the far back of the bus on a hot and humid July day. The packed bus, referred to as a *daladala* in Tanzania, travelled on a severely potholed road that made the journey especially challenging. Upon reaching a sizable pothole, which the bus was unable to traverse, a man with a bucket appeared outside the van at the driver's window. The man said he would fill the pothole for a fee. The driver paid him, and the man filled the pothole with crushed stone and sand. The bus crossed over the filled pothole and continued its journey.

After dropping off a few passengers, the bus turned a corner and moved along another road, whereupon it came to another large pothole. Standing next to this pothole was the same man with his bucket. This was a different road, nearly a mile from the last. The passengers started to laugh and make up stories about how the man reached the second pothole so quickly. Perhaps he tunneled through the potholes to get from one place to another; perhaps he was training for soccer and running with a bucket full of rocks to each spot where a car needed to pass; perhaps he had magic powers connected to the potholes.

Ultimately, many people were impressed with the man's scheme: filling potholes when a bus came, receiving a tip to fill the hole, and then removing the rocks from the hole to take to the next pothole in hopes of another tip. They did not blame him for the potholes and instead laughed about the inability of the Tanzanian government to repair local roads. Several jokes emerged about austerity measures and the rebuilding of a new, prosperous Tanzania through the man with the bucket. The humor continued for the rest of the trip as riders marveled at both the heroics of the man and the deplorable state of infrastructure in Tanzania. No person disembarked from the bus without a smile on his or her face.

Similar to other parts of the world, life in urban areas of East Africa can be challenging: frequent traffic jams, long lines at government offices, electricity blackouts, high unemployment, and crime make these urban areas both socially and economically difficult. Despite these challenges, or perhaps because of them, people use humor to laugh at their situations and enjoy the communities in which they live. There are comedians who perform at packed clubs; television, internet, and radio shows that feature humorous comedy sketches; cartoons that appear daily in local newspapers; jokes that circulate widely; songs that provide witty insights into daily life; and a proliferation of social media that features humorous posts. Though it is impossible to avoid problems in urban areas, it is also difficult to miss the smiling faces, the witty banter, the thoughtful play on words, and jocular encounters that people have daily. Even on crowded buses on potholed streets on a hot day, people use laughter to both critique and improve the world around them.

Humor is an important form of social engagement found among all human communities. Studies suggest that humor may have emerged as a means for people to form intimate bonds within a group, to demonstrate sophisticated language and cognitive abilities, or as a method of courtship.[1] In East Africa, humor reveals a great deal about problems that people see within society. The comedy that receives the most attention in popular media, such as radio and newspapers, focuses on personal narratives that demonstrate the absurdity of situations. People laugh at a man with a bucket of rocks because they all know and understand the decay of the country's infrastructure and the incompetence of political leaders. The name of the president never needs to be mentioned, nor the specific funding agencies that deal with road works. Instead, laughing at someone filling potholes with a large bucket demonstrates a shared attitude that these things should not occur, and that the government should do more to take care of roadways. Interestingly, conversations on public transport rarely turn political in the sense of individual comments on or condemnation of a political leader. Humor is enough to reveal people's attitudes and underlying beliefs.

Humor exists in many aspects of daily life within East Africa. Comedy films, in particular, are both popular and widely circulated. Many consider the artist King Majuto, whose real name is Amri Athuman, the most successful film comedian in Tanzania. His hundreds of films over the past thirty years have made him one of the most reliable and entertaining comedians working in the country. Audiences can rent or buy his films in almost any major market in the country. His films are shown on long bus rides that traverse the region and in daladalas that travel between rural towns. Proprietors of hair salons, barbershops, hotels, and large apartment complexes have televisions that show his films along with a mix of other local and foreign movies. There are film houses, referred to as *mabanda ya kuonyesha video*, where audiences can pay a small fee, around ten cents, to see a Majuto film. Even in squatter communities throughout Dar es Salaam, televisions found in communal areas show his comedy films. While Majuto is not the only successful actor in the country, there is a reliability in both the regularity of his films (on average, Majuto acts in over thirty films per year) and the consistent humor of his characters, even when he takes on challenging roles.

We interviewed King Majuto at his home in Tanga, Tanzania, in March 2017 to talk about his approach to humor (sadly, Majuto passed away the following year). We asked him where he came up with ideas for his comedy sketches, and he explained, "Many times, my ideas for humor come to me from the news or from things that happen among people in society. For example, I might see people who steal bags from people inside a daladala. I then write this down somewhere, and then gather some of my collaborators, and we create a comedy sketch from this issue that I saw inside the daladala." After coming up with ideas, the group of artists will run through the sketches to see the effectiveness of the story and humor.

Majuto's films are low-budget, costing around $50 per scene. The average film has around seventy scenes. The scenes are done quickly, without much rehearsal or retakes, which adds an air of spontaneity to the comedy routines. There are no laugh tracks in the films, or even the types of pauses or side-glances that hint at humor in many Western films. The humor comes more organically, which can convey a sense of conversation, drawing the viewer in as part of the moment. The films also appear slow to many Western viewers, as the characters sometimes stretch scenes to get to the heart of a situation. This differs from meticulously scripted scenes where the actors' dialogue tends to be well edited to push the plot forward. Majuto's films, as with many other East African films, give more space to the actors to find the richness of an idea. It may be best to think of them as something between soap operas, improvisational comedy, and dramas: there is a plot, but it can be overly dramatic and frequently improvised.

In the movie *Duplicate*, a friend of his wife's finds out that Majuto's character is having an affair with a young woman.[2] That friend confronts Majuto while wearing bright orange leggings. Majuto does not recognize the woman and seems confused by her presence (he has also consumed too much alcohol, adding to the absurdity of the situation). He then says to the young woman who confronts him, "I seem to remember you." Looking down at her leggings, he continues:

> Halafu kama nimekukumbuka wewe; si nikikuona na hichi kisuruali chako cha soksi? Bado hujaoana nae? Halafu nyie mnatabu sana. Ukitoka Bara, mnavaa vizuri. Mkiingia huku Coast, mnaanza kuvaa visoksi hivi. Halafu kama anaingia nanii, kwenye suruali, nanii siafu. Inakuwaje?

Didn't I see you in these small trouser-like socks? Have you
not changed? You really have a problem. When you are in
the country, you dress very well. When you come to the coast
[city], you wear . . . [he pauses and looks at her leggings
again] these socks that start to look like trousers. What is it
supposed to be?

The humor is multilayered here, which we will explain in a moment.
While the audience is drawn into the story about his affair, Majuto's
drunken character gives voice to people's thoughts about leggings.
Leggings are popular among women in Tanzania, but many people
are unsure if they are a safe, practical, or decent form of dress.

To understand the humor, the viewer of Majuto's comedy needs
to understand that East Africa has had many periods of conflict
over women's dress. From the burning of miniskirts in the 1960s to
concerns over tight outfits in the early 2000s, many people have an
opinion about appropriate clothing in society. Some argue that the
criticism of women's dress reflects men trying to control women's
bodies, though it should be noted that many news reports also criticize men who wear tight clothing. Others argue that tight or short
outfits do not reflect social norms or decent behavior. In many markets in Tanzania, one can hear young men hiss or boo at women who
wear clothing too short or too tight. In some circumstances, women
have also had their clothing torn from them if young men believe the
outfits to be inappropriate. While these occurrences remain rare, they
reflect deep conflicts that exist over dress, sexuality, and identity in
Tanzanian society.

Leggings represent a particular point of contention among many
Tanzanians. Health experts have called tight-fitting pants dangerous and unhealthy due to compression of limbs, which, they argue,
can limit blood flow. Radio commentators have expressed everything
from admiration to outrage for the outfit. Majuto takes a different
approach, to draw out the humor that he sees in this form of dress. In
looking at the woman's leggings in the scene, he becomes confused
as to what they are. Are they socks? Trousers? Small pants? Un-
derwear? In addition, the word "sock" can mean condom in Swahili,
which adds another meaning to the potential sexuality symbolized by
the pants. In the end, he seems completely baffled about what to call
them. Part of the humor here lies in the lack of language to refer to
a popular item that does not appear, according to Majuto's character,
to fit into Tanzanian society. It should be noted that, earlier in the

film, Majuto's character sees the same woman in the same dress and compliments her on how nice she looks. In his drunken state, however, he attempts to make sense of the lack of Swahili terms that can be used to refer to this item of clothing. Interestingly, when we asked people in Dar es Salaam what they called the outfit, many were also unsure. Most referred to them as either "tight trousers" or "tights," while others could not think of a good term.

The authors asked a dozen people (six men and six women between the ages of twenty-five and forty-five) in Dar es Salaam to explain the humor of this scene. The combination of copying foreign fashion styles and the loss of traditional dress featured prominently in their comments. One forty-three-year-old male stated, "The humor here lies in the fact that urban life changes people's habits. The film shows that life in the city is governed by imitating foreign cultures, especially from the United States. Here, Majuto explains that a woman from the country wears nice clothes, but in the city, she starts to wear 'socks.' As people integrate into city life, they live a life of imitation. In my opinion, it is better to not copy bad things." For this individual, the humor focused on imitating both foreign and urban forms of dress, which some view as being un-African and inappropriate. There is a strong desire among many people in East Africa to maintain cultural forms that derive from local traditions. Leggings, to these viewers, contradict the styles, patterns, and norms of dress expected in the country.

Many women also held similar views about the humor in the film and the inappropriateness of leggings. One thirty-one-year-old female stated, "The film shows some of the habits that we women imitate from Europe. For example, tight forms of dress are a style that many women like to wear because men are very attracted to it. In the film, the woman wears the [tight] clothes to show that she is from the city and not from the country, so that she can find a partner." This interviewee gives voice to the reason that leggings remain popular: to attract a partner, particularly a person who may live in urban areas and therefore, according to people's expectations, have more wealth and opportunities. Many other men and women were more direct in commenting about the inappropriateness of woman in leggings who appeared to be walking around "nude" just to find a partner. The humor for each of these individuals derives from their contempt of imitation of foreign forms of fashion, as well as the focus on sexuality over decency.

Other individuals picked out humor in another aspect of the scene: the fact that Majuto's character was too ignorant to realize that the woman standing before him in the leggings was a friend of his wife's. In effect, he was caught having an affair but remained too ignorant to notice. For them, the legging diatribe only demonstrated the ignorance of the character that Majuto played and was not the source of the humor.

The four possible forms of humor in the film—the confusion over the terminology for leggings; the differences in dress between town and city; issues over sexuality and fashion; and Majuto's character missing the fact that he was caught having an affair—demonstrate the forms of humor that can be drawn from one scene. Someone who supports an individual's ability to wear whatever he or she wants uses the scene to show that Majuto's character acts as a drunken fool in his ignorant comments. Others see Majuto's character as openly expressing something which they also feel: a dislike of contemporary clothing that repudiates social norms. Majuto's skill is that he can make each of these individuals laugh, even as they find humor in different moments. To put this another way, regardless of a person's political or social views, Majuto makes use of comedy that can make them laugh.

Comedy is an integral part of life in eastern Africa. People use humor to relieve the pressures of everyday life, to commiserate about social problems, and to connect with those who hold similar views. When passengers ride public transportation, humor can relieve personal anxieties about daily life in urban African cities, while also creating a shared sense of value and purpose. In film, humor provides a means to confront social issues and problems, such as conceptions of urban dress, sexuality, marriage, and labor. In understanding different forms of humor, we can learn a great deal about the types of actions and behaviors that make people laugh. We can see that people want to laugh at themselves and each other. And we can look at humor to see underlying beliefs, values, and ideologies. For many readers of this essay, however, it will be important to know that East Africans laugh and find humor even in challenging situations. To be funny and laugh represents a central part of living and enjoying daily life in East Africa.

Notes

1. Many authors discuss the reasons for humor, including Eric R. Bressler and Sigal Balshine, "The Influence of Humor on Desirability," *Evolution and Human Behavior* 27, no. 1 (2006): 29–39; Matthew M. Hurley, Daniel

C. Dennett, and Reginald B. Adams Jr., *Inside Jokes: Using Humor to Reverse-Engineer the Mind* (Cambridge, MA: MIT Press, 2013); Jon E. Roeckelein, *The Psychology of Humor: A Reference Guide and Annotated Bibliography* (Westport, CT: Greenwood, 2002); Robert Lynch, "It's Funny Because We Think It's True: Laughter Is Augmented by Implicit Preferences," *Evolution and Human Behavior* 31, no. 2 (March 2010): 141–48; and Stan Wilk, *Humanistic Anthropology* (Knoxville: University of Tennessee Press, 1991). Other studies focus on the role of humor in African societies, including recent articles in Stephanie Newell and Onookome Okome, eds., *Popular Culture in Africa: The Episteme of the Everyday* (New York: Routledge, 2014); Ebenezer Obadare, *Humor, Silence, and Civil Society in Nigeria* (Rochester, NY: University of Rochester Press, 2016); and Rotimi Taiwo, Akinola Odebunmi, and Akin Adetunji, *Analyzing Language and Humor in Online Communication* (Hershey, PA: Information Science Reference, 2016).

2. The full name of the film is *Duplicate: Majuto Mawili*. It can be viewed online, though we opted to not post the website addresses as the only copies that exist online are illegal. Majuto does not earn any revenue from online films, nor does he have the means to fight against the practice of posting films online. In addition, some versions have English translations that are either inaccurate or incomplete.

20

Chilimika
Dancing In the New Year in the
Nkhata Bay District of Malawi

LISA GILMAN

Baseball caps in place, the front row of five girls and young women stared straight ahead, their eyes framed in colorful sunglasses, their mouths fixed into frozen grins. They stepped rhythmically, each in her own characteristic style, while swinging handkerchiefs back and forth to the beating drums. With their skirts and blouses smartly tucked behind wide black belts, folded colorful cloth formed sashes across their chests. Jestina Tembo blew a whistle shrilly, signaling to the dancers to change their foot pattern as they moved in row and column formation around the mango tree. This team of *chilimika* dancers hosted and participated in a 1999 competition in the Nkhata Bay District of northern Malawi, where I was living and doing research on local dance forms.

In Malawi as in many African countries, urbanization, globalization, and technological transformations are impacting the cultural landscape. In rural and urban areas, Malawians are embracing Western and other foreign lifestyles. Many in the country are concerned that traditional cultural forms will gradually fade away as people adopt new or foreign ways of life. These cultural shifts and associated concerns have precipitated efforts by individuals, local associations, governments, and international bodies to try to preserve and revitalize traditional cultural practices. Yet, despite these very real concerns, some forms that are valued locally as traditional, such as chilimika, continue to thrive into the time of writing in 2018 because of the important role that they have for individuals and communities.

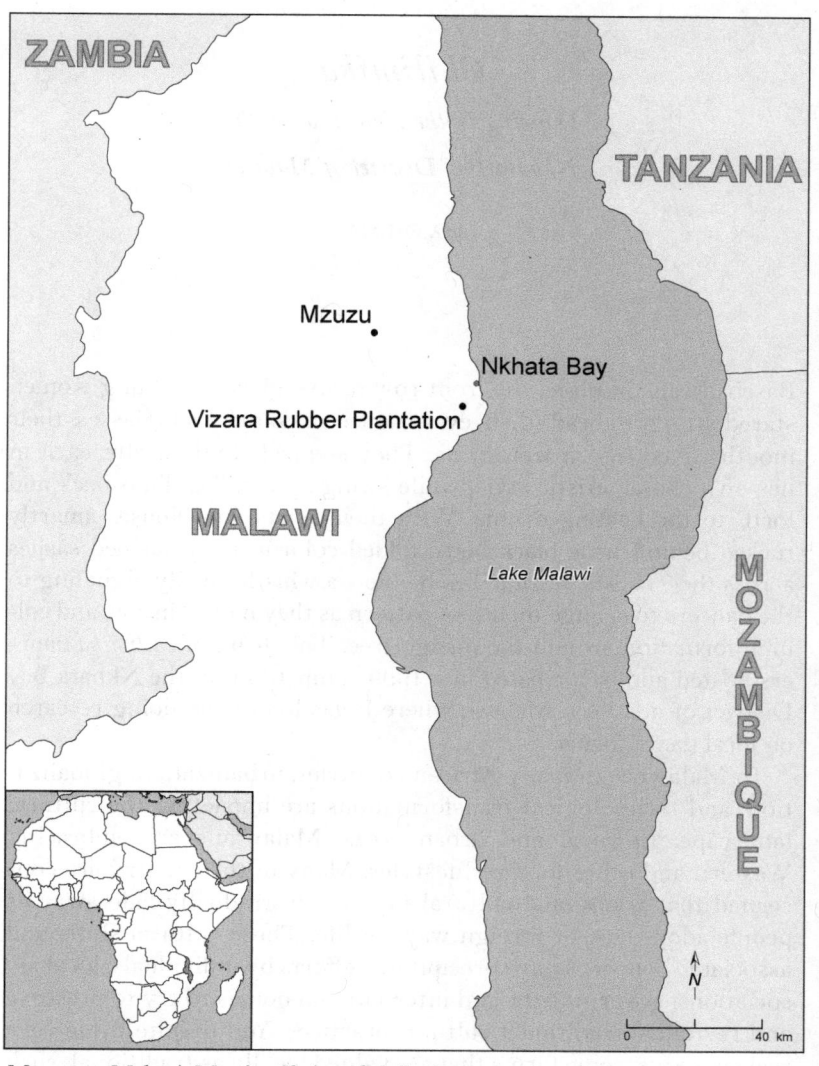

Map 20.1. Malawi. Map by Christopher Becker.

Making Friends and Building Community through Competition

A small country in southern Africa that shares borders with Tanzania, Mozambique, and Zambia, Malawi's population comprises multiple ethnic groups. Its economy and tourist sector rely on Lake Malawi—fifty-two miles wide and 365 miles long—which stretches the length of much of the country. The Nkhata Bay District is situated in the northern region along the lakeshore. People of the Tonga ethnic group make up the majority in the district. However, its boundaries are fuzzy, and residents also include those from the neighboring Tumbuka ethnic group. People from other Malawian districts and countries have also come to work or settle in the beautiful lakeside district. As teams of visiting dancers walked, biked, or took public transport to traverse the miles to this chilimika competition, they passed rows and rows of rubber trees, little cups attached to their sides to catch the dripping goo. Mweluzi, the team hosting the competition, lived in a village settlement on the Vizara Rubber Plantation. Chilimika (in Chitonga, the language spoken by the Tonga people) translates literally as "New Year." Dancers organize competitions that start on and around the first of January and often extend through February. Chilimika is a tradition of the Tonga people and the Nkhata Bay District. Yet, my hosts at this event, members of the Tembo family and daughters of the legendary performer Zabweka Tembo, are Tumbuka. Most members of the Mweluzi *boma* (dance team) were born and grew up on the rubber plantation, their parents having come to work there before most were born. The multiethnic village on the plantation is now their home. They maintain their own ethnic identities and continue to participate in the cultural celebrations of their own ethnic groups in addition to adapting to the locally dominant Tonga culture.

On typical days in this village, children go to school, most women work on their farms and take care of their homes, and men and some women work low-wage jobs for the plantation or run small businesses. Before, after, and in between, people hang out on front porches, take walks, gather water, attend churches of various denominations, or meet in the local small restaurants and bars to socialize. During the weekend of this competition, the village was transformed. The Mweluzi boma had invited five other groups to come to the village for two days of festivities. The teams came from as close as the adjacent village to as far as five miles away.

Chilimika is one dance form within a larger constellation of similar dances across southern Africa, including *mganda*, *malipenga*, and *beni*

Figure 20.1. Mweluzi *chilimika boma* at a competition in Malaza Village, Nkhata Bay District, Malawi. January 16, 1999. Source: Lisa Gilman.

dances in Malawi. Though each is distinct, they share some features. Dancers are typically organized into teams that are named, and each team is led by a hierarchy of leaders. The primary contexts for performances are intra- or intervillage competitions. Row-and-column formations and military-like marching moves are prevalent, though not shared by all. The costumes tend to be Western wear. The dress and steps often, but not always, refer to European military uniforms and marching styles. Each of these dance forms has its own distinct history, though some of the features that are shared by multiple ones are the result of similarities across cultures and historical experience. For example, the incorpora- tion of European military themes is rooted in African participation in the European colonial armies during the world wars.[1] Chilimika teams are made up of twenty to thirty members, mostly girls and women ages eight to their early thirties. Many teams also have two to three male members who dance and two to three male members who drum.

Knapsacks busting at the seams with spare clothing and costume items, teams coming from afar usually walk great distances to make it to the hosting village. The hosts are responsible for providing them with accommodation and food during the competition. On this weekend, members of Mweluzi and others in the village opened their homes to their guests. The local butcher slaughtered a cow so that hosting families could provide plenty of food.

On Saturday morning, the first day of the competition, hosts and guests wandered through the village socializing and gathering last-minute materials to refine their costumes. Dancers enjoyed lunches at their hosts' homes, eating the Tonga staple food of *kondowole*, a porridge made from cassava flour. They appreciated the special treat of grilled meat from the freshly butchered cow. Once full, dancers gathered in the *bwalo*, a central space in every village for important community activities. The drum beaters from each team built small fires to heat up and tune leather drum heads. They practiced their rhythms on the large drums, beaten on the sides (modeled after a marching band's bass drum), and cowbells. Dance teams took turns rehearsing their formations, made sure their costumes looked sharp, and woke up their voices by singing a few songs. At around 1:30 p.m., Esther Phiri, the chairwoman of Mweluzi, posted a clock and a schedule with the order of the performances on the mango tree in the center of the bwalo.

As the drumming intensified, more and more people from the surrounding area arrived. The audience created a wide circle around the mango tree, leaving an open space, the arena for the dancers. Each team positioned itself in a cluster in a spot around the periphery of the circle. When everyone was in place, the dance leader of the first group listed on the schedule blew her whistle. The rest of the team gathered in row and column formation to enter into the arena, their facial expressions fixed, their torsos slightly bent forward, their shoulders moving rhythmically back and forth while they swung their handkerchiefs.

Chilimika song themes cover a wide range of topics. I have heard the following song or variations of it at many competitions:

> Leader: Taza, ama
> All: Tafika tazamukondwesa saza
> Leader: Mukatio
> All: Mukationi zani mumufumbe
> Leader: Kuti wambi
> All: Kuti wambi zani mumufumbe
> Leader: Taza, ama
> All: Tafika tazamukondwesa saza
>
> Leader: We have come, mother
> All: We have come to make the occasion colorful
> Leader: You should see
> All: You should see, come and ask
> Leader: That she should sing
> All: That she should sing, come and ask her
> Leader: We have come, mother
> All: We have come to make the occasion colorful[2]

Chilimika lyrics are a fluid form and allow for improvisation and adaptation to make them suitable for a particular occasion. At this event, many contained self-praise for the team or criticized opponents. A team's accomplishments were glorified, and some songs listed places to which a team had purportedly traveled. Exaggeration was common, for example, claiming that a team went as far as London or Germany. Other songs praised people for whom the dancers performed, such as the hosting team or the chief of the hosting village. Some were original compositions. Others were copied or adapted from the songs of other chilimika teams or adopted from other musical and dance genres.[3]

As each team danced rhythmically in formation around the bwalo, the audience members played an active role. They ululated, called out, and sometimes joined in the dancing. Most importantly, if they liked what the team was doing or were impressed with a particular dancer, they entered the arena to offer a coin or small bill. Some, like me, entered quickly and handed over the money. Others did it with great fanfare, adding to the entertainment through their flamboyant movements or attempts to get the front-row dancers to break their frozen gazes.

As the day progressed, the energy level of the performances and thus of the audience response grew. Hundreds of people crowded around by the late afternoon. Mweluzi's "police," one of the positions in the team's leadership, was tasked with keeping the bwalo clear. He walked around with a menacing long stick, threatening to hit members of the encroaching audience who were craning their necks and bodies to see. As he brandished his weapon, children laughed gleefully while shoving back to allow room for the dancers.

When the last group performed, the arena collapsed as everyone moved in and around the space to talk to the dancers and to one another. Young kids picked up discarded drums and tried their hand at beating chilimika rhythms while other children squealed and danced their own moves. Performers gradually made their way to their hosts' homes, some arguing over who had been that day's winner. That night, guests enjoyed steaming plates of beef, vegetables, beans, and kondowole with their host families. Later in the evening, they stayed and chatted or made their way to public venues where larger numbers gathered to socialize.

The second day of the competition went much as did the first, though the enthusiasm generated by the success of the first day inspired even greater energy. It ended in the mid-afternoon, to give guests time to make the journey back to their homes. Guests packed up, said their goodbyes, already talking about who would host the next event. As they made their way down the road, sounds of drumbeating and excited singing faded as they dissolved into the distance.

I asked the Tembo sisters who had won. They laughed and asked my opinion. I offered that they had been the best, so they must be the winners. Jestina explained that, as the hosts, Mweluzi could not win. That would be disrespectful to their guests. I suggested another group. They laughed at me again. It quickly became clear that winning was not the point. Everyone left with their own idea of who had won, and all enjoyed arguing about it. There were no judges, and thus no designated victors. Though the dancers came to compete and hoped to stand out, the event was clearly an opportunity for sharing generously, creating bonds, and forging community.

Chilimika and Cultural Preservation Efforts

Though it developed in its current form fairly recently in the 1960s, Tonga people consider chilimika to be "traditional," and value it as an important part of their cultural heritage.[4] The Mweluzi competition discussed here took place in 1999. When I visited the Nkhata Bay District in 2013, I was told that I had just missed a lively chilimika season and that the tradition was alive and well.

In the course of doing research and living intermittently in Malawi to conduct folklore and ethnomusicological research over the last twenty-three years, I have frequently heard Malawians express concern that traditional culture is fading. Malawi's government with its Department of Culture, along with the United Nations Educational, Scientific and Cultural Organization (UNESCO) through its 2003 Convention for the Safeguarding of the Intangible Cultural Heritage, have been involved in efforts to try to revitalize and promote traditional culture.[5] Yet, chilimika seems to thrive without any efforts or funding by outside sources. Why does it continue amid so much concern about cultural decay? There are many answers to this question. Here, I will offer a few suggestions as a way to explore the important role that traditional cultural forms like chilimika have for individuals and communities.

Culture is dynamic. Even those cultural forms considered to be traditional and thus rooted in the distant past are always in flux. People continually adapt their traditions based on their needs and in response to their physical and social environments. They choose to participate in those traditions that are significant or continue to have value at an individual or group level, while they simultaneously discontinue or change those things that have lost relevancy.

Why do Tonga people continue to hold chilimika events while perhaps changing or rejecting some other traditional phenomena? As with any cultural form, chilimika is fluid and dynamic. Dancers constantly add new costume elements and elaborate steps, compose new songs, and find new venues for performance, thus contributing to its relevancy over time. Participants value chilimika because it is fun and lively and provides a way to celebrate an important event, the entering of the new year. They enjoy the opportunity to develop and perfect their dancing, drumming, singing, and song composition skills. They appreciate the recognition they get from others in their communities for their creativity. Competitions provide social occasions for young people, especially girls and women, to travel and stay in different villages, enjoy their autonomy, and make friends. These relationships can be lifelong; several people have shared with me that they met their future spouses at such events.

Like many people living in Malawi's rural areas, many chilimika dancers are poor. They would benefit from the government's or UNESCO's efforts at cultural revitalization and would appreciate the resources to buy costume items, properly host their guests, or organize large-scale competitions or festivals. Yet, they do not *require* the government or outside forces to help them keep the tradition alive. Because it is meaningful and important to them, dance team members and their village communities do what they can to find the resources to make performances possible, and thus contribute to cultural sustainability. At the time of the 1999 competition, the Tembo sisters were living with their parents. The family's income came mostly from subsistence agriculture and some assistance from one of their brothers who worked as a truck driver. They lived in a small three-bedroom village house. Throughout the competition season, Mweluzi members participated in what they called *fandi* (from the English "fund"). They raised money through small jobs, often by helping someone cultivate their fields. They used the small amounts earned to pay for costume items, food for their guests, and travel expenses. They kept these costs low by buying only the minimum and by walking great distances.

This example is illuminating because it provides a model for thinking about cultural preservation. In government efforts in Malawi and elsewhere to get people to revitalize culture, there is often an emphasis on organizing opportunities for showcasing arts and culture, such as festivals or exhibits. The objective of such efforts is often to provide incentives for people to participate in their cultural practices and opportunities to display their creativity. For these initiatives, organizers

cover transportation and sometimes costume costs and pay performers small stipends. These strategies are valuable and do contribute to
cultural revitalization. But, in Malawi, a country that generally has
not prioritized arts and culture, these events are few and far between
and only provide occasional spurts of inspiration or remuneration.
Their impact is limited because they provide opportunities for people
to perform their dances outside of the cultural context in which they
are significant, rather than energizing what are already meaningful
events. My examination of chilimika suggests that efforts at cultural
revitalization could be more successful if they injected incentives and
resources into cultural practices, such as chilimika, that already continue to be valuable and meaningful in their local contexts.

Notes

1. See Frank D. Gunderson and Gregory F. Barz, eds., *Mashindano! Com-
petitive Music Performance in East Africa* (Dar es Salaam, Tanzania: Mkuki na
Nyota, 2000); Lisa Gilman, "Putting Colonialism into Perspective: Cultural
History and the Case of Malipenga Ngoma in Malawi," in Gunderson and
Barz, *Mashindano!*; Christopher F. Kamlongera, "An Example of Syncretic
Drama from Malawi: *Malipenga*," *Research in African Literatures* 17, no. 2
(Summer 1986): 197–210; David Kerr and Mike Nambote, "The Malipenga
Mime of Likoma Island," *Critical Arts: A Journal for Media Studies* 3, no. 1
(1983): 9–28; J. Clyde Mitchell, *The Kalela Dance: Aspects of Social Relation-
ships Among Urban Africans in Northern Rhodesia* (Manchester: Manchester
University Press, 1956); Daniel Mpata, "The Malipenga Dance in Nkhata
Bay District," *Society of Malawi Journal* 54, no. 1 (2001): 23–28; and Ter-
ence Ranger, *Dance and Society in Eastern Africa, 1890–1970: The Beni Ngoma*
(Berkeley: University of California Press, 1975).

2. I recorded this variant sung by the American State Boma from Msani
Village on January 5, 1999.

3. For more information about the composition and adaptability of song
texts, see Lisa Gilman, *The Dance of Politics: Gender, Performance, and Democratization in Malawi* (Philadelphia: Temple University Press, 2009).

4. Group interview with Joseph Msamwera Chirwa, Mejere Chirwa, and
Robert Chirwa, February 10, 1999.

5. Lisa Gilman, "Demonic or Cultural Treasure? Local Perspectives
on Vimbuza, Intangible Cultural Heritage, and UNESCO in Malawi," in
UNESCO on the Ground: Local Perspectives on Intangible Cultural Heritage, ed.
Michael Dylan Foster and Lisa Gilman (Bloomington: Indiana University
Press, 2015).

Map 21.1. Mozambique. Map by Christopher Becker.

21

Portrait of a Playful Man

Mustafa, Master of Mapiko

PAOLO ISRAEL

This chapter presents a vista on the twentieth-century transformations of Mozambican mapiko masquerading through the life story of one of its practitioners.[1] Why a story, and why this story? African traditional masquerades have long been held to be the impersonal product of timeless "tribes," especially in colonial anthropology; it is therefore important to show that their dynamism was fueled by the vision of creative individuals. The person whose story I tell was both normal and exceptional: steeped in the collective experiences of his generation, yet endowed with a unique artistic personality.[2] His story is also an opportunity to explore the practice of "resurrecting" older masks, which is at the heart of mapiko's constant inventions and reinventions.

I.

Mustafa son of Bonde was born around 1930 in a remote hamlet located in the lowlands of Lipelwa, a fertile swale sitting below the southeastern ramparts of the Makonde Plateau in the province of Cabo Delgado in northern Mozambique. Less than a decade earlier, shortly after the plateau was occupied by the Portuguese in 1917—the last unsubdued patch of their colony—a Catholic mission had been established on the edge of the rampart. In the early 1930s the mission was little more than a wooden house by a well, but soon it would cast its shadow far and wide, so that Lipelwa was inevitably drawn into its orbit.

Mustafa's parents were peasants who had privileged the proximity of water over an entrenched cultural attachment to the highlands, which had defined their kin for generations. Their forebears' identity and livelihoods were shaped by a collective resolution to ensconce themselves on the thorny plateau that they called Makonde—"fertile drylands"—to escape the slaving raids which ravaged the Rovuma River valley. When at the beginning of the twentieth century Indian Ocean slavery finally tapered out, some Makonde began to appreciate the advantages of flowing water and wet soils, settling in the lowlands below the plateau or by the nearby Messalo River. Their idiom developed a few idiosyncratic twists, and their dances bloomed—some say, because the hordes of mosquitoes rising from the wetlands kept them awake all night.

At the age of eleven Mustafa was carried on his maternal uncle's shoulders toward a bush hut where he would be circumcised, taught manly skills such as hunting and trapping, and exposed to the secrets of mapiko masks.[3] You had to pass through two rows of whacking and yelling men and gather the courage to dash toward the masked figure that stood threateningly at the end of the tunnel—a spirit summoned from the grave, the elders swore—then grab it and tug at its ugly head, only to discover that a light wooden mask gave way, revealing a familiar face: "Uncle!" Once the doors to adulthood were disclosed through suffering and revelation, a boy's apprenticeship would begin in earnest. Elders tried out children to gauge where their inborn artistry was stronger. Dancing? Drumming? Singing? Carving? Costuming? They called it *ulanda*: talent in performance, inherited through the mother's womb—the same womb which bestowed lineage—implying also an inclination toward sociable life. Artistic ineptitude, *udagwa*, was the mark of an ungainly soul. Mustafa succeeded at most things. His elders decreed: this child will become a playful man.

Mustafa's elders also told him stories about how the ancestral masks had originated and evolved. The earliest mapiko had been a matter of fright and confusion, the dancer dragged by strong men into the hamlet as if he were a rabid animal, and so infuriated by one too many taunts about his father's penis and his mother's vagina, received while being squeezed hard into tight cloths, that he really behaved as one, flailing a scythe and dashing at the attendants. Back then, the dance wouldn't last more than a few minutes, and the women, as much as they might recognize the costumed man from gait or gesture, were frightened in earnest as if faced with an apparition from the netherworld. Since time immemorial the masks were the men's jealously guarded secret, but a secret in which elderly women—who danced their own clay masks in the depth of the bush for the girls' final puberty ordeals—had always partaken.

After Portuguese conquest, despite the brutalities and the forced labor, mapiko thrived. Elders came together across lineages to dance in large ensembles; this, they called *nyama ni nyama*, "flesh is flesh"—a person is a person, irrespective of kin. Sculptors carved new masks with elegant downward eyes and mouths, decorated with beeswax scarifications. The dance acquired a broader scope and was divided into separate movements. The drum orchestra was expanded to comprise different kinds of instruments, playing complex rhythmic counterpoints. Singers introduced new songs: winding recitative poems about current events, extravagant provocations to rivals, sapiential verse, rhythmic wordplay, satirical or self-praising tunes. Each group of artists developed their creations in relative autonomy. The result was a modernist performance, smoothly integrated in sound and movement, yet without an overarching unity of intent. The mask's movements were led by the chalice-shaped *likuti* drum, whose guttural sound gave the name to the genre—*du-tu! du-tu!*

From the 1940s mapiko players introduced a new genre called "youthly," or *nshesho*, from the Kiswahili *kucheza*, "to play." They carved naturalistic portrayals of a range of figures—from colonial policemen to Jesus Christ—executed with a taste for detail and polish. The drum orchestra was expanded and the pace become slower. After returning from the bush as a man, Mustafa was integrated into an ensemble of this genre. His favorite role was to guide the masked dancer with the baritonal *ligoma* drum through complex mimetic choreographies, but he would also compose songs for the great swaying choirs that animated the performance from a distance.

There had always been characters, too. In the Messalo lowlands, stories circulated about one of the oldest: Mbangi the fool, a *lipiko* cloaked in leaves which was deployed as a decoy against the Portuguese invaders. It would dash out of the bushes and prance around clumsily, rustling the leaves and shaking its ugly head; as the white soldiers were distracted—*toh!*—the Makonde fired with arrows and blunderbusses, then vanished back into the bushes. Mustafa's father would perform a character called Mpamola, an elder who danced together with his wife by a woven-rope bed. When Mustafa asked him where he'd learned this rare art, his father replied, "I copied the master Nampyopyo."

When he was twenty or so, Mustafa had the chance to watch Nampyopyo himself, who came down from the plateau to challenge his rival Shumu. Women went around the hamlets to announce: Nampyopyo against Shumu! Screwer versus Poison! The contest took place in the hamlet of kuna-Nkalau, by the marshes of Myangalewa. Nampyopyo's crew walked in burdened by dozens of sacks full of masks; Shumu's boys carried even more. They were greeted by the owner of the house, who laid before them pots upon pots of sour millet beer and sugarcane schnapps. Each master's crew set up its workshop in a separate clearing of the bushes at the hamlet's outskirts. Unfortunately, Mustafa's stubble was too thin to grant him admission to the place where the mapiko were prepared, for those elders of yore protected their secrets jealously.

The following morning the masks came out, one by one, all day long, till the sun sank down—*piii!* Each mask was introduced by a song that sketched a little story about the character, drove home a moral point, or poked fun at vices and social types. The battle was tireless. Shumu triumphed for sheer inventiveness and the capacity to astonish. His masks were often monstrous or surrealistic. There was Smoke, a huge, fuming headpiece; Shimmyae, a woman with a live cat strapped on her back; Buffalo, covered in hides and squirting out steaming piss; and the abstract Flood. Nampyopyo won on account of elegance of carving and exactness of reproduction. Never mind the pictures the fathers took at the mission—if Nampyopyo chose you as subject, you would see your replica prancing around to the bright sound of five elongated *nneya* drums. Nampyopyo's characters veered toward realist caricature: the stingy Coastal Woman, who doesn't let her guests sit by the mango tree for fear they might pilfer its fruits; Those-Who-Laugh-With-You, but stab you in the back; the Native Policemen; and then the most famous of all, the Germans-in-the-Hamlet, stylish white people with wooden removable hats.[4] After three days, the festivities ended, and the two masters parted ways with a handshake. Mustafa would never again see anything that stimulated his imagination as did that great contest.

II.

In the late 1950s Mustafa packed his bags and crossed the border to seek employment in Tanganyika. He followed in the footsteps of many who had sought relief from the brutality of Portuguese colonialism

in the neighboring British territory. But things were rapidly changing in Tanganyika as well. The country was about to become independent under the leadership of Julius Nyerere.[5] Mozambican exiles
were also coming together in political organizations that promoted
the cause of independence. In 1964 Mustafa got tired of laboring
in sisal plantations and enrolled in the Front for the Liberation of
Mozambique (Frelimo). He was sent back to fight in his homeland,
which was to become the main battlefield of the liberation war. In the
next ten years Mustafa lived the life of the simple soldier: obeying
orders, hauling war materials across rivers and marshes, ambushing
the enemy, keeping watch, surviving bombs from above and friendly
fire from behind, staying clear of accusations of betrayal, and, most
of the time, starving. Of dance and music there was little, except for
marching anthems and fleeting moments of diversion, like singing
songs to the rhythm of rudimentary rattles—cans filled with dried
maize, the soldiers' everyday food. Except for public holidays in the
liberated zones, all drums had to lay still, so as not to alert the enemy
to the location of the guerrillas.

After independence in 1975, the new revolutionary government
deployed the majority of its Makonde soldiers outside of their homeland, to avert a military insurrection as well as to use them as vectors
of propaganda. Mustafa got stationed in the town of Montepuez in
the hinterland of Cabo Delgado. He labored in a collective farm where
he learned techniques of agricultural extension and irrigation from
eastern European *cooperantes* (solidarity aid workers). Finally he could
return to the beloved drums. In obeisance to the party's program to
"kill the tribe to give birth to the nation," mapiko groups included
people from various lineages and ethnicities, as well as women, at
least in the choirs.[6] Mustafa played in a group of the "youthly" genre
that he'd performed before the war, but soon grew weary. The new
songs and choreographies extolled the heroism of leaders, decried
the vileness of traitors, commemorated the deeds of the anticolonial
struggle, and prompted everyone to embrace the values of socialism.
There was little of the bubbling inventiveness and irreverence that
Mustafa had witnessed in the last days of colonial rule.

After a while, though, a refreshing novelty was brought from the
village of Mapate. The new mask, called Neijale—"Don't wander
off"—was a reinvention of the decoy Mbangi. Endowed with exceptionally large ears that symbolized unwillingness to hear, Neijale was
a mischievous soldier who disobeyed his superior's orders, skiving off

every political meeting and stumbling through military drills. Rhythms and songs came straight from the times of the armed struggle—not celebratory anthems, but tunes that soldiers had sung in their fleeting moments of diversion, often relating comical anecdotes. Mustafa set up his own Neijale group, which danced for a few years, until he was allowed to return home.

By the ancient mission, now emptied of priests and repurposed as a military warehouse, he found a bustling new communal village called Mwambula. Willy-nilly, all the people had had to abandon their hamlets and resettle into large villages—hundreds of houses built in orderly rows, embryos of future socialist cities in the bush. Nobody was allowed to live in isolation in their ancestral lands. Mustafa acquired a plot, built a house, and married. Meanwhile, a civil conflict brewed in the country, which would soon turn into a proxy battlefield of the Cold War. The armed bandits, as the government called them, soon spread to Cabo Delgado and settled in the lowlands, from which they attacked the plateau in deadly incursions. Mustafa's ancestral fields in Lipelwa became too dangerous to be plowed. For almost a decade, he worked infertile collective fields and survived on little. He didn't join the village mapiko group, in which, despite much talk of unity, he felt like a foreigner. When peace finally came in 1992, Mustafa was a thin man with little to show for himself.

III.

One day, visiting Lipelwa, Mustafa mulled over the lessons in irrigation he'd had from the cooperantes in Montepuez. Could he not apply them to his ancestral fields? Channel God's waters to a place where God had put none? With the help of his children, he dug an irrigation system regulated by wooden sluices to divert a nearby rivulet into a broad field, which he turned into a paddy. In the space of a few years he became the district's foremost rice producer. For the cherry on top, he was awarded a veteran's pension. He acquired a spacious plot along the village's main avenue and built an extravagant house with multiple wings, modeled on one he'd seen in Tanganyika during his years as a sisal worker. Now that, against all odds, he had become in his sixties an established man, Mustafa's thoughts turned once again to dance. In the enthusiasm for peace, mapiko thrived anew. The old genres coexisted alongside widely imitated new ones, such as the

Figure 21.1. Mustafa son of Bonde, Mwambula, Mozambique, 2009.
Source: Rui Assubuji.

wild-animal masks invented by a bunch of youngsters in Matamba-
lale. Mustafa mulled it over. Could he leave a permanent mark in the
ancestral tradition, in the same way as Shumu and Nampyopyo had
done? Why was it that nobody built on those masters' achievements?
Could he come up with something as baffling and as unique?

Kutakatuwa—to resurrect or to make stand anew—was the word that ancient mapiko masters had used to describe their reprises and re-inventions of older traditions.[7] In the same way, Mustafa set to reprise Nampyopyo's masks, albeit with a personal twist. Lacking Nampyopyo's carving talent, Mustafa crafted a set of masks out of old truck tires. The rubber made them elastic and unfathomable, approaching Shumu's inclination for the ugly and the mysterious. Then he carved two puppets, which he fastened on top of tall, hollow poles that concealed strings to maneuver them: one dancing, the other drumming. The rubber masks embodied three different characters: Shuku Nwele, "Ill in the Rainy Season," a parody of lazy people who pretend to be sick at the time of agricultural labor, only to enjoy its fruits later; Kunyatilika Anyoke Nnume, "Annoyed by the Husband's Mother," a parody of women who cannot deal with their mothers-in-law; and Shanguku, a colonial policeman yet reminiscent of a Frelimo officer. All wore foot rattles made of dried *meeve* fruit, typical of the lowlands, and wielded blunderbusses. Dancers and drummers wore animal-hide backpacks and hunting accoutrements. Dressed in flowing garb and wielding a spear, Mustafa introduced the characters with a fable about lazy peasants, unsociable wives, and brutal policemen. The choir intoned songs largely drawn from the Neijale repertoire. One especially stood out, a liberation anthem, modeled on a widespread lullaby, that extolled the virtues of precolonial resistance fighters Malapende—a Makonde chief—and Nungunyana, emperor of the southerly Gaza kingdom.

> *Vashitenda ing'ondo, ing'ondo, ing'ondo*
> *Yakulyambola*
> *Yakala*
> *Ing'ondo*
> *Ya-Ngungunyane*
> *Namuje Malapende*
> *Vashitenda ing'ondo*
> *Yakulyambola Moshambiki*

> They were making a war, a war, a war
> Of self-liberation
> Long ago
> The war
> Of Ngungunyana
> And his friend Malapende
> They were making a war
> To liberate Mozambique

Figure 21.2. (*top*) Puppets dancing on a pole, Mwambula, Mozambique, 2003. Source: Paolo Israel.

Figure 21.3. (*right*) Shanguku, the policeman, rubber mask. Mwambula, Mozambique, 2003. Source: Paolo Israel.

The resulting performance paid homage to Nampyopyo's lost art, which one song explicitly acknowledged; to Western technology, which Mustafa appropriated through the use of industrial materials; and to lowland peasant culture and its values of solidarity. At the same time, it offered a version of liberation history that highlighted anticolonial resistance more than revolution, with a veiled critique of revolutionary violence. Shuku Nwele enjoyed wide popular acclaim, all the while remaining inimitable, for none managed to figure out exactly how Mustafa had crafted the stretchable masks and moveable puppets.

Meanwhile, Mustafa reprised another form of colonial-era artistry: *vilanga*, the winding poems that mapiko masters used to intone in the interval between the dance's movements, to comment on current events or satirize specific incidents and individuals. At a cultural festival, he observed a performer from the south playing a *xitende* musical bow,[8] an instrument that does not exist in the north. He crafted one for himself and learned how to play it, marking the upbeat with a metal ring. On the syncopated rhythm thus generated, he sung poems in which he dispensed moral advice, evoked ancient proverbs, told stories of the time of colonialism and war, and lamented the decay of culture and language. His favorite was a lamentation on the lost opportunity to study, which would have enabled him to master technology and bolster his inventiveness.

> Atunatango' vyoe
> Tukashamidye atunatango' vyoe
> Tunkushi doni:
> "Likambale avanampinda ajumile"
> Kala atushimanya
> Iradio tushishema mandandosha avajungu
> Shinema tushishema vanu vakumoka
> Kala atushimanya
> Kenga myaka vandavalanga
> Lipundishe tundamanya wé

> Let's not talk too much
> Us who didn't study, let's not talk much
> They say:
> "You can't bend a catfish when it's dry"
> Once upon a time we didn't know
> The radio, we called it the white man's undead
> The cinema, we called it ghosts
> Once upon a time we didn't know
> That years can be counted
> Let's study, we will learn

IV.

In old age, Mustafa mulled over the future of mapiko. The old patronage provided by lineage heads had been weakened by the revolutionary onslaught on tribalism. But in the new democratic dispensation, the government turned its back to the old ideals of solidarity and pursued only money. Increasingly, artists refused to dance gratis, even for ordained state festivities. Wouldn't mapiko inevitably die out? Perhaps, Mustafa considered, mapiko masters should follow the example of soccer teams, which sponsored the fencing of fields so as to charge an entrance fee. He made plans to build an enclosure by his house where mapiko would be performed for a paying audience. Wouldn't people be willing to spare a penny to watch?

Mustafa died before he could realize this dream. His fragile legacy is a unique, idiosyncratic invention, still remembered dearly in his homeland; a body of recorded song-poems, sometimes broadcast by the local radio; and a faith in the power of artistic creation to traverse the ages, reprised in new guises through the work of daring, visionary individuals.

Notes

1. The full story is told in my monograph *In Step with the Times: Mapiko Masquerades of Mozambique* (Athens: Ohio University Press, 2014). I carried out three recorded interviews with the protagonist of this story in 2003, 2004, and 2005. The background draws from over a hundred interviews with mapiko practitioners, recording of over two thousand songs, and archival research.

2. The concept of "exceptional normal" was coined by micro-historian Eduardo Grendi. On the value of storytelling in history, see Joan W. Scott, "Storytelling," *History and Theory* 50, no. 2 (May 2011): 203–9.

3. From the verb *kupika*, "magical transformation." The singular *lipiko* refers to the masked dancer. In matrilineal societies, the maternal uncle is the main figure of parental authority.

4. Germans were the first colonizers of Tanganyika (1884–1918), and the owners of sisal plantations in northern Mozambique.

5. Tanganyika would become Tanzania in 1964, when it was fused with Zanzibar.

6. Frelimo turned early on into a Marxist-Leninist movement, committed to non-racialism and the eradication of tribalism, sexism, and "obscurantism" (religion and beliefs, as well as traditional authority).

7. This concept finds a scholarly echo in V. Y. Mudimbe's concept of *reprendre*. See his *The Idea of Africa* (Bloomington: Indiana University Press, 1993): 154–208.

8. The musical bow is a traditional African instrument, consisting in a wooden bow, on which a string is pulled taut. The string is struck with a stick. In the xitende from southern Mozambique the bow is attached to a coconut shell, and the string is divided into two uneven sections. It is similar to the Brazilian *birimbau*.

Part 6

Technology and Media

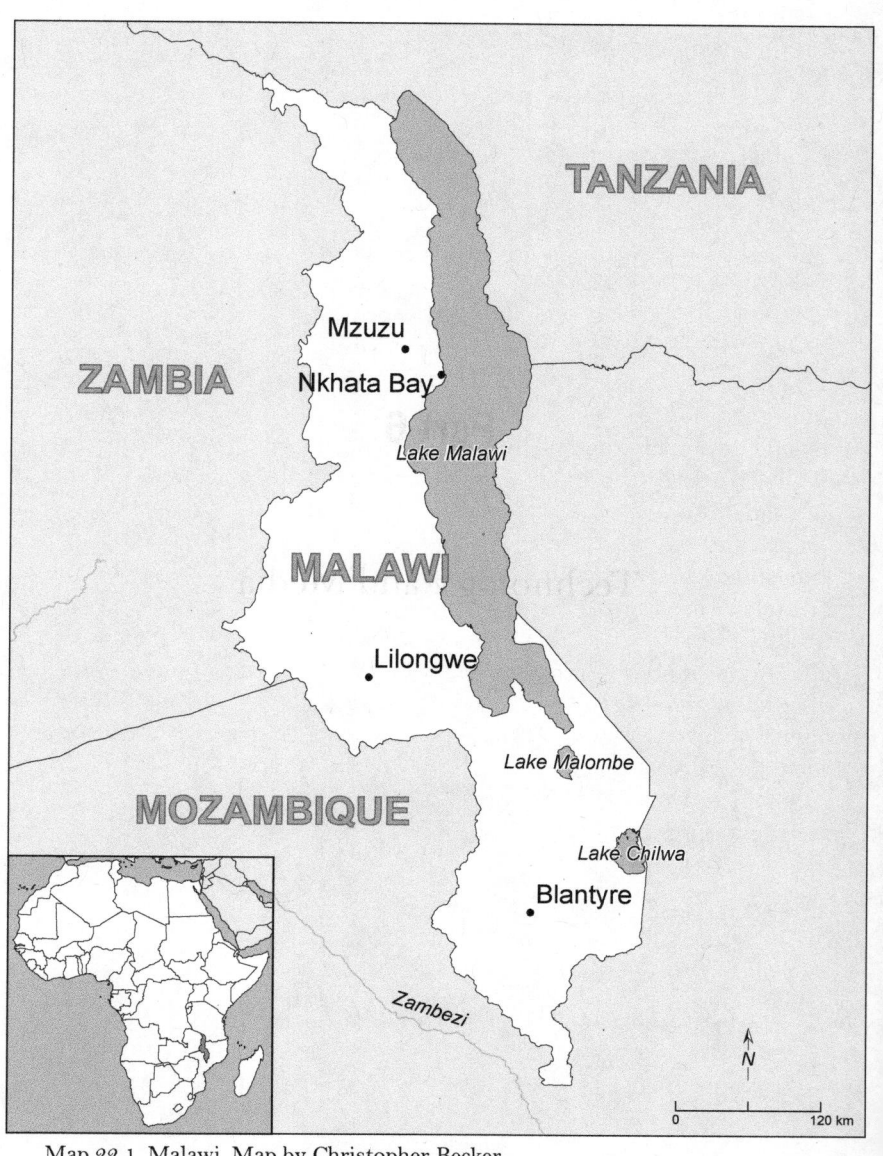

Map 22.1. Malawi. Map by Christopher Becker.

22

Mobile Malawi and Everyday Handsets

As elsewhere on the African continent, the mobile phone is a pervasive feature of daily life in Malawi. Between 2000 and today, mobile telephone infrastructure, availability, and use has grown tremendously across the country, echoing more general global patterns and documented increases in communications access.[1] Mobile phone use in Malawi extends across sectors and domains of social life, serving key functions in the economy (formal and informal), government, community organizations (NGOs and informal associations), and journalism. In that mobile phones appear at the center of everyday life in Malawi in pragmatic ways, they also operate as catalysts for cultural expressivity, as a "cultural technology."[2] On the one hand, the ubiquity of mobile handsets offers ready and reliable communication of extant values, practices, and creativity. On the other hand, the dynamic qualities of cellular technologies and the ways users deploy them have given rise to emergent cultural forms and habits that can augment and/or disrupt those already in place.

Based on general observations I've made across multiple ethnomusicological research visits to Malawi since 2000, as well as in specific fieldwork I conducted in 2013 on the use of mobile phones by a cultural heritage organization and a community radio station, I structure this essay around a series of vignettes and reflections on the everyday presence of mobile phones in Malawian social and cultural life. These vignettes draw on examples from both urban and rural contexts, pulled from my own observations and experiences, as well as narratives I gathered during interviews and conversations. Ultimately, the essay describes the mobile phone infrastructure in Malawi—which manifests every day in a range of ways, from the visual to the economic—in order to provide context for my core point:

the daily presence of mobile phones as vehicles for creative expression on the social-cultural landscape of Malawi.

Overview of Telephone Infrastructure in Malawi

For many years, Malawi has had an insufficient landline telephone system. Technical trouble with the system has been the norm, and phones have been limited to more urban areas or district population centers in general. As of 2016, the population of Malawi was just over seventeen million, while there were only about 550,000 landlines—a ratio in line with the historical imbalance underlying issues of access to telephone communications for large portions of those living or staying in the country. By contrast, in 2016 there were over five and a half million mobile subscribers throughout Malawi. However, with an estimated 34 percent mobile penetration rate, Malawi sits at a lower adoption rate than regional neighbors.[3] This low rate is largely due to economic factors and related weaknesses in technological infrastructure. Nonetheless, far more people across the country have access to phone-based communication due to cellular networks than has ever been the case.

As of the time of writing, there are two main cellular providers based in Malawi: Telecom Networks Malawi (TNM) and Airtel (formerly two different companies, Celtel Malawi and Zain). Calling across the networks incurs extra charges, so many people opt to have a SIM card for each network. An estimated 95 percent of all calls in the country occur in-network, demonstrating the dual monopoly that TNM and Airtel enjoy. While there are plans for a third provider to launch services in 2017, the lack of competition leads to high costs for users. A recent BBC article indicated that Malawians spend on average upwards of 56 percent of their monthly income for cellular network access, making it one of the most expensive countries in Africa for mobile usage. In Kenya, by comparison, mobile users spend an average of 5 percent of their monthly income.[4]

Cost is a component of the daily presence mobile phones have in Malawian social and cultural life. While it is possible to purchase monthly plans that offer features such as unlimited calling and bulk data, these plans are unaffordable to many. Instead, most users opt for the "pay as you go" option common throughout the continent. In this model, users purchase airtime—sometimes referred to as units

Figure 22.1. People are selling prepaid scratch tickets or access to a phone to make a call. It's a source of cash income for the reseller, great marketing and sales for the cell provider, and a convenient service for everybody. Malawi, 2008. Source: Rob Flickenger, Creative Commons.

or minutes—in any amount they can afford or need. Often this means buying airtime every day, possibly even multiple times a day, usually in small batches. Scratch cards are the means for getting airtime, and these are available practically anywhere: in tuck shops (small convenience stores selling food and other goods), at corner stands, from roving vendors, or from the official stores of TNM or Airtel. As such, the logos and banners from these companies are fixtures of the daily visual landscape in Malawi, alongside the ubiquitous scratch cards. Advertising for the companies is everywhere, seen on billboards, buses, in print ads in newspapers, and on the umbrellas identifying corner vendors selling airtime.

Since 2000 or so, I have observed the growth of mobile phone usage in Malawi across several trips to the country. Although spaced at irregular intervals, these visits have enabled me to see changes from afar over a decade and half, and the changes have had remarkable impact on everyday cultural experience. Between 2000 and 2004, cell phone technology remained primarily in the hands of upper and elite classes and areas of connectivity centered on large urban centers. By 2010, the prominence of mobile phones was striking and obviously on the rise. In both urban and rural settings and across socioeconomic classes, many Malawians had at least one mobile handset; those who could afford two handsets had one for TNM and one for Airtel. By the time of my most recent visit, 2013, mobile phones were ubiquitous, used for all forms of communication and coordination across a range of sectors: politics, economics and business, health, and arts and culture.

Descriptive Examples: Fieldwork and Daily Observations

I now turn to a series of illustrations of mobile phone presence that I have gathered since 2000. These vignettes illustrate the multiple ways mobile phones have functioned within the flow of culture, communication, and creativity in Malawi. I offer them in roughly chronological order, tracing the arc of change as cellular technology has become more and more commonplace.

In the summer of 2000, I was wrapping up the fieldwork for my dissertation, conducting interviews with fans and performers of rap in Blantyre. Through this project I had met youth from across the socioeconomic span of Malawi society. I worked with a hip-hop collective from a high-density neighborhood that had extreme poverty alongside middle-class comfort, and I worked with a group of youth who were from families in the political elite. The latter all had mobile phones, while the former did not. One of the members of the more privileged group was the son of the country's vice president at the time. His friends were cell phone users, though not all of them had the same level of financial independence. Late one afternoon, I was chatting with Q (a pseudonym) and other members of their rap group when he received a call on his phone. After one short ring, the caller hung up. It happened again almost instantly, and Q muttered, "It's a dead ringer." The others all laughed. I assumed it had been a wrong number, but asked what he meant anyway. Everyone laughed again, as it was obvious I wasn't part of the quickly emerging mobile phone youth scene. Q explained that a dead ringer is someone who wants to talk to you but does not have enough airtime or credit on their phone. Calling and hanging up a few times sends a signal to the recipient that they should call back—the assumption being that the recipient is able (and willing) to spend their airtime. The slang term had not been in effect too long according to Q and the rest of the group, and by my next visit to Malawi in 2004 it appeared to have faded from use.

By the summer of 2010, mobile phones were far more prevalent than in the preceding decade. No longer limited to urban population centers, cellular technology expanded into rural towns and villages across Malawi. During a short visit to the Nkhata Bay District in the northern part of the country, my family and I were able to easily and efficiently communicate with friends we wanted to visit who were unreachable via land-based telephone lines. And while not all rural residents had mobile phones, there was a common understanding of the value and opportunity the devices held. During a visit to a rural elementary school, we met a class of students during their art lesson. That day they were building in clay, and a young boy proudly displayed his creation: a life-sized mobile handset, complete with numerical buttons and display screen.

Over the course of 2013, I had two extended visits to Malawi and the rest of my examples stem from those trips. Through ethnographic fieldwork opportunities and more informal travel and observation, I encountered a much more robust daily presence of mobile phones compared to 2010. The following vignettes illustrate the ways in which mobile phones manifest as cultural and communication technologies to varying scales and in diverse contexts.

One of the constant challenges for cell phone users anywhere outside the major metropolitan centers—and sometimes even within them—is charging phone batteries. Where electricity is undependable or only narrowly available, entrepreneurial people have set up charging businesses. Open-air stalls feature car batteries rigged with phone charging cables, while more permanent businesses that have electricity may offer charging services behind the counter. In a small grocery just off M1, the main north-south highway, I spotted a power strip behind the counter dedicated to charging customer phones.

In addition to charging services, many businesses offer a suite of phone repair services. These businesses exist within larger shops, as market stalls, or as mobile and temporary setups. Such momentary businesses could be a small table in the shade of a building, a chair and overturned box just outside the entrance to an outdoor market, or a piece of cloth spread out under a mango tree featuring a display of phones and components. Across all of these business configurations, the repair services vary from simple battery replacement to more complicated swapping of parts, such as screens or keypads.

Depending on their agility with the software-based aspects of cell phones, the largely self-taught technicians might be able to unlock a handset, upgrade its operating system, or install features and apps.

In 2013, I conducted research into the ways a community radio station and an ethnic heritage association used cellular phones for their cultural work in Mzimba (northern Malawi). The speed and ubiquity of mobile phone technology made planning and organizing a cultural festival or gathering and reporting news on cultural events much easier than even a few years earlier. For example, there was no internet connection at the radio station, so reporters relied on web access through their personal smartphones in order to gather stories on national and international culture. And organizers of the Umtheto Festival—a harvest festival important to the ethnic identity and heritage of Ngoni people living in Mzimba—depended on cell phones for daily communication with each other, Ngoni leaders, and governmental officials when it came to planning the event.[5] Prior to cell phones, the complex negotiations around the festival occurred through the postal system or messages hand delivered via transport on the national long-distance bus system. The delay built into these options was offset by their dependability, a feature not found in landline telephones or email (which requires both a computer and a landline internet connection).

But the speed and ubiquity of mobile phones existed in tension with some aspects of traditional forms of communication. One day I was discussing the Umtheto Festival with Mr. Thole, one of the organizers. After emphasizing the efficiency in organizing brought about by cell phones because of the speed of communication, he paused and sat back in his chair. He then reflected on the danger of this speed in a specific cultural context for communication: the death of a relative. His hypothetical example was this: it was entirely feasible for him to receive an SMS while sitting at the table with me that informed him an uncle had died. He told me that, should that happen, he would quite possibly fall out of his chair that very moment. His point was that the instantaneous notification would shock him physically in a way that the traditional manner for delivering news of death would not. The cultural norm around such news is that other relatives or close associates deliver it in person, coming to you in a formal way that provides some comfort. Mr. Thole's contrasting examples illustrate tension between the immediacy provided by cellular technology and the cultural expectations around certain forms of communication in Malawi.

The Umtheto Festival itself represents a dynamic intersection of cellular phones and cultural practices. The history of the festival is complex and beyond the scope of this chapter, and although I was not able to attend Umtheto I had an opportunity to be at the 2013 N'cwala Festival in Zambia. The organizers of Umtheto modeled it after the N'cwala event, so there are many similarities. As noted above, mobile phones figure centrally in the long process of organizing and planning the festival. Notably, cellular phone carriers have sponsored both Umtheto and N'cwala events over the past several years with financial contributions. With Umtheto, the Malawian carrier TNM provided corporate sponsorship in 2012 and, while I conducted my fieldwork, discussions were underway with Airtel regarding sponsorship in 2013 (ultimately, the festival did not take place that year).

During the festival, cultural participation and enjoyment of the event goes hand in hand with cell phones. As phones with camera capability have become increasingly common, more people are able to visually document their experience at Umtheto. Social media—especially the popular WhatsApp platform—has enabled attendees to share the event instantaneously with friends and relatives not in attendance. In my discussion with Mr. Thole, he stated several times that he often saw people holding their phones overhead in order to simulcast a performance to those on the other end of the call. In addition to using their phones to transmit the sounds of Umtheto, attendees also make audio recordings on their phones for future sharing and listening. The ubiquitous mobile devices become a means for extending the experience of cultural heritage by offering multiple ways to share and document.

Discussion and Conclusion:
Cell Phones as Cultural Technologies

As the examples surrounding the Umtheto Festival illustrate, cellular technology operates as a "cultural connector" in the realm of heritage advocacy, planning, and experience. Attention to heritage often operates as a daily phenomenon in Malawi—especially at the radio station in Mzimba, with its focus on local community and cultural values—and the place of mobile phones as tools in cultural heritage work is central.

Additionally, the wider and ever-increasing prevalence of cell phones on the social landscape suggests that these devices more broadly function as cultural technologies on a daily basis in Malawi. Cellular handsets are a constant presence as a communications technology, and have also become vehicles for cultural continuity and creativity.

A question to consider in light of the preceding examples and discussion is this: what do mobile phones do in everyday life in Malawi? In the very practical and technical sense, cellular phones enable widespread communication for individuals and communities—communication that is both vital and quotidian throughout social life as people make plans with friends, seek health information, close business deals, or establish political alliances.

In the more abstract cultural sense, though, mobile handsets and the network technologies behind them are channels for cultural expression. In the examples described above, cultural expressions manifest in a range of ways via mobile phones. People use mobile phones to document traditional cultural events, learn forgotten songs, organize around heritage, or pass along culturally framed information or knowledge. In these instances, we can recognize existing cultural content—concepts, beliefs, language—moving through the new technology, sometimes modified and sometimes not. Mobile phones have given rise to new or emergent cultural forms and expressions, such as slang or other linguistic expressions as well as modes for participating in radio. Additionally, mobile phones have shifted the general culture of communication in Malawi with regards to time and expectations around availability and access to individuals.

As such, mobile phones are simultaneously vehicles for continuity and catalysts for change in culture and expressivity. The devices are fixtures in the everyday technological experience for many Malawians, but they are also, necessarily, a pervasive component of everyday cultural participation. It is not sufficient to declare that mobile phones are impacting, or even altering, culture in Malawi because they are so prevalent. Instead, it is more useful to approach mobile phones as integral elements of daily life that have become integral components of cultural expression precisely because they are so available on a daily basis. This is a nuance worth embracing, so that distinctions between pervasive and causal do not become overly deterministic, making us lose sight of the many ways we can understand everyday life in Africa.

Notes

1. Manuel Castells, Mireia Fernández-Ardèvol, Jack Linchuan Qui, and Araba Sey, *Mobile Communication and Society: A Global Perspective* (Cambridge, MA: MIT Press, 2007).

2. Anandam Kavoori and Kalyani Chadha, "The Cell Phone as a Cultural Technology: Lessons from the Indian Case," in *The Cell Phone Reader: Essays in Social Transformation,* ed. Anandam Kavoori and Noah Arceneaux (New York: Peter Lang, 2006).

3. Henry Lancaster and Peter Lange, *Malawi: Telecoms, Mobile and Broadband: Statistics and Analyses,* accessed February 9, 2017, https:// www.budde.com.au/Research/Malawi-Telecoms-Mobile-and-Broadband -Statistics-and-Analyses.

4. Emmanuel Igunza, "Malawi's Expensive Mobile Phone Habit," BBC News, February 20, 2015, http://www.bbc.com/news/world-africa-31533397.

5. See Lisa Gilman, "The Politics of Cultural Promotion: The Case of the Umthetho Festival of Malawi's Northern Ngoni," in *Public Performances: Studies in the Carnivalesque and Ritualesque,* ed. Jack Santino (Logan: Utah State University Press, 2017).

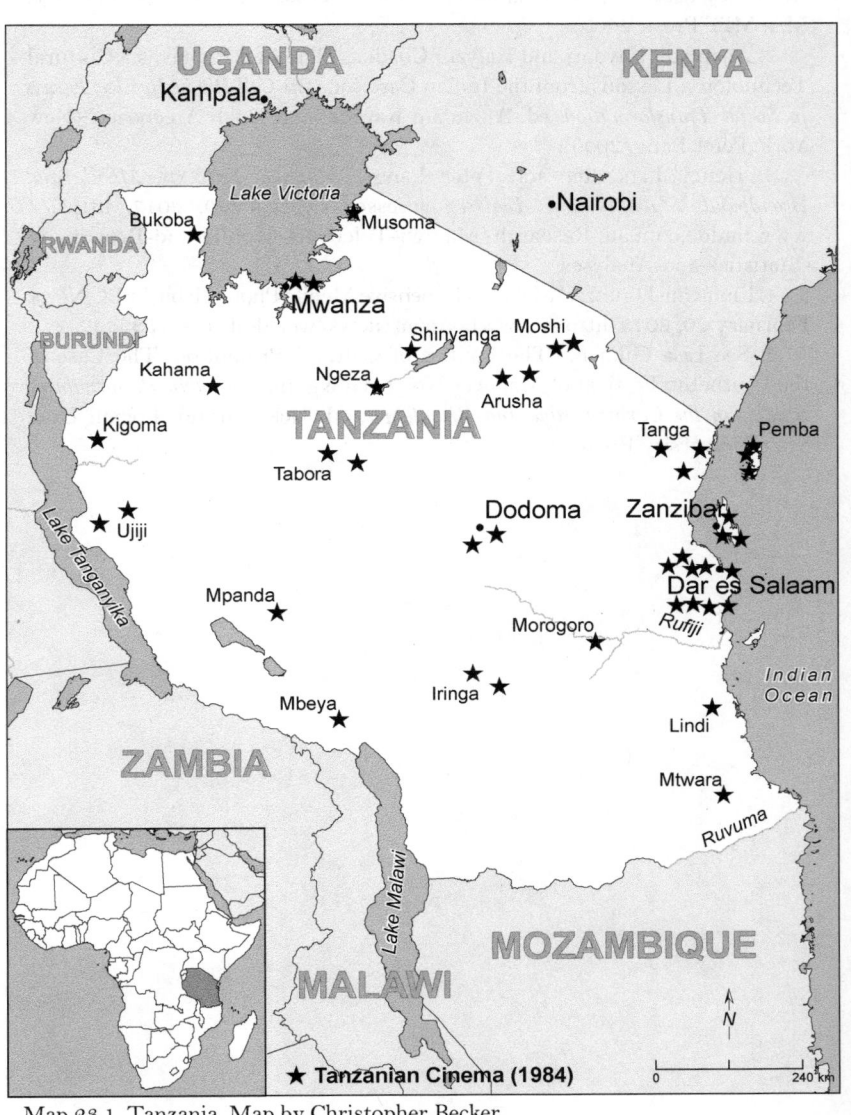

Map 23.1. Tanzania. Map by Christopher Becker.

23

Meeting Up at the Movies in Tanzania

LAURA FAIR

Imagine growing up in a place and at a time when at least once a week, *everyone* you knew, and hundreds you did not, gathered together to frolic in the city center. When each Sunday, over the course of your entire adolescence, cousins, siblings, schoolmates, and neighbors, along with everyone's aunts, uncles, parents, and out-of-town guests walked down the main street to the local theater to take in the latest film to hit the town. Think about the social impact on yourself and your community if young and old, rich and poor, male and female, as well as those of every conceivable color and religious affiliation went to the same place for entertainment and watched the same thought-provoking movie. What would it mean if, before and after the film, a thousand people—individuals, families, and small groups—hung out for hours, greeting each other, catching up on local gossip and news, eating ice cream, socializing in the streets, and debating the meaning of the film? This is what Sundays were like for several generations of urban Tanzanians.

Contemporary readers might take large, urban, integrated spaces for granted. But in colonial Africa, this was often far from the case. From approximately 1890 to 1960, across the continent, European powers tried to limit Africans' rights to live in the cities and did their upmost to curtail their freedom of movement in town at night. However, colonial authorities' ability to keep Africans out of the cities varied across the continent. In South Africa, Zimbabwe, and Kenya, Africans had to carry passes and were legally allowed inside city limits only for work. In Zambia and the Congo, control was not so strict, although it was still next to impossible for Africans to enter a commercial cinema prior to independence. But in Tanzania, Europeans' ability to keep Africans away from the movie houses was more constrained.[1] Here, from as early as the 1910s, Africans enjoyed urban moviegoing on a regular basis. By the 1950s, going to the cinema was by far the most popular urban pastime in the nation. Exploring the creative ways Tanzanians engaged with global films, how young people utilized cinematic space for distinctly generational pleasures, and how cinemas figured into romantic relationships are the three central themes addressed in this essay.

The author of this chapter is a historian, which means she is not only interested in the past, but in understanding both change and continuity over time. My research involved analyzing records from colonial and postcolonial government officials as well as business records from individual cinemas, including box-office receipts. Interviews with those who worked at or went to the cinemas were also critically important. In addition to interviews in the Swahili language with more than a hundred men and women, I also conducted surveys and ran essay contests in numerous towns to learn about Tanzanians' favorite stars, films, and memories of going to the movies, as well as how cinematic habits and preferences varied over space and time.

Historical Background

Zanzibar, one of many Swahili city-states along the East African coast, rose to prominence in the nineteenth century as the main commercial center linking goods and peoples from East Africa with others from across the Indian and Atlantic Oceans. Its position intensified after 1830, when the Sultan of Oman moved his capital to the isles and began inviting merchants from what are today India and Pakistan to settle there. Even after the British declared Zanzibar part of their empire in 1890, Zanzibar remained an important point of commercial activity in the region. It was the epicenter from which local traders and businessmen spread cinematic entertainment throughout East Africa, as well as the first place in the region to have a permanent modern venue dedicated specifically for cinematic entertainment, built by a Zanzibari immigrant entrepreneur in 1921.

Zanzibar's importance in the movie industry stemmed not only from its prominent position in trade, but also because in 1900 the city had a population of nearly fifty thousand, making it one of the most urbanized places on the continent. Dense populations provided assurance of potential customers at a time when everyone who went walked to the show. In the 1940s and 1950s, as newer regional towns grew and local entrepreneurs amassed capital, they, too, invested in civic and artistic culture, spreading cinemas across the Tanzanian mainland.

In colonial Africa, moviegoing was largely an urban phenomenon. But before independence, in the early 1960s, less than three percent of Tanzania's total population of just under nine million lived in towns. During the coming decades urban populations soared, as did the percentage of young people living in towns. By 1978, Tanzania's urban population had increased nearly five-fold and almost 75 percent of all migrants to towns were in their teens and twenties. By the late 1970s, youth outnumbered those over forty by five to one in many Tanzanian towns. Demographically speaking, the city was a great place to be if you were young.[2]

As early as the 1950s, moviegoing was so popular in many cities that tickets frequently sold out. In Zanzibar and Dar es Salaam, demand for tickets was so intense that it spurred a vibrant black market. Numerous men lived their entire adult lives, even building homes, on the earnings they made from scalping cinema tickets in these two towns. From the 1950s through the 1980s, Sunday moviegoing was the quintessential form of family entertainment across Tanzania. On Tuesday, tickets were released for the coming Sunday show, and most people booked their seats to avoid dealing with scalpers later in the week. Midweek was spent in anxious anticipation of the stars and themes featured in the coming attraction. By Friday, attention turned to what to wear, what to cook for the communal meal before the outing, and which neighbors, friends, and classmates might be going as well. The Sunday movie and associated festivities were the highlight of many people's week.

From the earliest days, young people also went to the movies with groups of friends, Monday through Saturday. Boys as young as eight or nine years old took in Laurel and Hardy comedies and Charlie Chaplin films in the 1920s and 1930s, or cowboy and action films as the years wore on. If their parents were not wealthy enough to give them money for admission, they earned their entrance running errands for neighbors or local shopkeepers, collecting soda bottles that they returned for deposit, or pestering the local cinema owner until he let them in for free. Most theaters also sold tickets for the seats closest to the screen for just a few pennies, making moviegoing easily affordable for young boys. Known as the "ruffian rows," this was where boys and teens gathered inside the theaters and interacted with life on the screen. They shouted, threw punches at the villains, and sang and danced along with the lovers in the film. Girls, too, went to the movies with their friends, but before the 1970s they were rarely as free as boys to wander the town. Most had to secure both money and permission from their parents to see a show. Along the coast, where the majority of the population is Muslim, theater owners offered special shows where men were not allowed. Known as "ladies' shows," these screenings brought three, four, or five hundred female teens and women down to the theater for matinees each week. For the old as well as for the young, male and female, the cinema was where urban Tanzanians went to see and be seen.

Films from Egypt, Europe, Japan, Hong Kong, and the United States were screened in Tanzania, but, across generations, it was Indian films that stole the show. Indian films featured numerous song and dance sequences, which East African audiences adored, and the stories also appealed to Tanzanian crowds. Indian melodramas from this era dealt explicitly with struggles between the poor and the wealthy, political corruption, and the heartache of youth who wanted to marry across class and communal divides. Indian films were also told visually, so that even if you could not understand the dialogue you could understand the drama and the key debates in a film. But each generation of moviegoers also had additional genres and national film styles that caught its fancy. After the show, Tanzanian audiences took their interpretations of the film onto the streets, where they engaged in animated debates about the film, the characters, the themes, and their relevance, or not, to local lives and society. The most popular films provided viewers with material they could blend, bend, and refashion to speak to their own dreams and desires.

Independence at the Show

In the postindependence era, cinemas took on a new youthful vibe. Nowhere else in the city was there a space capable of holding five hundred to a thousand people where youth could gather, socialize, and consort largely beyond the gaze of adults. By the early 1980s, 60 percent of youthful moviegoers in the capital city of Dar es Salaam went to the movies at least once a week, and half of those went twice a week or more. Many of the men I interviewed said they went to the movies almost every night. For kids born after independence, the social and cultural experience of moviegoing helped to distinguish them from their elders' largely rural ways and time.

With the help of accommodating theater owners and managers, young people increasingly took over cinemas, making them their own every day except Sunday. The Avalon Cinema in Dar es Salaam, which opened in 1945, became the venue for regular battle-of-the-bands competitions beginning in the mid-1960s. There were nearly a dozen different categories in the competition, from local genres to jazz and rock 'n' roll. Organized and run by youth themselves, these annual competitions catapulted many to the status of local stars. Ali, a Muslim teen who served as the lead singer in a group of Elvis impersonators, recalled how terrifying it was to perform before more than eight hundred screaming, very judgmental peers at the Avalon. But he and his friends won first place in the category of rock 'n' roll two years in a row. Afterwards, neither he nor his bandmates could walk down the street without being greeted with "Hey, man, you were great at the Avalon!" In Dar es Salaam, it was Ali and his pals, not Elvis, who rocked.

Figure 23.1. Avalon Cinema, Dar es Salaam, c. 1945. Source: Personal collection of Asad Talati.

Figure 23.2. The Big Five, Elvis tribute band, on the stage of the Avalon cinema, Dar es Salaam. Source: Photo courtesy of Ali Ghafoor (*center*), the lead singer.

During these same decades, city youth also convinced the managers of the drive-in to turn over the theater to them on Wednesday night for charity shows. Ostensibly, the purpose of the evening was to raise money for orphans, the Red Cross and Red Crescent, or the children's ward at a local clinic and hospital. Schools, classes, and social clubs competed to see who could raise the most money, providing a wonderful excuse for thousands of kids looking to stay out past midnight on a school night. Admission was also paid per vehicle, not per person, adding an additional element of competition to the event: how many people could you squeeze into a car? Soccer teams filled pickup trucks with thirty or more players and fans. One woman recalled regularly filling the family station wagon with no less than twenty of her closest friends for these events. When *Herbie* films were screened, everyone inside a Volkswagen Beetle got in for free. Several people described their experiences, laughing hysterically as they recalled cramming eight to ten people inside a VW Bug. Once inside, everyone spilled from the vehicles, setting out blankets and mats or simply wandering around to socialize. No one I spoke to remembered the movies they saw at these events. What they recalled was the thrill of being part of the largest late-night gathering of youth in town, seeing friends en masse, and meeting kids from other schools and parts of town. In Moshi and Morogoro, too, youth convinced movie house managers to offer back-to-back-to-back features on holidays and for charity, allowing youth to stay out until dawn at the cinemas.

In the 1970s and 1980s, while many youth went to see the latest Indian family-centered melodrama with their parents on Sunday, Tuesday through Saturday they also went with small groups of friends to see films their parents might likely disapprove of. Studios across the globe began producing films directed specifically at a rebellious young demographic. Social, political, racial, and sexual tensions were portrayed on screen like never before. *Hare Rama Hare Krishna* (Anand, 1971) centered on a girl who ran away from a neglectful father and found refuge in a commune of dope-smoking Hare Krishna hippies in India. *Disco Dancer* (Shubash, 1982), infused with psychedelic swirling colors and youth dancing in ways that would surely shock the elders, took Tanzania by storm, ushering in a new era of disco dance clubs. Blaxploitation films, featuring R&B and funk soundtracks and black actors who defeat corrupt white police and city officials, were considered cool, racy, and popular. Bruce Lee's films were also hot. Actresses like Angela Mao (*Lady Whirlwind*, 1972, and *Enter the Dragon*, 1973) and Pam Grier (*Coffy*, 1973, and *Foxy Brown*, 1974), who played smart, capable female martial artists, were also hugely popular. Tanzanian youth of all gender identities were inspired by cinematic martial artists and many took up martial arts themselves. These new genres of film—featuring strong women and winning men of color—turned white colonial narratives and Hollywood stereotypes of race and gender on their heads. Such images spoke directly to Tanzanians who were actively asserting their own ability to forge a new social, economic, and political world through their support of transnational black liberation movements.

Dating at the Movies

Tanzanians across generations made use of both the physical and imaginary space of moviegoing to date and debate the meaning of "true love." Filmgoing provided opportunities to engage imaginative possibilities and fostered dreams about alternative ways of living and loving. Films also instigated intensive debates among families and friends about the choices, constraints, and ethics of specific characters and their dilemmas. In a social context where teens and parents went to the movies together, film texts fostered gendered and generational deliberations about patriarchy and power as well as how to manage filial, romantic, and other types of love.[3]

Gay or straight, nearly every East African gets married and has children at some point in their life, and up until the 1990s, most marriages were arranged by family elders, not by individuals in a conjugal couple. One of the many reasons Indian films were so popular in East Africa is that similar family traditions were also common in India, and the stresses and strains of life under patriarchal authority were common themes in films. When families emerged from the Sunday movie, they immediately set about debating the heroes, villains, subplots, and scenes. In some cases, these contests of opinion would continue for days and weeks. In the process, individuals of all ages were able to think through their own positions on a host of issues, publicly assert positions about their own romantic dreams and domestic desires, and discursively define the boundaries they wanted others to respect.

Theaters were also common urban spaces where couples rendezvoused for a date. As hundreds of people gathered outside of the theater before and after the show, young people might smile and at least visually flirt with someone they found attractive. In the 1960s, adventurous youth might even make a clandestine plan—arranged via friends, siblings, and cousins—to meet their romantic interest at the local theater to see a particular film. Rarely would they sit together, but many said simply sneaking to see the same film constituted a date. By the 1970s, bold couples might arrange to meet during a Sunday screening by feigning the need to use the bathroom when the third song-and-dance number began. Near the bathrooms they might exchange a few words before rejoining their elders, who remained oblivious to their secret romantic rendezvous. Charity-night shows at the drive-in were another frequent space for young couples to meet. No one I interviewed ever confessed to kissing, or anything else, at these shows. As one man said when asked if youth used the opportunity to make out, "Are you kidding? With four thousand prying eyes looking for something to gossip about? No way!" Another woman assured me that if you did something like that, word would reach home to your parents before you did, and you would be barred from the movies entirely. At charity shows, a far more typical physical expression of love was for a young man to corral a few of his friends into helping him serenade a girl he fancied with a popular love song from the film, as she sat with her siblings and friends. Youth in these days generally still accepted and respected cultural and religious mores that made premarital sexual experimentation rare. Romance during these years was about emotions, not about physical sex.

In the context of arranged marriage, newlyweds also used the space and time of the show to bring their emotional relationship to a higher plane. Most couples lived with their in-laws, or large extended families, and rarely had space outside of their bedroom to be alone. Sunday Indian films gave them the opportunity to take off, alone, in the late afternoon to spend the rest of the evening together at the show. As slowly as possible, they strolled back home. To paraphrase one man who regularly went to the movies with his wife when they were newlyweds, "This was the only time we had to be alone. We made a habit of getting out of the house together and going to see Indian films. These films always left us talking about love, what true love was, and what a good domestic relationship looked like. This wasn't something we usually talked about after seeing an action film."

By the 1980s, however, youth began to push at earlier social and sexual norms. Dating before marriage became something that many increasingly aspired to do. For those enrolled at the university, going to the movies on Friday or Saturday night with a date became the epitome of "cool." In one survey conducted in the early 1980s, 70 percent of the Friday night crowd at a Dar es Salaam cinema was there with a date. Dance clubs, discos, and bars were also common places to go, but for those who found such venues too rambunctious, or who eschewed places where alcohol was served, going to the movies was a common place to date. At the movies, a couple could be "alone" but simultaneously surrounded by several hundred others. Both men and women said that they found this reassuring, as it removed the pressure or expectation of physical contact. Dating, for most, involved a night out on the town, talking, and perhaps ice cream.

But in the 1980s, movies were also becoming increasingly risqué, and many youth across the globe (including the author) looked to these rather explicit films for something approaching sex education. In many communities in Tanzania there were long-standing traditions of initiation, where children approaching puberty were instructed by particular elders from their community about matters of physical maturation, moral expectations, sexual desires and gratification, as well as how to enhance the chances for getting pregnant and how to prevent pregnancy. But as more and more teens began going to boarding school after independence, and increasing numbers moved to town, these earlier traditions began to wane. So, as new genres of erotica began to hit global screens, many Tanzanian youth went to the movies to look and to learn. The lessons provided by film were far less thorough than the instruction provided by community-based sexual health instructors of the past, but it filled a pressing need. *Young Lady Chatterley* (1977) and *Endless Love* (1981) were two films of this type that legions of young people in Tanzania went to see. These films were so popular that many students ended up buying tickets on the black market and paying two to three times the ticket-window price to watch actors make love on screen.

Even here, however, there were continuities. Both youth who went through initiation in the countryside and those who snuck off to see erotic films, bonded as a cohort. Both groups also emerged with more possibilities to ponder, new things to debate with their friends, and, if they dared, more ways to needle and press their parents.

Notes

1. Laura Fair, *Reel Pleasures: Cinema Audiences and Entrepreneurs in Twentieth-Century Urban Tanzania* (Athens: Ohio University Press, 2018); Odile Goerg, *Fantômas sous les tropiques: Aller au cinéma en Afrique colonial* (Paris: Vendémiaire, 2015); James Burns, *Cinema and Society in the British Empire, 1895–1940* (New York: Palgrave Macmillan, 2013); James Burns, "John Wayne on the Zambezi: Cinema, Empire, and the American Western in British Central Africa," in "Leisure in African History," ed. Emmanuel

Akyeampong and Charles Ambler, special issue, *International Journal of African Historical Studies* 35, no. 1 (2002): 103–17; Charles Ambler, "Popular Films and Colonial Audiences: The Movies in Northern Rhodesia," *American Historical Review* 106, no. 1 (2001): 81–105.

2. M. A. Bienefeld and R. H. Sabot, *The National Urban Mobility, Employment and Income Survey of Tanzania (NUMEIST)* (Dar es Salaam: Ministry of Economic Affairs and Development Planning and Economic Research Bureau, 1971); P. P. Namfua, "Age, Sex, Marital Status," in *Analysis of the 1978 Population Census*, ed. Bureau of Statistics (Dar es Salaam: Ministry of Planning and Economic Affairs, 1982); United Republic of Tanzania, Bureau of Statistics, *Kilimanjaro Region Socio-economic Profile* (Dar es Salaam: National Bureau of Statistics and Kilimanjaro Regional Commissioner's Office, 2002), 12–13; United Republic of Tanzania Bureau of Statistics, Morogoro Regional Socio-economic Profile (Dar es Salaam: National Bureau of Statistics and Morogoro Regional Commissioner's Office, 2002), 16–17.

3. Brian Larkin, "Indian Films and Nigerian Lovers: Media and the Creation of Parallel Modernities," *Africa: Journal of the International Africa Institute* 67, no. 3 (1997): 406–40; Laura Fair, "Making Love in the Indian Ocean: Hindi Films, Zanzibari Audiences, and the Construction of Romance in the 1950s and 1960s," in *Love in Africa*, ed. Jennifer Cole and Lynn M. Thomas (Chicago: University of Chicago, 2009).

Map 24.1. Tanzania. Map by Christopher Becker.

24

Retelling the World in Swahili

Revisiting the Practice of Film Translation in Tanzania

BIRGIT ENGLERT WITH NGINJAI PAUL MORETO

On a late afternoon in August 2009, we walk by a wooden shack in the Chamwino neighborhood in Morogoro, a regional town in central Tanzania. The covers of six films are on display outside, including titles such as *Unstoppable* with Wesley Snipes and *Tears of the Sun* with Bruce Willis. "Imetafsiriwa Kiswahili" (It has been translated into Swahili) is written in large letters on the film covers.

Voices talking in English can be heard from a television screen and then—quite abruptly—another voice can be heard speaking in Swahili, which is spoken by the vast majority of the Tanzanian population and is a national language in this East African country. A few seconds later, English becomes audible again, only to be overlaid by the Swahili-speaking voice shortly thereafter. This overlapping of languages goes on and on, intermingled with laughter and comments from the audience.

The room is packed with young people, most of them men, but there are also some women sitting on the small wooden benches, some of them with young children on their knees. The film that they are watching has been translated into Swahili by a man known as DJ Mark. Over the last decade, he has been one of the most popular film translators in the country, and his work has contributed enormously to the boom that the film translation business has experienced in this period.

Although DJ Mark has become famous for his film translations from English into Swahili, he is far from fluent in English. In fact, he can barely speak it, but he developed a good passive command of the language "on the job" when he started to translate films while working as a small-scale miner in northern Tanzania.[1]

In this regard, DJ Mark is no exception in the Tanzanian film translation business, which is characterized by practices that are somewhere between the processes of translation and the re-narration of films. Films in foreign languages undergo a series of transformations that help to increase their appeal to their predominantly young Tanzanian audiences. As a result, the translators also refer to themselves as *MaDJs* (deejays or disc jockeys). In the strict sense of the word, the term veejay (video jockey) would be a better fit and is used in some of the literature and in a documentary film on this subject; the term "film narrators" has also been employed.[2]

We will first give a brief overview of the context in which these films are being watched and will then focus on the translation practices by which international film productions are transformed into Tanzanian products of popular culture. Further, we will discuss some of the changes which have shaped the translation business since it first aroused our attention.

This chapter is written from an African Studies perspective and is based on field research that focused on qualitative methods. It included interviews and informal conversations with film translators, owners of video shops and video parlors, and film consumers, as well as participatory observation conducted in various video parlors. This research was carried out by Birgit Englert and Nginjai Paul Moreto in the towns of Masasi and Morogoro during two stays in 2009; in 2017, additional field work in Tanzania was carried out by Moreto in Mwanza and Morogoro, and on the internet by Englert.

Background

The existence of cinemas in Tanzania has dwindled since colonial rule by the British ended in 1963.[3] Nevertheless, watching films plays an important role in how Tanzanians spend their leisure time. Outside the home, this mostly takes place in so-called video parlors, where video films are shown on TV screens for low entrance fees.

As most video parlors are located in urban neighborhoods, they are not only affordable but also easily accessible, often mixed in with market stalls and places where beer and coffee are sold. All of the owners of video parlors that we talked to emphasized that it was crucial to show translated films, as otherwise they would fail to attract an audience.

Figure 24.1. Audience watching translated movies in a video parlor located in a neighborhood in Morogoro, Tanzania. Source: Birgit Englert.

Figure 24.2. Entrance to a video parlor in Morogoro, Tanzania, with the films scheduled for the day on display. Source: Birgit Englert.

Over the last few years, the watching of films in video parlors has somewhat declined, which is due to more and more people having television sets and computers in their own homes and the enormous increase in the availability of translated films. Unlike a couple of years ago, they are now sold on CDs by street hawkers who compete with video shop and video parlor owners.

The number of film translators or MaDJs has also grown. The young men who are involved in this business either work as independent entrepreneurs or are employed by entrepreneurs. Most of them are based in Tanzania's largest urban center, Dar es Salaam, from where translated films are distributed to other towns across the country such as Morogoro, which is located just a three-hour drive away.

However, in towns that are further away from Dar es Salaam, MaDJs have established themselves and cater to the local market. This is the case in Mwanza, the second-largest city in Tanzania, which is located on the shore of Lake Victoria in the northwest, and also in Masasi, a small city in the very south of the country.[4] With the improvement of roads, these places have become better connected to Dar es Salaam and the availability of translated films from the country's metropolis has increased accordingly.

A couple of years ago, live translations could still be experienced in certain video parlors in Dar es Salaam.[5] These performances of translators talking live into a microphone while the original film is running in the background appear to have since vanished. All of the video parlors in Mwanza, Morogoro, and Masasi that we visited for the purpose of this study rely exclusively on translations recorded on CDs. Live translations were primarily remembered as a practice of the past, although they were said to continue in a small town called Katoro in the Geita District by someone known as DJ Mzigo wa Ndevu.

When we first conducted research on this topic in 2009, films in English, Hindi, or Urdu were the most in demand. However, by 2017, their popularity had clearly decreased in favor of films in Korean and Chinese. Video parlor owners stressed that one of the factors that makes Korean films so popular is that they are often part of a series, which is highly valued by the viewers. The stories themselves also appeal to many Tanzanians and are suitable for the whole family to watch. An added attraction is the fact that they are widely available on the market and at low prices.

On the Practices of Film Translation

The oral translations provided by the film translators are neither proper dubbings nor voice-overs, but rather what could be termed as "delayed dubbing" (i.e., the voice of the translator is inserted after the original voice). Both the original dialogue and the translation remain to a large extent audible, although the voice of the translator might sometimes overlap with the original voice.

In a first instance, the film translators help the viewers to understand what the actors are saying. However, they actually do much more than just translate the text. In many cases, they also translate the context by giving additional explanations, which are often comparisons between what is happening on the screen and Tanzanian realities. For example, a translator might change the names of geographical places in the film to well-known locations in Tanzania, thereby turning foreign places into places within Tanzania. Furthermore, translators often guide their audience through the film by making references to what has come before and to what is going to happen in the story. They also provide their audience with background information on the film itself, such as when and where it was shot and by whom. Even details about the personal lives of the actors are often included in the narration of the translator.

The translator is not judged on whether they provide the most accurate translation but on whether they provide a translation that is able to convey the original intention of the director to the audience, while also adding a certain *vionjo* (flavor) to the film that makes it more entertaining to the audience.

As Emmanuel, a video parlor employee in Mwanza, emphasized in 2017, there are "some parts where they betray the viewers very much, but we do not mind since we get entertainment due to the specific flavor of talking. It is as if he tells a story which we are seeing ourselves, this indeed is enjoyable, . . . even though you might understand the film better than [the translator] himself." However, if the translation is seen to lack vionjo, mistakes may also be perceived as annoying and the DJ may be labeled with the pejorative name "DJ Muongo" (DJ Lie).

Although film translators are known and appreciated for adding new information to films, they are also known for cutting parts of the original information. DJs censor films by either simply not translating certain things or by deciding to cut certain images if they regard them as unsuitable for their audience. Censorship, which affects sex scenes in particular, can also take the form of advertisements for other films that they have translated, which appear over certain sequences of the film that they decide should not be seen.[6]

Competition among film translators is high, and obviously new generations of translators emerge over time. In 2009, DJ Mark had just recently replaced Lufufu, the pioneer of film translation in Tanzania, because DJ Mark's style was considered more "youthful."[7] He has turned himself into a trademark, not only by introducing himself in each film under various additional names, such as *sauti ya simba* (the voice of a lion), but also through his particular style of translation, which even includes the occasional coining of his own terms. In 2017, DJ Mark is facing competition from a number of translators, such as DJ Murphy, DJ Ommy, or Kenyan DJ Afro, all of them male. They entered the market more recently and are valued for their more accurate translations, which are due to them having better foreign language skills, as Star Mbwiso, a video parlor owner in Morogoro, stressed in an interview in 2017.

Some translators however, occupy a special niche in the film translation business, such as Juma Khan, who has held onto his reputation as the best translator of Indian films for years, or King Rich, who made a name for himself as a translator of Nigerian video films. In legal terms, the translated films are obviously illegal products whose production is based on violation of copyright law. Ironically, though, the film translators who work with this pirated material make an effort to ensure the rights to their own work by inserting a warning that the translated film must not be copied.[8]

New Developments

Just recently, translated films have begun to appear on the video platform YouTube, which has become the main archive for different forms of popular culture production over the last decade.[9] One YouTube channel by a popular DJ who specializes in productions from China and Korea went online in mid-2016. Due to the copyright violations that are inherent in the practice of film translation, it was taken down by YouTube and re-emerged shortly thereafter under a different name. However, as few Tanzanians have access to an internet connection that is strong enough to stream films, it is mostly university students who use the internet on campus who are able to watch films directly on YouTube.

Translators also face competition from another side: in November 2016, the Chinese ambassador to Tanzania presented a new initiative of the Chinese government to cooperate with a company, StarTimes, in translating Chinese films into Swahili.[10] It remains to be seen what impact this will have on entrepreneurs in the film business and on the prevalence of Chinese productions on the market.

Furthermore, in Kenya, another professional translation business, African Voices Dubbing Company, was founded in 2014 for the production of dubbed films in Swahili and also in a number of other African languages, such as Kikuyu, which is spoken by segments of the Kenyan population, or Luganda, which is widely spoken in Uganda.[11] These high-quality translations—in terms of accuracy and technical standards—do not appear to have had an impact on the Tanzanian market (yet).

In Tanzania, very few films are translated into African languages other than Swahili, which is spoken by virtually everyone who resides in urban areas. However, Ibra, a video parlor owner in Mwanza, spoke of a film called *Bushman* that had been translated into Sukuma and became a great success in the Sukuma-speaking villages around Mwanza.

As film translation practices are changing and new actors are emerging in this area, new leisure practices also appear to be having an impact on the culture of watching films. In recent years, football betting, in which people bet on the results of soccer games in European leagues, has gained enormous popularity, to the extent that many video parlors have turned to screening soccer matches and selling betting cards, which provides a better income than that generated by the screening of translated films. Some video parlor owners in Morogoro have even considered switching professions altogether, as interviews with Sanga and Star Mbwiso conducted in 2017 revealed.

Revisiting this field after eight years showed many new developments. Most significant are how popular culture practices and leisure habits are changing, as well as the emergence of new media enabling new habits of production and consumption. The everyday habit of consuming films in Tanzania serves the same purpose as it does in Europe or the United States: people relax and entertain themselves by watching films. I find it important to underline that, through their translations, the MaDJs aim to provide their Tanzanian audiences with an enjoyable and meaningful experience. It is their audiences that they target with their work; their "retellings" must not be understood as subversive practices aimed at the centers of global film production.

Apart from the entertainment aspect, most of the film viewers we spoke to emphasized the fact that these films provide them with a window to the world and allow them to learn more about life outside of Tanzania, especially in a context where very few Tanzanians ever get to travel abroad due to economic and legal reasons. These translated films are a good example of transnational cultural products that are being appropriated and turned into Tanzanian cultural products. The films bear witness to the creativity of the translators, whose work goes far beyond translation in the more conventional sense of the word, as they add several additional layers of expressivity to them.

Notes

The chapter was written by Birgit Englert, whereas the research on which it is based has been conducted by Birgit Englert and Nginjai Paul Moreto. An earlier version of this text has been published in Chinese in China Media Report 17, no. 4 (2018): 58–63. It is based on twelve interviews with video parlor owners or employees and film translators in Tanzania between 2009 and 2017.

1. For more background on DJ Mark, see Birgit Englert, "In Need of Connection: Reflections on Youth and the Translation of Film in Tanzania," Stichproben: Vienna Journal of African Studies 10, no. 18 (2010): 137–59.

2. See Sandra-Katharina Groß, "Die Kunst afrikanischer Kinoerzähler: Video Jockeys in Dar es Salaam" (MA thesis, Johannes Gutenberg University Mainz, 2010); Andrés Felipe Carvajal Gómez and Sandra-Katharina Groß, Veejays in Dar es Salaam: Filamu kwa Kiswahili), documentary video, 50 min (Germany/Colombia/Tanzania, 2012); and Matthias Krings, "Turning Rice into Pilau: The Art of Video Narration in Tanzania," working paper no. 115 (Department of Anthropology and African Studies, Johannes Gutenberg University Mainz, 2010).

3. James Brennan, "Democratizing Cinema and Censorship in Tanzania, 1920–1980," International Journal of African Historical Studies 38, no. 3 (2005): 507–9.

4. For more details on film translation in Masasi, see Birgit Englert with Nginjai Paul Moreto, "Inserting Voice: Foreign Language Film Translation

as a Local Phenomenon in Tanzania," Journal of African Media Studies 2, no. 2 (August 2010): 225–39.

5. Groß, "Video Jockeys in Dar es Salaam"; Carvajal Gómez and Groß, Veejays in Dar es Salaam.

6. Englert, "In Need of Connection," 137–59.

7. For detailed accounts of the work by Lufufu, see Krings, "Turning Rice into Pilau"; and Matthias Krings, African Appropriations: Cultural Difference, Mimesis, and Media (Bloomington: Indiana University Press, 2015).

8. See Englert with Moreto, "Inserting Voice," 225–39.

9. Birgit Englert, "Popular and Mobile: Reflections on Using YouTube as an Archive from an African Studies Perspective," Stichproben: Vienna Journal of African Studies 16, no. 31 (2016): 27–56.

10. See "Startimes Kuonesha Filamu Za Kichina Zilizo Tafsiriwa Kwa Kiswahili," YouTube, November 8, 2016, posted by "SIMU TV," video, 02:00, https://www.youtube.com/watch?v=t9rhdoMaPXg.

11. See "African Voices Dubbing Company," YouTube channel established July 25, 2015, https://www.youtube.com/channel/UCIEWVjE -ATun7XTcTb7scKg/about.

Map 25.1. Democratic Republic of Congo. Map by Christopher Becker.

25

The Listeners' City

Radio, Congolese Rumba, and the Appropriation of
Urban Space in the Belgian Congo in the 1950s

CHARLOTTE GRABLI

On January 1, 1949, the general governor of the Belgian Congo, Eugène Jungers, inaugurated radio broadcasts specially designed "for the Congolese," the Radio Congo Belge pour Africains (RCBA, Belgian Congo Radio for Africans).[1] Significantly, during his address to Congolese listeners, the governor introduced radio as a substitute for a "tribal" mode of communication, "the tom-tom of the Bula Matari" ("break rocks" in the Kikongo language).[2] In African history, such a comparison of radio technology with the "tom-tom," or the talking drums, has been frequently used to evoke the sound of a message spreading and its reception through hearing. However, the governor also appropriated the Congolese expression *bula matari*, coined in the late nineteenth century to refer to the use of dynamite by the first European explorers who crossed Central Africa. In the 1950s, Congolese people called any Belgian official Bula Matari, and this name still remains in the collective memory as a symbol of the violence of the colonial state. As the Belgian authority began broadcasting in indigenous languages primarily to serve its own propaganda, calling the radio "the tom-tom of the Bula Matari" represented an attempt to introduce broadcasting as an emanation of colonial power.[3] The drum-roll sound that every RCBA program opened with gave the inaugural address its musical form, symbolizing and reiterating the announcement of acoustic colonization.[4]

Regarding Congolese popular culture, however, what makes radio such a fascinating object of research is its "autonomous power" that lets the listener's imagination run wild, and results in listening behaviors radio programmers did not expect.[5] As the Cameroonian musician and writer Francis Bebey recalled, African cities' first listeners were fascinated with the "marvelous" musical broadcasts and the anonymous voices "that make the broadcast thing mysterious."[6] On the other hand, early listeners had an ambiguous, sometimes defiant attitude toward the news or other programs made to educate the "masses" of colonized people. A focus on the moment when radio was first introduced in the *cité indigène*, the native quarters of Leopoldville where Africans were compelled to stay, is helpful in understanding the integration of radio within everyday musical life. Leopoldville was the capital city of the Belgian Congo. The city was renamed Kinshasa after independence in 1960, and the country has been successively called République du Congo (1960–71), Zaïre (1971–97), and today République Démocratique du Congo (RDC). In this metropolis, known as the cradle of "Congolese rumba"—a dance music that grew in popularity throughout the continent in the 1950s—African listening habits allow us to demonstrate how radio escaped colonial power to quickly become an emblem of this urban musical culture. In fact, until 1960, when the announcement of independence renewed Congolese interest in spoken news and led the RCBA to diversify its programs, the radio set remained above all a source of music, working as a collective gramophone.

The musical focal point of this study stands out from the academic literature on radio in Africa, as it has mostly considered this media in relation to language and communication.[7] I shall rather explore the history of radio as a social object related to music, place, and territory—a field that has predominantly been focused within anthropology. This study is based on archival research in the Africa Archives of the Belgian Ministry of Foreign Affairs and in the Royal Library of Belgium. It was informed by a series of interviews made during 2014 fieldwork in Kinshasa among musicians of the two great musical ensembles of the 1950s—African Jazz, led by the singer Joseph Kabasele, and OK Jazz, led by Franco Luambo, bands that, despite their names, played music bearing little resemblance to jazz.

As the success achieved by the RCBA set off debates within the public sphere, colonial officials, missionaries, and Congolese journalists produced a great number of articles and surveys on radio. In particular, in the weekly newspaper *Actualités africaines* (African news), created in 1956, the *évolués* ("civilized natives," the legal name referring to the Congolese nascent bourgeoisie) regularly criticized RCBA programs and the increase of musical broadcasting.

Figure 25.1. Franco and the OK Jazz's drummer, Leopoldville, ca. 1956–60.
Source and copyright: Jean DEPARA / Courtesy Revue Noire.

The essay begins with a brief historical sketch of broadcasting in Leopoldville, before moving on to an analysis of the Congolese reception of the RCBA broadcasts and the medium itself. As most of the city dwellers could not afford a radio and private listening thus remained a marginalized experience through the colonial period, this essay focuses on collective listening behaviors and discusses the role of the Congolese audience in the making of the musical broadcasts, which constituted the new city soundscape, or the musical landscape of the colonial town.

The Making of the Musical Function of the Colonial Radio Set

According to the prevailing view among colonial governments, the Belgians perceived radio as a means to reach the "masses" in their homes. The colonial administration thus sought to make radio more accessible in the cité, where, until the late 1940s, radios were reserved for the African nascent bourgeoisie. Indicative of this limited audience, half of the Congolese women living in Leopoldville had never heard a radio in 1945, and when one was lucky enough to own a radio, "one hastened to give a demonstration."[8] Consequently, the colonial government encouraged the manufacturers of radios to "lower their price within the reach of the natives' purse," while at the same time they commercialized the "saucepan special," a cheap wireless set, so called because the prototype was built in the shell of a metal saucepan, then used for the design.[9]

Resulting from the Belgian attempt to thwart the anti-imperialist propaganda of Egyptian channels, RCBA adapted its programs with the simple intention of bringing as much of the Congolese population into the audience as possible.[10] Although the information was carefully controlled, the station passed it off as Congolese by hiring African announcers who read local and international news reports, broadcasted on various topics such as sports or Congolese natural resources, and performed short sketches aiming at improving mass education, hygiene, and housing, every day in a different language (Kikongo, Lingala, Swahili, Tshiluba, and French). However, a large part of the listeners only understood one of the African languages, and most of the time listened to musical programs.[11]

Between 1950 and 1959, musical broadcasts therefore increased from 57 percent to 73 percent of total broadcast hours.[12] The RCBA played the most appealing records from abroad, such as the Cuban musical genre *son* or Puerto Rican mambo, as well as Congolese rumba. Perceived as a musical technology, advertising in the Congolese press associated radios with the old gramophone, a musical technology that already symbolized urban Africa.[13] In 1960, this process resulted in the market launch of the "radiophono" (for *radiophonographe*, the French name for gramophone), an instrument of the brand Erres combining the functions of the gramophone and the radio.[14] The name echoed an expression coined by the Congolese elite, according to whom radio was failing to fulfill its educative mission by turning into "an entertainment machine," which they pejoratively nicknamed "radiophono."[15]

For most of the audience, however, RCBA successfully played with the sensory tie, specific to broadcasting technology, between voice, language, and music. Listeners called the RCBA "our radio" and demonstrated a genuine attachment to their programs, which became a vehicle for a sense of cultural sovereignty in the cité.[16] The success achieved was such that the expansion of the Congolese programs went so far as to exceed European broadcasting time in 1958 (ten hours a day during the week, fifteen on Saturday, and seventeen on Sunday). The RCBA personnel also significantly increased. Limited to two Belgians and six Congolese in 1949, there were ten Europeans and forty-eight Congolese working at the RCBA by the eve of independence.

The Right to the Musical City

Despite government efforts to democratize radios in African homes, radio listening remained, to a large extent, a collective experience. Throughout colonization, listeners associated broadcasting less with the mobility entailed by wireless sets than to the making of public places. The "crowd of interested listeners" that formed the popular classes gathered every day around the public address (PA) system installed in "strategic places" of the cité. Although loudspeakers had been used by the colonial administration, the Force publique (Public Force, the combined police and military force), and missionaries during the 1940s, the majority of the PA systems were installed after the launch of the African programs. In 1951, sixteen PA systems were working in the cité.[17] This kind of gathering grabbed the attention of a European journalist passing through Leopoldville in 1951: "Of the new Congo's many modern scenes, none is more impressive than the spectacle of hundreds of African men, women and children crowding together under the loudspeaker when the first bars of '*Uélé*,' the call tune known throughout the colony, resounds in the hot tropical night. In silence they listen to the voice transmitted from afar, and sometimes at the first notes of a Congolese tune their feet move restlessly in the old Congo dancing rhythms."[18] Putting the clichés on the African tropical nights and the old dancing rhythms aside, this description highlights the success achieved by the PA system and suggests a certain intensity of listening.

In an interview in Kinshasa in 2014 with the former bassist of African Jazz, Augustin Moniania, better known as Roitelet (Little King), he mostly remembered these daily radio excursions as musical leisure. "They were radio in the streets, on every corner, they were the public address. As soon as 6 p.m. you can see the people coming. They settle themselves there. When it's playing, the entire neighborhood can hear: 'Hello, hello, this is Belgian Congo Radio. Belgian Congo Radio invites you to listen to the music.'" In the cité, many other sound sources, such as record dealers and bars, which installed loudspeakers in the streets and played music all day long, accentuated the feeling of musical ubiquity that Roitelet suggested. In 1957, one even worried about the use of radios by bus drivers who sought to attract new passengers by turning their vehicles into "warm dancing venues," either moving or not.[19] Unlike "'musicalized' wanderers taking shelter from the sonic ecology present in the city," Leopoldville's listeners asserted their presence and actively participated in the sound ecology of the city.[20]

While radios integrated the African material culture by referring to the gramophone, the use of public address systems was similarly shaped by the preexisting model of open-air movie projections started in 1944 in Leopoldville.[21] The capacity of public cinema and broadcasting to create a window to the outside made these leisure activities particularly appealing in the context of segregation. Moreover, like street projections, public radio momentarily erased the social hierarchy usually visible during musical shows. In fact, among music-loving city dwellers, those who were too poor or too young to be admitted in musical venues were known as the *n'guembo* (the bats), because they "contented themselves with perching on the walls to applaud their idols."[22] Conversely, public address systems linked the listening experience to the appropriation of space by allowing all the cité inhabitants to listen to broadcasts of local music. This explains the city dwellers' claims regarding safety: "Many Congolese who do not reside near the public address are afraid of going out after nightfall and taking poorly lit streets to get to loudspeaker spots, which are, themselves, sometimes in the dark."[23] Beyond providing musical pleasure, the creation of collective listening practices met African claims to appropriate public spaces as well as nightlife.

A Collective Gramophone

The right to the city was not a matter of taking over spaces in the city alone. The choice of musical broadcasts and sounds that permeated the cité's everyday life were just as important. From the outset of the RCBA, listeners demonstrated their will to participate in the shaping of programs. In 1951, the new media outlet received three hundred letters a week, the vast majority consisting of requested records. For the dedicated program called *The Requested Records*, the announcers made selections and prepared the comments that introduced each song. As this program became the most popular radio broadcast, not only were listeners using *The Requested Records* as a means to celebrate Congolese music, but they also hijacked the program. Some quarrels occurred when a man requested the RCBA to broadcast a record to get the attention of a married woman.[24] The RCBA promoted this correspondence by responding during other programs such as *Our Listeners' Hour* and *The Listeners' Mail*.[25] Indeed, besides requesting records, listeners sent eclectic questions reflecting the national and global anxiety of the time, such as "What is the hydrogen bomb?" Or, "How can the state which manufactures money be in debt?" Or, "Is Hitler really dead?"

A 1954 survey by the RCBA offered an interesting insight into the urban musical scene and the way such programs conveyed a sense of "cultural sovereignty." Indeed, in a context in which people had little control over anything except cultural life, the listeners' participation in the making of the programs can be understood as a search for autonomy. Not surprisingly, the thirty thousand letters the RCBA had received over the previous year "consisted, in the proportion of 90 percent, of requests for Congolese music," while a few of them expressed interest in European recordings such as Line Renaud's "Chien dans la vitrine" (a French version of the 1952 American novelty song "(How Much Is) That Doggie in the Window?") and the "Hallelujah" chorus from Handel's Messiah.[26] During this year, twenty records by Congolese musical ensembles, mostly based in the cité, topped the ranking, with five thousand requests. While songs by the band leader Joseph Kabasele, the musician and painter Guy-Léon Fylla, or the singer-guitarist Léon Bukasa were very popular, the audience clearly established Antoine Mundanda's "Mabele ya Paul" (The land of Paul) as the greatest success of 1954, with 863 requests.

Mundanda had won an Osborn Award for the best recording of African music in 1953, a South African award created by the British ethnomusicologist Hugh Tracey in 1952 to promote African records, so his music had been frequently broadcast by the RCBA. Unlike most of the Congolese urban ensembles in which electric guitar was the key instrument, Mundanda and his musicians played *likembe* (thumb piano), also known as *sanza* and *mbira* in Central and Southern Africa. It was ubiquitous in the southern Congo before being supplanted by the guitar in the 1940s. The lyrics were a tribute to another great musician who passed in 1950, Paul Kamba, who had been the first to establish himself as a Congolese rumba celebrity on both sides of the Congo River. With its celebration of the local scene and its distinct likembe sound, this song reflected the urban soundscape's complexity, and thus best expressed the inherent contradictions of African modernity.

The study of early colonial radio shows that listeners used it to make the cité their own and imbue it with particular types of sociability and sounds. It emphasizes the importance of the imaginaries at play in listening practices in our understanding of the city dwellers' "struggle to create a new order of time and space."[27] Indeed, the audience participation in the making of the programs such as *The Requested Records,* as well as the public address system, allowed the inhabitants to produce overlapping ambient fields and organize the everyday soundscape. At the heart of the invention of the listeners' city was the relationship between musical spaces and time. Up to today, an intimate, symbolic association of Congolese rumba, loudspeaker technology, and urbanity remains central to the African imaginary of the city. As the Kenyan writer Binyavanga Wainaina observed, "this music, this style, this metallic sound has become the sound of our time."[28]

Notes

1. This essay is based on a broader study: Charlotte Grabli, "La ville des auditeurs: Radio, rumba congolaise et droit à la ville dans la cité indigène de Léopoldville (1949–1960)," *Cahiers d'études africaines*, no. 233 (2019): 9–45.

2. Eugène Jungers, General Governor, Address to the RCBA, January 1, 1949, folder 4622, Pauwels-Boon papers, Africa Archives, Ministry of Foreign Affairs, Brussels (hereafter, "Pauwels-Boon papers"). Unless otherwise noted, all translations are my own.

3. Richard Fardon and Graham Furniss, eds., *African Broadcast Cultures: Radio in Transition* (Oxford: J. Currey, 2000), 23.

4. Greta Pauwels-Boon, *L'origine, l'évolution et le fonctionnement de la radiodiffusion au Zaïre de 1937 à 1960* (Tervuren, Belgium: Musée Royal de l'Afrique Centrale, 1979), 119.

5. On the "autonomous power" of technologies, see Brian Larkin, *Signal and Noise: Media, Infrastructure, and Urban Culture in Nigeria* (Durham, NC: Duke University Press, 2008), 4.

6. Francis Bebey, *La radiodiffusion en Afrique noire* (Issy-les-Moulineaux: Éditions Saint-Paul, 1963), 7.

7. See Liz Gunner, Dina Ligaga, and Dumisani Moyo, eds., *Radio in Africa: Publics, Cultures, Communities* (Johannesburg: Wits University Press, 2012).

8. Suzanne Comhaire-Sylvain, *Femmes de Kinshasa: Hier et aujourd'hui* (Paris: Mouton, 1968), 36–37.

9. Van Herreweghe, Head of the African programs, "Radio Congo Belge—émissions pour Africains," November 14, 1951, folder 4622, Pauwels-Boon papers.

10. On anticolonial radio propaganda, see Gunner, Ligaga, and Moyo, *Radio in Africa*, 7.

11. "Rapport annuel d'activités du service de l'information," 1957, folder 4622, Pauwels-Boon papers.

12. Pauwels-Boon, *L'origine*, 140.

13. Georges Balandier, *Sociologie des Brazzavilles noires*, 2nd ed. (Paris: Presses de la Fondation Nationale des Sciences Politiques, 1985), 225.

14. *Actualités africaines*, January 11, 1960.

15. *Actualités africaines*, February 2, 1956.

16. See David B. Coplan, "South African Radio in a Saucepan," in Gunner, Ligaga, and Moyo, *Radio in Africa*, 136.

17. See UNESCO, ed., *L'information à travers le monde: Presse, radio, film, télévision*, UNESCO publication 701 (Paris : UNESCO, 1951).

18. "Broadcasting for the Congolese," *The Belgian Congo To-day* 1, no. 3 (1952): 105.

19. *Actualités africaines*, November 14, 1957.

20. Rowland Atkinson, "Ecology of Sound: The Sonic Order of Urban Space," *Urban Studies* 44, no. 10 (September 2007): 1907.

21. Paul Coppois, "Le cinéma pour indigènes au Congo belge," *Congopresse*, November 15, 1947.

22. Sylvain Bemba, *Cinquante ans de musique du Congo-Zaïre (1920–1970): de Paul Kamba à Tabu-Ley* (Paris: Présence Africaine, 1984), 127.

23. K. Theunissen, "Rapport sur les émissions africaines de RCB," December 12, 1952, folder 4622, Pauwels-Boon papers.

24. *Actualités africaines*, January 10, 1957.

25. Pauwels-Boon, *L'origine*, 116.

26. Report of the Natives Affairs and Labor Force, Stanleyville, 1955, folder 4622, Pauwels-Boon papers; *Essor du Congo*, March 1, 1955.

27. Phyllis M. Martin, *Leisure and Society in Colonial Brazzaville* (Cambridge: Cambridge University Press, 1995), 3.

28. Binyavanga Wainaina, *One Day I Will Write about This Place: A Memoir* (London: Granta, 2011), 77.

Part 7

Labor and Livelihoods

Map 26.1. Tanzania. Map by Christopher Becker.

26

Mechanical Expression in a Broken World

Repair, Fun, and Everyday Life in Tanzanian Garages

JOSHUA GRACE

"Let's Go Test": A Day in a Tanzanian Garage

The test drive came at the end of a hot January day in Dar es Salaam, Tanzania's largest city. Saidi (a young mechanic and my immediate advisor) and I had been working on a new Toyota Land Cruiser since mid-morning. The driver, who worked for a government official, requested an oil change and a brake check. A quick removal of the tires showed completely worn brake pads and drums. "You'll need to replace everything except the calipers," Saidi said.

The driver agreed with the assessment. He then called a taxi and went, himself, to a parts dealer to purchase the drums and pads. This procedure was common. Beginning in the early 1990s, market liberalization brought parts and cars from Dubai, India, Japan, South Korea, and, later, China to Tanzania on an unprecedented scale. It led to a choice between three types of parts at stores: used, "original" new (*orijino* in Swahili), and "fake" (*feki*). The latter, cheaper knock-off brands manufactured in China, create uncertainty for mechanic and customer alike. Mechanics do not want their reputations tied to cheap parts, and customers do not want to pay for orijino but receive feki while mechanics pocket the cost difference. For the case at hand, the driver solved this conundrum by purchasing the parts himself.

We changed the oil in the meantime. The Land Cruiser's filter was surrounded by hoses and wires. Saidi, a wiry boxer with long arms, could touch the filter, but could not grip it well enough to loosen it.

After a quick dig at the engineers who designed the vehicle, Saidi praised his own creativity and dedication to his craft. He said that annoying designs had stumped him before and that they occupied his mind at home, sometimes keeping him from rest—sometimes even causing him to dream about possible fixes. Saidi then claimed to have invented a method for loosening and tightening filters by making a slipknot out of a long piece of rope, which he then carefully placed around the filter after lowering it through layers of hoses and parts. After tightening both ends of the rope, the filter slowly turned as we moved the rope. We changed the oil and replaced the filter with the same technique. By that time, the driver had returned with the brake pads and drums. The repair took a couple of hours but went off without a hitch.

"Let's go test," Saidi said. We had repaired the Land Cruiser in a small section of an unregistered garage called a "mute garage" (*gereji bubu*) that spanned about 265 yards on a dirt side road off two busy city streets.

Saidi drove past other parts of the garage to the main road and stomped on the gas pedal. As we flew down a two-lane road through a neighborhood called Tandale, I peered over at the speedometer: seventy kilometers an hour. Having fastened my seatbelt upon entering, I asked, "Saidi, why aren't you wearing your seatbelt?" "I need to feel the car," he responded. Saidi then tapped the brakes three times. We came to a quick stop. "They work," he said, smiling. We took off again and then veered off the road into a gravel lot where Saidi locked up the brakes, sending us skidding toward a fence as we turned in a half-donut.

We came to a stop. The gate opened, and young assistant mechanics dressed in dirty overalls walked out. "This is where I learned mechanics." A decade earlier, Saidi had entered this garage as a *spanaboi,* or "wrench boy," who traded labor for knowledge. Now a budding mechanic, he had just fixed and test-driven a $30,000 vehicle. He did not own it, of course, but its functioning depended upon his knowledge.

After exchanging greetings, we returned to our garage slowly— Saidi tapping the brake pedal often to mimic bumper-to-bumper traffic. Saidi returned the keys to the driver and confidently told him, "The brakes work." Saidi negotiated the final price with the driver. He likely took home between twenty and thirty dollars before doling out some of his earnings to the garage's head mechanics. I grabbed a cup of coffee with one of these mechanics, Kondo, in the shade of a cabinet

Figure 26.1. Author (*center*) with Kondo (*second from left*), Saidi (*second from right*), and other members of the garage at the beach on a Sunday. This garage used Sundays to wash overalls, clean the garage, and rest. Source: Joshua Grace.

used to store parts. As I sipped from the small cup, I mentioned Saidi's rope technique in passing. "That dumbass. I taught him that. He's always stealing my ideas. He told you he came up with that in a dream. Saidi," he yelled, "you need my ideas to pretend to be a mechanic!"

Oil changes and brake repair occur every day in garages. Any aspiring *fundi* (mechanic) must know how to do them. However, even simple innovations like the rope trick point to a history of technological innovation and maintenance rarely associated with Africa. Before returning to Saidi and Kondo's stories, let's look briefly at the origins of *bubu* ("mute") garages and mechanics and why their lives help unsettle the conventional wisdom about technology in independent Tanzania.

Background and Argument:
The Historical Stakes of Breakdown and Repair

For Tanzania, which earned political independence in 1961, technological breakdown plays an important role in histories of African-initiated modernization schemes precisely because stories about this period often end with failure.[1] Consider, for example, the quick shift in international discourse between the 1960s and the 1980s. At the dawn of independence, most development consultants claimed Tanzania desperately needed more technology to grow its economy. At this time, some within international institutions like UNESCO (the United Nations Educational, Scientific and Cultural Organization) and the World Bank noted that colonial policies rooted in racial segregation had left new nations with few industrial resources or institutions to sustain economic growth in world markets and to provide services to citizens.[2]

As Tanzania's economy slowed in the mid-1970s, however, the focus on technology shifted from need and an indictment of British colonialism to assumptions about the miscalculations of African modernizers over the preceding decade and a half. Some charged that bureaucrats had prioritized their own well-being over the nation by siphoning money from development projects; others viewed decisions to invest in costly infrastructure as economically unsustainable and therefore technologically "inappropriate."[3] In both cases, material brokenness, evident in unfinished roads, stationary railway cars, or, in the case at hand, piles of car parts and modified vehicles in a bubu garage, served as a sign—indeed, a sort of everyday archive for citizens—of the independent government's failures. In addition to the above charges, it suggested that Tanzanian modernization schemes did not work because the nation lacked the capacity to produce, invent, or use industrial technologies.[4] British officials made similar statements throughout the colonial period.

But the indictment of the mid-1970s added a more specific critique of Tanzania's technological culture. It charged that an independent African society directing its own development could not receive already-built technologies that worked elsewhere, put them to use effectively, and then care for them through maintenance. The International Monetary Fund (IMF) and World Bank, for example, used a version of this story to justify the structural adjustment of Tanzania's socialist economy in the 1980s. Pervasive brokenness, they argued, showed that a strong independent state could not—or, at least, had not—allocate or care for technological resources in ways that brought sustained economic growth through technological function.

Against this backdrop, Tanzanian garage histories matter for two reasons. First, garages remind us that technological brokenness is neither an unchangeable state nor uniquely African. As American historian Kevin Borg writes, "The repair shop is where the weaknesses of technology are laid bare; where progress is stalled, repaired, and sent back on the road; where technological failure is the stock-in-trade and the ideal of the well-oiled machine meets the reality of our entropic world."[5] We do not know if economists at the IMF and World Bank could fix their own vehicles. But we do know that Kondo and Saidi, like mechanics in Borg's work, read technological failure differently. Because they saw dysfunction as an opportunity to be creative, to seek social mobility, and to have fun, their lives alert us to a different set of possibilities regarding technology and personhood during the independent era.

Second, though there is a rich record of scholarship on dress, art, music, dancing, sport, and written and oral literatures—as this volume attests—scholars have written much less about Africans' ability to appropriate, modify, and express themselves mechanically through industrial technologies such as motor vehicles.[6] Where and how have Africans expressed themselves as industrial agents in the twentieth century? As the next section illustrates, the answer to this question takes us to "unofficial" (*si rasmi*) spaces, bodies, and minds rarely associated with the cutting edge of technology or development.

Methods and "Mute" Histories

As a historian, I joined a garage because colonial and national archives contain very few documents pertaining to the nuts-and-bolts process of car repair and even fewer from a mechanic's perspective. I also hoped to see firsthand what mechanics had told me in interviews about garages as spaces of social mobility, expertise, and even fun for young Tanzanian men. Oral histories revealed that African mechanics left private and government British garages to open shops in their own neighborhoods and homes beginning in the late 1930s. By the early 1960s, the product of this movement, gereji bubu, had become the most popular site of automotive training in Tanzania.[7]

Gereji bubu gained this reputation, on the one hand, because they offered young men without formal education an opportunity to become intimate with vehicles and their parts. Without needing to read or to hold certificates—a process most young men could not afford—bubu apprentices learned by cleaning parts, by taking vehicles apart and reassembling them, and through modification, a process in which mechanics join parts from different vehicles and makes—sometimes making an entire vehicle from scratch.

Readers in the Global North may consider this an undesirable alternative to formal training or modification, yet bubu mechanics saw and see their training as the most effective form of technological practice because it comes from, and thus matches, the landscape of vehicles and parts they inhabit. In fact, when I first entered some garages, mechanics thought I was a spy from American car companies who had come to poach their ideas. My head mechanic, Kondo, told them otherwise by phone. But these episodes demonstrate that bubu garages drew young men like Kondo and Saidi into a space where they could not only learn about a globally relevant machine, but also put their own stamp on local auto design in the course of careers that historically spanned decades, as Kondo's had by 2012.

In 1978, Kondo, who had recently finished secondary school, joined a garage run by retired mechanics because "college wasn't possible due to money" and because he "loved auto mechanics." The garage was located just yards from where Saidi and I fixed the Land Cruiser and on the other side of the wall from where Kondo and I talked about his career. That space is now occupied by a school, but in the late 1970s and early 1980s Kondo learned there by assisting in repairs and modifications for several years. This "hand expertise" (*utaalum wa mikono*) gave retired mechanics what they needed: cheap and sometimes free labor to fix vehicles. And it gave young men what they wanted: access to knowledge about an important machine that they could use to build lives as adults.

Kondo found this approach to repair especially useful during severe part shortages in Tanzania after the mid-1970s. He described scarcity-induced modification as an opportunity to make something new, a chance to learn, and a source of pride: "[Mechanically], we did everything. We could take out one type of engine and fit another from any other make into the car. . . . If the government orders cars from Japan, we learned about cars from Japan. In auto mechanics you have to be like a doctor; you have to change with the times. If Japanese cars come, you have to change with them because that is the current system. My responsibility is to fix, to learn, and to know about the ways the system changes." According to Kondo, this took "heart," "patience," and "intelligence." And it was fun. When mechanics described the day-to-day process of work, they often said that "work doesn't go without cursing" (*kazi haiendi bila matusi*) or joking. For the latter, they cited the common act of joining "male" and "female" parts together during modification. For example, placing a transmission from one model into the metal housing of another model or brand required mechanics to thrust a "male" transmission, and its input shaft in particular, into the engine and its housing: in this case, the "female" part. For the first several tries, mechanics would likely fail to properly join the parts, leading to jokes about impotence until the lead mechanic addressed the obstacles to successful modification—salvaging the car as well as the mechanic's masculinity.

My point is this: to maturing mechanics like Kondo, broken things brought good news for two reasons. First, used things provided opportunities to substantially remake and redesign vehicles when they broke down. The more parts one collected from idle vehicles, the more creative one could get with designs and modifications. Second, as the Tanzanian shilling declined in value during the 1970s and 1980s, repurposing parts allowed comparative social stability. Economist Ngila Mwase found that "homemade" parts sold for two to three times as much as new parts in the late-1970s.[8] To many in the Global North, bubu shops probably look like disorganized piles of useless scrap produced by scarcity and lack of skill and resources. But young men approached piles of broken parts as a way to build knowledge, to shape the function of an important technology, and to create economic security.

Kondo came of age in this environment, eventually becoming a head mechanic at the shop in which he first learned *ufundi*. His apprentices call him "uncle" (*mjomba*), and he receives the first cut of all repairs in his part of the shop. As Kondo and I talked in 2012, however, he worried that the type of social mobility that allowed him to age well no longer existed. "The parts are cheap and don't last." This not only makes modification risky, he said, but also devalues mechanics' labor and knowledge by turning them into "screw off, screw on" laborers who simply replace broken with new parts—a form of work with minimal joy, technological creativity, or monetary payout.

Which brings us back to Saidi. Shortly after we fixed the Toyota's brakes, Saidi left the garage for a long-haul trucking job in Zambia. He called often, but kept pushing back his return date. Disappointed but not surprised, Kondo charged that "mechanics these days don't know work. They just chase money." He added that young men did not develop a depth of knowledge held by previous generations because most of them couldn't afford to pass up more lucrative career opportunities, such as driving, and thus missed decades of learning by doing.

Saidi's and Kondo's lives as mechanics point to the contradictory nature of mechanical expertise in Tanzania's recent past. Though the 1970s and 1980s are most closely associated with economic decline and the failure of postcolonial modernization in Tanzania, parts shortages caused by fiscal crisis actually raised the value of bubu mechanics' mental and physical labor in a manner that allowed Kondo to achieve the status of "uncle" in his garage. Similarly, though some read the growing import economies of the 1990s and 2000s, including imports of "original" and "fake" spare car parts, as signs of financial health and recovery, current economies of knowledge value a less skillful mechanical activity, driving, over a recognizable form of industrial expertise: repairing and modifying cars themselves.

Auto repair rewarded Saidi and Kondo differently, but each mechanic used garage work to integrate himself into a global narrative of car expertise that often treats independent Tanzania, and Africa more broadly, as places where brokenness is the final state of technologies that work elsewhere. Fun and creativity are not always enough to keep maturing mechanics around garages. Still, the durable presence of repair in bubu shops shows that we must not let disrepair or brokenness have the final word on the possibilities of African mechanical expression.

Notes

1. The title of this chapter draws on "broken world thinking" as formulated in Steven Jackson, "Rethinking Repair," in *Media Technologies: Essays on Communication, Materiality and Society*, ed. Tarleton Gillespie, Pablo Boczkowski, and Kirsten A. Foot (Cambridge, MA: MIT Press, 2014).

2. Howard Stein, *Beyond the World Bank Agenda: An Institutional Approach to Development* (Chicago: University of Chicago Press, 2008).

3. World Bank, *Accelerated Development in Sub-Saharan Africa: An Agenda for Action* (Washington, DC: World Bank, 1981), http://documents.worldbank .org/curated/en/702471468768312009/Accelerated-development-in-sub -Saharan-Africa-an-agenda-for-action.

4. Gabrielle Hecht, *Being Nuclear: Africans and the Global Uranium Trade* (Cambridge, MA: MIT Press, 2014).

5. Kevin L. Borg, *Auto Mechanics: Technology and Expertise in Twentieth-Century America* (Baltimore: Johns Hopkins University Press, 2007), 4.

6. Examples include Kurt Beck, "The Art of Truck Modding on the Nile (Sudan): An Attempt to Trace Creativity," in *The Speed of Change: Motor Vehicles and People in Africa, 1890–2000,* ed. Jan-Bart Gewald, Sabine Luning, and Klaas van Walraven, 151–74 (Boston: Brill, 2009); Jojada Verrips and Birgit Meyer, "Kwaku's Car: The Struggles and Stories of a Ghanaian Long-Distance Taxi-Driver," in *Car Cultures,* ed. Daniel Miller (London: Berg, 2001); and Jennifer Hart, *Ghana on the Go: African Mobility in the Age of Motor Transportation* (Bloomington: Indiana University Press, 2016). On stories of creativity, see Clapperton Chakanetsa Mavhunga, *Transient Workspaces: Technologies of Everyday Innovation in Zimbabwe* (Cambridge, MA: MIT Press, 2014).

7. Joshua Grace, *African Motors: Automobility and the History of Development in Tanzania, 1860s–2015* (Durham, NC: Duke University Press, forthcoming).

8. Ngila Mwase, "The Supply of Road Vehicles in Tanzania: The Problem of Suppressed Demand," *Journal of Transport Economics and Policy* 17, no. 1 (January 1983), 83.

Map 27.1. Tanzania. Map by Christopher Becker.

27

Male Friendship and the Writing Life in Dar des Salaam, Tanzania

EMILY CALLACI

Sometime around 2009, I became obsessed with Swahili detective novellas from the 1970s. At the time, I was living in Dar es Salaam, Tanzania: a city where used book sellers spread out their wares on tables or on blankets on the ground on street corners throughout the city. Sorting through the piles of "How to get rich quick!" advice manuals, pamphlets promising cures for impotence and skin rashes, and evangelical autobiographies of sin and redemption, I would sometimes find one of the treasures I was looking for. The detective novellas were immediately recognizable by their cover artwork—once brightly colorful, but now faded—which took inspiration from action-film posters and featured ninjas in mid-kick; scantily clad women either weeping, swooning, or aiming a gun; and men sporting 1970s-style bell-bottoms and Afros astride motorcycles, jumping over cars. These novellas were printed on thin paper and were often crumbling into dust by the time I got my hands on them. The stories themselves were written in a slangy style of Swahili, and, though they stole liberally from the story lines of James Bond, Bollywood, spaghetti westerns and kung fu films, the stories all took place in the streets of Dar es Salaam and had Tanzanian characters. The novellas were produced by and for young urban migrants. As historical artifacts, they offer a glimpse into the imaginations of young Tanzanians of earlier decades.[1]

I collected these books from scattered locations throughout the city and studied them for clues about the characters and contours of the 1970s literary scene that produced them. The back covers of the books displayed a biographical note and photograph of the author, a synopsis of the story, and several quotes of bombastic praise of the author from other young writers. The same names would appear again and again in dedications of the books, where the author would name the fellow writers who had loaned him money, helped to produce the book, or provided camaraderie throughout the process. After reading about 150 of these novellas over several years, I spent the summer of 2013 tracking down their authors. I walked the dusty city in the hot sun, asking around at used booksellers, bars, and newsstands until finally I met Farid, whose father was the late Hammie Rajab, one of the most prolific and popular of the authors. Farid helped me to track down the sons of the late Edi Ganzel and Elvis Musiba, and they in turn helped me to find Jumaa Mkabarah, Kajubi Mukajanga, and several of the other writers in their network who were still alive.

I learned that the world that these men shared extended far beyond their literary output. At the time that they wrote, the authors were young men—often teenagers—who had recently arrived in the city and were struggling to survive and make a meaningful life as the first generation in their families to leave their rural homes. As urban newcomers, they relied on each other in nearly all aspects of their lives. Through our conversations, they taught me about the history of their literary movement, and, through that, the history of postcolonial Dar es Salaam. For them, however, our conversations served an additional purpose. For them, I was there to help collect and distribute news and greetings among old friends who had lost touch over the past four decades. I was inadvertently helping to stage a reunion of sorts.

This is a story about a group of friends—about ten to fifteen men in Dar es Salaam, a city that quadrupled in size over the course of the 1970s. In the face of high levels of unemployment, the collapse of government services, and economic insecurity, friendships were something people not only enjoyed but also relied on. Yet, like all relationships, friendships could also be fraught with the burdens placed on them. Friendship was, to borrow a phrase from anthropologist Jane Dyson, a "contradictory resource": a source of sustenance, but also of social pressure and, at times, steep obligations.[2] Within a broader social fabric, friendships reproduce some dominant social norms and divisions, while providing a basis from which to challenge others. The bonds of friendship can, for example, serve to retrench gender norms or consolidate class privilege. At other times, they can be sites of experimentation and boundary crossing, undermining the political power of older generations or challenging racial divisions.

Figure 27.1. The writer Hammie Rajab, date unknown. Source: Courtesy of Farid Hammie Rajab.

Certain aspects of friendship appear timeless. We can read Shakespearean portrayals of affection, devotion, and betrayal among friends and recognize the rewards and frustrations of our own relationships—and, yet, friendship is also forged within and indelibly marked by

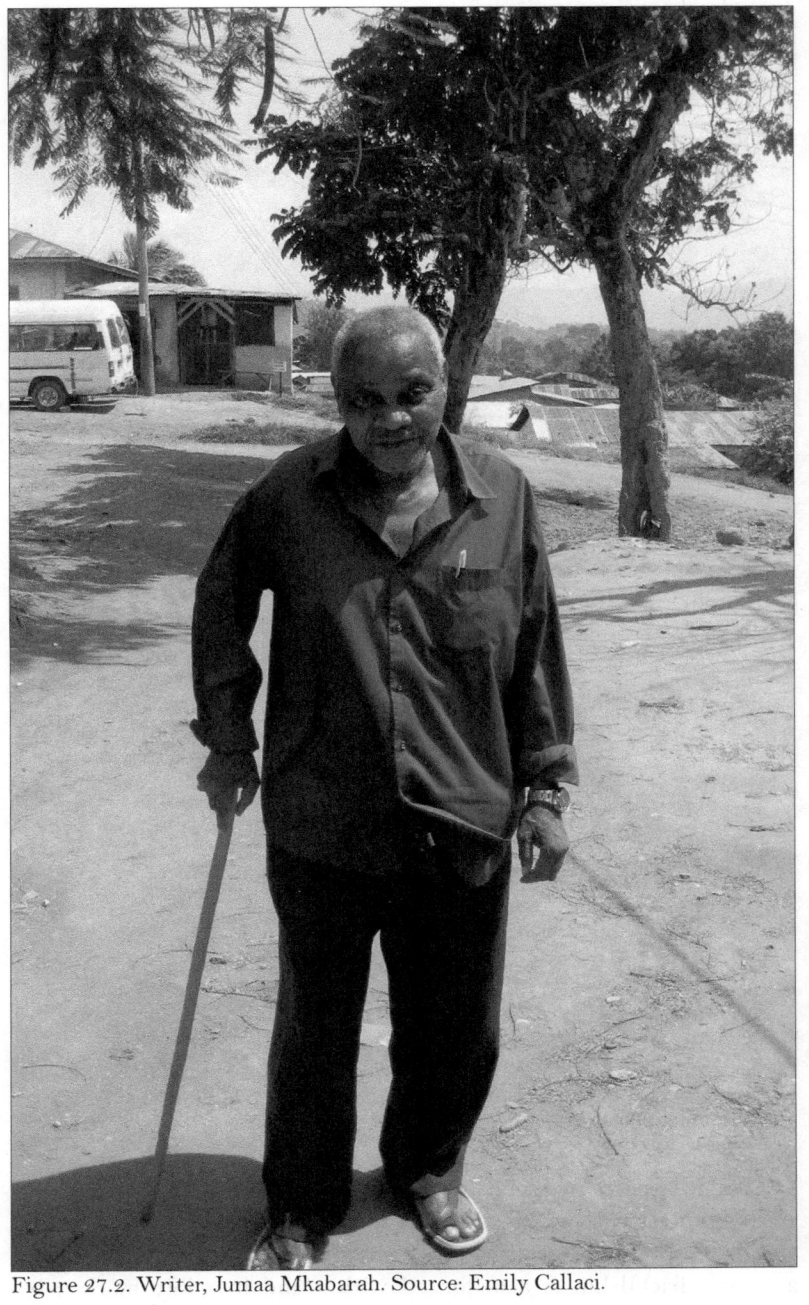

Figure 27.2. Writer, Jumaa Mkabarah. Source: Emily Callaci.

historical context. For example, among working class "lads" in 1970s Britain, the rituals of friendship—competitive performances of wit, troublemaking, and disruption—were shaped by the contours of working-class life and served to prepare young people for the challenges they would face as factory workers in adulthood.[3] In the ancient Greek city, women formed friendships within the confines of gendered expectations about the role of women as upholders of community morality.[4] Amid a tumultuous and rapidly changing world of colonialism, independence, and the upheavals of economic decline in northern Zambia over the course of the twentieth century, young male friends sought spaces of emotional security and belonging in cliques.[5] In contemporary rural North India, girls responsible for collecting leaves as bedding for their families' cattle herds express notions of friendship and affection in relation to the formation of work teams, as they find friends with whom they work well on this daily task.[6]

The friendships of the men I interviewed were simultaneously heartfelt and structured by economic and historical context. They took shape within an urban revolution in the global south that began in the 1970s, in which, for the first time in world history, urban growth occurred in the absence of economic growth and improving standards of living.[7] The vast majority of Africa's new urban areas were squatter settlements where inhabitants, lacking legal rights to the land they occupied, were vulnerable to eviction, police harassment, or slum demolitions. The simultaneous increase in urban populations and decrease in the number of wage-labor jobs led to the growth of the informal sector, in which people found off-the-books ways of making a living outside the formal economy of wage and salaried labor.[8] In Tanzania, these trends were particularly pronounced. In the 1970s, Dar es Salaam was the third-fastest-growing city in the world. By 1971, 83 percent of Dar es Salaam's residents were recently arrived migrants from elsewhere. The squatter population grew dramatically each year, making up 65 percent of the urban population by the end of the decade.[9]

Several factors made friendship especially important in this context. First, many young Tanzanians had migrated to the city in search of jobs, yet jobs were disappearing while at the same time the value of wages decreased dramatically. Youth increasingly could not rely on wage labor to survive in the city. Forging a life in the city meant forging a livelihood in the informal sector, which meant cultivating relationships with people in the urban economy. Second, many politicians and media commentators blamed the problems of urban life on unemployed youth, who they portrayed as hooligans, as layabouts, and as criminals. In defending themselves against these stereotypes, young men came to identify closely as a group. Third, the relationships between young migrants and their families in rural areas were under increasing strain as unemployed youth struggled, and failed, to meet the demands of their elders that they send resources home. Meanwhile, rural communities, also feeling great economic strain, demanded greater amounts of bridewealth— the gifts given by a man's family to his fiancée's family—making marriage too expensive for many young people. The paths to adulthood, status, and respectability that previous generations had forged through marriage, cultivating the land, and accumulating wealth were increasingly difficult to attain. In response, young people forged alternative kinds of status, identity, and belonging in the city, relying less on relationships with family and employers and more on relationships with their friends.

The network of friends that I interviewed were born in the 1940s and migrated to the city in their late teens and early twenties. They had been children during the final years of colonial rule and were young men in 1961, when Tanzania gained independence from Great Britain. This was a generation of youth who expected to become adults in a prosperous, modern, and independent Africa. The following decade, a global economic recession, combined with a collapsing national economic program of socialism, deflated their ambitions.

These urban migrant men were excluded from many of the spaces of elite urban life. Dar es Salaam residents faced a severe housing shortage, and the government agency that controlled access to public housing reserved spaces almost exclusively for men who had wives and children. Moreover, private landlords were suspicious of young single people and tended to discriminate against them in the rental market. Many young men lived together in cramped rooms that they shared. These men had also been excluded from higher education, as admission to the University of Dar es Salaam, the nation's only major university at the time, was prohibitively competitive. Young men could not afford to go to the restaurants, bars, and nightclubs where the city's elites hung out and drank imported bottled drinks. Instead, they spent much of their time at "groceries," which were cheap illegal drinking establishments run by women who made home-brewed alcohol.

Scarcity was no barrier to style, however. At the time, as part of a policy of national economic self-sufficiency, the Tanzanian government restricted foreign imports and instead promoted local textile industries. Public service advertisements called on youth to be patriotic and wear clothing made in local factories, but young men preferred secondhand clothes in the cosmopolitan styles of the time: bell-bottoms, tight-fitting shirts and vests, and platform shoes. As the writer Freddy Macha explained, "Nice disco clothes had to be imported. So . . . you had to have the right stuff bought from dealers and guys from street corners. Those days you had to dig deep. I recall having to travel to Nairobi in Kenya just to get clothes, or buying clothes from foreigners and even freedom fighters from South Africa and Zimbabwe." Secondhand clothing came into Tanzania through ports and borders with Kenya, Zaire, and Mozambique, via enterprising men like Macha, and found their way into urban black markets. To wear secondhand clothing was not only to signal your elegance, but also to demonstrate knowledge of how to attain highly coveted items despite restriction and scarcity. A young urban man with social status was someone whose very appearance revealed that he knew how to live in the urban underground economy.

While young urban men wanted to look well-connected and savvy, they did not aspire to look wealthy, for to appear "wealthy" during a time of austerity and material scarcity was to be associated with the ill-gotten spoils of political corruption. It was an open secret that the young men who cut a stylish figure on the street lived in ramshackle accommodations and often skipped meals during the week in order to afford to go out with friends on the weekends. They often did not own all of their own clothes, but traded and borrowed items of clothing with each other. As Telson Mughogho told me, you would often find three or four men jointly owning a pair of bell-bottoms that they would take turns wearing. This way of living may have been a necessity born of scarcity, but young men took pride in it. Young men saw this economy of recycled elegance as distinct from the kinds of wealth associated with the corruption of a wealthier older generation. Consider this poem by Kajubi, another pulp fiction writer who came of age in the 1970s:

When I put on a big bugaloo[10]
Dirty and literally made up of patches
And tight slim-fit shirts
That are torn and without buttons,
When I wear long hair
That is combed only when God is happy,
When I enter the cinema and dance halls
At night
By forging and jumping over the wall
It is all hooliganism.
But when you
An age mate of my father,
Delude my sister
Confusing her with your Datsun,
And hypnotising her
By showing her bundles
Of one hundred shilling notes
And then using her
And making her pregnant
Then, like the coward you are,
Eluding her
So that you are clear
To hunt for others,
It is not hooliganism.
That is logic.[11]

This poem conveys a male elegance made from material trappings of
the city and the creativity that was necessary in a time of economic
scarcity. Kajubi celebrates a kind of frugal cosmopolitanism shared
by young urban men of his generation. Contesting the mainstream
portrayal of his generation of young men as "hooligans," his poem
redirects blame for social and sexual ills to the behaviors of wealthy
men of an older generation.

In their everyday lives, the young writers travelled along paths
in the city that were distinct from what would appear on any official
map, circulating from their cramped living quarters to the food stalls
and "groceries," to street corners and black-market clothing sellers. It
was in these spaces and exchanges that friendships were forged.

In the second half of the 1970s, Tanzanians struggled to access
basic necessities like tea, rice, and soap, let alone paper and ink for
printing books. Yet it was in these constrained circumstances that

young men started an underground novella-publishing industry. They would write their first drafts by hand in a notebook, and then give it to a friend who had access to a typewriter through an office job and could type up the manuscript on the sly at work. After discussing and editing several drafts with their friends, the author would obtain a final typed manuscript and enlist an illustrator to design the cover artwork. When they couldn't scrape together enough money from among their friends to meet production costs, authors had to find a shop owner or other investor to loan them money for printing costs in exchange for a future cut of the profits. They had two options for printing. The first was to take their manuscripts to one of Dar es Salaam's few small, privately owned printing presses, whose main trade was in Christian or Islamic texts. The second option was to take their manuscripts to one of the government cooperative printing presses, but for this option to work, the writer needed a connection inside the print factory who could, for a fee, illicitly push his manuscript to the front of the queue.[12] The novellas had an initial print run of between three and ten thousand copies, and books by the more popular authors would typically sell out in less than a month. The authors circulated the city on foot, hawking their books on street corners or through newspaper stands in the market. To be successful in Dar es Salaam's underground publishing industry required being frugal, being "in the know," having friends and connections, and being able to make a life in the informal urban economy.

The writers rarely made any significant profit from their novellas. So, why did they bother? When I posed this question, Kajubi Mukajanga, switching momentarily from Swahili to English, told me, "We were basically hustlers." Then, switching back to Swahili, he went on to explain, "but everybody knew us, and that was good." Kalindimya agreed, telling me his life was in no way materially bettered by his writing. "You got a name for yourself, and that's it. This is what the economy was like." What they gained from their publishing industry was a reputation, and each book that circulated through the city enhanced the group's reputation as well-connected, cosmopolitan men with lots of friends. The words of praise from fellow writers plastered across the back of their books not only complimented the stories but also displayed the social connections of the authors. Writers also included cameo appearances by their friends in their books, always in a way that made them look heroic, masculine, and patriotic. They dedicated their books to each other and helped promote each other's work in the streets. Through blurbs, cameo appearances, and dedications, they publicly expressed affection for each other.

One example of such a cameo appearance appears in Ben Mtobwa's book, *Dar es Salaam Usiku* (Dar es Salaam by night). A female character, Rukia, sees a group of writers out at a bar,

> The table was now occupied by five men. One of them, Rukia recognized. Wasn't that Sam Kitogo? Yes, isn't that the stout young man, the writer of books? And that one, isn't that Hammie Rajab? Rukia had never met him, but she didn't need to be told. His face was recognizable from his books and magazines. Without a doubt, that must be Kajubi Mukajanga, because he and Hammie never left each other's sides. Those others . . . that one was maybe Nicco ya Mbajo . . . and that one could be John Rutayisingwa. Rukia saw the barmaid approach them to take their order. Kitogo said something that made the barmaid laugh. Hammie said something that made her giggle. Now, she was stroking Kitogo's beard. And when she left to go fetch their beers, her gait was different. She tossed and swayed her ass. The writers laughed and toasted their glasses.[13]

This book was published in 1990, about a decade after the heyday of the underground Swahili fiction industry, but it expresses nostalgia for not only the friendship of young men, but also their reputation as a group, recognized by others as they moved through the spaces of the city.

While this image captures the conviviality of male bonding, it also raises the question: what was the role of the fictional female character in this scenario? While writers promoted male friendship as a key feature structuring urban life, they also reproduced and entrenched the separate social roles of men and women. Women were not members of this literary network and would not be seated at the table with them in this fictional scene or in real life.

In the novellas themselves, girls and women are portrayed in stark caricature, as dishonest, sexually promiscuous, and greedy; or, in the other extreme, as helpless victims in need of a male savior.[14] In this way, the novellas reflected the gender politics of the time. Young women came to cities in unprecedented numbers in the 1960s and 1970s, and, with the expansion of educational opportunities to girls, many young women were now qualified for jobs that had previously been reserved for men, particularly in office work. Many young men found women's newfound mobility and economic autonomy disconcerting, and perceived women as the cause of their own economic and romantic difficulties. The late 1960s were a time of great controversy over so-called modern girls and women. Throughout the 1960s and 1970s, it was a fairly common occurrence for mobs of young men to attack or harass young "modern" women in Dar es Salaam's public spaces.[15]

The writers used caricatures of women to bolster their own identity as heroic. In some stories, female characters are greedy, materialistic, and morally weak, submitting to the lust of "sugar daddies" rather than pursuing romantic entanglements with their virtuous but broke age-mates. In other stories, it is conservative rural elders who selfishly marry girls off to older, wealthier men in order to access their wealth. In these tales, the young, frugal, fashionable protagonists defend and save helpless women from the predations of those older men.[16] Yet the resolution of the story is never that girls or women having ambitions or motivations of their own. Their ultimate destiny is to become the girlfriend or wife of the heroic male protagonist, modeled after the author and his friends. While the reputations, commercial networks, and literary production of these friends produced bonds of friendship, they also solidified male prerogatives as the defining moral story of the city.

The writer Mpufu Katojo captures this experience of male bonding in a 1973 editorial for the Dar es Salaam *Daily News*. He describes going out on the town one night with his three best friends, hoping to meet women. The men are educated, virtuous, and looking for love, but they don't have much money. They lament that young women want nothing to do with them, but instead seek out wealthier sugar daddies or prudishly stay at home in the evenings. Katojo describes the men's disappointment and romantic frustration, but then goes on to describe an evening shared by male friends drinking, talking about politics, dancing together, and commiserating about the difficulties of life in the city.[17]

For the generation of migrants who made their lives in Africa's rapidly growing cities of the 1970s, friendship was a vital resource that was simultaneously economic, social, and emotional. For the network of young men who created Dar es Salaam's underground fiction publishing industry, male friendship offered a secure space from which to challenge generational hierarchies, cast light on the economic hardships faced by young people, and carve out new forms of social recognition and status. At the same time, male friendship also became a place for the entrenchment of masculine ideals and the defense of young men's prerogatives and privileges over those of young women.

Notes

1. My research on this publishing industry appears in two separate publications. See Emily Callaci, "Street Textuality: Socialism, Masculinity, and Urban Belonging in Tanzania's Pulp Fiction Publishing Industry, 1975–1985," *Comparative Studies in Society and History* 59, no. 1 (January 2017): 183–210; and Callaci, *Street Archives and City Life: Popular Intellectuals in Postcolonial Tanzania* (Durham, NC: Duke University Press, 2017).

2. Jane Dyson, "Friendship in Practice: Girls' Work in the Indian Himalayas," *American Ethnologist* 37, no. 3 (August 2010): 482–98.

3. Paul E. Willis, *Learning to Labor: How Working Class Kids Get Working Class Jobs* (New York: Columbia University Press, 1981).

4. Claire Taylor, "Women's Social Networks and Female Friendship in the Ancient Greek City," *Gender and History* 23 no. 3 (November 2011): 703–20.

5. James A. Pritchett, *Friends for Life, Friends for Death: Cohorts and Consciousness among the Lunda-Ndembu* (Charlottesville: University of Virginia Press, 2007).

6. Dyson, "Friendship in Practice."

7. Garth Myers, "Introduction," in *African Cities: Alternative Visions of Urban Theory and Practice* (New York: Zed Books, 2011).

8. Keith Hart, "Informal Income Opportunities and Urban Employment in Ghana," *Journal of Modern African Studies* 11, no. 1 (March 1973): 61–89; Karen Tranberg Hansen and Mariken Vaa, "Introduction," in *Reconsidering Informality: Perspectives from Urban Africa*, ed. Karen Tranberg Hansen and Mariken Vaa (Uppsala: Nordiska Afrikainstitutet, 2004).

9. Richard Stren, Mohamed Halfani, and Joyce Malombe, "Coping with Urbanization and Urban Policy," in *Beyond Capitalism vs. Socialism in Kenya and Tanzania*, ed. Joel D. Barkan (Boulder, CO: Lynn Rienner, 1994).

10. Slang for bell-bottom pants.

11. Kajubi, "Logic," in *Summons: Poems from Tanzania*, ed. Richard S. Mabala (Dar es Salaam: Tanzania Publishing House, 1980), 46.

12. Walter Bgoya, *Books and Reading in Tanzania*, Studies on Books and Reading 25 (Paris: UNESCO, 1984).

13. Ben R. Mtobwa, *Dar es Salaam Usiku* (Dar es Salaam: Heko, 1998), 24.

14. For example, see John Simbamwene, *Mwisho wa Mapenzi* (Dar es Salaam: Longman, 1971); and Hammie Rajab, *Dunia Hadaa* (Dar es Salaam: Busara, 1982).

15. Andrew Ivaska, *Cultured States: Youth, Gender, and Modern Style in 1960s Dar Es Salaam* (Durham, NC: Duke University Press, 2011).

16. For example, see Jumaa Mkabarah, *Kizimbani* (Dar es Salaam: Black Star Agencies, 1974); Kajubi D. Mukajanga, *Mpenzi* (Dar es Salaam: Grand Arts Promotions, 1984); Mukajanga, *Tuanze Lini?* (Dar es Salaam: Grand Arts Promotions, 1983); and Hammie Rajab, *Ufunguo wa Bandia* (Dar es Salaam: Eastern Africa Publications, 1979).

17. Mpufu Katojo, "On the Rampage with Eligible Bachelors," *Daily News* [Dar es Salaam], May 27, 1973.

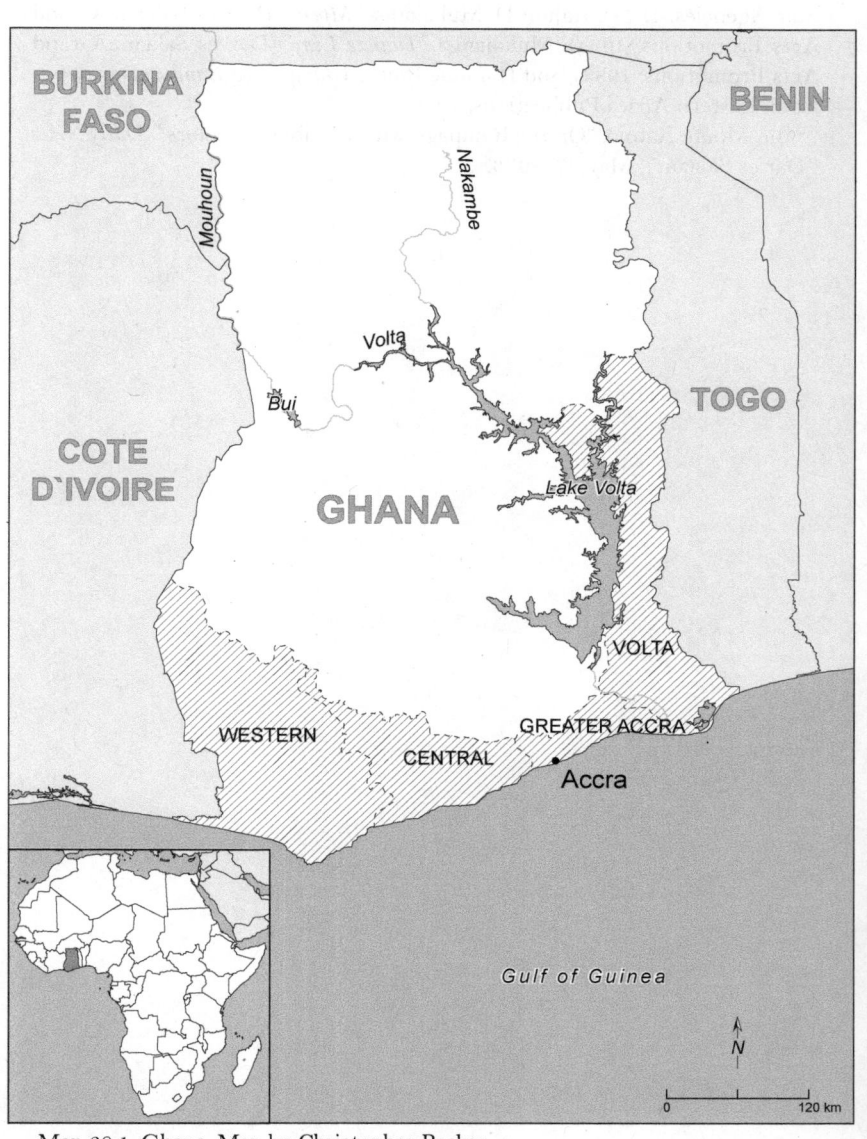

Map 28.1. Ghana. Map by Christopher Becker.

28

Work and Happiness

Songs of Indigenous Ghanaian Fishermen

ERIC DEBRAH OTCHERE

For six days in a week, dawn breaks on a group of people whose work usually begins after midnight and continues, depending on unpredictable factors such as weather conditions, the nature of the sea's waves, and availability of helping hands, until around midday or later. These people, the indigenous fishermen of the southern coast of Ghana, on the Atlantic Ocean's Gulf of Guinea, have continued a traditional trade that goes back in time to long before recorded history. Spanning across four administrative regions of southern Ghana—Volta, Greater Accra, and the Central and Western Regions (from east to west)—fishermen have mostly practiced a form of seine net fishing, also referred to as seine-haul fishing or dragnet fishing. The seine or dragnet is cast into the water so that it hangs vertically. Weights pull down the bottom part while floating buoys hold up the top. Attached to two of these vertically hanging nets is a third net, usually sack-like in shape and enclosed except for the part that hangs from one end of the two vertical seines. After casting them, the fishermen return to shore and haul the nets using long ropes that are tied to the other ends of the vertical seines. Any fish that tries to escape the embrace of the enclosing seines get trapped in the adjoining enclosed net.

The process of going out to cast the net and coming back to haul it to shore is not as simple and romantic as the description above suggests. It is an arduous, grueling, time-consuming, and physically exacting endeavor with no promised rewards, since getting a great catch is fortuitous. Yet, day in and day out, with the exception of Tuesdays (it is a common belief among Ghanaian coastal dwellers that Tuesday is a day for the spirits of the sea to rest and enjoy some solitude), fishermen have persisted and succeeded in getting fish to their respective local markets.

Meanwhile, they have something that helps them to endure the hardship, distract them from the hard labor, and make the time pass quickly. It synchronizes their individual energies, heightens their work, mutually ignites their spirits, and keeps them united. It voices their concerns, expresses their views on sensitive issues, attracts extra helping hands from watching crowds, moderates and manages their emotions, pushes the frontiers of their creative imaginations, amicably settles their differences, keeps them healthy and refreshed, helps them manage the putrid effluvium of decay from the detritus of the previous day's fish sales, draws potential buyers to their camps, and creates a safe haven. This thing also provides a space for negotiating the complex nexus of politics, identity, religion, gender, and social inequality. They have music.

The focus of this chapter is on the music that accompanies these Ghanaian canoe fishermen's work. While casting light on the immeasurable value of music in the daily activities of the fishermen, the chapter focuses on the poetic dimensions of the song lyrics. I illustrate how the fishermen employ a combination of linguistic and paralinguistic devices to own their physical and expressive spaces, as well as for social commentary.

Contextualization

Along the roughly 528-kilometer coast of Ghana are about two hundred communities whose major traditional occupation is fishing. Ghana's fishing industry employs an estimated 10 percent of the country's population, or about 2.6 million people. The fisheries subsector accounts for about five percent of the country's agricultural production. Fishing in rivers, lakes, lagoons, and the sea is done by big multinational fishing companies as well as medium- and small-scale fishermen in Ghana. There are also established fish farms that use artificially created ponds. This chapter focuses only on the practice of the small-scale maritime fishermen, since they are known for their singing. The word "fishermen" suggests the gendered nature of this occupation, a predominantly male affair. The part played by women mostly comes after the catch, when they are responsible for processing and marketing.

Figure 28.1. Women waiting patiently with their containers to carry the fresh fish directly to the market or for processing. Source: Eric Debrah Otchere.

The four coastal regions are inhabited by people with distinct cultural, language, and ethnic identities. The Volta region, sharing a border with Togo, is dominated by the Ewe ethnic group.[1] The Greater Accra region, where the current capital city of Ghana (Accra) is located, is dominated by the Ga. The Central Region, where the former capital city of Ghana (Cape Coast) is located, is dominated by the Fante. The Western Region, which shares a border with Ivory Coast, has people of the Fante, Ahanta, and Nzema ethnic groups. Ewe, Ga, Fante, Ahanta, and Nzema refer to both the people and their languages. Even though these cultural and ethnic identities are reflected strongly in the fishermen's songs, the attendant influences resulting from years of migration and intermingling among the fishermen are also decipherable in the song repertoires of many of the fishing groups. Consequently, an interesting hodgepodge of languages, tonal styles, pitch combinations, and subject matter are a pervasive feature.

In the course of my extensive ethnographic fieldwork, I have recorded many fishing songs. To get "cleaner" recordings devoid of the attendant din at the shores, I selected fishermen from different ethnic groups and recorded their songs in a professional studio. I later played back these recordings during interview sessions for the fishermen to tell me the exact words in each. Once they were written down, we discussed the content and meanings of the lyrics. Experts in each of the local languages translated the songs into English.

Fishing Songs

Ewe

Ame si ƒo detsi vivi mate ŋu aklɔ asi ko adzo le
Egbɔ maɖɔmaɖɔkpɔe o Wobe kutrikuku
Metsonu ye nye dzidzedzekpɔkpɔ. Ne ɖee
Wònye nyateƒea manye afi sia manɔ egbe o
Mele dzamevui dzem zã kple keli
Gake nyemate ŋu atɔ asi naneke dzi be eya ye
Nye viɖe si mekpɔ tso nye kutrikuku me o
Kese wɔ dɔ, fiẽ ɖu
Tsɔ wò ɖɔ kple ɖɔkplɔti
Miayi tɔ dzi, Miayi tɔ dzi
Afi aɖe kpɔkpɔ nyo wu yame kpɔkpɔ

The one who prepares a sumptuous meal
Does not just wash his hands and walk away
"Success should be the outcome of hard work," they say
If that were true, this is not where I should be
I keep toiling night and day
But I have very little to show for it
Monkey dey work, baboon dey chop
Pick up your nets, get your paddles
To the sea, to the sea
A bad job is better than none at all

This text is a translation of a song sung by a migrant Ewe group living in Cape Coast. The first two lines refer to a traditional proverb, which implies that when one has worked hard on something, s/he must get a taste of the outcome. Lines three and four highlight a hiatus between *what ought to be* and *what is*. In lines five and six, the singer places himself within the context provided in the first four lines by pointing out how his propitious and yet grueling routine has earned him practically nothing worthwhile. He supports his claim in the next line, where he quotes a popular metaphor that highlights the social inequality within set structures. In all likelihood, the "baboon" in line seven of the text refers to the owner(s) of the fishing equipment. In spite of the injustice, lines eight and nine signal the singer acquiescing to the exigencies of his reality. He is then consoled by the fact that "a bad job is better than none at all" (line 10). The fishermen are obliged to give from one-fifth to one-quarter of their daily catch to these owners. The remainder of the catch is then distributed among the crew and the people who are active in pulling the catch ashore.

This is the general tone of many of the songs. They address serious issues in a lighthearted manner, which might completely elude the casual observer. While a few of the songs make references to the work of fishermen (as in the example above), many focus on other topics, including commentaries on pertinent sociopolitical, religious, and economic issues from a point of view that is often sidelined. Most of the fishermen have little formal education. Therefore, their views on topical issues in the news are hardly heard or considered beyond their immediate communities. By studying fishing-song texts, we get perspectives of the fishermen on stories and "mainstream" narratives. The song themes, like other work songs, are part of the text of meanings produced by this subculture, attempting to form a cohesive version of what is realized incompletely in the authoritative discourse.[2] In other words, the content of the fishing songs serves as commentary on various issues that make headlines in the media and thereby make these stories fuller.

This song, like many others, stimulates thought about several things. The language is generally cryptic and indirect, employing a number of figurative expressions and literary devices such as metaphors, allusions, anthropomorphisms, and intended ambiguities. Interpreting the song texts is therefore complex, as it is difficult to decipher the exact intentions of the singers. Apart from the difficulty that arises from the linguistic and literary structures, these fishermen have developed a distinctive sublanguage of their own, what I refer to as the "fisher's tongue." This sublanguage carries most of the lexical words of the dominant language of the particular fishing group (for example, the languages Ewe, Ga, Fante, or Nzema) and a very high number of borrowed words (from English and other local Ghanaian languages) that are the result of the years of code-mixing among the fishermen. The bigger distinctive feature lies more in the way words are pronounced and joined to produce meaning than on the complexity of the individual words themselves.

How the singers use the words and structure the phrases makes it difficult to understand, even if one is a speaker of the dominant language. Many words sound muffled, consonants are attenuated or elided, words are deliberately used in contexts that are incongruous to the "regular" language, and many of the borrowed words are (mis) appropriated so that, even when you recognize the language from which the words were borrowed, they do not necessarily mean the same thing. Furthermore, several words are laden with ambiguities and are often interspersed with singers' own jargon and nonlexical vocalizations (sounds that do not have any referents or meanings in themselves). These vocalizations are often used as embellishments or as repetitive response patterns that help to keep the rhythmic flow. The following Fante song text summarizes many of the features of the fisher's tongue. Rather than a faithful respect for the correct Fante orthography, I have written the text in a way that reflects the sounds and articulation patterns being discussed.

> A'aa ny'n, a'aa ny'n, ofir' εpom' kyekyengogo
> Pagigingigin kyekyengogo
> Kolomboa. ɔr'hwehwε asaase fofor'
> Na dze
> Eyi akoko nyin' na ɔpε
> Unc Kwesi tsena boka
> Wɔmbɔ no hwe kyekanindini
> Ano' asεm bεba
> Besia yi shamɔlɔ

> There she is, there she is, coming from the north *kyekyengogo*
> *Pagigingigin kyekyengogo*
> Like Columbus, she is looking for a new land
> Among other things
> What she is interested in is a cock
> Uncle Kwesi sits to the east
> Send word to him *kyekanindini*
> Otherwise there will be trouble
> This particular lady is a whore

In the first line, the words *ofir'* and *εpom'* are the only ones that might be recognized by a regular non-fishing Fante speaker. *Ofir'* means "comes from" and *εpom'* means "in the sea" in regular Fante. In the fishing tongue, however, *εpom'* means "north," in much the same way as *boka* in line five means "east." These directions do not, however, correspond to the standard cardinal points on a compass. They are arbitrary, depending on the speaker's relative position at the time. The repeated words that come before the *ofir'* are an approximation, a contracted form of the phrase *ɔno nyen*, which means "there s/he is." The last word of the first line, *kyekyengogo*, as well as other words in the song such as *pagigingigin* (line two) and *kyekanindini* (line six), are embellishing sounds that have no lexical meanings whatsoever (non-lexical vocalizations). These words may, however, have contextual connotative meanings. *Kolombo* in the beginning of the third line is a reference to Christopher Columbus (the Italian explorer and naviga-tor who embarked on several voyages, including across the Atlantic Ocean). *Unc* is the shortened form of the English borrowing "uncle," which among the Fante is usually used as a sign of respect for any adult male. *Shamɔlɔ* in the last line is a borrowed word which means "bed-wetter" in the Ga language. In the context of the song, it means "prostitute."

I cannot stress enough how difficult it would be for an outsider to carry out meaningful, in-depth study of the fishing songs by just observing or listening to the fishermen; this is probably a reason why these songs have long been neglected in academic circles. For the fishermen, it is liberating to build this kind of expressive world where they can freely express themselves and vent their emotions. Through singing, they can talk about people in their presence without them having the slightest clue. It also helps them to select direct recipients of specific messages. Their arbitrary expressions of geographical po-sitions and the panoply of ambiguous jargon words can give the ca-sual listener a false sense of place, assuming they are able to make out the words at all. The shores are open places where anybody can visit at any time. Without the fisher's tongue, fishermen have little privacy. Thus, the fisher's tongue helps the fishermen to establish their own expressive space where they can freely share thoughts, admonish and reprimand each other, and make and laugh at their own jokes without undue interference.

The use of ambiguities and figurative expressions allows the fisher-men to manipulate symbolic meanings for their own purposes. This manipulation often takes the form of repudiating the messages that are expressed through the music, enabling them to freely express themselves: if necessary, they can deny any interpretations that might cause inconvenience, embarrassment, or even serious religious or political complications. The potential for self-distancing or denial of personal involvement with song texts gives the fishermen room to air their views, even those that might be considered sensitive or offensive. Consider the element of repudiation in the following Fante song:

> Ma metse ara nye yi
> Morotow ndwom biara kεkε
> Ma moho afɔw dabaa ntsi,
> Metsew mfifir' mpo a obiara nkεhu.
> Menhyεε bɔ biara dε wɔntow aba mmam'
> Na sε ɔketsew kedzi ne moko na
> atwεr bεtsew ho mfifir dzaa
> Ɔno εwɔ dεε yεka ho asεm
> Abaadze mpo na merekeka yi?
> Morotow ndwom bi ara kεkε oo
>
> Ma metse ara nye yi
> Morotow ndwom bi ara kεkε
> Emi menhyehyεε moho bereketsee ntsi
> Wɔrehwehwε a, wonnhu m'
> Ɔnnyε emi na medze 'madze y' kεgyee adze'
> Mbom sε wɔdze edziban no si egua no do,
> Na wɔdze 'pon no yε egua dzaa
> Ɔno εwɔ dεε yεka ho asεm
> Abaadze mpo na mere keka yi?
> Morotow ndwom bi ara kεkε oo
>
> I am just a simple man
> Singing just a simple song
> Because I get wet from the sea,
> My sweat is hardly noticed
> I am not the one who made promises for votes
> But when the frog feels the heat from the pepper
> that the lizard has eaten,
> It is worth talking about
> I don't know what I am even saying,
> Just singing my simple song
>
> I am just a simple man
> Singing a simple song
> Because I am not all dressed up in a suit and tie,

I am hardly noticed
I am not the one who gave my "something for something"
But when the food is put on the chair
and the table is used as the seat
It is worth talking about
I don't know what I am even saying,
Just singing my simple song

In the last line of each verse, the singer expressly denies knowledge of whatever the previous lines are alluding to and acknowledging that he is only singing a song. Meanwhile, the events alluded to are common-knowledge mainstream news. The first stanza speaks to the attitude of politicians who make promises during campaigns and fail to deliver once elected. In the second verse, the song alludes to some women who were given presidential appointments "out of the blue." There were allegations that some paid their way to the top through sex.

Fishing songs are generally in the call-and-response style (one person sings a part and the group responds with a fixed recurrent pattern, which is usually different from what the leader sings, like a question and answer), as well as cantor-and-chorus form (one person sings and the group repeats exactly what the leader sings, sometimes with minor melodic differences). These styles encourage participation even from people outside the group, since no rehearsals are necessary. Most of the response parts in the songs are made up of short repetitive phrases as well as nonlexical vocalizations that can be learned easily while singing. As evident in the irregular meter in the song texts above, it is the response parts rather than the call (main text) that provide the points of reference for coordinated work.

Parts of the call usually overlap the responses, which are usually evenly spaced. The well-timed ad-libs, witty interpolations, overlapping rhythmic phrases, interlocking pitches, and the collective spontaneity are some of the remarkable attributes of these otherwise stylistically plain tunes. Sometimes, the songs serve as frames within which people voice their displeasure with others, and, through this, disputes are resolved. As the fixed responses go on, people take turns to introduce new content, which can be about anything from the hot gossip within the local community to international news. In this light, the content of Ghanaian fishing songs unequivocally serves as social commentary.[3] Common themes around which fishing songs revolve include politics, morality, religion, belief systems, and general philosophy of life.

Apart from serving as useful accompaniments to the work and providing reference points for synchronizing movements, the fishing songs serve as a privileged form of social criticism. Within the context of the songs, issues are raised and resolved, information is disseminated, life lessons are learned, announcements are made, progressive identities are negotiated, and safe creative and expressive spaces are formed. Studies of the song texts illuminate deeper meanings about such concepts as migration, memory, cultural transformation, and space. Furthermore, the songs provide information about the lives of the fishermen beyond their work and the communities within which they live. Everything else aside, it is a complete delight to watch, engage with, and listen to these witty, expressive men as they work and sing.

Notes

1. For a detailed discussion of the maritime culture of the Ewe, see Emmanuel K. Akyeampong, *Between the Sea and the Lagoon: An Eco-Social History of the Anlo of Southeastern Ghana, c. 1850 to Recent Times* (Athens: Ohio University Press, 2001).

2. Gerald Porter, "'Work the Old Lady out of the Ditch': Singing at Work by English Lacemakers," *Journal of Folklore Research* 31, no. 1/3 (January–December 1994): 35–55.

3. Kwasi Ampene, *Female Song Tradition and the Akan of Ghana: The Creative Process in Nnwonkoro* (Burlington, VT: Ashgate, 2005); Msia Kibona Clark, "Hip Hop as social Commentary in Accra and Dar es Salaam," *African Studies Quarterly: The Online Journal of African Studies* 13, no. 3 (Summer 2012): 23–46, https://sites.clas.ufl.edu/africa-asq/files/Clark-V13Is3.pdf; Nate Plageman, *Highlife Saturday Night: Popular Music and Social Change in Urban Ghana* (Bloomington: Indiana University Press, 2013).

29

Leisure at the Edge of Legality

Cannabis in Twentieth-Century Swaziland and South Africa

BILL MCCOY

Grandmas Growing Gold?

Being a small country in Southern Africa whose population is made up of fewer than 1.5 million siSwati speakers, Swaziland (renamed eSwatini in 2018) doesn't exactly dominate the global news cycle. But, in August 2012, the country made the front page of the *New York Times* with the headline "Where Grandmas Grow Gold." The story introduced readers to the phenomenon of "Swazi Gold," an apparently high-quality strain of cannabis that grows in Swaziland. The focus of the story, however, was not really on the crop itself, but rather on the producers, many of them elderly Swazi women who found themselves caring for their grandchildren orphaned by HIV/AIDS. The story dramatically explored the plight of "thousands of peasants eking out a meager living in the rural areas of this kingdom at Africa's southern tip by growing marijuana, . . . embracing it as a much-needed income boost that is relatively hardy and easy to grow."[1]

There's nothing inherently wrong with this bit of investigative journalism, though it does follow a certain formulaic pattern that is consistently evident in international journalism about Swaziland. Most obviously, it connects the cannabis production directly to Swaziland's very high rate of adult HIV/AIDS infection, which has had undeniably serious social and economic consequences for the country. It is, of course, interesting to think about the socioeconomic connections between cannabis production in Swaziland and the problem of HIV/AIDS, but, as a historian, that wasn't the first thing I noted

Map 29.1. Swaziland (eSwatini)/South Africa. Map by Christopher Becker.

about this story. What stood out to me was the manner in which the story treated this phenomenon of Swazi women growing cannabis, or *dagga* in local parlance, as something quite novel, an opportunity that has apparently (and quite literally) sprung out of the ground as a means of dealing with the HIV/AIDS crisis. This implication of novelty, I knew, was misleading, because it reminded me in many ways of an incident from 1952 that I had uncovered quite by accident while doing research on the history of leprosy care in Swaziland. Drawing chiefly on the documentary evidence surrounding this older story and its larger context, I hope that we will be able not only to see the stories of modern Swazi grandmothers in a different light, but also to consider the results when leisure activities exist on the margins of what is legal.

Dagga at the Mbuluzi Leprosy Hospital

In 1952, Swaziland was in its fiftieth year under the rule of the British Empire, though the influence of British governance on ordinary Swazis was uneven at best. As in most other parts of their empire, the British employed a model of indirect rule in Swaziland, with a resident commissioner and a handful of other officials working in parallel with the traditional hierarchy of the Swazi monarchy, which had consolidated its rule over the area starting in the middle of the eighteenth century. As a result, most matters affecting the daily lives of Swazis remained in the hands of other Swazis, though their options were obviously limited by British oversight. In the mid-1940s, as part of their mission to "civilize" the Swazis, the British had funded the construction of the Mbuluzi Leprosy Hospital as a place to isolate and treat patients affected by leprosy. Just as the hospital prepared to open in 1948, its daily operations were handed over to Christian missionaries representing the Church of the Nazarene, a last-minute expedient based on a financial crunch that became the permanent arrangement until the hospital closed its doors in 1982.

Mbuluzi was always a small institution, by patient population if not by acreage. The hospital site lay on over five hundred acres astride two mountaintops a few miles northeast of Mbabane, the seat of the British government. In 1952, the hospital had about seventy residents receiving treatment, most of whom would spend a period of at least six months at Mbuluzi because of the slow and uncertain progression

Figure 29.1. A view of the Mbuluzi Leprosy Hospital site as it appeared in 2010, nearly 30 years after the hospital closed. In the foreground are patient housing structures, while the structures visible on the next hilltop are the church building, clinic, kitchen, and staff housing areas. At the time of the photo, an NGO had turned the site into an agricultural demonstration site. Source: Bill McCoy.

of leprosy treatment at the time. The small size of the patient community probably helped ensure Mbuluzi's relatively tranquil history, though this is not to suggest that the patients never raised objections to the conditions of life there. Although segregation at Mbuluzi was at least nominally voluntary, the isolation was real, and the missionaries worked vigorously to shape the life of the settlement according to their social and moral norms. Not everyone was willing to accept the resulting curtailment of their choices. Some patients ran away, alleging neglect and very poor living conditions. Others slipped away during the night for sexual liaisons or access to alcohol. Still others simply refused to participate in church services.

Elizabeth Cole, the resident missionary nurse representing the Nazarene mission at Mbuluzi, had a major role to play in supervising community norms. In one chapter of her short book about Mbuluzi, she crafted a series of four stories exploring the various ways in which patients rebelled against the institution's rules. She first recounted how a search for "witchcraft paraphernalia" in the patient residences had left hospital staff "loaded with sacks and tins containing horns, bones, foul-smelling concoctions, huge teeth, and many weird objects."[2] This was, in turn, followed by the uncovering of a scheme for brewing traditional Swazi beer in one of the men's villages and the confiscation of "eight gallons of very intoxicating liquor." Not long after this, Cole learned from the incensed wife of a male patient that young women from "just over the mountains" were visiting the men's villages at night, which led to yet another intervention. Finally, Cole discovered that patients were growing dagga around their residences, and it is on this story that I want to focus.

In her book, Cole suggests patients were growing the dagga for themselves. But her personal letters from that time indicate that Cole was convinced that the patients were growing dagga at the direction of Hugh Mason Ntisane, a former employee who had worked at Mbuluzi as a government agricultural demonstrator before being dismissed for his own violations of the community norms. Now, Cole believed, he was sneaking back into the colony at night to remove the dagga and export it to South Africa for sale. In describing the

Figure 29.2. A 2010 view of the remnants of the patient housing area at the site of the Mbuluzi Leprosy Hospital, from the opposite hillside. The patients were secretly growing dagga in the areas between their housing units. Source: Bill McCoy.

incident, Cole was very careful in her choice of words, as she believed that not only Ntisane but also the man who was serving as the colony's schoolteacher was involved. She was afraid that there would be trouble in the colony if the information was revealed prematurely, including possible reprisals against the patient who had been her informant.[3]

In combination, these incidents help us understand something of the gap that existed between Swazi culture and missionary ideals. There is no evidence, for example, that the patients of Mbuluzi ever completely left behind traditional healing practices during or after their time at Mbuluzi. Beer brewing and consumption were likewise firmly entrenched components of traditional Swazi social life, especially during the rainy season (as was the case in this incident), when beer was the essential reward for participation in communal work parties that undertook the difficult labor of preparing and maintaining fields for the year's crops.[4] What Cole condemned as both illegal and immoral behavior, the patients involved likely saw as merely a reasonable reward for their completion of the labor that Cole and her associates compelled them to do.

The Swazi perspective on dagga was in some ways similar to the beer issue. Dagga had a long history in the region, with evidence dating its migration into Southern Africa via Indian Ocean trade routes to a period at least several centuries prior to the fifteenth-century European voyages of exploration. By the twentieth century, there is abundant evidence that its use was commonplace throughout the region. For example, at the same time as Cole was engaged in her struggle to stamp out dagga production at Mbuluzi, James Walton in South Africa was completing an extensive catalog of the different types of dagga pipes in use throughout the region, ultimately inventorying several dozen types ranging from animal horns to clay pots.[5] Walton and others describe a pattern in which dagga smoking was chiefly recreational and usually reserved for adult men.

In Swaziland specifically, this pattern seems to have been borne out across the twentieth century. The anthropologist Brian Marwick described the smoking of dagga as "a habit very firmly entrenched" in the 1930s, especially as a leisure activity among older men and as a stimulant for men in the army before entering into battle.[6] In P. A. W. Cook's 1931 collection of *tibongo* (praise poems) connected with the men who had ruled as the Swazi monarch, dagga and the implements used for smoking it appear in two of the poems in a totally matter-of-fact fashion.[7] Similarly, a proverb used among the Swazi declares, "indzaba itfungelea egudwini," which roughly translates, "He is a topic for discussion over dagga smoking pipes."[8] These attitudes seem to be consistent with those found across the twentieth century. In his research into the subject in the 1970s, for example, Brian du Toit encountered a ninety-five-year-old Swazi man who smoked dagga three times daily and who regarded it as "purely social," saying that it was "part of the entertainment when he and his friends get together to discuss the affairs of his people."[9] It seems clear that moderate dagga consumption was a relatively common occurrence in Swaziland and across the region, which might legitimately lead to confusion or consternation amongst Mbuluzi's patients at the harsh condemnation of the practice by the missionary staff.

Cannabis in the Southern African Context

Examining the broader context further illuminates the incident at Mbuluzi. In the same year as the incident, for example, South Africa's *Drum* magazine ran a feature story painting a picture of a very lively dagga trafficking system operating throughout the region, arguing that it constituted a public menace that needed to be corrected.[10] Also in 1952, the South African government published a major study on dagga abuse in the country, which included an investigation of the traffic by way of Swaziland and other neighboring territories. The report stressed the view that police forces across the region needed to crack down on trafficking as a public menace. Of the surrounding territories, the investigation found Swaziland to be the greatest source of imports. However, it was unclear how much was locally grown and how much Swaziland served as a conduit for trafficking dagga from Portuguese East Africa and Zululand into South Africa's urban areas, especially around the city of Johannesburg, where a number of gangs had opportunistically seized the chance to sell alcohol and dagga to the mining laborers concentrated in the area.[11]

Swaziland's dagga trade flourished not just on its environment's ecological suitability for growing the plant, but also on the exceptionally high regard for the quality of its product around the region. The 1952 government investigation noted that Swazi dagga commanded a higher price than that from other areas because of its popularity.[12]

Similarly, in the 1970s, Brian du Toit's study of the regional cannabis trade found numerous individuals who placed "their only faith in cannabis from Swaziland," and referenced one informant who reported that "he always gets his cannabis from Swaziland because his 'wise' forefathers . . . used to make an expedition to Swaziland to get dagga for the Royal family and '*indunas*' (chiefs) because it was believed it was the best obtainable in the country."[13]

High demand meant that individuals continued to grow the crop in the face of police action aimed at disrupting the illegal traffic, and this seems to have been what was happening at Mbuluzi. The 1952 and 1953 annual reports of Swaziland's police commissioner indicated that his force had made a concerted effort in those years to disrupt dagga production, which the authorities believed was having the desired effect. The report for 1953 concluded, "Police patrols are now engaged in obviating this traffic at its source by seizing and destroying plants before they reach maturity. Reports reveal that growers are now resorting to growing plants in containers suspended in the branches of large trees in an endeavour to conceal them from Police patrols. Obviously only a very small quantity can be produced in this way."[14] Interestingly, in the South African government's report on the police patrols in Swaziland and the other High Commission territories, it noted that they relied significantly upon "officials of the Veterinary Department" to help them identify areas for patrol, since their activities naturally took them into the rural contexts where people commonly grew the plant.[15] In other words, the police strategy relied upon the help of men such as Hugh Mason Ntisane, which may well have provided him with the confidence to attempt to develop his own dagga trafficking business on a government-controlled piece of property. The potential financial gains clearly outweighed the obvious risks, and Ntisane was not the only one who saw it this way. In 1956, *Drum* published a two-part exposé on the dagga trade in and around the South African town of Bergville, where a 1954 police raid had resulted in widespread violence and the eventual execution of twenty-two men. Even with the tragedy fresh in everyone's memories, the *Drum* reporter found a flourishing dagga trade in the area, as the lure of ready profits proved too much for people to resist.[16] In the absence of any significant cultural condemnation of dagga production or consumption, people like Ntisane and the Mbuluzi patients who aided him seemingly found this particular act of subterfuge quite appealing.

Leisure at the Edge of Legality

It is easy to see in retrospect just how illustrative this small incident at Mbuluzi was of a much larger set of social and economic dynamics at work across this region, and it is a good reminder of just how thin the lines often are that separate leisure activity from the political and economic realm. How much Elizabeth Cole and her missionary colleagues understood about this larger context is uncertain, but it certainly played no role in their response to the discovery of the dagga being grown at Mbuluzi. In Cole's undoubtedly stylized book narrative, the guilty patients, when confronted by the police with their wrongdoing, had suddenly become "very religious," protesting that the destruction of the plants should be delayed because it happened that the police had come on a Sunday, the day of rest. In Cole's telling, her quick prayer for an answer to this plea was answered by the sudden recollection of the Gospel of John's account of Jesus driving moneychangers from the temple: "The scripture was quoted and a comparison was made between the Temple that had been built for God at Jerusalem, and Tembelihle, which was built for God at Mbuluzi." In this way, the deceitful intentions of the patients were overcome, and "the old giant dagga . . . was literally chopped to death" under the watchful eye of the police and the chaplain.[17]

The story, as framed by Elizabeth Cole, dramatizes the mission's perception of their work as a fundamentally spiritual one, reinforcing her particular narrative in a manner not unlike the way that the *New York Times* used the story of dagga production in contemporary Swaziland to round out a narrative of Swazi poverty and suffering in the wake of HIV/AIDS. I don't necessarily intend to condemn or invalidate either narrative, but it is important to ask ourselves whether the Swazis producing the cannabis would recognize themselves in either story. Given the historical evidence unpacked in this chapter, it seems reasonable to think that the dramatic appeal of these stories may be chiefly a product of audience preoccupations rather than a particularly accurate depiction of how Swazis themselves might recount these stories. In this light, we are all invited to be mindful of the ways in which we sometimes overlook the more complex realities of human life, in which even a leisure activity may become grounds for contesting the boundaries of legality and much more.

Notes

1. Lydia Polgreen, "Grandmas Grow Gold in Swaziland," *New York Times*, August 14, 2012, http://www.nytimes.com/2012/08/15/world/africa /grandmothers-grow-marijuana-in-swaziland-to-support-families.html. The print version of the story ran on August 15, 2012. A very similar story also ran on *BBC News* less than a year after the *Times* story, see "Swaziland's cannabis 'gold,'" *BBC News*, July 25, 2013, http://www.bbc.com/news/av /world-africa-23445677/swaziland-s-cannabis-gold.

2. Elizabeth Cole, *Give Me This Mountain* (Kansas City, MO: Nazarene Publishing House, 1959), 57–60.

3. Elizabeth Cole to David Hynd, "Unprocessed Correspondence," January 1952, Box 2499, David Hynd Collection, Nazarene Archives, Lenexa, Kansas.

4. On the role of beer in communal work parties, see Hilda Kuper, *An African Aristocracy: Rank among the Swazi* (New York: International African Institute, 1980), 144–48. On Swazi methods of beer brewing, see Brian Allan Marwick, *The Swazi: An Ethnographic Account of the Natives of the Swaziland Protectorate* (London: Frank Cass, 1966), 79–80.

5. James Walton, "The Dagga Pipes of Southern Africa," *Researches of the National Museum* 1, no. 4 (December 1953): 85–113.

6. Marwick, *The Swazi*, 80.

7. P. A. W. Cook, "History and *Izibongo* of the Swazi Chiefs," *Bantu Studies* 5, no. 2 (1931): 189, 201.

8. C. L. Sibusiso Nyembezi, *Zulu Proverbs* (Johannesburg: Witwatersrand University Press, 1974).

9. Brian M. du Toit, *Cannabis in Africa: A Survey of Its Distribution in Africa, and a Study of Cannabis Use and Users in Multi-ethnic South Africa* (Rotterdam: A. A. Balkema, 1980), 122.

10. "Dagga!," *Drum*, September 1952, 12–15.

11. *Report of the Inter-Departmental Committee on the Abuse of Dagga*, U.G. no. 31/1952, (Pretoria: Government Printer, Union of South Africa): 91–92.

12. *Report of the Inter-Departmental Committee*, 92.

13. Du Toit, *Cannabis in Africa*, 172, 107.

14. L. W. Clarke, "Annual Report of the Commissioner of Police, Swaziland for the Year 1953." African Government "J" Documents Collection, African Studies Library, Boston University, J720 P6 1952-63.

15. *Report of the Inter-Departmental Committee*, 207.

16. G. R. Naidoo, "I Go Back to Bergville," *Drum*, October 1958, 26–30.

17. Cole, *Give Me This Mountain*, 60–62.

Bibliography

Abrahams, Roger D. "Toward an Enactment-Centered Theory of Folklore." In *Frontiers of Folklore*, edited by William R. Bascom, 79–120. Boulder, CO: Westview, 1977.

Abruzzini, Marissa. "The Evolution of After-Tears Parties in South Africa." Blog post, SevenPonds.com, January 5, 2017. http://blog.sevenponds.com/cultural-perspectives/the-evolution-of-after-tears-parties-in-south-africa.

Adam, Issahaku. "Leisure Aspirations of People with Visual Impairment in the Kumasi Metropolis, Ghana." *Annals of Leisure Research* 21, no. 3 (2018): 347–63.

Adams, Melinda. "Colonial Policies and Women's Participation in Public Life: The Case of British Southern Cameroons." *African Studies Quarterly: The Online Journal of African Studies* 8, no. 3 (Spring 2006): 1–22. https://sites.clas.ufl.edu/africa-asq/files/Adams-Vol8Issue3.pdf.

Adebanwi, Wale, ed. *The Political Economy of Everyday Life in Africa: Beyond the Margins*. Suffolk, UK: James Currey, 2017.

Aderinto, Saheed. "Introduction: Colonialism and the Invention of Modern Colonial Childhood." In *Children and Childhood in Colonial Nigerian Histories*, edited by Saheed Aderinto, 1–18. New York: Palgrave Macmillan, 2015.

Adichie, Chimamanda Ngozi. "The Danger of a Single Story." Produced by TED. YouTube, October 7, 2009. Video, 19:16. https://www.youtube.com/watch?v=D9Ihs241zeg.

Adler, Patricia A., Peter Adler, and Andrea Fontana. "Everyday Life Sociology." *Annual Review of Sociology* 13 (1987): 217–35.

"African Voices Dubbing Company." YouTube channel, est. July 25, 2015. https://www.youtube.com/channel/UCIEWVjE-ATun7XTcTb7scKg/about.

"Africa Women Cup of Nations Kicks off in Cameroon." *Guardian*, November 20, 2016, https://www.theguardian.com/world/2016/nov/20/africa-women-cup-of-nations-cameroon-opening-ceremony-football.

Agbenyega, Joseph S. "The Power of Labelling Discourse in the Construction of Disability in Ghana." Paper presented at the Australian Association for Research in Education Conference, Newcastle, New South Wales, Australia, 2003.

Akyeampong, Emmanuel. *Between the Sea and the Lagoon: An Eco-Social History of the Anlo of Southeastern Ghana c. 1850 to Recent Times.* Athens: Ohio University Press, 2001.

Akyeampong, Emmanuel, and Charles Ambler. "Leisure in African History: An Introduction." In "Leisure in African History," edited by Emmanuel Akyeampong and Charles Ambler. Special issue, *International Journal of African Historical Studies* 35, no. 1 (2002): 1–16.

Alegi, Peter. *African Soccerscapes: How a Continent Changed the World's Game.* Athens: Ohio University Press, 2010.

———. *Laduma! Soccer, Politics and Society in South Africa.* Pietermaritzburg, South Africa: University of KwaZulu-Natal Press, 2004.

Allman, Jean, ed. *Fashioning Africa: Power and the Politics of Dress.* Bloomington: Indiana University Press, 2004.

Ambler, Charles. "Popular Films and Colonial Audiences: The Movies in Northern Rhodesia." *American Historical Review* 106, no. 1 (2001): 81–105.

Ampene, Kwasi. *Female Song Tradition and the Akan of Ghana: The Creative Process in Nnwonkoro.* Burlington, VT: Ashgate, 2005.

Andreas, Neshani. "Neshani Andreas: A Passion for Writing." Interview by Erika von Wietersheim, originally published October 2004 in *Insight Namibia* (Windhoek). The Free Library, December 1, 2004. https://www.thefreelibrary.com/Neshani+Andreas:+a+passion+for+writing-a0131994511.

Anikpo, Mark O. C., and Josiah D. Atemie, eds. *Introduction to Nigerian Socio-Cultural Heritage.* Port Harcourt, Nigeria: Osia International, 1999.

Annan, Jeannie, Christopher Blattman, Khristopher Carlson, and Dyan Mazurana. *The State of Female Youth in Northern Uganda: Findings from the Survey of War-Affected Youth (SWAY).* Boston: Feinstein International Center, 2008.

Askew, Kelly. *Performing the Nation: Swahili Music and Cultural Politics in Tanzania.* Chicago: University of Chicago Press, 2002.

Atkinson, Rowland. "Ecology of Sound: The Sonic Order of Urban Space." *Urban Studies* 44, no. 10 (September 2007): 1905–17.

Babcock, Barbara A., ed. *The Reversible World: Symbolic Inversion in Art and Society.* Ithaca, NY: Cornell University Press, 1978.

Bahgat, Ahmad. *Ramadan Diary.* Translated by Nermeen Hassan. Cairo: General Egyptian Book Organization, 1988.

Baker, William J., and James A. Mangan, eds. *Sport in Africa: Essays in Social History.* London: Africana, 1987.

Balandier, Georges. *Sociologie des Brazzavilles noires.* 2nd ed. Paris: Presses de la Fondation Nationale des Sciences Politiques, 1985.

Balogun, Oluwakemi M., and Kimberly Kay Hoang. "Refashioning Global Bodies: Cosmopolitan Femininities in Nigerian Beauty Pageants and the Vietnamese Sex Industry." In *Global Beauty, Local Bodies*, edited by Afshan Jafar and Erynn Masi de Casanova, 1–21. New York: Palgrave Macmillan, 2013.

Barber, Karin. *A History of African Popular Culture: New Approaches to African History*. Cambridge: Cambridge University Press, 2018.

———, ed. *Readings in African Popular Culture*. Bloomington: Indiana University Press, 1997.

Bascom, William. *The Yoruba of Southwestern Nigeria*. Prospect Heights, IL: Waveland, 1984.

Bebey, Françis. *La radiodiffusion en Afrique noire*. Issy-les-Moulineaux: Éditions Saint-Paul, 1963.

Beck, Kurt. "The Art of Truck Modding on the Nile (Sudan): An Attempt to Trace Creativity." In *The Speed of Change: Motor Vehicles and People in Africa, 1890–2000*, edited by Jan–Bart Gewald, Sabine Luning, and Klaas van Walraven, 151–74. Boston: Brill, 2009.

Bemba, Sylvain. *Cinquante ans de musique du Congo-Zaïre (1920–1970): De Paul Kamba à Tabu-Ley*. Paris: Présence Africaine, 1984.

Berger, Iris. *Women in Twentieth-Century Africa*. New York: Cambridge University Press, 2016.

"Best of Journal Rappé 2 (Invités) avec Xuman et Keyti." YouTube, October 25, 2013, posted by JT Rappé. Video, 7:39. https://www.youtube.com/watch?v=MiGgqskvFlc.

Bgoya, Walter. *Books and Reading in Tanzania*. Studies on Books and Reading 25. Paris: UNESCO, 1984.

Bienefeld, M. A., and R. H. Sabot. *The National Urban Mobility, Employment and Income Survey of Tanzania (NUMEIST)*. Dar es Salaam: Ministry of Economic Affairs and Development Planning and Economic Research Bureau, 1971.

Blacking, John. "Games and Sport in Pre-Colonial African Societies." In *Sport in Africa: Essays in Social History*, edited by William J. Baker and James A. Mangan, 3–22. London: Africana, 1987.

Blinde, Elaine M., and Diane E. Taub. "Women Athletes as Falsely Accused Deviants: Managing the Lesbian Stigma." In *Sociological Perspectives on Sport: The Games outside the Games*, edited by David Karen and Robert E. Washington, 503–11. New York: Routledge, 2015.

Bloch, Maurice. "Death, Women and Power." In *Death and the Regeneration of Life*, edited by Maurice Bloch and Jonathan Parry, 211–30. Cambridge: Cambridge University Press, 1982.

———. "Zafimaniry Birth and Kinship Theory." *Social Anthropology* 1, no. 1b (February 1993): 119–32.

Boer, Martin, and Robin Sherbourne. *Getting the Most Out of Our Diamonds: Namibia, De Beers, and the Arrival of Lev Leviev*. Institute for Public Policy Research Briefing Paper 20. Windhoek, Namibia: IPPR, 2003.

Böhme, Claudia. "Film Production as a 'Mirror of Society': The History of a Video Film Art Group in Dar es Salaam, Tanzania." *Journal of African Cinemas* 7, no. 2 (2015): 117–35.

———. "White Elephant: Die Aushandlung von Kultur in der tansanischen Videofilmindustrie." PhD diss., Institut für Ethnologie und Afrikastudien, Johannes Gutenberg-Universität Mainz, 2016.

Borg, Kevin L. *Auto Mechanics: Technology and Expertise in Twentieth-Century America*. Baltimore: Johns Hopkins University Press, 2007.

Bosire, Mokaya. "What Makes a Sheng Word Unique? Lexical Manipulation in Mixed Languages." In *Selected Proceedings of the 39th Annual Conference on African Linguistics: Linguistic Research and Languages in Africa*, edited by Akinloyè Ojó and Lioba J. Moshi, 77–85. Somerville, MA: Cascadilla Proceedings Project, 2006.

"Boxing Sensation: Woman Licks Male Opponent." *Cameroon Times*, October 6, 1964, 1.

Brennan, James. "Democratizing Cinema and Censorship in Tanzania, 1920–1980." *International Journal of African Historical Studies* 38, no. 3 (2005): 481–511.

Bressler, Eric R., and Sigal Balshine. "The Influence of Humor on Desirability." *Evolution and Human Behavior* 27, no. 1 (2006): 29–39.

Bronner, Simon J. "Folklore Movement." In *American Folklore: An Encyclopedia*, edited by Jan Harold Brunvand. New York: Routledge, 2006.

Brown, Carolyn. "Race and the Construction of Working-Class Masculinity in the Nigerian Coal Industry: The Initial Phase, 1914–1930." *International Labor and Working-Class History*, no. 69 (Spring 2006): 35–56.

Burns, James. *Cinema and Society in the British Empire, 1895–1940*. New York: Palgrave Macmillan, 2013.

———. "John Wayne on the Zambezi: Cinema, Empire, and the American Western in British Central Africa." In "Leisure in African History," edited by Emmanuel Akyeampong and Charles Ambler. Special issue, *International Journal of African Historical Studies* 35, no. 1 (2002): 103–17.

Caisse Nationale de Prévoyance Sociale. *Guide de la femme camerounaise (AGRACAM)*. Yaoundé, Cameroon: CNPS, 1976.

Callaci, Emily. *Street Archives and City Life: Popular Intellectuals in Postcolonial Tanzania*. Durham, NC: Duke University Press, 2017.

———. "Street Textuality: Socialism, Masculinity, and Urban Belonging in Tanzania's Pulp Fiction Publishing Industry, 1975–1985." *Comparative Studies in Society and History* 59, no. 1 (January 2017): 183–210.

Carsten, Janet. *After Kinship*. Cambridge: Cambridge University Press, 2004.

Castells, Manuel, Mireia Fernández-Ardèvol, Jack Linchuan Qui, and Araba Sey. *Mobile Communication and Society: A Global Perspective*. Cambridge, MA: MIT Press, 2007.

Central Intelligence Agency. "Senegal." *The World Factbook.* Accessed February 16, 2017. https://www.cia.gov/library/publications/the-world-factbook /geos/sg.html.

Chahin, Salah. *Azjal Sihafiyah.* Cairo: Al-Ahram Center for Translation and Publishing, 2007.

Cheney, Kristin E. *Pillars of the Nation: Child Citizens and Ugandan National Development.* Chicago: University of Chicago Press, 2007.

Chernoff, John M. *Hustling Is Not Stealing: Stories of an African Bar Girl.* Chicago: University of Chicago Press, 2003.

"Children's Xmas Tree." *Oranjemund* [Namibia] *Newsletter,* December 4, 1987.

Churchill Show (NTV Kenya). "Brigeddia Poet—Special Dedication to Ladies (Spoken Word)." YouTube, April 24, 2015. Video, 4:09. https:// youtu.be/d0tcaG8V2J4.

Cissé, Mamadou. "Langues, état, et société au Sénégal." *SudLangues: Revue électronique internationale de sciences du langage,* no. 5 (December 2005): 99–133.

Cissé, Momar. *Parole chantée et communication sociale chez les Wolof du Sénégal.* Paris: Harmattan, 2009.

Clark, Msia Kibona. "Hip Hop as Social Commentary in Accra and Dar es Salaam." *African Studies Quarterly: The Online Journal of African Studies* 13, no. 3 (Summer 2012): 23–46. https://sites.clas.ufl.edu/africa-asq /files/Clark-V13Is3.pdf.

———. *Hip-Hop in Africa: Prophets of the City and Dustyfoot Philosophers.* Athens: Ohio University Press, 2018.

Clarke, Kamari Maxine. *Fictions of Justice: The International Criminal Court and the Challenge of Legal Pluralism in Sub-Saharan Africa.* Cambridge: Cambridge University Press, 2009.

Cleveland, Todd. *Following the Ball: The Migration of African Soccer Players across the Portuguese Colonial Empire, 1949–1975.* Athens: Ohio University Press, 2017.

Cole, Elizabeth. *Give Me This Mountain.* Kansas City, MO: Nazarene Publishing House, 1959.

Cole, Jennifer, and Lynn M. Thomas, eds. *Love in Africa.* Chicago: University of Chicago Press, 2009.

Comaroff, Jean, and John L. Comaroff. *Of Revelation and Revolution.* Vol. 2, *The Dialectics of Modernity on a South African Frontier.* Chicago: University of Chicago Press, 1997.

Comhaire-Sylvain, Suzanne. *Femmes de Kinshasa: Hier et aujourd'hui.* Paris: Mouton, 1968.

Constitution of the Republic of Zambia (1996.) Accessed June 26, 2017. www .zambialaws.com/Principal-Legislation/CHAPTER-1CONSTITUTION -OF-ZAMBIA-ACT.html.

Cook, P. A.W. "History and Izibongo of the Swazi Chiefs." *Bantu Studies* 5, no. 2 (1931): 181–201.

Cooper, Frederick. "Industrial Man Goes to Africa." In *Men and Masculinities in Modern Africa,* edited by Lisa A. Lindsay and Stephan F. Miescher, 128–37. Portsmouth, NH: Heinemann, 2003.

Coplan, David B. "South African Radio in a Saucepan." In *Radio in Africa: Publics, Cultures, Communities,* edited by Liz Gunner, Dina Ligaga, and Dumisani Moyo, 134–48. Johannesburg: Wits University Press, 2012.

Currier, Ashley. *Out in Africa: LGBT Organizing in Namibia and South Africa.* Minneapolis: University of Minnesota Press, 2012.

Darcy, Simon. "Inherent Complexity: Disability, Accessible Tourism and Accommodation Information Preferences." *Tourism Management* 31, no. 6 (December 2010): 816–26.

Del Negro, Giovanna P., and Harris M. Berger. "New Directions in the Study of Everyday Life: Expressive Culture and the Interpretation of Practice." In *Identity and Everyday Life: Essays in the Study of Folklore, Music, and Popular Culture,* edited by Harris M. Berger and Giovanna P. Del Negro, 3–22. Middletown, CT: Wesleyan University Press, 2004.

Durham, Deborah. "Did You Bathe This Morning? Baths and Morality in Botswana." In *Dirt, Undress, and Difference: Critical Perspectives on the Body's Surface,* edited by Adeline Masquelier, 190–212. Bloomington: Indiana University Press, 2005.

———. "Love and Jealousy in the Space of Death." *Ethnos* 67, no. 2 (2002): 155–79.

———. "Soliciting Gifts and Negotiating Agency: The Spirit of Asking in Botswana." *Journal of the Royal Anthropological Institute,* n.s., 1, no. 1 (March 1995): 111–28.

Du Toit, Brian M. *Cannabis in Africa: A Survey of Its Distribution in Africa, and a Study of Cannabis Use and Users in Multi-ethnic South Africa.* Rotterdam: A. A. Balkema, 1980.

Dyson, Jane. "Friendship in Practice: Girls' Work in the Indian Himalayas." *American Ethnologist* 37, no. 3 (August 2010): 482–98.

Eades, J. S. *The Yoruba Today.* Cambridge: Cambridge University Press, 1980.

Ebben. Comment on "The Tank Park." Oranjemund Online, forum post, July 17, 2007. http://www.oranjemundonline.com/Forum/index.php?topic=25.0.

Ebeogu, Afam. "Onomastics and the Igbo Tradition of Politics." *African Languages and Cultures* 6, no. 2 (1993): 133–46.

Eckert, Andreas, and Adam Jones. "Introduction: Historical Writing about Everyday Life." In "Everyday Life in Colonial Africa," edited by Adam Jones. Special issue, *Journal of African Cultural Studies* 15, no. 1 (June 2002): 5–16.

Egole, Anozie. "Clubbing, Night Life, Only Way to Ease Stress—Lagosians." *Vanguard* (Lagos), August 4, 2012. https://www.vanguardngr .com/2012/08/clubbing-night-life-only-way-to-ease-stress-lagosians.

Ellemers, Naomi, Russell Spears, and Bertjan Doosje. "Self and Social Identity." *Annual Review of Psychology* 53, no. 1 (2002): 161-86.

Ellis, William. *History of Madagascar.* 2 vols. London: Fisher, Son, 1838.

Emeagwali, Gloria. "Intersections between Africa's Indigenous Knowledge Systems and History." In *African Indigenous Knowledge and the Disciplines: Anti-colonial Educational Perspectives for Transformative Change,* edited by Gloria Emeagwali and George J. Sefa Dei, 1–17. Rotterdam: Sense Publishers, 2014.

Emecheta, Buchi. *The Wrestling Match.* Oxford: Oxford University Press, 1980.

Engelke, Matthew. "Past Pentecostalism: Notes on Rupture, Realignment, and Everyday Life in Pentecostal and African Independent Churches." *Africa: Journal of the International African Institute* 80, no. 2 (2010): 177–99.

Englert, Birgit. "In Need of Connection: Reflections on Youth and the Translation of Film in Tanzania." *Stichproben: Vienna Journal of African Studies* 10, no. 18 (2010): 137–59.

———. "Popular and Mobile: Reflections on Using YouTube as an Archive from an African Studies Perspective." *Stichproben: Vienna Journal of African Studies* 16, no. 31 (2016): 27–56.

Englert, Birgit, with Nginjai Paul Moreto. "Inserting Voice: Foreign Language Film Translation as a Local Phenomenon in Tanzania." *Journal of African Media Studies* 2, no. 2 (August 2010): 225–39.

Epprecht, Marc. *Hungochani: The History of a Dissident Sexuality in Southern Africa.* Quebec: McGill–Queen's University Press, 2004.

Ewumbue-Monono, Churchill. *Youth and Nation-Building in Cameroon: A Study of National Youth Day Messages and Leadership Discourse (1949–2009).* Oxford: African Books Collective, 2009.

Fadipe, Nathaniel Akinremi. *The Sociology of the Yoruba.* Ibadan, Nigeria: University of Ibadan Press, 1970.

Fair, Laura. "'It's Just No Fun Anymore': Women's Experiences of Taarab before and after the 1964 Zanzibar Revolution." In "Leisure in African History," edited by Emmanuel Akyeampong and Charles Ambler. Special issue, *International Journal of African Historical Studies* 35, no. 1 (2002): 61–81.

———. "Kickin' It: Leisure, Politics and Football in Colonial Zanzibar, 1900s–1950s." *Africa* 67, no. 2 (1997): 224–51.

———. "Making Love in the Indian Ocean: Hindi Films, Zanzibari Audiences, and the Construction of Romance in the 1950s and 1960s." In *Love in Africa,* edited by Jennifer Cole and Lynn M. Thomas, 58–82. Chicago: University of Chicago, 2009.

———. "Ngoma Reverberations: Swahili Music Culture and the Making of Football Aesthetics in Early Twentieth-Century Zanzibar." In *Football in Africa: Conflict, Conciliation and Community,* edited by Gary Armstrong and Richard Giulianotti, 103–13. New York: Palgrave Macmillan, 2004.

———. *Pastimes and Politics: Culture, Community, and Identity in Post-Abolition Urban Zanzibar, 1890–1945.* Athens: Ohio University Press, 2001.

———. *Reel Pleasures: Cinema Audiences and Entrepreneurs in Twentieth-Century Urban Tanzania*. Athens: Ohio University Press, 2018.

Falola, Toyin, and Augustine Agwuele, eds. *Africans and the Politics of Popular Culture*. Rochester, NY: University of Rochester Press, 2009.

Falola, Toyin, and Daniel Jean-Jacques. *Africa: An Encyclopedia of Culture and Society*. 3 vols. Santa Barbara, CA: ABC-CLIO, 2015.

Fanon, Frantz. "This Is the Voice of Algeria." In *The Sound Studies Reader*, edited by Jonathan Sterne, 329–35. New York: Routledge, 2012.

Fardon, Richard, and Graham Furniss, eds. *African Broadcast Cultures: Radio in Transition*. Oxford: J. Currey, 2000.

Faulkner, Donald. *Social Welfare and Juvenile Delinquency in Lagos, Nigeria*. London: Howard League for Penal Reform, 1952.

Faye, Ousseynou. "Sport, argent et politique: La lutte libre à Dakar (1800–2000)." In *Le Sénégal contemporain*, edited by Momar-Coumba Diop, 309–40. Paris: Karthal, 2002.

Feeley-Harnik, Gillian. "Childbirth and the Affiliation of Children in Northwest Madagascar." *Taloha: Revue de l'Institut de Civilisations—Musée d'Art et d'Archéologie, Antananarivo* 13 (2000): 135–72.

Feierman, Steven. "Africa in History: The End of Universal Narratives." In *After Colonialism: Imperial Histories and Postcolonial Displacements*, edited by Gyan Prakash, 40–65. Princeton, NJ: Princeton University Press, 1995.

Ferguson, James. *Expectations of Modernity: Myths and Meanings of Urban Life on the Zambian Copperbelt*. Berkeley: University of California Press, 1999.

Ferrari, Aurélia. *Emergence d'une langue urbaine: Le sheng de Nairobi*. Louvain: Peeters, 2012.

Firestone, Matthew D., Michael Benanav, Thomas Hall, and Anthony Sattin. *Lonely Planet: Egypt*. 10th ed. Franklin, TN: Lonely Planet, 2010.

Fortes, Meyer. *Marriage in Tribal Societies*. Cambridge: Cambridge University Press, 1962.

Fourchard, Laurent. "Lagos and the Invention of Juvenile Delinquency in Nigeria, 1920–60." *Journal of African History* 47, no. 1 (2006): 115–37.

Gennaro, Michael. "Nigeria in the Ring: Boxing, Masculinity, and Empire in Nigeria, 1930–1957." PhD diss., University of Florida, 2016.

Ghana Statistical Service. *2010 Population and Housing Census Report: Disability in Ghana*. Accra: Ghana Statistical Service, 2014.

Gilman, Lisa. *The Dance of Politics: Gender, Performance, and Democratization in Malawi*. Philadelphia: Temple University Press, 2009.

———. "Dancing for Our Mother: Performance, Maternalism, and Joyce Banda's Brief Presidency in Malawi." *Africa Today* 64, no. 1 (Fall 2017): 29–52.

———. "Demonic or Cultural Treasure? Local Perspectives on Vimbuza, Intangible Cultural Heritage, and UNESCO in Malawi." In *UNESCO on the Ground: Local Perspectives on Intangible Cultural Heritage*, edited by Michael Dylan Foster and Lisa Gilman, 59–76. Bloomington: Indiana University Press, 2015.

————. "The Politics of Cultural Promotion: The Case of the Umthetho Festival of Malawi's Northern Ngoni." In *Public Performances: Studies in the Carnivalesque and Ritualesque*, edited by Jack Santino, 164–88. Logan: Utah State University Press, 2017.

————. "Purchasing Praise: Women, Dancing, and Patronage in Malawi Party Politicking." *Africa Today* 48, no. 4 (2001): 43–64.

————. "Putting Colonialism into Perspective: Cultural History and the Case of Malipenga Ngoma in Malawi." In *Mashindano! Competitive Music Performance in East Africa*, edited by Frank D. Gunderson and Gregory F. Barz, 319–45. Dar es Salaam: Mkuki na Nyota, 2000.

Gluckman, Max. *Order and Rebellion in Tribal Africa*. London: Cohen and West, 1963.

Goerg, Odile. *Fantômas sous les tropiques: Aller au cinéma en Afrique colonial.* Paris: Vendémiaire, 2015.

Gómez, Andrés Felipe Carvajal, and Sandra-Katharina Groß. *Veejays in Dar es Salaam: Filamu kwa Kiswahili.* Documentary video, 50 min. Germany/Colombia/Tanzania, 2012.

Grabli, Charlotte. "La ville des auditeurs: Radio, rumba congolaise et droit à la ville dans la cité indigène de Léopoldville (1949–1960)." *Cahiers d'études africaines*, no. 233 (2019): 9–45.

Graboyes, Melissa. "Chappati Complaints and Biriani Cravings: The Aesthetics of Food in Colonial Zanzibari Institutions." *Journal of Eastern African Studies* 5, no. 2 (May 2011): 313–28.

————. *The Experiment Must Continue: Medical Research and Ethics in East Africa, 1940–2014.* Athens: Ohio University Press, 2015.

————. "Good Food, Ridiculous Diets, and a Well-Fed Swahili: Food and Diet in Colonial Zanzibari Institutions." *Journal of Colonialism and Colonial History* (forthcoming).

Grace, Joshua. *African Motors: Automobility and the History of Development in Tanzania, 1860s–2015.* Durham, NC: Duke University Press, forthcoming.

Graeber, David. "Dancing with Corpses Reconsidered: An Interpretation of *Famadihana* (in Arivonimamo, Madagascar)." *American Ethnologist* 22, no. 2 (May 1995): 258–78.

Green-Simms, Lindsey B. *Postcolonial Automobility: Car Culture in West Africa.* Minneapolis: University of Minnesota Press, 2017.

Gripaldo, Rolando M. "The Person as Individual and Social Being." In *The Dialogue of Cultural Traditions: A Global Perspective*, edited by William Sweet, George F. McLean, Tomonobu Imamichi, Safak Ural, and O. Faruk Akyol, 37–44. Washington, DC: Council for Research in Values and Philosophy, 2008.

Groß, Sandra-Katharina. "Die Kunst afrikanischer Kinoerzähler: Video Jockeys in Dar es Salaam." MA thesis, Johannes Gutenberg University Mainz, 2010.

Gunderson, Frank D., and Gregory F. Barz, eds. *Mashindano! Competitive Music Performance in East Africa.* Dar es Salaam, Tanzania: Mkuki na Nyota, 2000.

Gunner, Liz, Dina Ligaga, and Dumisani Moyo, eds. *Radio in Africa: Publics, Cultures, Communities.* Johannesburg: Wits University Press, 2012.

Gyekye, Kwame. *African Cultural Values: An Introduction.* Philadelphia: Sankofa, 1996.

Hansen, Karen Tranberg, and Mariken Vaa. "Introduction." In *Reconsidering Informality: Perspectives from Urban Africa,* edited by Karen Tranberg Hansen and Mariken Vaa, 7–24. Uppsala: Nordiska Afrikainstitutet, 2004.

Hart, Jennifer. *Ghana on the Go: African Mobility in the Age of Motor Transportation.* Bloomington: Indiana University Press, 2016.

Hart, Keith. "Informal Income Opportunities and Urban Employment in Ghana." *Journal of Modern African Studies* 11, no. 1 (March 1973): 61–89.

Heap, Simon. "'Their Days Are Spent in Gambling and Loafing, Pimping for Prostitutes, and Picking Pockets': Male Juvenile Delinquents on Lagos Island, 1920s–1960s." *Journal of Family History* 35, no. 1 (2010): 48–70.

Hecht, Gabrielle. *Being Nuclear: Africans and the Global Uranium Trade.* Cambridge, MA: MIT Press, 2014.

Henderson, Richard N. *The King in Every Man: Evolutionary Trends in Onitsha Ibo Society and Culture.* New Haven, CT: Yale University Press, 1972.

Hinton, Alexander Laban. "Introduction: Toward an Anthropology of Transitional Justice." In *Transitional Justice: Global Mechanisms and Local Realities after Genocide and Mass Violence,* edited by Alexander Laban Hinton, 1–22. New Brunswick, NJ: Rutgers University Press, 2010.

Hodgson, Dorothy L. *Being Maasai, Becoming Indigenous: Postcolonial Politics in a Neoliberal World.* Bloomington: Indiana University Press, 2011.

———. *The Church of Women: Gendered Encounters between Maasai and Missionaries.* Bloomington: Indiana University Press, 2005.

———. *Gender, Justice, and the Problem of Culture: From Customary Law to Human Rights in Tanzania.* Bloomington: Indiana University Press, 2017.

———. *Once Intrepid Warriors: Gender, Ethnicity, and the Cultural Politics of Maasai Development.* Bloomington: Indiana University Press, 2001.

Hodgson, Dorothy L., and Judith A. Byfield, eds. *Global Africa: Into the 21st Century.* Berkeley: University of California Press, 2017.

Hodgson, Dorothy L., and Sheryl A. McCurdy, eds. *"Wicked" Women and the Reconfiguration of Gender in Africa.* Portsmouth, NH: Heinemann, 2001.

Hurley, Matthew M., Daniel C. Dennett, and Reginald B. Adams Jr. *Inside Jokes: Using Humor to Reverse-Engineer the Mind.* Cambridge, MA: MIT Press, 2013.

Igunza, Emmanuel. "Malawi's Expensive Mobile Phone Habit." BBC News, February 20, 2015. http://www.bbc.com/news/world-africa-31533397.

Israel, Paolo. *In Step with the Times: Mapiko Masquerades of Mozambique.* Athens: Ohio University Press, 2014.

Insoll, Timothy. *The Archaeology of Islam in Sub-Saharan Africa.* New York: Cambridge University Press, 2003.

Internet World Stats. "Internet Users in Africa: June 2016." Accessed February 16, 2017. http://www.internetworldstats.com/stats1.htm.

Ivaska, Andrew. *Cultured States: Youth, Gender, and Modern Style in 1960s Dar es Salaam.* Durham, NC: Duke University Press, 2011.

Jackson, Steven. "Rethinking Repair." In *Media Technologies: Essays on Communication, Materiality and Society,* edited by Tarleton Gillespie, Pablo J. Boczkowski, and Kirsten A. Foot, 221–39. Cambridge, MA: MIT Press, 2014.

Jackson, Steven, Alex Pompe, and Gabriel Krieshok. "Repair Worlds: Maintenance, Repair, and ICT for Development in Rural Namibia." In *Proceedings of the ACM 2012 Conference on Computer Supported Cooperative Work,* edited by Steven Poltrock, 107–16. New York: Association for Computing Machinery, 2012.

Jahin, Salah. *Azjal Sihafiyah.* Cairo: Al-Ahram Center for Translation and Publishing, 2007.

James, Deborah. *Money from Nothing: Indebtedness and Aspiration in South Africa.* Stanford, CA: Stanford University Press, 2014.

Jessup, Glenda Madeleine, Anita C. Bundy, and Elaine Cornell. "To Be or to Refuse to Be? Exploring the Concept of Leisure as Resistance for Young People Who Are Visually Impaired." *Leisure Studies* 32, no. 2 (2013): 191–205.

"Journal Rappé [S01] EP 9 avec Xuman et Keyti." YouTube, June 21, 2013, posted by JT Rappé. Video, 5:27. https://www.youtube.com/watch?v=yHevxCIF4d4.

"Journal Rappé [S01] EP 24 avec Xuman et Keyti." YouTube, October 4, 2013, posted by JT Rappé. Video, 5:36. https://www.youtube.com/watch?v=KqfND-ynq2o.

"Journal Rappé (S03, ép.01) avec Xuman et Keyti." YouTube, May 8, 2015, posted by JT Rappé. Video, 7:32. https://www.youtube.com/watch?v=lgUQ_xBsOnQ.

"JTR Medley (English Subtitled)." YouTube, May 22, 2015, posted by JT Rappé. Video, 10:01. https://www.youtube.com/watch?v=2kfiq8mpn14.

Jua Cali [Paul Julius Nunda]. "Jua Cali—Ngeli Ya Genge." YouTube, November 13, 2011. Posted by "GengeNairobi." Video, 4:14. https://youtu.be/U2lseD8eLME.

Kalekin-Fishman, Devorah. "Sociology of Everyday Life." *Current Sociology* 61, no. 5/6 (2013): 714–32.

Kalugila, Leonidas. *More Swahili Proverbs from East Africa.* Uppsala: Nordiska Afrikainstitutet, 1980.

Kamlongera, Christopher F. "An Example of Syncretic Drama from Malawi: *Malipenga.*" *Research in African Literatures* 17, no. 2 (Summer 1986): 197–210.

Karp, David A., William C. Yoels, Barbara H. Vann, and Michael Ian Borer. *Sociology in Everyday Life*. 4th ed. Long Grove, IL: Waveland, 2016.

Katebe, John. "A Guide to Conducting a Zambian Funeral." Kwite Online, November 4, 2011. http://kitweonline.com/kitweonline/discover-kitwe/culture/a-guide-to-conducting-a-zambian-funeral.html.

Kavoori, Anandam, and Kalyani Chadha. "The Cell Phone as a Cultural Technology: Lessons from the Indian Case." In *The Cell Phone Reader: Essays in Social Transformation*, edited by Anandam Kavoori and Noah Arceneaux, 227–39. New York: Peter Lang, 2006.

Kerr, David, and Mike Nambote. "The Malipenga Mime of Likoma Island." *Critical Arts: A Journal for Media Studies* 3, no. 1 (1983): 9–28.

Kipury, Naomi. *Oral Literature of the Maasai*. Nairobi: Heinemann Educational Books, 1983.

Kirshenblatt-Gimblett, Barbara. "The Future of Folklore Studies in America: The Urban Frontier." *Folklore Forum* 16, no. 2 (1983): 175–234.

Koepping, Elizabeth. *Food, Friends and Funerals: On Lived Religion*. Berlin: Lit Verlag, 2008.

Konde, Emmanuel. *African Women and Politics: Knowledge, Gender, and Power in Male-Dominated Cameroon*. Lewiston, NY: Edwin Mellen, 2005.

Konings, Piet, and Francis B. Nyamnjoh. *Negotiating an Anglophone Identity: A Study of the Politics of Recognition and Representation in Cameroon*. Leiden: Brill, 2003.

Krings, Matthias. *African Appropriations: Cultural Difference, Mimesis, and Media*. Bloomington: Indiana University Press, 2015.

———. "Turning Rice into Pilau: The Art of Video Narration in Tanzania." Working paper no. 115. Department of Anthropology and African Studies, Johannes Gutenberg University Mainz, 2010.

KTN News Kenya. "KTN Life and Style: Artistic Tuesday, Spoken Art—Virusi Mbaya 06/12/2016." YouTube, December 8, 2016. Video, 28:38. https://www.youtube.com/watch?v=VAsibu_VkbM.

———. "Life and Style: Spoken Art with Kenneth [*sic*] B and Kuni Mbichi." YouTube, January 24, 2017. Video, 28:21. https://youtu.be/z9OU2CC—qw.

Kuper, Hilda. *An African Aristocracy: Rank among the Swazi*. New York: International African Institute, 1980.

Lancaster, Henry, and Peter Lange. *Malawi: Telecoms, Mobile and Broadband: Statistics and Analyses*. Accessed February 9, 2017. https://www.budde.com.au/Research/Malawi-Telecoms-Mobile-and-Broadband-Statistics-and-Analyses.

Larkin, Brian. "Indian Films and Nigerian Lovers: Media and the Creation of Parallel Modernities." *Africa: Journal of the International Africa Institute* 67, no. 3 (1997): 406–40.

———. *Signal and Noise: Media, Infrastructure, and Urban Culture in Nigeria*. Durham, NC: Duke University Press, 2008.

Larson, Pier M. "Austronesian Mortuary Ritual in History: Transformations of Secondary Burial (*Famadihana*) in Highland Madagascar." *Ethnohistory* 48, no. 1/2 (Winter/Spring 2001): 123–55.

Lindsay, Lisa A. "'No Need . . . to Think of Home'? Masculinity and Domestic Life on the Nigerian Railway, c. 1940–61." *Journal of African History* 39, no. 3 (1998): 439–66.

———. "Trade Unions and Football Clubs: Gender and the 'Modern' Public Sphere in Colonial Southwestern Nigeria." In *Leisure in Urban Africa*, edited by Paul Tiyambe Zeleza and Cassandra Rachel Veney, 105–24. Trenton, NJ: Africa World Press, 2003.

"Listen to Ghetto Radio on TuneIn." Podcast. TuneIn. Accessed October 12, 2017. https://tunein.com/radio/Ghetto-Radio-895-s77900/.

Livingston, Julie. "Suicide, Risk, and Investment in the Heart of the African Miracle." *Cultural Anthropology* 24, no. 4 (November 2009): 652–80.

Lloyd, Peter Cutt. "The Yoruba of Nigeria." In *Peoples of Africa*, edited by James L. Gibbs Jr., 549–82. New York: Holt, Rinehart and Winston, 1965.

Longman, Chia, and Tamsin Bradley, eds. *Interrogating Harmful Cultural Practices: Gender, Culture and Coercion*. Burlington, VT: Ashgate, 2015.

Lynch, Robert. "It's Funny Because We Think It's True: Laughter Is Augmented by Implicit Preferences." *Evolution and Human Behavior* 31, no. 2 (March 2010): 141–48.

Mabala, Richard S., ed. *Summons: Poems from Tanzania*. Dar es Salaam: Tanzania Publishing House, 1980.

Mabogunje, Akin L. *Urbanization in Nigeria*. London: University of London Press, 1969.

Makama, Godiya Allanana. "Patriarchy and Gender Equality in Nigeria: The Way Forward." *European Scientific Journal* 9, no. 17 (June 2013): 115–44.

Manga, Clara. "Women and Sports." *Cameroon Champion*, May 29, 1962, 3.

Mangan, J. A. "The Education of an Elite Imperial Administration: The Sudan Political Service and the British and the British Public School System." *International Journal of African Historical Studies* 15, no. 4 (1982): 671–99.

Manuel, Peter. *Popular Musics of the Non-Western World: An Introductory Survey*. Oxford: Oxford University Press, 1988.

Marris, Peter. *Family and Social Change in an African City: A Study of Rehousing in Lagos*. Evanston, IL: Northwestern University Press, 1962.

Martin, Phyllis M. *Leisure and Society in Colonial Brazzaville*. Cambridge: Cambridge University Press, 1995.

Marwick, Brian Allan. *The Swazi: An Ethnographic Account of the Natives of the Swaziland Protectorate*. London: Frank Cass, 1966.

Matabeni, Zethu. *Reclaiming Afrikan: Queer Perspectives on Sexual and Gender Identities*. Athlone, South Africa: Modjaji Books, 2014.

May, Vivian M. *Pursuing Intersectionality, Unsettling Dominant Imaginaries*. New York: Routledge, 2015.

Mavhunga, Clapperton Chakanetsa. *Transient Workspaces: Technologies of Everyday Innovation in Zimbabwe.* Cambridge, MA: MIT Press, 2014.

McLaren, Anne E. *Performing Grief: Bridal Laments in Rural China.* Honolulu: University of Hawai'i Press, 2008.

Mitchell, J. Clyde. *The Kalela Dance: Aspects of Social Relationships among Urban Africans in Northern Rhodesia.* Manchester, UK: Manchester University Press, 1956.

Mkabarah, Jumaa. *Kizimbani.* Dar es Salaam: Black Star Agencies, 1974.

Moraa, Anne. "Spoken Word in Kenya: A Hunger for the Word." The Spoken Word Project—Stories Traveling through Africa. Accessed October 10, 2017. http://www.goethe.de/ins/za/prj/spw/plc/nai/enindex.htm.

Morsi, F. *Mawsouat Ramadan* [Ramadan encyclopedia]. 4th ed. Cairo: General Egyptian Book Organization, 2013.

Mougoué, Jacqueline-Bethel Tchouta. "Intellectual Housewives, Journalism, and Anglophone Nationalism in Cameroon, 1961–1972." *Journal of West African History* 3, no. 2 (Fall 2017): 67–92.

Mpata, Daniel. "The Malipenga Dance in Nkhata Bay District." *Society of Malawi Journal* 54, no. 1 (2001): 23–28.

Mtobwa, Ben R. *Dar es Salaam Usiku.* Dar es Salaam: Heko, 1998.

Mudimbe, V. Y. *The Idea of Africa.* Bloomington: Indiana University Press, 1993.

Mukajanga, Kajubi D. *Mpenzi.* Dar es Salaam: Grand Arts Promotions, 1984.

———. *Tuanze Lini?* Dar es Salaam: Grand Arts Promotions, 1983.

Mwangi, Evan. "Masculinity and Nationalism in East African Hip-Hop Music," *Tydskrif vir letterkunde* 41, no. 2, 2004.

Mwase, Ngila. "The Supply of Road Vehicles in Tanzania: The Problem of Suppressed Demand." *Journal of Transport Economics and Policy* 17, no. 1 (January 1983): 77–89.

Myerhoff, Barbara G. *Number Our Days.* New York: Dutton, 1979.

Myers, Garth. "Introduction." In *African Cities: Alternative Visions of Urban Theory and Practice,* 1–20. New York: Zed Books, 2011.

Namfua, P. P. "Age, Sex, Marital Status." In *Analysis of the 1978 Population Census,* edited by Bureau of Statistics, 57–91. Dar es Salaam: Ministry of Planning and Economic Affairs, 1982.

Nana-Fabu, Stella. "An Analysis of the Economic Status of Women in Cameroon." *Journal of International Women's Studies* 8, no. 1 (November 2006): 148–62.

Ndi, Anthony. *Southern West Cameroon Revisited (1950–1972).* Vol. 1, *Unveiling Inescapable Traps.* Mankon, Bamenda, Cameroon: Langaa Research & Publishing CIG, 2014.

Nelson, Sarah. "The New Type of Senegalese under Construction: Fadel Barro and Aliou Sané on *Yenamarrisme* after Wade." *African Studies Quarterly: The Online Journal of African Studies* 14, no. 3 (March 2014): 13–32. https://asq.africa.ufl.edu/files/Volume-14-Issue-3-Nelson.pdf.

Newell, Stephanie, and Onookome Okome, eds. *Popular Culture in Africa: The Episteme of the Everyday.* New York: Routledge, 2014.

Nolte, Insa, Olukoya Ogen, and Rebecca Jones, eds. *Beyond Religious Tolerance: Muslim, Christian and Traditionalist Encounters in an African Town.* Woodbridge, UK: James Currey, 2017.

"Nigeria Reclaim African Women's Title." BBC Sport, October 25, 2014. https://www.bbc.com/sport/football/29739296.

Nonini [Hubert Mbuku Nakitare]. "Nonini—Kataa Hio (Official Video)." YouTube, November 18, 2009. Posted by "Nonini MgengeTrue." Video, 4:03. https://youtu.be/-8GxtU1Rsjg.

Nourse, Erin. "'Birth Is Our Spear Battle': Pregnancy, Childbirth and Religion in a Northern Malagasy Port City." PhD diss., University of Virginia, 2014.

————. "Turning 'Water Babies' (Zaza Rano) into 'Real Human Beings' (Vrai Humains): Rituals of Blessing for the Newly Born in Diégo Suarez, Madagascar." *Journal of Religion in Africa* 47, no. 2 (January 2018): 224–56.

Ntarangwi, Mwenda. *East African Hip Hop: Youth Culture and Globalization.* Urbana: University of Illinois Press, 2009.

Ntarangwi, Mwenda, David Mills, and Mustafa Babiker, eds. *African Anthropologies: History, Critique, and Practice.* London: Zed Books, 2006.

Nwosu, I. E. "Gender Role Perceptions and the Changing Roles of Women in Nigeria." *International Journal of Agriculture and Rural Development* 15, no. 3 (2012): 1240–46.

Nwoye, Chinwe M. A. "Igbo Cultural and Religious Worldview: An Insider's Perspective." *International Journal of Sociology and Anthropology* 3, no. 9 (September 2011): 304–17.

Nyembezi, C. L. Sibusiso. *Zulu Proverbs.* Johannesburg: Witwatersrand University Press, 1974.

Obadare, Ebenezer. *Humor, Silence, and Civil Society in Nigeria.* Rochester, NY: University of Rochester Press, 2016.

Obi, T. J. Desch. *Fighting for Honor: The History of African Martial Art Traditions in the Atlantic World.* Columbia: University of South Carolina Press, 2008.

Ogunniyi, Cassandra. "Perceptions of the African Women's Championships: Female Footballers as Anomalies." In *Women's Sport in Africa*, edited by Michelle Sikes and John Bale, 89–101. New York: Routledge, 2016.

Oha, Obododimma. "Praise Names and Power De/constructions in Contemporary Igbo Chiefship." *Culture, Language and Representation* 7 (2009): 101–16.

Okpewho, Isidore. *Once Upon a Kingdom: Myth, Hegemony, and Identity.* Bloomington: Indiana University Press, 1988.

Oloya, Opiyo. *Child to Soldier: Stories from Joseph Kony's Lord's Resistance Army.* Toronto: University of Toronto Press, 2013.

Omonubi-McDonnell, Morolake. *Gender Inequality in Nigeria.* Ibadan, Nigeria: Spectrum Books, 2003.

Organisation des Femmes de l'Union Nationale Camerounaise. *La Femme Camerounaise*. Paris: EDICEF, 1972.

Osborn, Chase Salmon. *Madagascar: Land of the Man-Eating Tree*. New York: Republic, 1924.

Pauwels-Boon, Greta. *L'origine, l'évolution et le fonctionnement de la radiodiffusion au Zaïre de 1937 à 1960*. Tervuren, Belgium: Musée Royal de l'Afrique Central, 1979.

Peek, Philip M., and Kwesi Yankah, eds. *African Folklore: An Encyclopedia*. New York: Routledge, 2004.

"Pinching Spot in Our National Team, The." *Cameroon Telegraph*, December 20, 1968, 5.

Plageman, Nate. *Highlife Saturday Night: Popular Music and Social Change in Urban Ghana*. Bloomington: Indiana University Press, 2013.

Polgreen, Lydia. "Grandmas Grow Gold in Swaziland." *New York Times*, August 14, 2012.

Porter, Gerald. "'Work the Old Lady out of the Ditch': Singing at Work by English Lacemakers." *Journal of Folklore Research* 31, no. 1/3 (January–December 1994): 35–55.

Pritchett, James A. *Friends for Life, Friends for Death: Cohorts and Consciousness among the Lunda-Ndembu*. Charlottesville: University of Virginia Press, 2007.

Rajab, Hammie. *Ufunguo wa Bandia*. Dar es Salaam: Eastern Africa Publications, 1979.

———. *Dunia Hadaa*. Dar es Salaam: Busara, 1982.

Raji, Olalere Waheed, and Rasaq Atanda Ajadi. "A Stylistic Analysis of Ekun Iyawo." *Research on Humanities and Social Sciences* 3, no. 9 (2013): 143–48.

Randrianja, Solofo, and Stephen Ellis. *Madagascar: A Short History*. Chicago: University of Chicago Press, 2009.

Ranger, Terence. *Dance and Society in Eastern Africa, 1890–1970: The Beni Ngoma*. Berkeley: University of California Press, 1975.

Riaño-Alcalá, Pilar, and Erin Baines. "Editorial Note." In "Transitional Justice and the Everyday," edited by Pilar Riaño-Alcalá and Erin Baines. Special issue, *International Journal of Transitional Justice* 6, no. 3 (November 2012): 385–93.

Rice, Kate. "Ukuthwala in Rural South Africa: Abduction Marriage as a Site of Negotiation about Gender, Rights and Generational Authority among the Xhosa." *Journal of Southern African Studies* 40, no. 2 (2014): 381–99.

Roeckelein, Jon E. *The Psychology of Humor: A Reference Guide and Annotated Bibliography*. Westport, CT: Greenwood, 2002.

Rosenoff Gauvin, Lara. "In and Out of Culture: Okot p'Bitek's Work and Social Repair in Post-Conflict Acoliland." *Oral Tradition* 28, no. 1 (March 2013): 35–53.

Ross, Eric S. *Culture and Customs of Senegal*. Westport, CT: Greenwood, 2008.

Rudd, Philip W. "Sheng: The Mixed Language of Nairobi." PhD diss., Ball State University, 2008.

Sahlins, Marshall. "What Kinship Is (Part One)." *Journal of the Royal Anthropological Institute* 17, no. 1 (March 2011): 2–19.

Scott, Joan W. "Storytelling." *History and Theory* 50, no. 2 (May 2011): 203–9.

"Senegal Mobile Subscribers Reach 14.7 Million at End-March." *Telecompaper.* Last modified July 6, 2015. https://www.telecompaper.com/news /senegal-mobile-subscribers-reach-147-million-at-end-march—1091056.

Setsiba, T. H. S. "Mourning Rituals and Practices in Contemporary South African Townships: A Phenomenological Study." PhD diss., University of Zululand, 2012.

Shaw, Rosalind. "Displacing Violence: Making Pentecostal Memory in Postwar Sierra Leone." *Cultural Anthropology* 22, no. 1 (February 2007): 66–93.

Shaw, Susan M., Douglas A. Kleiber, and Linda L. Caldwell. "Leisure and Identity Formation in Male and Female Adolescents: A Preliminary Examination." *Journal of Leisure Research* 27, no. 3 (1995): 245–63.

Sheff, Elisabeth. "Polyamorous Families, Same-Sex Marriage, and the Slippery Slope." *Journal of Contemporary Ethnography* 40, no. 5 (2011): 487–520.

Sheldon, Kathleen. *African Women: Early History to the 21st Century.* Bloomington: Indiana University Press, 2017.

Simbamwene, John. *Mwisho wa Mapenzi.* Dar es Salaam: Longman, 1971.

Simons, Gary F., and Charles D. Fennig, eds. *Ethnologue: Languages of the World.* 20th ed. Dallas, TX: SIL International, 2017.

Sissako, Abderrahmane, dir. *La vie sur terre.* VHS. San Francisco: California Newsreel, 1998.

Sofola, Johnson Adeyemi. *African Culture and the African Personality: What Makes an African Person African.* Ibadan, Nigeria: African Resources, 1973.

Solway, Jacqueline. 2017. "'Slow Marriage,' 'Fast *Bogadi*': Change and Continuity in Marriage in Botswana." *Anthropology Southern Africa* 40, no. 1 (2017): 309–22.

Sounaye, Abdoulaye. *Islam et modernité: Contribution à l'analyse de la ré-islamisation au Niger.* Paris: Harmattan, 2016.

Spronk, Rachel. *Ambiguous Pleasures: Sexuality and Middle-Class Self-Perceptions in Nairobi.* New York: Berghahn Books, 2012.

"Startimes Kuonesha Filamu Za Kichina Zilizo Tafsiriwa Kwa Kiswahili." YouTube, November 8, 2016. Video, 02:00. https://www.youtube.com /watch?v=t9rhdoMaPXg.

Stebbins, Robert A. 2005. "Choice and Experiential Definitions of Leisure." *Leisure Sciences* 27, no. 4 (2005): 349–52.

Stein, Howard. *Beyond the World Bank Agenda: An Institutional Approach to Development.* Chicago: University of Chicago Press, 2008.

Stren, Richard, Mohamed Halfani, and Joyce Malombe. "Coping with Urbanization and Urban Policy." In *Beyond Capitalism vs. Socialism in Kenya and Tanzania*, edited by Joel D. Barkan, 175–200. Boulder, CO: Lynn Rienner, 1994.

Taiwo, Rotimi, Akinola Odebunmi, and Akin Adetunji. *Analyzing Language and Humor in Online Communication*. Hershey, PA: Information Science Reference, 2016.

Tamale, Sylvia. *African Sexualities: A Reader*. Nairobi: Pambazuka, 2011.

Tang, Patricia. *Masters of the Sabar: Wolof Griot Percussionists of Senegal*. Philadelphia: Temple University Press, 2007.

Taylor, Claire. "Women's Social Networks and Female Friendship in the Ancient Greek City." *Gender and History* 23, no. 3 (November 2011): 703–20.

Taylor, Scott D. *Culture and Customs of Zambia*. Westport, CT: Greenwood, 2006.

Tchebwa, Antoine Manda. *Terre de la chanson: La musique zaïroise, hier et aujourd'hui*. Louvain-la-Neuve: Duculot, 1996.

Tembo, Mwizenge. "Funerals and Burials in Zambia." Accessed January 10, 2017. http://people.bridgewater.edu/~mtembo/menu/zambia/funeralsburials .shtml#.

Thompson, Virginia, and Richard Adloff. *The Malagasy Republic: Madagascar Today*. Stanford, CA: Stanford University Press, 1965.

Tignor, Robert, L. *Egypt: A Short History*. Princeton, NJ: Princeton University Press, 2010.

Tripp, Aili Mari. *Women and Power in Post-Conflict Africa*. New York: Cambridge University Press, 2015.

Trudell, Barbara. "Practice in Search of a Paradigm: Language Rights, Linguistic Citizenship and Minority Language Communities in Senegal." *Current Issues in Language Planning* 9, no. 4 (November 2008): 395–412.

Turner, Edith. *Communitas: The Anthropology of Collective Joy*. New York: Palgrave Macmillan, 2012.

Turner, Victor. *The Ritual Process: Structure and Anti-Structure*. Chicago: Aldine, 1969.

Uchendu, Victor C. "'Kola Hospitality' and Igbo Lineage Structure." *Man* 64 (March/April 1964): 47–50.

Uchino, Bert N. "Social Support and Health: A Review of Physiological Processes Potentially Underlying Links to Disease Outcomes." *Journal of Behavioral Medicine* 29, no. 4 (August 2006): 377–87.

Ugandan Ministry of Health. *Health and Mortality Survey among Internally Displaced Persons in Gulu, Kitgum and Pader Districts in Northern Uganda*. Kampala, Uganda: Ministry of Health, 2005.

United Nations, Department of Economic and Social Affairs, Population Division. "World Population Prospects." Accessed October 12, 2017. https://esa.un.org/unpd/wpp/Download/Standard/Population/.

United Nations Development Programme. *Human Development Report*.

United Republic of Tanzania, Bureau of Statistics. *Kilimanjaro Region Socio-economic Profile.* Dar es Salaam: National Bureau of Statistics and Kilimanjaro Regional Commissioner's Office, 2002.

"Unveiling the 6 Hottest Clubs in Lagos." Encomium, April 19, 2015. http://encomium.ng/unveiling-the-6-hottest-clubs-in-lagos.

van Binsbergen, Wim. "Making Sense of Urban Space in Francistown, Botswana." In *Urban Symbolism,* edited by Peter J. M. Nas, 184–228. Leiden: Brill, 1993.

van Dijk, Rijk. "The Social Cocktail: Weddings and the Innovative Mixing of Competences in Botswana." In *Transforming Innovations in Africa: Explorative Studies on Appropriation in African Societies,* edited by Jan-Bart Gewald, André Leliveld, and Iva Peša, 191–207. Leiden: Brill, 2012.

van Onselen, Charles. *The Seed Is Mine: The Life of Kas Maine, a South African Sharecropper 1894–1985.* Cambridge, UK: James Currey, 1996.

Van Wolputte, Steven. 2016. "Sex in Troubled Times: Moral Panic, Polyamory and Freedom in North-West Namibia." *Anthropology Southern Africa* 39, no. 1 (2016): 31–45.

Verrips, Jojada, and Birgit Meyer. "Kwaku's Car: The Struggles and Stories of a Ghanaian Long-Distance Taxi-Driver." In *Car Cultures,* edited by Daniel Miller, 153–84. London: Berg, 2001.

Vidacs, Bea. "Through the Prism of Sports: Why Should Africanists Study Sports?" *Africa Spectrum* 41, no. 3 (2006): 331–49.

Wainaina, Binyavanga. "How to Write about Africa." *Granta* 92 (Winter 2005): 91–96.

———. *One Day I Will Write about This Place: A Memoir.* London: Granta, 2011.

Wallace, Marion. *A History of Namibia: From the Beginning to 1990.* Oxford: Oxford University Press, 2013.

Waller, Richard. "Rebellious Youth in Colonial Africa." *Journal of African History* 47, no. 1 (2006): 77–92.

Walton, James. "The Dagga Pipes of Southern Africa." *Researches of the National Museum* 1, no. 4 (December 1953): 85–113.

Warga, Jake. "Rapping the News in West Africa." NPR, *All Things Considered.* Podcast, 3:30. Accessed February 16, 2017. http://www.npr.org/2015/01/15/377527029/rapping-the-news-in-west-africa.

Wasike, Chris. "Jua Cali, Genge Rap Music and the Anxieties of Living in the Glocalized City of Nairobi." *Muziki* 8, no. 1 (July 2011): 18–33.

Weiss, Brad. *Street Dreams and Hip Hop Barbershops: Global Fantasy in Urban Tanzania.* Bloomington: Indiana University Press, 2009.

Wilk, Stan. *Humanistic Anthropology.* Knoxville: University of Tennessee Press, 1991.

Willis, Paul E. *Learning to Labor: How Working Class Kids Get Working Class Jobs.* New York: Columbia University Press, 1981.

Win, Everjoice J. "Not Very Poor, Powerless or Pregnant: The African Woman Forgotten by Development." In *Feminisms in Development: Contradictions,*

Contestations and Challenges, edited by Andrea Cornwall, Elizabeth Harrison, and Ann Whitehead, 79–85. London: Zed Books, 2007.

"Women Are Incapable Referees." Letter to the editor, *Cameroon Times*, July 15, 1967, 2.

Women's Cameroon National Union. *The Faces of Cameroonian Women.* Yaoundé, Cameroon: WCNU, 1975.

"Women Too in the World of Sports." *Cameroon Champion*, June 12, 1962.

World Bank. *Accelerated Development in Sub-Saharan Africa: An Agenda for Action.* Washington, DC: World Bank, 1981. http://documents.worldbank.org/curated/en/702471468768312009/Accelerated-development-in-sub-Saharan-Africa-an-agenda-for-action.

World Health Organization. *World Report on Disability.* Geneva: World Health Organization, 2011.

Wright, Marcia. *Strategies of Slaves and Women: Life-Stories from East/Central Africa.* Cambridge, UK: James Currey, 1993.

Yankah, Kwesi. *Speaking for the Chief: Okyeame and the Politics of Akan Royal Oratory.* Bloomington: Indiana University, 1995.

Yankholmes, Aaron Kofi Badu, and Shanshan Lin. "Leisure and Education in Ghana: An Exploratory Study of University Students' Leisure Lifestyles." *World Leisure Journal* 54, no. 1 (March 2012): 58–68.

Youngstedt, Scott M. "The 5th Francophonie Sports and Arts Festival: Niamey, Niger Hosts a Global Community." *African Studies Quarterly: The Online Journal of African Studies* 10, no. 2/3 (Fall 2008): 129–51. https://sites.clas.ufl.edu/africa-asq/files/Youngstedt-Vol10Issue23.pdf.

———. *Surviving with Dignity: Hausa Communities of Niamey, Niger.* Lanham, MD: Lexington Books, 2013.

Zeleza, Paul Tiyambe. "Introduction: The Creation and Consumption of Leisure: Theoretical and Methodological Considerations." In *Leisure in Urban Africa*, edited by Paul Tiyambe Zeleza and Cassandra Rachel Veney, vii–xli. Trenton, NJ: Africa World Press, 2003.

Contributors

Hadeer Aboelnagah is a professor of English literature at Prince Sultan University in Riyadh. She is a principal fellow at the Higher Education Academy (United Kingdom) and an affiliated researcher and former faculty member at the University of Ottawa and Carleton University, Ottawa, Canada. She has authored a series of nine English books introducing the culture of the Middle East and translated numerous books and articles. Her research interests include Arabic and Islamic culture, Islam and the West, and women in Islam. She blogs for the *New York Times* and is a frequent contributor to newspapers in North America.

Issahaku Adam is a senior lecturer in tourism management in the Department of Hospitality and Tourism Management at the University of Cape Coast, Ghana. He has interest in accessible tourism, leisure, disability and wellbeing, safety and security in international tourism, and ICT applications in tourism. He has worked on research projects tangential to these interests and is currently working on a book on accessible tourism in Africa as well as research projects on digital leisure among international tourists, leisure as a sociocultural space for integration among West African migrants in Ghana, and the sexual and reproductive health and leisure needs of young people with disability in Ghana.

Abiola Victoria Ayodokun is an information retrieval specialist with Nigeria Watch. She holds a master's degree in peace and conflicts studies from the University of Ibadan. She is the cofounder of Epot Integrated Concept, a research consultant and logistics solution provider firm based in Ibadan, Nigeria. She is a chartered mediator and the assistant national coordinator of IFRA-Nigeria Research Fellowship. She specializes in gender and environmental insecurity.

Osuolale Joseph Ayodokun is the head of operations at Epot Integrated Concept, a research consultant and logistics solution provider firm based in Ibadan, Nigeria. He holds a master's degree in anthropology from the University of Ibadan and currently is on his PhD program in anthropology at the University of Ibadan. He is interested in the study of the interface of the biological component of the environment and the culture of the society.

Omotoyosi Babalola is a lecturer in African history at the Directorate of Educational Services and Training (DEST), Redeemers University, Ede, Osun State, Nigeria. Her research interests include Nigerian and African history, gender studies, and Pentecostalism. She is currently in the PhD program at the Institute of African Studies, University of Ibadan, Nigeria.

Oluwakemi M. Balogun is an assistant professor in the Department of Women's, Gender, and Sexuality Studies and the Department of Sociology at the University of Oregon. Her research interests include gender, globalization, nationalism, embodiment, race/ethnicity, and migration. She is the author of *Beauty Diplomacy: Embodying an Emerging Nation* (Stanford University Press, forthcoming).

Mokaya Bosire teaches Swahili at the University of Oregon, Eugene. As a linguist and Africanist, he has conducted research on Swahili and urban youth languages in East Africa, where he explores language contact outcomes, and has written widely on Sheng, a youth language of Nairobi. His current research looks at translanguaging and the teaching of Swahili as a foreign language.

Emily Callaci is an associate professor of African history at the University of Wisconsin, Madison. She is the author of *Street Archives and City Life: Popular Intellectuals in Postcolonial Tanzania* (2017). She is currently working on a second book about the history of biomedical contraception and the search for reproductive justice in Africa.

Deborah Durham is an anthropologist who has conducted field research in Botswana from 1989 to the present, focusing on Herero people's minority identity and liberal democracy, and on discourses of youth, and has published widely on both. She is currently writing about the affective dimensions of the new material culture in Botswana. She is coeditor of *Generations and Globalization: Youth, Age, and Family in the New World Economy* and *Figuring the Future: Globalization and the Temporalities of Children and Youth*, with Jennifer Cole, and *Elusive Adulthoods: The Anthropology of New Maturities*, with Jacqueline Solway.

Birgit Englert is associate professor of African history and society in the Department of African Studies at the University of Vienna, Austria. She has published on land rights, gender, popular music, and film, primarily in relation to Tanzania. Further, she directed a research project on popular culture in trans-local spaces in which her own regional focus was on Marseille and the Comorian diaspora. She has edited several volumes and is a founding member and managing editor of the Africanist journal *Stichproben: Vienna Journal of African Studies*.

Laura Fair is a professor of history at Michigan State University. Her research focuses on urban social, cultural, and gender history in Zanzibar and Tanzania. She is author of *Pastimes and Politics: Culture, Community, and Identity in Post-Abolition Urban Zanzibar, 1890–1945* and *Reel Pleasures: Cinema Audiences and Entrepreneurs in Twentieth Century Urban Tanzania*.

John Fenn's academic training is in folklore and ethnomusicology (PhD, Indiana University, 2004). He is currently the head of Research and Programs at the American Folklife Center in the Library of Congress. Prior to this, he was an associate professor at the University of Oregon and on the faculty in the Arts and Administration Program as well as the Folklore Program. He has conducted fieldwork on expressive culture in Malawi (Southeast Africa), China, Indiana, and Oregon, exploring a wide range of practices, traditions, and communities.

Michael Gennaro is instructor of history at Bossier Parish Community College. He is currently turning his dissertation research about the history of boxing in colonial Nigeria into a monograph. He co-edited (with Saheed Aderinto) *Sports in African History, Politics, and*

Identity Formation (Routledge, 2019). He has published on a variety of topics in Nigerian history ranging from the history of table tennis, to boxing promoters as colonial sporting entrepreneurs, to the movement of African athletes in the Black Atlantic.

Lisa Gilman is professor of folklore and public humanities in the English Department at George Mason University. Her research interests include performance, intangible cultural heritage, gender, and politics in southern Africa and the United States. Her monographs include *The Dance of Politics: Gender, Performance, and Democratization in Malawi* (2009), the coedited volume (with Michael Dylan Foster) *UNESCO on the Ground: Local Perspectives on Intangible Cultural Heritage* (2015), *My Music, My War: The Listening Habits of U.S. Troops in Iraq and Afghanistan* (2016), and the *Handbook for Folklore and Ethnomusicology Fieldwork* (with John Fenn, 2019). She also produced the documentary *Grounds for Resistance* about the antiwar activism of US veterans of the Iraq and Afghanistan wars.

Charlotte Grabli is completing her PhD in the History and Civilizations program at the École des Hautes Études en Sciences Sociales (EHESS) in France. Her research focuses on the sound and musical cultures of two segregated spaces: the native quarters of Leopoldville (now Kinshasa) in the Belgium Congo, and the suburb of Sophiatown in Johannesburg, Union of South Africa, from 1930 to 1960. She is the author of the book chapter "Atlantic Voices: Imagination and the Formation of a Sound Dialogue between Congolese and Cuban Singers in the 1950s," in *Cuba & Africa: Engagements, Circulations and Racial Representations in the 20th Century* (Wits University Press, forthcoming).

Melissa Graboyes is an assistant professor in the Clark Honors College at the University of Oregon. She is a historian of modern Africa who draws upon a variety of historical and anthropological methods to investigate topics related to history, global health, and medical ethics. She is the author of *The Experiment Must Continue: Medical Research and Ethics in East Africa, 1940–2014* (2015). She is currently working on projects related to the history of failed malaria elimination attempts in East Africa, and the history and ethics surrounding the development of the DHS (Demographic Health Survey).

Joshua Grace is an assistant professor in the Department of History at the University of South Carolina, where he teaches African history and histories of development and sustainability. His research explores the technopolitics of development in Tanzania from the late 1800s to the present. Grace is currently finishing *African Motors: Automobility and the History of Development in Tanzania, 1860s to 2015* (under contract with Duke University Press), which explores the history of cars in Tanzania from the repair shop to the open road to post-OPEC oil trading.

Dorothy L. Hodgson is dean of the School of Arts and Sciences and professor of anthropology at Brandeis University. As a historical anthropologist, she has conducted research for over thirty years in Tanzania on such topics as gender, ethnicity, development, colonialism, indigenous peoples, and human rights. Her most recent books are *Gender, Justice, and the Problem of Culture: From Customary Law to Human Rights in Tanzania* (2017) and *Global Africa: Into the Twenty-First Century* (2017, coedited with Judith Byfield).

Habib Iddrisu is a traditionally trained dancer, musician, and historian from Northern Ghana, born into the Bizing family of court historians and musicians of the Dagbamba/Dagomba people. He has diverse experience as a performer, teacher, choreographer, and scholar. He earned his PhD in Performance Studies from Northwestern University and his research interests include West African music and dance practice and performance, cultural studies, postcolonial independence history, political economy, oral history, and African diaspora studies.

Paolo Israel is associate professor and chairperson of the Department of History at the University of the Western Cape. He is the author of *In Step with the Times: Mapiko Masquerades of Mozambique* (2014). Since 2000, he has been carrying out fieldwork and historical research in and on Mozambique. His research interests encompass performance, orality, liberation struggle history, and witchcraft. He is currently working on two projects: a narrative history of the Mueda massacre of 1960, and a creative nonfiction book titled *The Magical Lions of Muidumbi.*

Akwasi Kumi-Kyereme is an associate professor in the Department of Population and Health of the University of Cape Coast, Ghana. His research interests include reproductive health, social dimensions of health, health care financing, and disability studies. He has authored over forty publications (articles, books, and technical reports) and is currently working on the sexual and reproductive health and leisure needs of young people with disability in Ghana.

Prince F. M. Lamba is an arts and cultural affairs officer in the Department of Arts and Culture in Zambia. As an ethnomusicologist, his interests include urban ethnography, African musical arts, cultural economics, and development. Prince has written articles found online at http:www.musicinafrica.net/users/prince-fm-lamba. He has also worked in different institutions including the American Embassy in Zambia, University of Zambia, Evelyn Hone College of Applied Arts, the Zambian Open University, and St. Andrews High School in South Africa. He is the founder and artistic director of the Pamodzi Dance Troupe in Zambia, and current folklore graduate student at the University of Oregon.

Cheikh Tidiane Lo specializes in West African folklore and heritage, with a focus on Senegalese expressive cultures. He is a Fulbright scholar from Senegal and has recently completed a PhD in folklore with a minor in cultural anthropology at Indiana University Bloomington. He has published articles on heritage tourism, folklore, and Wolof oral tradition.

Bill McCoy is an associate professor of history and director of the Honors Scholar Society at Eastern Nazarene College in Massachusetts. His primary interests are in the history of medicine and Christianity in Africa, with his research work focused primarily on the history of leprosy care in South Africa and Swaziland during the twentieth century.

Nginjai Paul Moreto studied mass communication at St. Augustine University of Tanzania in Mwanza, and journalism at the Dar es Salaam School of Journalism. His main interests are film and communication and he has been involved in research projects on popular culture more generally since 2005.

Jacqueline-Bethel Tchouta Mougoué is assistant professor of gender and sexuality in African cultural studies at the University of Wisconsin–Madison. She is the author of *Gender, Separatist Politics, and Embodied Nationalism in Cameroon* (2019). She is currently working on her second book, which probes the connection between changing ideals of manhood and the Bahá'í faith movement in Cameroon.

Martha Ndakalako-Bannikov is a PhD candidate in comparative literature at the University of Oregon. She specializes in Namibian literatures in the context of African literary history and global anglophone and world literature. She is interested in the way national culture and identity are developed and expressed in Namibia, and the role of history, memory, and the publishing industry in these expressions.

James Nindi is a sociologist and journalist based in Dar es Salaam, Tanzania. He has published hundreds of articles on issues related to music, art, and culture in newspapers such as *Mwananchi, Mtanzania,* and *Uhuru,* as well as over ten arts-related publications. He has also worked for many nonprofit organizations on conferences and events that address art, labor, and law. He collaborated with Alex Perullo on the two editions of the book *The Music Business in Tanzania: Copyright Law, Contracts, and Collective Management Organizations.*

Erin Nourse is assistant professor of religious studies at Regis University in Denver, Colorado. She is a historian of religion who employs an ethnographic approach to the study of religion. Her research has focused on birth rituals and rites of initiation for the newly born in the pluralistic city of Diego Suarez, Madagascar. Her interests include ritual, African religions, and the manner in which people construct religious identities in pluralistic religious communities.

Eric Debrah Otchere is a senior lecturer in the Department of Music and Dance, University of Cape Coast, Ghana. He is an AHP (2015) fellow and an ASA (2016) presidential fellow. Currently, he is an *Iso Lomso* Fellow of the Stellenbosch Institute for Advanced Studies. His research covers several areas of music such as in education, in health, music and emotions, and everyday use of music. He is currently coediting a book about memory, power, and knowledge in African music and beyond.

Alex Perullo is a professor of anthropology and music and director of the Global Studies Program at Bryant University. His publications include the ethnography *Live from Dar es Salaam: Popular Music and Tanzania's Music Economy* and a manual on copyright law titled *Artistic Rights: Copyright Law for East African Musicians, Artists, Writers, and Other Authors.* He has also published articles on intellectual property rights in Africa, genres of popular music, and human rights. His forthcoming book is tentatively titled *These Rights Are Ours: Value, Labor, and Law in African Music.*

Lara Rosenoff Gauvin is an assistant professor in the Department of Anthropology at the University of Manitoba. She is a scholar, artist, activist, and curator whose work centers the knowledge and practices of survivors of conflict and forced displacement, particularly in Northern Uganda. Her research and teaching interests include indigenous knowledge, land rights, intergenerational relations, social repair, and responsive methodologies.

Daniel Jordan Smith is professor of anthropology at Brown University. He conducts research in Nigeria focusing on a range of issues, including HIV, social change, political culture, kinship, and masculinity. He won the 2008 Margaret Mead Award for his first book, *A Culture of Corruption: Everyday Deception and Popular Discontent in Nigeria* (2007), and the 2015 Elliott P. Skinner Award for his second book, *AIDS Doesn't Show Its Face: Inequality, Morality, and Social Change in Nigeria* (2014). His most recent book is *To Be a Man Is Not a One-Day Job: Masculinity, Money, and Intimacy in Nigeria* (2017).

Maya Angela Smith is an associate professor of French in the Department of French and Italian Studies at the University of Washington. Studying topics related to multilingualism, migration, and race, she is a sociolinguist who works primarily on the francophone African diaspora. Her book *Senegal Abroad: Linguistic Borders, Racial Formations, and Diasporic Imaginaries* (2019) explores the relationship between language and the construction of national, transnational, postcolonial, racial, and migrant identities among members of the Senegalese communities in Paris, Rome, and New York.

Steven Van Wolputte is professor of social and cultural anthropology at the Institute for Anthropological Research in Africa (IARA),

Katholieke Universiteit Leuven. His research concentrates on northern Namibia, and he has published in the fields of material and popular culture, political anthropology, and the anthropology of the body. Currently, his research investigates the impact on intimacy and close relationships of rapid urbanization and far-reaching social, economic, and ecological change.

Scott M. Youngstedt is professor of anthropology at Saginaw Valley State University. He has been conducting ethnographic field research in Niger over the past thirty years, focusing on migration, diasporic communities, conversation, festivals, and water. Youngstedt is the author of *Surviving with Dignity: Hausa Communities of Niamey, Niger* (2013), coauthor of *Water, Life, and Profit: Fluid Economies and Cultures of Niamey, Niger* (2019), and coeditor of *Saharan Crossroads: Exploring Historical, Cultural, and Artistic Linkages between North and West Africa* (2014). He currently serves as president ex-officio of the West African Research Association.

Index

364 / Index